Social Theory and Education Research

Social Theory and Education Research is an advanced and accessible text that illustrates the diverse ways in which social theories can be applied to educational research methodologies. It provides in-depth overviews of the various theories by well-known and much-debated thinkers – Michel Foucault, Jürgen Habermas, Pierre Bourdieu and Jacques Derrida – and their applications in educational research.

Updated throughout and with new extended introductions to each theorist and a new chapter on the application of socio-theoretical concepts in education research methodologies and the how-to of research practice, this second edition assists education practitioners and researchers in their acquisition and application of social theory. This book contextualises the various theories within the broader context of social philosophy and the historical development of different forms of thought.

Social Theory and Education Research will be incredibly useful to postgraduate students and early career researchers who wish to develop their capacity to engage with these debates at an advanced level. It will also prove of great interest to anyone involved in education policy and theory.

Mark Murphy is Reader in Education and Public Policy at the University of Glasgow, UK.

D1453241

Social Theory and Education Research

Understanding Foucault, Habermas,
Bourdieu and Derrida

Second edition

Edited by
Mark Murphy

Routledge
Taylor & Francis Group

LONDON AND NEW YORK

Cover image: © Getty Images

Second edition published
by Routledge
4 Park Square, Milton Park, Abingdon, Oxon OX14 4RN

and by Routledge
605 Third Avenue, New York, NY 10158

Routledge is an imprint of the Taylor & Francis Group, an informa business

First edition published by Routledge 2013

British Library Cataloguing-in-Publication Data
A catalogue record for this book is available from the British Library

Library of Congress Cataloging-in-Publication Data
A catalog record has been requested for this book

ISBN: 978-0-367-74201-0 (hbk)
ISBN: 978-0-367-74202-7 (pbk)
ISBN: 978-1-003-15655-0 (ebk)

DOI: 10.4324/9781003156550

Typeset in Bembo
by Taylor & Francis Books

Contents

Illustrations

Contributors

Julie Allan is Professor of Equity and Inclusion at the University of Birmingham, UK, and was formerly the Head of School. Her research interests are in inclusion, equity and rights, and she has provided expert advice to governments and published widely in these areas. Recent publications include the *World yearbook of education 2020: Schooling, governance and inequalities* (edited with Valerie Harwood and Clara Jørgensen and published by Routledge) and *Psychopathology at school: Theorizing mental disorders in education* (written with Valerie Harwood and published by Routledge).

Cristina Costa is an Associate Professor in Education at Durham University, UK. She has a strong interest in exploring the intersection of education and emergent social phenomena through different social theory lenses. She has conducted research on digital literacies and digital inequalities, curriculum innovation, digital scholarship practices, and widening participation, with an emphasis on student estrangement in higher education.

Elizabeth Green is the Provost of Tyndale University, Toronto, Canada; Fellow of the Royal Society of the Arts and a Senior Fellow at the Canadian Think Tank, Cardus. Elizabeth gained her doctorate in education from the University of Oxford, UK, and her ethnographic research into a City Technology College and Academies sponsored by a Christian foundation was the first such study in the UK. Previously she has worked as a history teacher in UK secondary schools. Her publications include *Innovative Christian Education Research* co-edited with Joannes Luetz (Springer Press) and *Christian Faith in English Church Schools* with Trevor Cooling, Andrew Morris and Lynn Revell (Peter Lang).

Andrew Hope is a Professor of Sociology and Dean of the School of Arts at Federation University Australia. He has an international research reputation in the areas of school surveillance and risks faced by young people online. Previously, he has held positions at Adelaide, Manchester Metropolitan, Sunderland, Huddersfield and Durham universities.

Jones Irwin is an Associate Professor in Philosophy and Education at St Patrick's College, Dublin City University, Ireland, where he is Co-Director of the MA in Human Development. He has published the monograph *Derrida and the writing of the body* (Ashgate, 2010) and the book *Paulo Freire's philosophy of education: origins, development, impacts and legacies* (Bloomsbury, 2012). He has specific research interests in philosophy with children and continentalist philosophy of education.

Irene Kleanthous completed her PhD studies in Mathematics Education at the University of Manchester, UK, in 2012. She explored adolescent students' dispositions towards mathematics and perceptions of parental influence by applying Bourdieu's theory and using mixed research methods in her thesis. Her doctoral studies were funded by the School of Education (University of Manchester) and the A.G. Leventis Foundation (Cyprus). She was involved in various research projects at the University of Manchester, where she worked as a Research Assistant. Irene was also employed by the European University of Cyprus, where she taught Educational Research methods and Didactics of Mathematics for the BEd in Primary Education. She is currently working as a researcher at the Centre for Educational Research and Evaluation (Cyprus Pedagogical Institute), where she is coordinating various research projects.

Bob Lingard is a Professorial Fellow in The Institute for Learning Sciences and Teacher Education at Australian Catholic University, Australia. He is also an Emeritus Professor at The University of Queensland, Australia. He has also held the Andrew Bell Chair in Education at the University of Edinburgh, UK (2006–2008) and was Research Professor at Sheffield University, UK (2003–2006). He is a Fellow of the Academy of Social Sciences in Australia and also a Fellow of the UK Academy of Social Sciences. He researches and publishes in the sociology of education and education policy. His most recent books include, *Globalisation and education* (Routledge, 2021), *Digital disruption in teaching and testing* (Routledge, 2021), *Global–national networks in education policy: Primary education, social enterprises and 'Teach for Bangladesh'* (Bloomsbury, 2021), and *Globalizing educational accountabilities* (Routledge, 2016).

Terence Lovat is Professor Emeritus at the University of Newcastle, Australia, Honorary Research Fellow at the University of Oxford, UK, Honorary Professor at the University of Glasgow, UK, and Adjunct Professor at Royal Roads University, Canada. In 2017, he was Visiting Professor at Yogyakarta University, Indonesia. He is a former Pro Vice-Chancellor, Dean and Executive Committee Member at the University of Newcastle. His research interests span Islam and Jewish–Christian relations, curriculum theory, values education and religion in schools. He has written over 30 books and 200 refereed articles and chapters.

Duncan P. Mercieca is a Senior Lecturer in Education at the School of Education and Social Work, University of Dundee, UK. Trained as a teacher, he has had experience teaching in mainstream and special schools. His interests are in the links between education and continental philosophy, particularly in the issues of the Other and becoming. He has published articles in various journals, including the *Journal of Philosophy of Education* and *Ethics and Education*.

Mark Murphy is Reader in Education & Public Policy, School of Education, University of Glasgow, UK. He has published widely in the field of social theory and applied research, with books including *Social theory: A new introduction* (Palgrave, 2021), *Habermas and social research: Between Theory and method* (Routledge, 2017), *Theory as method: On Bourdieu, education and society* (with C. Costa, Routledge, 2016) and *Bourdieu, habitus and social research: The art of application* (with C. Costa, Palgrave, 2015). Mark is the editor of the book series *Social theory and methodology in education research* (Bloomsbury Press) and is co-editor of the multi-authored website www.socialtheoryapplied.com.

Shaun Rawolle is a Senior Lecturer in the School of Education and the Centre for Research in Educational Futures and Innovation at Deakin University, Australia. Shaun's research and publications are located broadly in the areas of sociology of education and education policy. Shaun has co-authored a book with Professor Bob Lingard, *Bourdieu and the fields of education policy* (Routledge, 2021).

Ali Sameer is an Associate Tutor in the School of Education at the University of Glasgow, UK. He completed his PhD in 2020, and his thesis examined the role of securitisation and its impact on girls' education in Pakistan. Coming from an anthropological and development studies background, he has worked in the field for organisations such as Save the Children and Oxfam, GB, dealing with social equity issues. Coupled with his academic background and in-field experience, his current interest lies in pursuing ideas in the construction of knowledge, postcolonial studies, gender, security, Michel Foucault's work on power and discourses, and hybridising social theory and ideas.

Fredrik Sandberg is an Associate Professor in the Department of Sociology at Lund University, Sweden. In his research he draws inspiration from Jürgen Habermas' theory of communicative action and Axel Honneth's recognition theory.

Christine Winter is an Honorary Research Fellow in the School of Education in the University of Sheffield, UK, and Research Engagement Lead at the Geographical Association. Her research focuses on curriculum, curriculum policy analysis and enactment. She is interested in the constitution and politics of curriculum knowledge and its associated responsibilities expressed through the language of curriculum texts. She is particularly interested in the process of racialisation in school humanities subjects. Christine leads a British Academy/*Journal of Moral Education* Trust project 2018–2021 with the title: 'Is the geography GCSE curriculum in England white?' She is working on a number of projects focusing on decolonising the school and higher education curriculum and promoting anti-racist education. Her recent publications have been published in *Critical Social Policy, Journal of Education Policy* and *Journal of Curriculum Studies*.

Preface to the second edition

The first edition of this book has proven to be a popular text among academics and students and it is used on postgraduate education modules in different universities (which was a key aim of the original text). The same issues that the book engaged with – theory and methodology in education and the application of theoretical concepts in education research design – are still as relevant today, if not more so eight years on. The success of the original book suggests that there is a demand for a text like this and that there is a real need for books that help to explain the relation between theory and research practice. All too often this key aspect of research quality – an aspect that underpins the explanatory power of education research – is downplayed in other research textbooks, which is (still) something of an oversight.

Since the publication of the first edition of this text in 2013, I have done further work on the relation between social theory and education research. This includes establishing the website www.socialtheoryapplied.com as well as developing a book series on *Social theory and methodology in education research* (Bloomsbury). I have also published a thematic introduction to social theory (*Social theory: A new introduction* (Palgrave, 2021)), which outlines the significant role played by social theory in ideas around topics such as civil society, the economy, knowledge and the body. It is inevitable then that my own thoughts on the relation between social theory and education have also developed. I see a much clearer methodological context for this relationship, not just from the perspective of theory application, but also from the very foundations of methodological construction – its epistemological and ontological basis. The 'bigger picture' for theory application, specifically social theory, is one that positions method and methodology as an explicitly value-laden enterprise, one that rejects the value-free fantasies of positivist science and, instead, aims to critically interrogate the politics of educational practices.

This stance unites the work of all four theorists, whose ideas revolve in different ways around issues of justice, solidarity and freedom – no wonder that they prove so popular in education research. Researchers are drawn to the field of education precisely because of its consequences for justice, and as a result the same researchers seek out the theories of Bourdieu and the others because they speak to these concerns.

This period of reflection has resulted in the inclusion of a wholly new chapter (Chapter 2, written with Cristina Costa), which examines in depth some of the key issues involved in social-theory driven education research, including the role of conceptualisation, operationalisation, hybridisation and critical reflexivity. These issues have long required some further interrogation and I hope that the chapter provides some useful insights for readers. Alongside this, the other chapters (including the introductory chapter) have been significantly updated, with a new chapter from Ali Sameer (Chapter 5), who puts the ideas of Foucault to work in the context of education in Pakistan.

Mark Murphy, Glasgow, August 2021

Acknowledgements

I would like to express my gratitude to all the contributors in this collection, all of whom fully appreciated the significance and value of the project from its inception, having themselves spent considerable time applying social theory in their own educational research. This level of accumulated knowledge is strongly evident in the chapters and accounts of their work, providing inspiration for other researchers who look to the likes of Foucault, Habermas, Bourdieu and Derrida for ideas about research design and analytical frameworks.

The idea for the book came after many years of experience conducting my own education research and also supervising education students conducting research on various aspects of professional practice and education policy. Their contribution to this collection should also be acknowledged as they have provided much food for thought when it came to the book's rationale and design. My hope is that the book will be of use to future generations of researchers who wish to make the challenging journey from practice to theory, and back again.

Part I

Introduction

1 Social theory and education research

An introduction

Mark Murphy

Introduction

Ideas relating to educational policy and practice are underpinned by recourse to foundational disciplines, including philosophy and the social sciences. Educational research embeds itself in a wide variety of theoretical discourses, using them to explore issues such as professional and cultural identities, forms of educational management, changing work practices and priorities. They also form the basis for numerous debates relating to the user experience, including, for example, differential attainment and achievement, access and inclusion, and the relationship between culture and learning. Although education researchers have drawn on the work of a wide diversity of theorists, a number of these have been of special significance to education. While the likes of Karl Marx, Antonio Gramsci, John Dewey and Paulo Freire influenced previous generations of educational theorists, much of the more contemporary theory building has revolved around a quartet of well-known and much-debated thinkers – Jacques Derrida, Pierre Bourdieu, Michel Foucault and Jürgen Habermas.

However, while the influence of these thinkers has grown considerably over the last number of years, the application of their ideas to education can often prove challenging to the educational practitioner. This is unsurprising, given the manner in which these theories have developed from sometimes arcane debates in continental philosophy, far removed from the modern world of teaching practice that is embedded in concerns over performance, attainment and accountability. The field could do with suitable reading material that can appeal to the advanced practitioner market, while also providing a sufficiently in-depth overview of the various theories and their applications in educational research.

The main purpose of this edited collection is to help rectify this omission in educational theory and provide a text that is both advanced and accessible, offering the education practitioner/researcher a suitable book to assist their acquisition and application of social theory. This book has appeal to readers who have an interest in how theory can be effectively applied to educational problems, and which can illuminate the relationships between theory and practice, in a manner that offers some practically realisable solutions to educational issues.

DOI: 10.4324/9781003156550-2

Alongside the benefits to the individual researcher, there is much to be gained for the educational research community generally from taking advantage of the originality, rigour and intellectual insight of these authors. Their work, while certainly not without its critics, offers such a treasure-trove of ideas – about power and control, democracy, social organisation, language and communication, selfhood and subjectivities, the state and economy – that they can, when thoughtfully implemented, contribute to the delivery of higher quality educational research.

This is one of the reasons why all four thinkers, to varying degrees, have achieved an increasing level of visibility in educational research (this could also be said to be the case for other professional fields such as health and social work[1]). The chapters included in this collection are designed to provide examples of how this visibility has manifested itself in various aspects of educational research, illustrating the diverse ways in which continental theory of whatever stripe can be used to explore educational issues. From school surveillance to curriculum design, social theory can be adapted to shed light on 'practical' issues facing the sector, helping to widen and deepen discussion around these areas when they are in danger of being over-simplified.

As a preface to these contributions, this chapter is designed to provide a brief introduction to the field of social theory itself, as well as identifying some of the issues faced by educational researchers in applying the work of Derrida et al. The chapter also provides a summary of the core educational questions to which social theory has so far been applied (based on an overview of recent educational research output), finishing with an overview of the book's organisation and content.

The context(s) for this book

There are some contexts for this book that need to be mentioned: these contexts are political in nature, which reflects the ethos of social theory itself. One important aspect of this context relates to the politics of education: The field of education is unquestionably politicised, with the mildest of policy changes scrutinised and endlessly debated. This reflects the importance of education in people's lives, its impact on social mobility and life opportunities, alongside the political repercussions of unpopular policies. This has not prevented sweeping changes taking place in schools, colleges and universities, with vast swathes of the world witnessing the twin agendas of neo-liberalism and new public management instilling their questionable virtues into classrooms and lecture halls. These changes have seen policies such as marketisation, competition, school choice and privatisation taking hold in the sector, their consequences evidenced in the increased presence of curriculum narrowing, teaching to the test, professional discontent and most importantly widening educational inequality.

The realities of 21st-century political economies position education as a quick fix for the ills of a post-welfare state confronted with growing economic inequality, heightened social divide and often entrenched levels of social immobility. Educational institutions and professionals have to contend with a harsh political climate in which education has become an opportunistic public policy designed to offset the ravaging consequences of neoliberal economic upheaval. The hopes of a democratic polity seemingly rest on the workings of a highly regulated and surveilled education sector whose success is measured by test scores and other official metrics that serve competitive interests but do little to bolster democratic discourse and community, This highly instrumentalised approach to learning, teaching and scholarly life has little room for theory and theorising, while simultaneously crying out for powerful explanatory tools that can help to examine the causes of dysfunctional educational policies and practices as well as their consequences.

The second context relates to the politics of education *research*: A consequence of the political context detailed above is the sharp turn to social theories for ideas, concepts and frameworks that offer explanatory tools in the struggle to understand the relation between education, power and justice. Social theory-driven research adds a value-laden component to research design that more accurately reflects the often-harsh realities of education reform. Theory-driven research of whatever stripe makes explicit the social, political and economic drivers of educational policies, and questions the veracity and reach of education reforms that seek simple solutions to often highly complex problems.

Social theory-driven research has fierce competition in the shape of positivism and positivist education research, a methodology that persists in the face of criticism over the years due to its lauding of value-free science as the saviour of education. Often the default research paradigm of governments and think tanks, positivism has tended to skew debates on education quality while sidelining the broader social concerns mentioned above. Instead, positivist design, unwittingly or otherwise, sees school and teacher reform as the answer to these broader concerns, and hence the proliferation of research projects that seek to adjust school and teacher quality to address concerns over educational injustice, while falling in line with global trends of performance, regulation and accountability.

The third context relates to the politicised nature of social theory: Social theory in its numerous forms – feminism, Marxism, postcolonialism – is a necessary and inevitable response to conditions of subjugation, inequality and injustice across social life. These theories are a form of critical reasoning that seek to understand the sub-altern position of groups that live under these conditions, whether they be the working-class, women, ethnic minorities, people with disabilities, the LGBTIQ+ community, and so on. These theories reflect the political times we live in and develop in tandem with historical developments. The latter in fact precedes the former, with the early 21st century providing sufficient evidence of the need for theory in the face of a highly unstable world economy, a dangerously fragmented sense of social solidarity, a race to the bottom when it comes to education values combined with a de-professionalising of the teaching sector.

Social theory comes into its own when tackling such deep-rooted social problems, as it accepts and understands the political nature of sectors such as education – instead of aiming to depoliticise the field, social theory is explicit in framing the issues affecting education as already politicised and, as a result, offers researchers a conceptual apparatus that addresses the social roots of educational issues. These roots may surface via forms of language, culture, knowledge and governance systems, and hence the theories may differ in their focus, but when applied to a field such as education, they inevitably ask research questions that can unsettle taken-for-granted assumptions about schools, colleges and universities. At their best, applied social theories provide a direct and forceful alternative to the hegemonic power of league tables, teacher performativity, education markets and the dismantling of public education systems.

There is deeper historical and political context to social theory that should be outlined here, especially given the work of the four theorists in this book and the debt they owe to the European tradition of social theory. This is a context that was constructed out of 19th-century revolutionary fervour, political struggle and the world of ideas. The radical ideas of the Enlightenment paved the way for both the French and the American Revolutions. This influence is symbolised in the famous call to arms 'liberté, egalité, fraternité', a set of ideals which still resonate today. They certainly resonate in the field of social theory, the history of which is littered with efforts to deal with these ideals and the possibilities that they represent for society, no more so than in the case of Foucault, Habermas, Bourdieu and Derrida.

From this historical angle, social theory can be viewed as an intellectual and political project designed to situate the modern social world against these revolutionary ideals of the French Revolution, of the Republic and of democracy. Its various guises probe and question the workings of social institutions and tests their adherence to the principles that underpin modern societies. They test this adherence in the face of numerous competing principles such as efficiency, productivity, consumption, commodification, and individualism, as well as troubling conditions such as isolation and fragmentation. They also gauge the distance between the real and the ideal, and interrogate the willingness of, for example, the state to realise the promise of the Enlightenment. Such ideals act as guiding principles for social affairs and social conduct, held up as lofty principles to govern and deliver justice.

The content of this book, which covers the work of four thinkers, testifies to the persistence of these ideals and their power as a critical vantage point from which to judge education's success and failures. It starts precisely from a position of judgement and it is this judgement that needs to be considered in the context of a set of events and philosophies that came to being centuries earlier. This is what provides social theory with its critical edge and offers an explanatory power unmatched in other theoretical endeavours. Its various branches, paradigms and themes gather analytical ammunition via concerns over freedom, justice and solidarity. Without these, what would be the rationale for theories like this?

The four theorists in this book are situated in this confluence of ideas about justice, freedom and solidarity, each playing a role in the development of their thought. Education researchers have turned for example to Habermas because of his work on the public sphere, its decline in the 20th century and what this means for informed public debate. Habermas' work on discourse ethics speaks to the capacity of collectives to take seriously democratic dialogue and learning, while his sociological focus on lifeworld colonisation speaks to the fragile nature of socialisation processes and human communication and interaction and the damage that can be inflicted on these by the overreach of the state and the market. These issues reflect deeply held concerns about modern society and how democratic ideals can wither on the vine if not embedded in the practices of education.

What is social theory?

The field of social theory feeds off a desire to understand the world we live in, the collective experience filtered and mediated through the institutions and practises of family, community, education, work and politics. In contemporary social theory, certain core themes take precedence over others, themes such as the relations between the state, economy and civil society, the importance of culture and knowledge in social formations and social transformations, the power of language as a mechanism of social control and social, and the impact of socialisation on emotional life (Murphy 2021).

Alongside the existence of this broad range of issues, there are also a large number of what could be termed social theories – feminism and postcolonial theory for example could be labelled as such, likewise with critical race theories. Space precludes a more detailed examination of the field of social theory – there are other sources than offer such an overview.[2] Space also precludes the opportunity to explore the ideas of other prominent social theorists, such as Nancy Fraser, Julia Kristeva, Zygmunt Bauman, Judith Butler, Jean Baudrillard, Nobert Elias and Ulrich Beck. The authors included in this collection are not meant to represent an exhaustive list. Instead, they are the focus of this book as they are among the most prominent theorists of the modern age, and have proven popular in the field of educational research. It is also fair to say that their influence on other social theorists, philosophers and the academic world in general is immense, making major contributions to debates across a wide range of disciplines.

This contribution has been facilitated by the conceptual work undertaken by these four thinkers – concepts such as the public sphere, discourse ethics and colonisation (Habermas), governmentality, subjectivation, parrhesia (Foucault), cultural capital, doxa, habitus (Bourdieu) and différance, supplement and deconstruction (Derrida), have all become an established part of the academic lexicon, a testament to their impressive explanatory power. Scholars across the humanities and social sciences have adapted these concepts to help examine so many facets of modern life, and the education field is no different, developing a strong attachment to ideas such as cultural capital.

Their influence has also extended into the broader public sphere, these authors combining the role of social theorist with that of public intellectual. Intellectualising the problems and issues of the day, they provide spaces within which educational researchers as well as others can adopt an intellectual stance to their subjects with some level of legitimation and credibility. It is also evident that their theories are delivered with normative intent, whether it be Derrida's deconstructive approach, the critical theory of Habermas, the critical social science of Bourdieu or the archaeology and genealogies of Foucault. In this way, they could be viewed to some extent as the heirs to the tradition of social philosophy, a tradition that stretches at least as far back as Jean-Jacques Rousseau (1755/2004) and his *Discourse on the origin of inequality*. This tradition took as its aim the use of philosophy to examine problems in society, an aim not too dissimilar to the social theories included in this collection.

The work of all four social theorists are influenced in one way or another by the work of a 'classic' social theorist, Karl Marx. Marx was a pre-eminent social theorist in his own right, his ideas casting a considerable shadow over debates in modern social theory. A great deal of this theory owes some kind of debt to Marx's concepts of capital, class and exploitation, and his re-workings of post-Enlightenment notions of political economy and liberal democracy. This is evident in the work of Bourdieu, for example, whose work on cultural and social reproduction saw him cast as a neo-Marxist, his ideas helping to fill in some of the blanks in Marx's historical materialism (especially around the role of culture) (Fowler 2011). Marxism is a major starting point for Habermas, a figure strongly associated with the Frankfurt School of Critical Theory, which included in its ranks (neo)Marxists such as Erich Fromm and Herbert Marcuse (Kellner 1989). Habermas' work *The theory of communicative action* (Habermas 1984; 1987), was at base a project designed to reconstruct Marx's theory of historical materialism, in order to provide (in Habermas' opinion) a better diagnosis of the problems facing late capitalist society (Murphy 2009). Foucault, who later in his career moved decisively away from Hegelian dialectics, was 'considerably influenced by Marx' early on (Best 1995, 87), his first book *Mental illness and psychology* (Foucault 1976) was immersed in Marxist concepts of alienation and contradiction. Even Derrida, whose post-structuralist approach to deconstruction could never be confused with Marxian political economy, argued at one stage for a return to Marx, publishing his famous text *Spectres of Marx* (Derrida 1994) to a bemused academic world – the editor arguing that for Derrida, 'deconstruction' 'always already moves within a certain spirit of Marx' (Magnus and Cullenberg 1994, x).[3]

Foucault and Derrida broke more decisively with the Marxist tradition (more so than Bourdieu and Habermas), occupying central positions in the fabric of postmodern and post-structural thought, respectively. Their positions as pre-eminent French intellectuals on the post-1968 French left makes this somewhat inevitable, a context within which post-Marxist social theories proliferated as a form of break with the past (Best and Kellner 1991). For such a diverse set of thinkers, however, it could be argued (strongly) that the legacy of Marx lives on; a common thread in contemporary theory is a fascination, even obsession, with how the dynamics and forms of *power* play themselves out via institutions, linguistic traditions, texts, cultures and forms of selfhood. Above all else, Marx's concern with modern mechanisms of exploitation and how forms of oppression lurk behind the veils of modernisation and capitalist industry, provides a strong intellectual and normative backdrop to so much modern theory. His methodology of ideology critique arguably finds an echo in the work of all four theorists and also in the work of those inspired by such theorists (examples of which are numerous in this collection).

A special mention should be made in this section regarding the interdisciplinary nature of much modern social theory. Central to this nature is the distinction between sociological theory and social theory – while in many cases social theories have a background in the discipline of sociology, they are not one and the same thing. Social theories emanate and draw from a range of disciplines including sociology, but also philosophy, anthropology, history, media and communication studies, psychology and psychoanalysis, linguistics, cultural studies and literary criticism. Social theory is therefore positioned across and between the humanities and social sciences. The work of the theorists in this collection are utilised across these fields and belong to no one discipline, which makes sense given their own interdisciplinary leanings. This level of complexity is often one of the reasons why their work is so influential; it is also one of the reasons why educators can experience difficulty during the act of application, the lack of disciplinary belonging a burden as well as a benefit. Having said that, the fact that education theory draws from a range of disciplines should mean that, at least in principle, the educational researcher should be able to cope in this world of multiple sets of ideas.

A note on the purpose of theory

There is a famous saying by Karl Marx that, over the course of time, has come to confuse the purpose of theory in the minds of many, including those in the education field. It is taken from Thesis Eleven of Marx's Theses on Feuerbach, and goes like this:

> The philosophers have only interpreted the world in various ways; the point, however, is to change it.
>
> (Marx, in Marx and Engels 2011, 570)

As well as being the most famous of the eleven theses, it is also arguably the most misinterpreted of Marx's statements. This is sometimes misconstrued as some variant of 'act first, ask questions later (if at all)'. This is not the meaning intended by Marx when he developed his critique of Feuerbach and then later Max Stirner in *The German ideology* (Marx and Engels 1846/2011). Instead Marx's real target was the perceived need to deliver some kind of objective philosophical justification/legitimation for engagement with acts of social struggle (against oppression, exploitation, colonialism).

An excellent explanation of Marx's thinking around Thesis Eleven is provided by Cornel West (1991) in his book *The ethical dimensions of Marxist thought*. In the chapter 'Marx's adoption of radical historicism', West argues that

Thesis Eleven 'was not a rejection of rational dialogue, discourse, or discussion, nor is it a call for blind activism' (West 1991, 68). Rather, Thesis Eleven was a statement of Marx's desire to situate philosophical thinking about social problems within history rather than outside it – Marx, not for the first time, flipping conventional wisdom on its head. Thesis Eleven itself was the inevitable outcome of a process begun earlier in the Theses, most notably in Theses Six and Seven, where Marx made clear his shift from philosophy to a form of radical historicism, or what West refers to as the 'move from philosophic aims and language to theoretic ones':

> This means that fundamental distinctions such as objectivism/relativism, necessary/arbitrary, or essential/accidental will no longer be viewed through a philosophic lens. That is, no longer will one be concerned with arriving at timeless criteria, necessary grounds, or universal foundations for philosophic objectivity, necessity, or essentiality. Instead, any talk about objectivity, necessity, or essentiality must be under-a-description, hence historically located, socially situated and 'a product' of revisable, agreed-upon human conventions which reflect particular needs, social interests, and political powers at a specific moment in history. The task at hand then becomes a theoretic one, namely, providing a concrete social analysis which shows how these needs, interests, and powers shape and hold particular human conventions and in which ways these conventions can be transformed.
>
> (West 1991, 67)

For Marx, theorising social change went hand-in-hand with an understanding of social change as inevitably being 'under-a-description' as West puts it. Thesis Eleven, then, is the culmination of this thinking, providing a succinct indication of the consequences of the radical historical shift for social struggle, a shift that assumes

> the heightened awareness of the limitations of traditional philosophy will soon render that philosophy barren, a mere blind and empty will-to-nothingness. In its place will thrive a theory of history and society, able to account for its own appearance and status, aware of the paradoxes it cannot solve, grounded in ever changing personal needs and social interests, and beckoning for action in order to overcome certain conditions and realize new conditions. In this way, the radical historicist viewpoint enables Marx to make the philosophic to theoretic shift without bothering his philosophic conscience.
>
> (West 1991, 68)

This approach to social theorising is a very useful way to both think about the purpose of theory in relation to education research but also as a tool to consider the content and ideas expressed in this book. The message from Marx and from West is that theory most certainly has a purpose but what provides this purpose is its relation to practice. This practice can take many forms, but examples are distributed right throughout the education field: practices of classroom instruction, access and selection procedures, practices of education commodification, experiences of alienated pupils and disempowered teachers, the management of emotions, the struggles for educational rights and recognition. These education practices and our efforts to understand and explain their effects provides social theory with its radical and transformative edge. This edge is strengthened by the desire of social theorists to situate their analyses within history, within the ebb and flow and sometimes dramatic shifts in historical developments. Being the servant of history instead of attempting to stand outside of it and cast abstract judgements, is social theory at its best, this 'under-a-description' approach to theory as West puts it a superior way to generate the knowledge necessary to explain and transform society.

Social theory can engage researchers with what Richard Johnson (1979) called 'really useful knowledge'. Johnson resurrected the term to talk about the working class in the UK in the 1970s, while others used it to critique the new vocationalism at work at the time. The concept grew out of radical working-class educational associations in the 19th century and offered a framework from which to comprehend and also critique dominant forms of knowledge. The kinds of education it valued stemmed from the specific problems faced by working-class people at the time. The term has gone on to take on a life of its own, becoming a signifier in radical and popular education circles (see Crowther 2012). In a time of political confusion and economic uncertainty, the really useful knowledge of applied social theory can help educators and researchers make sense of their own social reality and that of others.

Reading the original texts

It is always sensible to read the original works alongside texts such as this. While these might themselves have received a process of interpretation from translators and publishers, as well as the authors, it is often the case that certain ideas about writers and their works, which are often based on a misreading of the text (as we saw above with Marx), get passed down through introductory courses and shorthand, and are often passed off as truth. And work that attempts to condense a wide range of material always faces the danger of oversimplification to the point of misrecognition. There are a large array of readers and textbooks that can help in this discovery of original work. I hope that this text assists in navigating the mix of ideas to be found in texts such as *The theory of communicative action* (Habermas 1984, 1987), *Of grammatology* (Derrida 1976), *Discipline and punish* (Foucault 1977) and *Language and symbolic power* (Bourdieu 1991).

Between (social) theory and practice: Dilemmas in educational research

As indicated above, the application of these theories brings its own set of issues. Some of these reflect issues of research design and implementation, including the development of tools such as data measurement and analytical criteria. Just as significant are the difficulties faced when grappling with the core concepts of social theory that already come with a range of contradictory meanings. Notions of 'power', 'culture' and 'practice' are challenging at the best of times, but these are compounded when they are aligned with the core educational concepts of teaching, learning, assessment, curriculum and support.

All forms of research, regardless of subject, come with a set of issues that need addressing in practical settings. Educational research is no different, its embeddedness in forms of professional practice (in many cases) adding a further layer of complexity. As a result, it should be emphasised from the outset that the movement from practice to theory is as challenging an intellectual journey, if not more so, than the journey from theory to practice. While the latter can often confound researchers who struggle to apply theoretical models and principles in contexts such as health organisations, business and social welfare, the former can often compound the problem for the educational researcher. Many of those engaged in educational research tend to arrive via the linked but distinct field of professional practice. While this can have certain advantages in terms of insight, providing a level of insider knowledge unavailable to the professional anthropologist (for example), it can also mean that intellectual judgement can be clouded by immersion in the hothouse of educational politics. Objectivity can often suffer as result.

This scenario is also compounded by the nature of professional training. Educators may be well versed in the application of educational theory to educational practice, but rarely are they required in any meaningful way to apply theories from other disciplines. This is a blessing and a curse of being an educational researcher – an *un*disciplined approach to the field of research can have drawbacks as well as benefits – providing professionals with a multi-disciplinary grounding while providing a disinclination to belong and to work within the parameters of any specific disciplinary paradigm.

Having said that, it often proves tempting when applying theory to research to try and stay true to the 'authentic' version of the theory being applied. Although the book is organised into four core parts exploring the application of each theorist, this is not a reflection of some notion that the work of people like Habermas and Foucault are and should be kept separate. The book is designed to provide some pointers in terms of introduction and application, but it is certainly not designed to discourage debate and cross-pollination between theories. Nowhere is it written that researchers cannot choose how and in what contexts they apply the work of theory. And while the overzealous might demand the 'pure' use of someone's work, regardless of context, it should not be forgotten that all of these theorists under discussion, have at various stages in their careers, cherry-picked from those who have influenced them. To suggest that there is a 'right' and 'wrong' way to understand and apply these theorists is to misinterpret the role of theory in research – the latter should never be made to bow down to the former. If anything, cherry-picking and cross-pollination should be positively encouraged – for how else do we arrive at original and innovative forms of knowledge, forms that can help us progress through the world of often stale and moribund arguments and paradigms in educational policy and practice?[4]

Another issue in educational research relates to the special status assigned to the concept of power in social theory. Evident in the educational research (including contributors in the current collection) is the attraction such thinkers have for those interested in the relationship between education and various mechanisms used to generate and distribute power. But given this close relationship between power and educational research, one needs to be even more careful in the pursuit of research objectives. One doesn't need to be a Foucauldian to understand that power is omnipresent, and that power and knowledge have a tight bond that is not easily broken. But the workings of power in educational settings should never be taken lightly or over-simplified, given that educational institutions and their assorted sets of practices, provide ideal environments for the interplay of multiple forms of power – cultural, social, structural – forms that in many cases are irreducible to the others.

Power is a notoriously difficult concept to pin down, and the researcher can all too easily fall into the trap of looking for power in the wrong places, or worse still, misrecognise their own capacity as power brokers in educational research settings. It is important for the researcher to recognise their own powerful presence in educational settings, while also accepting the fallibility of one theory of power in the face of complex and highly differentiated institutionalised arrangements. Erring on the side of intellectual caution does not do the educational researcher any harm, especially when combined with a recognition of the unfinished debates in social theory that form the backdrop to such forms of research in the first place.

Social theory applied: Core topics in educational research

As evidenced in this book, and in the general educational literature, ideas from social theory have been applied across the educational sector, from early years' education, through formal schooling, to adult and higher education settings. No field of education has proved immune from the pull of continental philosophy, including the more skills-based 'technical' end of the spectrum.[5] As well as this sector-wide immersion in notions of deconstruction, reproduction, colonisation and performativity, social theory has also been applied in a wide variety of research settings – and while there is considerable overlap between them, social theory has found favour in the following research topics:

- Inequality, inclusion and education
- Notions of educational selves and subjectivities
- Curricular and pedagogical practice
- Governance and management

Inequality, inclusion and education: The ways in which schooling and learning generally are mediated by, and impact on, issues of class, race and gender, have concerned education researchers for decades, with the ideas generated by social theory providing a valuable foundation for innovative methodologies. Much of social theory itself is designed to explore questions of power and privilege, and educational processes, systems and outcomes are intimately connected to these questions. The work of Bourdieu in particular lends itself well to themes of inequality and inclusion in education, which is unsurprising, as this was one of his research areas.[6] However, there are numerous other examples of educational research on inequality and inclusion that have borrowed heavily from the work of Foucault, Habermas and Derrida.[7]

Notions of educational selves and subjectivities: Questions of identity have come to the fore in social science research. Professional identity has received much attention, with the field of education proving a rich source of data. This is because educational identities are open to multiple interpretations and cover a wide range of professional formations and issues – becoming a teacher, transformations in teacher professionalism, sources of academic identity, to name but a few. Social theory has been widely applied to these research areas, with ideas from post-structuralism and postmodernism proving especially popular as conceptual schemas.[8] Another area of identity studies to which social theory has been applied is *student* identity. There is a growing body of research literature that examines the relationship between educational processes and forms of selfhood, with questions such as the formation of learner identities receiving a great deal of attention.[9]

Curricular and pedagogical practice: The field of teaching and learning has understandably proven a mainstay of educational research. The field, however, has undergone something of a transformation in the last two decades, moving away from its more psychological and instrumentalist routes to more recently embracing the intellectual traditions of social theorists such as Derrida and Habermas. The application of social theory in this field has been wide-ranging, covering topics such as the role of teacher efficacy in learning (Jennings and DiPrete 2010), the metaphorical nature of supervision (Lee and Green 2009), and the role of ethnography in assessment practices (Hill 2009).

Governance and management: Educational governance provides a political and economic context for the previous three thematic areas, but is also an important focus of research in its own right. In education, much of the governance research centres on policies of regulation, marketisation and accountability, and the impact of these on educational values, professionalism, provision and delivery. The ideas of all four theorists have been utilised to explore these themes, but the work of Michel Foucault has proven especially attractive to educators as a way of making sense of changing political imperatives, and the nature of performative and audit cultures.[10] Habermas has also proven to be popular in the field of policy and management studies.[11]

The organisation of the book

In developing the format of the book, the objective was to present the reader with an overview of the theorists and their influence in education, while also providing relevant examples of applied theory in research settings. With this objective in mind, the book is structured around four core parts, each comprising the following:

- A 'general' chapter which introduces the social theorist in question, detailing some of the ways the theory has been applied in educational settings, as well as providing a critical commentary on the theory and its application
- Two applied chapters providing case studies of applied education research using the relevant social theorist as a theoretical framework. Each chapter explores the significance of the theory to the chosen area of study, its influence on research design, while also exploring some of the challenges faced when applying social theory in empirical settings

The contributors have been carefully chosen so that as wide a range of sectors, subjects and issues as possible are included.

Chapter 2, by Mark Murphy and Cristina Costa, develops some of the issues raised in the current chapter and outlines some of the aspects of a methodology framed by social theoretical concerns. Subtitled 'From conceptualisation to operationalisation', the chapter argues that the field of education should consider more fully the ways in which social theory is utilised in contemporary forms of education research. At the centre of this consideration should be a concern to develop a form of critical research literacy that positions theory as at least the significant other of method in our efforts to advance *methodological* innovation. The quality of education research, especially in terms of intellectual advancement, would benefit greatly from the harnessing of social theory and its transformative potential. That said, there are concerns that need to be highlighted in the desire to merge theory and method in applied education research. Three issues need special consideration: (1) how to promote hybridised theory and conceptual interdisciplinarity in education research as a counterpoint to monological approaches to theory application; (2) how to encourage forms of critical reflexivity to counteract 'off-the-shelf' approaches to theory use; and (3) how to elevate the status of theory 'application' as a vital conduit in bridging concepts and research methods. These issues need special consideration as the field would ultimately benefit in the shape of greater conceptual originality and methodological rigour.

Julie Allan's chapter (Chapter 3) introduces Foucault and explores the interest his work has generated for researchers within education. Allan traces the development of Foucault's ideas, from his initial interest in structures and discourses, through to his archaeologies of knowledge, medicine and madness, in which he demonstrated how discourses produced particular truths. The chapter then charts Foucault's shift of focus onto genealogy, studying institutions such as prisons and schools and the issue of sexuality, and offering a critique of what was considered to be *normal*. His analyses of knowledge and power as interlinked, constructing individuals as objects of knowledge and as subjects who were controlled, even – and especially – by themselves, are explored. The fascination such genealogies have held for educational researchers, and the way in which they have been applied, is examined. Allan finishes her chapter with a discussion of whether there is such a thing as a legacy of Foucault and, if so, how this might be constituted.

In Chapter 4, Andrew Hope explores academic writing on panopticism, while also considering difficulties faced by researchers wishing to use this concept to make sense of the social impact of surveillance technologies within schools. Initially, Foucault's discussion of the panopticon in his influential text *Discipline and punish* (Foucault 1977) is examined, before some contemporary developments of (post)panoptic ideas are analysed. These insights are then applied as panoptic themes that could aid researchers focusing upon school observational practices. Some of the practical limitations of the panoptic metaphor are discussed as student resistance to school discipline is pondered. Ultimately, it is argued that while panopticism still holds some value for school surveillance researchers, an awareness of the inherent limitations should also encourage them to retool, as and when appropriate, through occasionally abandoning the concept and drawing on other insights. Staying within Foucault's writings, 'technologies of the self' and biopower are offered as two possible alternatives.

Ali Sameer, in Chapter 5, uses Foucault to examine issues of girls' education in a religiously driven postcolonial security state. As Sameer rightly states, postcolonial studies have used Foucauldian thought to frame its critical insights. However, it has to tackle the Eurocentric blind spots of Foucault, where he was accused of using French evidence to constitute epistemological frameworks to make assumptions about the rest of the world. This chapter addresses this methodological quandary when Foucault's notion of discourse is taken out of its context to examine issues of girls' education in the religiously driven postcolonial security state of Pakistan. Sameer suggests that the Foucauldian notion of discourse has definite strengths to comprehend the way power/knowledge works in society, but once applied out of its original western context it can exhibit certain limitations. Using Pakistan as a case study, Sameer argues that it is important to rearrange both theoretical and methodological choices by opting for a hybridised approach to social theory when applied outside its context. The chapter concludes by elaborating that in a postcolonial Pakistan, the working of discourses is diverse as compared to a European context. There is a duality of discourse, where visible discourses on girls' education not only empower them but also support their educational attainments. However, there are invisible discourses, the discourse of hypocrisy and the hidden curriculum that negate such empowerment and educational attainment.

According to Terry Lovat in his introductory chapter on Habermas (Chapter 6), many contemporary educational research agendas, be they in quality teaching, authentic pedagogy, values and citizenship education or service learning, are directed towards re-conceiving and re-constructing schools as transformational learning sites, which potentially entail more holistic developmental experiences for learners. Lovat argues that this is one of the main reasons why Habermas has proven popular in some areas of education research. The chapter claims that Habermas' theories of knowing and communicative action have the capacity to deepen our research understandings in several areas of education, including the role of the teacher and effective pedagogy, as well as the potential of schools to serve as sites of transformational learning. The chapter explores these themes, expounding on Habermasian theory and illustrating its pertinence to educational research through a number of contemporary applications.

Chapter 7 details some of my own ideas when working with Habermas in the field of education governance, specifically accountability and its impact on professional and institutional practice. A substantial amount of research evidence has been gathered regarding the pathologies of accountability, but less attention has been paid to the reasons why such pathologies occur in the first place. The chapter addresses this issue by exploring accountability in the context of Habermas' theory of lifeworld colonisation. The chapter explores the value of the colonisation thesis to modern-day issues associated with the 'regulatory state', that form of education governance with surveillance and enforcement strategies at its core. It takes seriously the contribution that Habermas can make to the field of public administration – a contribution that can position the field in its broader context of democratic governance. At the same time, it is accepted that there are limitations of the colonisation thesis as an explanatory device, with the chapter arguing that not all the consequences of accountability can be considered illustrative of a damaged communicative intersubjectivity. Specifically, the chapter turns to the concept of street-level bureaucracy for further refinement of Habermas' ideas around governance.

Drawing on data from a PhD research project exploring processes of recognition of prior learning (RPL) in the Swedish health care sector, Fredrik Sandberg outlines in Chapter 8 the kinds of dilemmas faced when applying Habermas' theory of communicative action in relation to issues of professionalism and professional accreditation. According to Sandberg, a Habermasian analysis raises issues about how actions and communication shape students understanding and learning, and how these processes connect to the relationship between system and lifeworld and the risk of colonisation. By reconstructing learning processes it is also possible to criticise actions that facilitate what Habermas terms the systemic 'colonisation of the lifeworld', but also point towards how processes can be developed by using communicative action as an ideal. Sandberg examines the problems of conducting a critical empirical analysis based on Habermas' normative theory, arguing that, in order to understand how people act, it is necessary to focus on methods that can capture such processes in action. At the end, discussions around hybridisation and how different critical social theories can be merged for analysis is pursued. Habermas and Axel Honneth's work on recognition is used as an example.

Shaun Rawolle and Bob Lingard's introductory chapter on Bourdieu (Chapter 9) outlines his 'thinking tools', namely field, habitus, capitals and practices, as well as his theoretical and methodological dispositions and commitment to relational thinking. On the latter, emphasis is given to the rejection of what Bourdieu calls 'epistemological innocence' and the need for a reflexive approach to all research and theorising, what Bourdieu refers to as the capacity for 'socioanalysis'.

In outlining Bourdieu's intellectual *oeuvre*, the chapter also provides a short biographical account of his life, then turning to a consideration of the utilisation of Bourdieu's work in the sociology of education and in what has been called policy sociology in education. The chapter outlines the ways in which his work, including his concepts of field and habitus, assist researchers in theorising and researching contemporary policy developments in education. These include the emergence of a global education policy field and its cross-field effects into specific national education policy fields.

In Elizabeth Green's applied chapter on Bourdieu (Chapter 10), a strong case is made for his theory of education, reproduction and distinction as a powerful tool in the analysis of faith-based education. Green's example of research in faith-based settings provides readers with an indication of how current educational research is broadening the traditional application of Bourdieu's social theory beyond the study of class. Drawing on empirical research carried out in faith-based Academies in the United Kingdom, Green's discussion of Bourdieu's work is grounded in a real and high profile research context allowing for a discussion of the obstacles encountered by researchers in their application of Bourdieu's concepts. The chapter also illustrates how to build on Bourdieu's theory by integrating concepts from other thinkers into educational research design. This is important because Bourdieu's writings are complex and this can mean that first encounters with his work are off-putting for new researchers.

Irene Kleanthous' chapter (Chapter 11) provides a second example of how Bourdieu can be applied in educational research. Drawing on her own work, Kleanthous reflects on the use of Bourdieu's theory in exploring adolescent students' perceptions of parental influence on their educational choices for future studies in higher education. The mobilisation of familial capital from middle-class parents to enhance their children's educational choices is well documented in the literature, and Kleanthous problematises the use of Bourdieu by asking whether capital is adequate as a tool to theorise parental influence. She argues that parental influence is a form of 'symbolic violence' after Bourdieu, which students and their parents 'misrecognise' because parental influence is largely unconscious. This new theoretical conceptualisation of parental influence is discussed in this chapter along with some current debates in the literature about familial habitus and familial doxa.

The final part of the collection is devoted to the work of Derrida, and Jones Irwin uses the introductory chapter (Chapter 12) to explore in detail Derrida's idiosyncratic conception of a philosophy of education, while also connecting his practical work on philosophy in schools with his later re-evaluation of the whole politics of education in *Who's afraid of philosophy?* (Derrida 2002). The chapter also explores the way in which his work has been adapted in educational research settings such as curriculum and pedagogy. The chapter examines the theoretical subtlety of deconstruction, its connection to issues of political justice and, lastly, its important role for reassessing research methods as they relate in education to social theory.

In Chapter 13, Christine Winter provides an account of how Derrida can be applied in educational research settings, in this case in studies of the UK geography school curriculum. After providing her own interpretation of deconstruction together with a brief account of the work of researchers who are concerned about 'applying' Derrida in education, Winter details her school-based research project and how Derrida's ideas were engaged in the development, teaching and evaluation of a curriculum unit for a class of students aged 12–13 in a state comprehensive school in the north of England. According to Winter, the project was not without its ups and downs, and these are recounted in the third section of the chapter. The conclusion summarises the contribution that Derrida's insights offer to curriculum research and to curriculum itself, in their invitation to strive for a more ethically responsible and inspirational approach to curriculum thinking and practice. Winter reflects on the project to provide a rationale for methodological decisions, to glimpse the issues researchers face in bridging the theory–method dyad, and to offer thoughts about future curriculum research.

In line with Jones' and Winters' chapters, the final chapter in the collection (Chapter 14) sees Duncan Mercieca arguing that Derrida can provide a number of useful concepts for reading the lives of teachers. His chapter does two things in this regard: first, a reading of published and/or produced teachers' narratives from a Derridean perspective with the aim of helping teachers read their own narratives; and second, detailing the possibility of presenting philosophical concepts developed by Derrida to practising teachers. Using Derrida's concept of 'aporia' as well as other related concepts such as 'trace' and 'supplement', Mercieca focuses on teachers who 'wander' on these ideas in relation to their own lives. This is done by teachers through reading/watching other teachers' narratives, seeing moments of aporia in the narratives and in their own work, and through noting that they are 'just' when they engage with 'blind spots' in their work.

Conclusion

It is often the case that books on educational research emphasise the correct approaches to using specific modes of research tool, such as interviews and questionnaires, or focus on the construction of a dissertation or research report and how the constituent parts are assembled to construct the finished product/project. This of course is invaluable guidance, but nevertheless there is a tendency to pay less attention to the role of theory in the construction of such projects, and the various ways in which social theory can be used to extract *meaning* from the research site under examination. The contributions included in this collection are intended as part of an effort to stymie this tendency, and to illustrate what a worthwhile activity it is to engage social theory with educational research, so long as the researchers themselves come armed with an understanding of the work that awaits them.

What the chapters in this collection indicate is not just the scope of ideas in continental theory, but also the varied sets of issues faced when applying such ideas in educational research contexts, a field of interwoven imperatives and practices in its own right. These challenges – epistemological, operational, analytical – can be seen to impact on researchers and their attempts to make sense of educational questions, whether these be questions of governance and political regulation, social reproduction, curriculum and pedagogical practices or professional identities. Above all, the contributions indicate that the application of a challenging set of ideas onto a multifaceted set of practices must be delivered with care and a strong consideration for both intellectual arguments alongside the concerns of the professional researcher.

Having said that, the relationship between theory and practice, in general (and not just in research terms), has never been straightforward. That is as true for policy issues as it is for practical issues faced in teaching and learning contexts. This makes the contributions of the research included in this collection all the more valuable, as they show that such connections can be made, while remaining respectful of both theory and practice as separate entities in their own right.

Notes

1 Useful overviews of the application of social theory to health and social work research can be found in McDonnell et al. (2009) and Gray and Webb (2012), respectively. Specific examples of individual theorists applied to health and social work include Chambon (1999) on Foucault and social work and Scambler (2001) on Habermas and health.
2 For a more general overview of the field of social theory, see my text *Social theory: A new introduction* (Murphy 2021).
3 See also Nancy Fraser's account of Derrida's 'dance' with Marxism (Fraser 1989), which was published prior to *Spectres of Marx*.
4 Examples of such cross-fertilisation of ideas do exist – see for instance the journal *Studies in Philosophy and Education*, a special edition of which explored Habermas 'in conversation with others' – the 'others' including the likes of Derrida and Lacan (Murphy and Bamber 2012).
5 Habermas, for one, has been applied in sectors such as distance education (Tilak and Glassman 2020), curriculum design in schools (Säily et al. 2020) and academic researcher programmes (Garland 2014).
6 Examples using Bourdieu in this regard include the likes of Adewumi (2019), Burke (2019) and Rampersad (2016). See also the edited collection on Bourdieu and Chinese education by Mu et al. (2018), which explores a range of exclusions and inequities.
7 The likes of Rasmussen (2002) and Ranson et al. (2004) have applied Habermas in their research exploring issues of inequality, while a good example of Derrida

applied in a similar fashion can be found in Allan et al. (2010). See the work of Done and Murphy (2018) and Peters and Besley (2014) for examinations of Foucault in relation to research on educational inclusion.

8 Jones et al.'s (2021) research uses Foucault to explore the impact of neoliberalism on academic work and identities. Costa (2016) explores changing academic identities resulting from digital media via the lens of Bourdieu. Love's (2008) work takes Derrida and applies his concept of the 'quasi-ideal' to critique consumerist academic identities in higher education; while Nelson et al. (2008) apply Habermas in research on what informs the values of novice school principals.

9 A useful example of research linking social theory to student/learner identity is provided in Gorely et al.'s (2003) work on Bourdieu and the gendered nature of physical education.

10 See, for examples of 'applied' Foucault, Day and Pirrie (2021), Gillies (2008) and Mifsud (2017).

11 Notable examples of educational management research that use Habermas as a theoretical framework include Mabovula (2010), who explores the relevance of communicative action in issues of governance in South African schools; Tveit (2017) who adapts Habermas' ideas to examine the role of parental involvement in schools; Murphy (2018) who applies Habermas' understanding of bureaucracy to debates over education governance; and Smith (2007) who uses Habermas to examine the impact of 'quasi-marketisation' on the world of English further education.

References

Adewumi, B. 2019. Bridging the gap: Using Bourdieu and critical race theory to understand the importance of Black middle-class parents' educational aspirations for their children. In *International perspectives on theorising aspirations: Applying Bourdieu's tools*, eds. G. Stahl, D. Wallace, C. Burke and S. Threadgold, 210–223. London: Bloomsbury.

Allan, J., N. Moran, C. Duffy and G. Loening. 2010. Knowledge exchange with Sistema Scotland. *Journal of Education Policy* 25, 3: 335–347.

Best, S. 1995. *The politics of historical vision: Marx, Foucault, Habermas*. New York, NY: Guilford Press.

Best, S. and D. Kellner. 1991. *Postmodern theory: Critical interrogations*. New York, NY: Guildford Press.

Bourdieu, P. 1991. *Language and symbolic power*. Cambridge: Polity Press.

Burke, C. 2019. Maybe it is for the likes of us: Reconsidering classed higher education and graduate employment trajectories. In *International perspectives on theorising aspirations: Applying Bourdieu's tools*, eds. G. Stahl, D. Wallace, C. Burke and S. Threadgold, 21–35. London: Bloomsbury.

Chambon, A. 1999. *Reading Foucault for social work*. New York, NY: Columbia University Press.

Costa, C. 2016. Academics online: Fighting for a new habitus. In *Bourdieu, habitus and social research: The art of application*, eds. C. Costa and M. Murphy, 151–166. London: Palgrave.

Crowther, J. 2012. 'Really useful knowledge' or 'merely useful' lifelong learning? In *International handbook of lifelong learning*, eds. D.N. Aspin, J.D. Chapman, K. Evans and R. Bagnall, 801–811. Dortrecht: Kluwer.

Day, S. and A. Pirrie. 2021. Tales from the Matrix: Student satisfaction as a form of governmentality. In *Social theory and the politics of higher education: Critical perspectives on institutional research*, eds. M. Murphy, C. Burke, C. Costa and R. Raaper, 45–64. London: Bloomsbury.

Derrida J. 1976. *Of grammatology*. Trans. G Spivak. Baltimore, MD: Johns Hopkins University Press.

Derrida, J. 1994. *Spectres of Marx: The state of the debt, the work of mourning, and the New International*. New York, NY: Routledge.

Derrida, J. 2002. *Who's afraid of philosophy?: Right to philosophy* I. Stanford, CA: Stanford University Press.

Done, E. and M. Murphy. 2018. The responsibilisation of teachers: A neoliberal solution to the problem of inclusion, *Discourse: Studies in the Cultural Politics of Education* 39, 1: 142–155.

Foucault, M. 1976. *Mental illness and psychology*. Berkeley, CA: University of California Press.

Foucault, M. 1977. *Discipline and punish: The birth of the prison*. London: Allen Lane.

Fowler, B. 2011. Pierre Bourdieu: Unorthodox Marxist? In *The legacy of Pierre Bourdieu: critical essays*, eds. S. Susan and B. Turner, 33–57. London: Anthem.

Fraser, N. 1989. *Unruly practices: Power, discourses and gender in contemporary social theory*. Minneapolis, MN: University of Minnesota Press.

Garland, P. 2014. What can the work of Habermas offer educational researcher development programmes? *Studies in Higher Education* 39, 1: 87–101.

Gillies, D. 2008. Quality and equality: The mask of discursive conflation in education policy texts. *Journal of Education Policy* 23, 6: 685–699.

Gorely, T., R. Holroyd and D. Kirk. 2003. Muscularity, the habitus and the social construction of gender: Towards a gender-relevant physical education. *British Journal of Sociology of Education* 24, 4: 429–448.

Gray, M. and S. Webb. eds. 2012. *Social work theories and methods*. 2nd edn. London: Sage.

Habermas, J. 1984. *The theory of communicative action, volume 1: Reason and the rationalization of society*. Boston, MA: Beacon Press.

Habermas, J. 1987. *The theory of communicative action, volume 2: Lifeworld and system: A critique of functionalist reason*. Boston, MA: Beacon Press.

Hill, M. 2009. Ways of seeing: Using ethnography and Foucault's 'toolkit' to view assessment practices differently. *Qualitative Research* 9, 3: 309–330.

Jennings, J. and T. DiPrete. 2010. Teacher effects on social and behavioral skills in early elementary school. *Sociology of Education* 83, 2: 135–159.

Johnson, R. 1979. 'Really useful knowledge': Radical education and working class culture, 1790–1848. In *Working Class Culture: Studies in History and Theory*, eds. J. Clarke, C. Critcher and R. Johnson, 75–102. London: Hutchinson.

Jones, A., J. Harris, N. Spina and J.M. Azordegan. 2021. Governing the 'good' casual academic: Institutionalised 'othering' practices. In *Social theory and the politics of higher education: Critical perspectives on institutional research*, eds. M. Murphy, C. Burke, C. Costa and R. Raaper, 167–184. London: Bloomsbury.

Kellner. D. 1989. *Critical theory, Marxism and modernity*. Baltimore, MD: Johns Hopkins University Press.

Lee, A. and B. Green. 2009. Supervision as metaphor. *Studies in Higher Education* 34, 6: 615–630.

Love, K. 2008. Higher education, pedagogy and the 'customerisation' of teaching and learning. *Journal of Philosophy of Education* 42, 1: 15–34.

Mabovula, N. 2010. Revisiting Jürgen Habermas's notion of communicative action and its relevance for South African school governance: Can it succeed? *South African Journal of Education* 30: 1–12.

Magnus, B. and S. Cullenberg. 1994. Editors' introduction. In J. Derrida, *Spectres of Marx: The state of the debt, the work of mourning, and the new international*, vii–xi. New York, NY: Routledge.

Marx, K. and Engels, F. 1846/2011. *The German Ideology: Including Thesis on Feuerbach*. New York: Prometheus books.

McDonnell, O., M. Cohan, A. Hyde and S. Porter. 2009. *Social theory, health and healthcare*. Houndmills: Palgrave Macmillan.

Mifsud, D. 2017. *Foucault and school leadership research: Bridging theory and method*. London: Bloomsbury.

Mu, G.M., K. Dooley and A. Luke. eds. 2018. *Bourdieu and Chinese education: Inequality, competition and change*. Abingdon: Routledge.

Murphy, M. 2009. Bureaucracy and its limits: Accountability and rationality in higher education. *British Journal of Sociology of Education* 30, 6: 683–695.

Murphy, M. 2018. Ever greater scrutiny: Researching the bureaucracy of educational accountability. In *Education governance and social theory: Interdisciplinary approaches to research*, eds. A. Wilkins and A. Olmedo, 193–207. London: Bloomsbury.

Murphy, M. 2021. *Social theory: A new introduction*. London: Palgrave.

Murphy, M. and J. Bamber. 2012. Introduction: From Fromm to Lacan: Habermas and education in conversation. *Studies in Philosophy and Education* 31: 103–107.

Nelson, S., M. de la Colina and M. Boone. 2008. Lifeworld or systemsworld: What guides novice principals? *Journal of Educational Administration* 46, 6: 690–701.

Peters, M. and T. Besley. 2014. Social exclusion/inclusion: Foucault's analytics of exclusion, the political ecology of social inclusion and the legitimation of inclusive education. *Open Review of Educational Research* 1, 1: 99–115.

Rampersad, R. 2016. Operationalising Bourdieu: Interrogating intersectionality and the underachievement of primary level Afro-Trinidadian boys. In *Theory as method in research: On Bourdieu, social theory and education*, eds. M. Murphy and C. Costa, 65–82. Abingdon: Routledge.

Ranson, S., J. Martin and C. Vincent. 2004. Storming parents, schools and communicative inaction. *British Journal of Sociology of Education* 25, 3: 259–274.

Rasmussen, P. 2002. Education for everyone: Secondary education and social inclusion in Denmark. *Journal of Education Policy* 17, 6: 627–642.

Rousseau, J.-J. 1755/2004. *Discourse on the origin of inequality*. New York, NY: Dover Press.

Säily, L., R. Huttunen, L. Hannu, T. Heikkinen, T. Kiilakoski and T. Kujala. 2020. Designing education democratically through deliberative crowdsourcing: The case of the Finnish curriculum for basic education. *Journal of Curriculum Studies* (Online First). doi:10.1080/00220272.2020.1857846.

Scambler, G. ed. 2001. *Habermas, critical theory and health*. London: Routledge.

Smith, R. 2007. Work, identity and the quasi-market: The FE experience. *Journal of Educational Administration and History* 39, 1: 33–47.

Tilak, S. and M. Glassman. 2020. Alternative lifeworlds on the internet: Habermas and democratic distance education. *Distance Education* 41, 3: 326–344.

Tveit, A.D. 2017. Parental involvement in school: Applying Habermas' theoretical framework. In *Habermas and social research: Between theory and method*, ed. M. Murphy, 109–121. Abingdon: Routledge.

West, C. 1991. *The ethical dimensions of Marxist thought*. New York, NY: Monthly Review Press.

2 Social theory and methodology in education research

From conceptualisation to operationalisation

Mark Murphy and Cristina Costa

Introduction

Social theory has provided a vital resource for intellectual debate, delivering an impressive panoply of theoretical approaches that have helped broaden the conceptual horizons of education researchers. This commitment to theory has undoubtedly provided scholars with a sharp set of tools via which to interrogate forms of professional and institutional practices. Without such tools, it is difficult to see how the field could offer a critical alternative to the instrumental demands of the educational improvement and what works agendas.

Education researchers are drawn to the transformative potential of social theory, as it offers tools to develop a counter-discourse to prevailing orthodoxies – this function is much prized and understandably so in a field that is inevitably politicised and wide-open to ideological manipulation. Social theories provide a suitable platform for developing this counter discourse as they share an unquestionable political orientation, while also providing a rich resource of material and concepts drawn from a diverse interdisciplinary base. Social theory comprises a range of analytical frameworks used to explain social phenomena, borrowing ideas from sociology, philosophy, history, literature, geography, cultural and gender studies, among others.

The discursive element of social theory is especially significant to the education field, as social theory itself is a form of language, a 'language that is able to illuminate, sometimes amplify, the understanding of the world we aim to explore' (Costa et al. 2018, 2). The seemingly endless linguistic resources provided by social theory have greatly enriched the field and have left no corner of education research untouched. That said, it is wise to take stock of this application of theory in education research, and to reflect on key challenges that need to be examined alongside the undoubted achievements of theory-driven applied research. We use this chapter to argue that three issues in particular need special consideration: (1) how to promote hybridised theory and conceptual interdisciplinarity in education research as a counterpoint to monological approaches to theory application; (2) how to encourage forms of critical reflexivity to counteract 'off-the-shelf' approaches to theory use; and (3) how to elevate the status of theory 'application' as a vital conduit in bridging concepts and research methods.

DOI: 10.4324/9781003156550-3

We argue that these issues need special consideration as the field would ultimately benefit in the shape of greater conceptual originality and methodological rigour. Most importantly, taking fuller advantage of the intellectual 'wide-lens' provided by social theory offers a much-needed vantage point from which to further enhance the quality of theory-driven education research. Before these issues are explored in more depth, it is important to situate theory-driven applied research in its historical context, specifically in relation to the role and status of positivism in education and social science research more generally. This contextualisation helps to illustrate the significance of the issues addressed in this chapter from an epistemological and ontological standpoint.

Positivism and research in the social sciences

As a force in social scientific research, positivism developed alongside the birth of capitalism and the Industrial Revolution, and as a philosophy and method draws heavily on the work of August Comte, the founder of sociology, as well as other 19th-century philosophers such as David Hume. While there are numerous offshoots of the theory, key tenets can be identified. These include the position that all factual knowledge is gained from experience, and that the analysis of these facts is dependent on the science of logic and mathematics. Evidence gained from observation and experience has an exclusive monopoly on this factual knowledge. The task of the social sciences is to research these social facts and then to develop from these facts a set of general laws of human behaviour and action, in a similar fashion to the methods of the natural sciences. This approach was deemed by Comte and others to be the only viable and logical way to escape the bias and prejudice of metaphysical and theological conceptions of knowledge, a set of affairs they viewed as outdated and incompatible with the modern emphasis on social and technological progress.

These aspects of positivism are well known and often detailed in textbooks on research methods. But alongside this and for the purpose of this chapter, the position of theory in positivism is worthy of special note. For positivists, theory is a secondary offshoot of the predictive effects of scientific method and is useful to the extent that it allows the researcher to move across data sets. Theories themselves play second fiddle to observable and verifiable facts and the data sets that accrue from them. This reflects the ontological assumption of positivism – that the world exists independently of people's perceptions and as a result could be investigated as an objective reality with the right methodological tools. The 'truth' of social behaviour was attainable, not through abstraction and theory, but by rigorous analysis of data gleaned through sensory experience.

Objectivity, disinterest and detachedness became guiding principles of scientific research, and as the father of modern sociology, Comte went on to have a considerable influence on what was considered appropriate and worthy (social) scientific research in the field. But positivism as a guiding force in fields such as sociology has not gone unchallenged over the decades and in particular has had to deal with its 'epistemological others' (Steinmetz 2005). These others have come thick and fast over the past 150 years, including approaches such as Marxism and psychoanalysis, post-structuralism, postcolonial and gender studies.

A key flaw highlighted by these epistemological others is the conception of sensory experience that is so central to the positivist tradition. Scholars such as Thomas Kuhn (1996) have highlighted the inherent bias that underpins this sensory experience: researchers will inevitably bring with them certain under-standings of the world that frame their social observations – observation and interpretation being intertwined. As a result, the prized objectivity of the detached and disinterested observer becomes open to question – the methods of data collection do not exist independently of the values the researcher brings to the research design. So for example in the design of a questionnaire or a focus group, the kinds of questions that are asked of respondents will them-selves be framed by particular ontological and epistemological beliefs.

This is arguably the key debating point when it comes to positivism and its epistemological others – the place of values in humanities and social science research. The notion of a value free science has often been held up as the gold standard of academic research, a vaulted position from which to make grand claims about the purity of research outcomes as well as the political sphere that seeks out research evidence supposedly free from ideological bias. Hence the generous funding for randomly controlled trials (RCTs) in schools in countries such as the United Kingdom and United States, an approach to research design that positions itself as untainted by values.

But such a view rests on distinctly uneasy foundations, one of which being the problematic assumption that a field such as education is amenable to research analysis using the same tools and approach as that deployed in chem-istry or biology. This is a serious error of judgement on the part of researchers, given that education is a decidedly social enterprise and a highly politicised one at that. While it is laudable that researchers aim to depoliticise a field and often view positivist approaches such as RCTs as a way to achieve this, politics and values are part of education's DNA and the denial of this is a form of what Bourdieu calls 'symbolic violence'. This is evident in the design of RCTs, a design that testifies to the fact that this approach is as biased as any other and produce 'knowledge based on what is deemed to count as knowledge' (Gale 2018, 211).

Social theory and the positivism debate

This paradigmatic stance inevitably means that positivism and the field of social theory are uneasy bed fellows, to put it mildly. In fact, there is often strong animosity between the two – anti-positivism is an identifiable thread that links numerous social theorists, such as the ones detailed in this book, as well as others such as Theodor Adorno, Donna Haraway, Judith Butler and Boa-ventura de Sousa Santos. For these authors, there is a political component to theory and theorising that is decidedly at odds with positivism. And for positi-vism and positivists, the space made available for theory and theorising is minimal – this side-lining of theory speaks to a politics of method and methodology that is an important aspect of this book. Steinmetz (2005, 29) talks of the 'uncanny persistence' of positivism even though it has been besieged by criticism at least since the great positivist debate of the 1960s (see Murphy 2021, Chapter 8). Part of this remarkable resilience is down to the prevalence of methodological fetishism, with methods and method training being 'a central site for the reinforcement of positivist hegemony in the social sciences' (Steinmetz 2005, 45).

This vaulted position of positivism is evident in the details of academic life. It is often the case that, for example, when 'researchers attempt to justify their methodology, they often appear to fail to explore the relationships between theory and method as science' (Bartlett 1991, 20). This methodological fetishism can be damaging for the quality of research outcomes, especially the assumption that methods are sufficient in themselves at uncovering meaning. As McCarthy puts it:

> If the method itself forms the objects of perception, defines the logic of analysis, legitimates particular social problems, and justifies the logic of science, then the theories which penetrate beneath the phenomenal appearances into the depth structures of society and call these structures into question are not valid forms of scientific knowledge.
>
> (McCarthy 2001, 231)

For education researchers, this hegemonic hold on the field can have real world consequences for the quality of research outcomes as the fetish for method overshadows paradigmatic concerns with research design. As Alvesson and Sköldberg (2000) (cited in Kumar Gir 2006, 232) put it, 'It is not methods but ontology and epistemology which are the determinants of good social science'.

The status of 'good' social science is what really matters, especially to the aims of this collection, as it embodies questions of research design, academic rigour, originality and significance – all powerful signifiers of quality research. The persistent denial of politics, of theory and values, highlight the short-comings of positivism as a methodological approach to education research in the 21st century, a historical context is which the politicisation of education and education research is stark and unrelenting. Burawoy (2005, 515) is correct to suggest that positivism is of little value in this rapidly changing world, one in which education institutions are subject to often highly unpredictable forces. These forces do not lend themselves to the scientific detached analysis of positivism, and instead result in the erosion of the 'conditions of the positivist illusion' (ibid, 516). Education academics who stick steadfastly to positivist science are placed in a difficult position, as social transformations such as marketisation impinge more and more on their own research environment. University researchers 'can no longer regard ourselves as outside history, projecting a universal knowledge from a non-existent Archimedian place … we have been living in a fool's paradise' (ibid, 516).

This fool's paradise is compounded by positivism's conflation of method and meaning, a situation that denies researchers access to the really-useful knowledge of social theory: the language required to formulate critical questions 'is not available' (McCarthy 2001, 231). Social theory offers such a critical language – hence why it is so valuable but also why it is such a threat to positivist social science.

That said, just because social theory offers this critical alternative does not mean that the field as well as its research applications are immune from critical scrutiny themselves – indeed, critical scrutiny is very much in keeping with social theory's own rationale. An opposition to positivism, while laudable in itself, provides an insufficient basis on which to build a strong case for theory-driven methodologies. This field of interpretive education research needs to develop some common understandings of what this form of research consists of, both its benefits and drawbacks – while positivism casts a long shadow, this should not be used as a reason to avoid a closer investigation of the field, and to suggest ways forward in order to enhance the quality and rigour of this form of education research. Ensuring that one's own methodological 'house' is in order is a more sustainable way to reclaim phrases such as research 'quality', and 'research rigour' from the hegemonic power of positivist approaches.

What follows is a contribution to this critical scrutiny in the context of education research, starting with a brief elaboration of theory as critical literacy.

Social theory as a form of critical literacy in education research

Language itself is central to the field of social theory as a professional practice. Social theory would struggle to express itself and develop without the explanatory power that language affords the user. Language not only allows for the communication of theory, but it also creates and shapes its conceptual architecture – see as examples the concepts of the shared third (Benjamin 2017), the broken middle (Rose 1992) and the hollowed-out state (Rhodes 2017). These are excellent examples of how language creates intellectual space for ideas to take shape. They also illustrate how language in the basic form of nouns and adjectives is surprisingly efficient at clarity and conciseness, even if at first sight it may be hard to grasp. Yet, perseverance in acquiring the theoretical language can often result in 'light bulb' moments that give researchers intellectual direction(s) through the newly acquired linguistic standpoint. The language of theory can help to thread together the researcher's ontological, epistemological and methodologically approach to help guide their critical enquiry.

In this way, theory offers a form of *critical literacy* for researchers to work with as a core aspect of 'doing' research. As a critical research literacy, theory can equip researchers with research lenses that give research phenomena a perspective from which to 'capture' reality as well as vocabulary for researchers to express their understanding of it. This is an essential step in research practice, one that individuals new to research or those less experienced in theory application can often struggle with when formulating their research and/or operationalising the different elements that comprise the research project. When researchers are already well versed with the knowledge of theory, then the concern shifts to the 'capturing' of reality. The question here then is not one of theoretical framing of what to capture, but a methodological concern of how to do the 'capturing' of reality (Costa et al. 2019). Here, in providing an answer, theory moves from intellectualisation of ideas to the conceptualisation and operationalisation of research through method.

Nevertheless, while its influence in education research has grown and its visibility all too evident, social theory faces a number of obstacles when it comes to realising its transformative potential in the education research field. In the remainder of this chapter we focus on three key issues in particular that need special consideration: (1) the place of hybridised theory and conceptual interdisciplinarity in education research; (2) the importance of critical reflexivity when dealing with social theory and education; and (3) the question of theory application in education research design.

1 Hybridised theory and conceptual interdisciplinarity

Social theory is a response to historical events, and historical forms of injustice. The *raison d'être* of social theory is to provide explanations for social transformations and their effects and also to account for the lack of change when it comes to issues of equity, freedom and solidarity. It therefore has little interest in identifying some kind of Archimedean point via which society can be judged – this is a thankless task and a waste of intellectual energy. But that said the lack of such an Archimedean point has posed difficulties for social theory and has asked questions of its capacity to deliver an effective form of social critique. It is better off without it, however, as changing historical circumstances cannot accommodate absolute certainties and fixed positions. This is why social theory should be approached as also subject to transformation in that theory should never be regarded as an off the shelf, one size fits all conceptual tool. Rather, it should be considered and used in light of the context that it is needed, hence the term 'theory application'. Theory application implies 'putting something to relevant use', in this case, placing theory at the service of the research phenomenon in need of exploration, understanding and explanation. This applies also to the numerous conceptual apparatuses that have been painstakingly constructed by scholars to help them explain society and its consequences. These theories and the theorists themselves are also products of historical circumstances and are not immune to change. On the contrary, they should be seen as historically contingent and not viewed as unalterable or outside critique. No social theory can or should be considered in such a manner. In this regard, Hope notes that Foucault and Deleuze (1980) made a similar argument (ibid, 208), reasoning that social theory 'should not be approached as something to genuflect before but rather as a tool kit that is used selectively depending on the analytical task at hand' (Hope 2022, 71).

The historical nature of theory is also of relevance to social theorists themselves. Social theorists often feel the need to defend a particular position against threats posed from other theories, and their anxiety is understandable given that so much depends on the assumed legitimacy of their conceptual work, both from a political and professional perspective. But this is unnecessary. It is also illogical as their own theories are generally built on an already existing set of ideas and concepts, without which it would be impossible to generate new concepts. Take Habermas for example: His work is a shining example of what we call hybridisation, his work weaving together a dazzling combination of thinkers and ideas to construct his own analysis of modern pathologies (Murphy 2017).

The same can be said for Pierre Bourdieu, Judith Butler, Gayatri Spivak and numerous others. The most effective theorists engage in this kind of conceptual interdisciplinarity, as a way to move debates forward and to untangle some previously knotty conceptual issues (Murphy 2017, 13–14). Fields such as the social sciences and humanities require hybrid work; take for example Stuart Hall's (1997) theory of culture, which expertly drew together ideas from Foucault, Fanon, Derrida and Said, using this fusion of ideas to respond to changing forms of diasporic identity, themselves rapidly evolving into hybrid forms of cultural signification. It is improper therefore to think that these latest versions of hybrid theory are themselves immune to change and represent the last definite word on whatever topic they examine. It is more likely that they will stay with us for a long time, but any efforts to preserve their purity are destined to fail or at best lead us down some suspect avenues. If nothing else, users of theory need to allow for the theory – often through certain key concepts – to infiltrate the contexts being researched and explore if and how far the theory can stretch as well as how it can be extended.

If the acquisition of theory can be compared to the process of language learning then, just like language acquisition, theory is the product of multiple influences. Most social theories seek inspiration in a multitude of sources. For example, Bourdieu's concept of habitus draws on ideas from Aristotle, Chomsky and Piaget, while Axel Honneth's typology of recognition combines Hegel's early work on recognition and Mead's interactionist principles of individual action, as well as the ideas of Jessica Benjamin. Many other theories currently used in social and education research originate from a variety of ideas that are put together to form a new one – this we call the process of *hybridisation*. In other words, theory is built on the hybridisation of ideas. In the art of theory making and theory application however this aspect can be overlooked as researchers seem too easily to adopt a research identity that pays homage to the 'Master' as Freirians, Foucauldians, Derridians, Habermasians or Bourdieuians, to name but a few forms of self-theoretical identification. By focusing on this issue it is not our intention to discourage deep study of these authors' work, but rather to question if such monological approaches to the theorisation of research is sufficient in the face of highly complex and rapidly shifting forms of educational practice, identity and governance. Instead, we should seek to make it commonplace to bring different theories together to complement our research. The need for such an approach is often identified when a given theory no longer stretches linguistically or empirically to decode the phenomenon at hand. This indicates that the further intellectualisation of research – conceptually and/or methodologically – requires inspiration from elsewhere.

A hybridised approach assists with both theory development and research design. Theory needs to 'test' and reconstruct itself based on changing forms of social practice. This is a key element of theorising, and this itself tends to strengthen the case for hybridisation in social theorising rather than weaken it. We suggest that education should be viewed through the intellectual wide-lens of social theory. On this point, Swedberg has done the field of social theory a great service by drawing our attention to the art of doing social theory (Swedberg 2014). According to Swedberg, to be successful at social theorising, you need to have 'the capacity to look at reality from a social perspective' (ibid, 169). He also adds that knowing some social theory and having the ability to engage with it effectively, to 'handle it well' is also important, a sentiment wholeheartedly shared by the authors. What Swedberg means by 'handle it well' is central to this debate:

> You may, for example, need to take a concept from one theory and combine it with a concept from another theory. You may want to eliminate some part of a theory and replace it with a new idea of your own, and so on.
>
> (ibid, 169)

This capacity to hybridise, he argues, means that researchers can develop the capacity to draw on a range of sources for inspiration. This is where knowledge of social theory comes in, knowledge that is not just about the accumulation of ideas, concepts and theoretical approaches; rather it is about having a depth of understanding as to what the 'social' means.

The capacity to be able to handle social theory well also requires a large dose of imagination on the part of the theorist. Talk of imagination and social theory sends us back to the work of C. Wright Mills and his classic text *The sociological imagination* (Mills 1959). His description of what this imagination entails and how to achieve it had a strong hybridising element. Mills argues that the sense of imagination 'is the combination of ideas that no one expected were combinable – say, a mess of ideas from German Philosophy and British economics' (ibid, 211). The mechanisms Mills identifies as stimulators of this imagination also speak to hybridity as crucial to effective theorising, which include scrambling and mixing up notes, searching out comparable cases, and seeking out the opposite of your own research subject (ibid, 212).

Swedberg builds on the work of Mills by providing some further avenues for exploring the creative social theory mind, which include free association and reverie. These are valuable ways of unearthing inspiration and budding theorists would be wise to consider them more fully. They should also accept that the basic building blocks of theorising are *other theories*. Building up this body of knowledge about specific themes/topics and the ways in which different theories have been constructed to help account for these is a crucial element to the development of social scientists, including education researchers.

Publications such as these produce new ways of thinking about specific topics that help to move academic debates forward, as well as helping to reorient our thinking about educational issues in changing historical times. Most importantly, hybridised research that adopts a reflexive attitude to theory application, works to the benefit of education practice, rather than purely serving particular theoretical silos. Theory is put to work to illuminate how practices, such as those related to curriculum, pedagogy and assessment, have particular effects (such as inequality), while also providing ideas about how best such effects can be tackled from a policy and practitioner perspective.

Education is not the only discipline to rely on theory from a range of other disciplines, organisation studies for example has a long history of 'borrowing' concepts from fields such as sociology and psychology (Oswick et al. 2011. 318). There are lessons that can be learnt from the experience of other fields, one of them being that conceptual borrowing can 'damage' the host field. Conceptual borrowing 'can overwhelm the more creative insights offered by the foreign theory, diminishing it to a rather "impotent" form of theory building' (ibid, 328). It is also the case that theory can mean very different things to different social scientists (Kroneberg 2019, 31), making comparisons across fields an even more challenging task. It is in this sense that not only epistemic and ontological vigilance remains central to research, but also reflexivity becomes a critical tool to researchers' research practice.

2 Social theory and critical reflexivity

The previous section highlighted the limits to monological approaches when it comes to theory building. There are also limits from a research design perspective. Evident in the education research literature is a tendency to not just depend on one key theorist, but also to act as if these specific theoretical toolkits solve all their problems – magically (and particularly true for Bourdieu and Foucault), concepts such as habitus, capital, field, subjectivation, discourse, panopticism, bio-power, heterotopia, and so on, can be taken down from the shelf and transposed onto seemingly simple and historically unwavering educational practices. This approach to theory application, which Allan calls 'lensification' (see Allan 2022, 48), can result in an uncritical acceptance of the virtues of specific social theories and their relevance to the education field.

This lensification approach is evident when it comes to the work of Bourdieu whose core concepts of habitus, field and capital are often used as a recipe to explain specific forms of education and social inequality. Such an approach is sometimes evident in different academic journals and is often accompanied by an uncritical approach to the use of these concepts. In the case of Foucault, Allan argues that this lensification sees researchers enticed by the 'apparent simplicity' of a Foucauldian lens, with such lens often 'serving as little more than a gloss' in educational research (Allan 2022, 48). What such careless use of theory usually leads to is the loss of the critical meaning that such concepts carry as part of the research process, thus reducing the significance and deep meaning that theoretical concepts encapsulate. It can also potentially lead to an impoverished view of the relation between theory and practice, one that tends to subjugate educational practice under the uber-explanatory power of habitus, discourse, rhizome, performativity, and so on.

Bourdieu himself warned against such a tendency, hence his insistence on a critical reflexivity in the research process (Bourdieu and Wacquant 1992). Talk of reflexivity has become commonplace in the research world, and alongside a focus on positionality offers a welcome guard against the excessive influence of personal bias and ideological position. But this tends to be geared towards issues of method and is much less prevalent in considerations of theory and its utility. Reflexivity should therefore not be confused with personal reflection of research practice. It is deeper than purely personal reflection in that as an intellectual tool, reflexivity aims to turn the research mirror on the researcher as a continuous form of intellectual accountability towards the entire research process – from its inception to conclusion – and not just the methodological construction of a research project.

Postgraduate students have been steadily immersed in issues of methodological rigour and/or trustworthiness, alongside an embedded obligation to consider the limits of their research design. This concern over limits does not always extend to theoretical issues, and Baur (2017, 51) helpfully reminds us that a requirement of theory-driven research is to explicate 'one's perspectivity', precisely because 'social theory plays both a major role in focusing the research question and in linking theory with the data' (ibid, 51). At the very least, explicating this theoretical perspective can help the field avoid the worst consequences of 'methodological fetishism' (Berger 2002) – i.e. the 'sprinkling' approach to theoretical analysis (Pierre 2017, 1081), or even more troubling, the failure 'to identify a conceptual framework at all' (Brosnan 2013, 5).

The adoption of a specific theorist or concept is not necessarily always a concern in the work of early career researchers or any researcher for that matter. Such an approach can provide greater depth and understanding of the value of particular concepts. It is appropriate to apply certain theoretical ideas but to do so calls for a critical eye – care needs to be taken when engaging with concepts in relative isolation. That said even when care is taken, a monological approach to theory application is not necessarily the best training for a career in academia and neither does it help move the education field forward in any significant way.

The use of such approaches is questionable at the very least in the context of producing quality research outputs. While the Research Excellence Framework (REF) in the UK does not have the final say on the topic of education research quality, the criteria used in the REF – originality, significance and rigour – are a useful way to consider what constitutes 'quality' research in education. Although the use of 'theory' is emphasised in '4 star' papers, this must be measured against these criteria, and it is arguably the case that monological approaches to theory can fall short in this regard. Any effective research assessment exercise needs to consider the extent to which the education research field benefits from continuous non-reflective application of one theorist or one concept/set of concepts to educational topics. It is difficult to characterise such work as original or laden with real significance.

The level of conceptual rigour is also open to debate: The degree of critical reflection on the utility of certain concepts or theories can be minimal, or evasive of its real significance and contribution to the field. Research rigour does not start or end with concerns over the design of research instruments but rather extends to the entire research process. In critical research, theory should be the marker and driver of rigour, with the caveat that rigour should be a guard against conceptual oversimplification. This has become common place when using the work of popular theorists, as is the case of Bourdieu, whose concept of capital is sometimes applied in research accounts as a vague catch-all term for forms of educational exchange, rendering its theoretical application meaningless. The same applies to the concept of habitus, whose etymological nature inevitably demands that researchers somehow engage with its complexity. Nonetheless, in attempts to simplify the concept, researchers can adopt a more than desired generic understanding of habitus as 'dispositions', without properly conceptualising these dispositions.

This is not useful as research outcomes can become unclear and vague, thus losing part of their essence and purpose in deriving originality. These examples illustrate the unreflexive side of the research(er) in trying to justify the applicability of theoretical concepts that demand an appreciation for the context of the research. After all, habitus as a theoretical tool was not conceived so it could be reduced to an elusive understanding of 'dispositions', but rather to be operationalised with a clear purpose and meaning in mind, one that is related to its context of application (see Costa et al. 2019), and whose meaning therefore changes from situation to situation, dependent on the research questions that motivate its application. Theoretic concepts are thus best understood as capsule definitions (Wacquant 2014, 4) developed to be transferable to different, yet specific contexts; contexts that are untangled into a complex system of inter-relations (Champagne and Duval 2018, 137). This is where reflexivity is most needed because this theory transferability from one context to another does not negate the fact that the meaning of concepts is not context dependent. Application of social theory requires an appreciation – as well as an awareness – of the relational nature of theoretical concepts.

Additionally, even when theories are duly applied to a research project, its applicability should not be approached as the be-all and end-all of theory–method approaches. Although at some point researchers will need to draw the line on the theories and concepts they will enlist for a given research project, the practice of reflexivity should not stop there. Reflexivity as part of the theory–method dialectic is not only concerned with theory application appropriateness, but also its extendibility to the research phenomenon as it is unveiled through the research process. For example, although neither Foucault nor Bourdieu have lived to explore the phenomenon that digital technologies have created, the legacy of their concepts have been extended to studies of digital practices, with reasonable success. Studies on datafication of education have drawn considerably on Foucault's concepts of subjectification and the panopticon, whereas studies on digital scholarship (Costa 2013; 2016) and digital education practices (Beckman et al. 2018) have taken inspiration from Bourdieu's conceptual triad of capitals, field and habitus. Nonetheless, it is always important to wonder if these research instruments extend the boundaries of the research sufficiently.

Such questions can be posed at the operationalisation stage of the research as well as at the analysis stage, thus making the case for an additional opportunity for theory hybridisation. Clues to this need often arise from the lack of vocabulary to explain, expand and/or do justice to the reality that the researcher aims to account for through their research. When the theoretical language at our disposal, as enlisted by our selected theoretical apparatus, no longer suffices to depict the problematics under focus, then it is important to seek theoretical help elsewhere. This can take at least different forms, by either seeking inspiration in other theories, developing our own concepts, and more often than not by doing both.

Ultimately, key to theory–method reflexivity is an awareness that all stages of the research process are intimately related as an intellectual project of meaning-making for which theory application becomes not only the conduit but also the glue that keeps it together. In this sense, critical reflexivity in education research can help overcome researchers' dogmatic views of what theory can offer to education research (Costa and Murphy 2016), which is more than adding an intellectual gloss to research findings. A critically reflexive approach enlists the power of social theory to unmask issues of injustice, while also keeping the researcher in check when it comes to issues of conceptual and methodological rigour. To be critically reflexive is then to remain vigilant of theory application across the entire research process.

3 The status of theory 'application' in bridging concept and method

The application of social theory to the exploration of education phenomena has never been more crucial than today given the highly politicised contexts of institutional and professional practice in the 21st century. That said, the notion of theory 'application' does not sit easily with everyone; for example Judith Butler (in Gane 2004, 74) expressed concern that the notion of applied theory overlooks the idea that theory is already a social practice. This is an important issue, but it does not negate the strong desire among researchers especially to 'fit' theory to method, and rightly so. 'Application' is at least a form of linguistic shorthand to engage with the 'problematic relationship between theories and data' as Habermas put it (Habermas 1967/1988, 100).

It is useful to bring Habermas into the discussion at this point. His presence in education research is less obvious than in the work of other theorists, which will have something to do with his lack of focus on educational matters over the years (Murphy 2010), but the same cannot be said when it comes to questions of theory and methodology on which subject he wrote about at some length in the 1960s. Investigation of this work indicates a shared concern over application, or what he calls 'operationalisation' (Habermas 1967/1988, 100). He called to account the 'arbitrariness of operationalisations' which he saw as undermining the credibility of social research, especially that which was grounded in interpretive approaches (ibid, 100). He argued that the arbitrary nature of application could be limited

> if we could make conscious the process whereby measurement procedures are adapted, after the fact, to a prescientifically grounded correspondence between sociological concepts and communicative experiences.
>
> (ibid, 100)

In part, Habermas here was responding to earlier claims made by Cicourel (1964), that the social sciences were plagued by a 'lack of methodological sophistication' (ibid, 21), which resulted in a disconnect between theory and method, in the lack of 'a precise or warranted correspondence between existing measurements systems and our theoretical and substantive concepts', a link Cicourel damningly states is only established by fiat.

It is evident therefore that concern with overcoming the dichotomy of theory/method is not a new one. But its significance when it comes to the craft and quality of research design remains. As we have argued in this chapter, theory should be elevated in research design because of its intrinsic relationship with research methods. How theoretical concepts are or can be applied to research practice is a question that new researchers often ask themselves. This is normally considered the 'black box' of research practice (Costa et al. 2019, 20), which consists of a set of challenges faced in research when 'bridging the gap' between theory and method. How researchers prepare for field work in light of the theoretical concepts that underpin their research (Costa and Murphy 2016; Murphy and Costa 2015) is rarely discussed explicitly in research publications. Accounts of how theoretical concepts can be brought to life in research settings are a valuable component of research design rationale, one that merits discussion and a place in teaching of research practice. Considering the theory–method relation allows for research practices to be positioned within a theory–praxis nexus while at the same time guiding research away from the temptation of perceiving the role of theory as an arbitrary, add-on to the discussion of research findings.

Social theorists themselves have supported stronger conceptualisation of research practice through the theoretical conceptualisation of research methods, with Bourdieu leading the way on such discussions (see, e.g. Bourdieu, Chamboredon and Passeron 1991; Bourdieu and Wacquant 1992). This approach aims to position theory and method as inseparable elements of research practice, of *methodology*. The theory/method dynamic points to a practice of addressing research methods beyond their role as tools for data collection and applying theory across the entire research process. This implies that disconnecting the conceptualisation of the research study from the methods of data collection is best avoided. Instead, a theory–method approach suggests that theory becomes central to the entire research process by making theory application central to the development of research instruments, not only with regards to the type of instrument, but also what shapes the contents of the research tool. An example of theory applied to method can be accessed through Nowicka's (2015) work on migrants' adaptation to a new environment. Drawing on the work of Bourdieu, Nowicka starts by conceptualising her inquiry through the concept of habitus that requires access to a suitable set of dispositions related to the phenomenon at hand. To unearth a deep understanding of 'adequate' dispositions to her study, she then seeks out ideas from intercultural studies and parallel fields to establish which dispositions are useful to employ in her study. This synergy between Bourdieu's theory and knowledge from Nowicka's applied field of research is then transferred to different research instruments to capture different dimensions of a specific set of dispositions that were operationalised to meet the purpose of her study. In other words, Nowicka's study is a good example of how theory can be applied to research design, i.e. to practice.

This type of theory application, however, should not be confused with ways of reproducing or re-testing theory, but rather as a form of theory 'stretching' in that the contribution of theory is only acknowledged when it enhances current knowledge through original and critical perspectives. Nowicka's work achieves this aspect by hybridising Bourdieu's concept of habitus with understanding of intercultural practices/learning. In essence, what theory as method does is to give researchers a *clearer* direction of their research and how it can be deployed empirically. This is an aspect that should be of central interest to researchers in that methodological choices are deeply rooted in theoretical discussions.

In short, theory application would benefit from being celebrated more visibly as an essential gateway into critical research. Theoretical language carries a given cultural perspective – it would be naïve to think theory is impermeable to change or progress, or that additional theoretical lenses should not be explored in tandem. Theory that remains relevant across time – just like language – is not only adjustable, but also dynamic enough to incorporate vocabulary (new concepts) necessary to express fresh reflections of social phenomena. That is the fundamental role of hybridisation in theoretical work, to welcome the influence of other areas of knowledge. Theory should not imprison researchers, but rather liberate them to conduct research in a suitably informed way whilst providing tools to explore pertinent phenomena and push the boundaries of theoretical work through the entanglement of different theories.

To make it clear, to adopt a theory as method approach to education research, i.e. how theory is used not just to help problematise and conceptualise the problem at hand, but also how it is then translated into the development of research instruments fit to 'capture' such reality (Costa et al. 2019), is to take a value-laden position pertaining to the research phenomenon at hand. However, this is not to be confused with adopting a biased stance to the research, to answer to positivist claims, but rather to establish from the onset that when it comes to critical education research value- and epistemologically neutral approaches are deemed illusory and unreflexive of their own ideological presumptions and values. As Bourdieu, Chamboredon and Passeron (1991) further remind us, claims of methodological objectivity serve only to hide a lack of epistemological, ontological and axiological concern when conducting education research:

> The endless debate about 'ethical neutrality' often serves as a substitute for a genuinely epistemological discussion of the 'methodological neutrality' of techniques, and, as such, it provides further support for the positivist illusion. By a *displacement* effect, interest in ethical presuppositions and ultimate values or ends diverts attention from critical examination of the theory of sociological knowledge that is engaged in the most elementary acts of practice.
>
> (ibid, 41)

To illustrate this issue in concrete ways, we will use the example of research on gender in education and the confusion between concepts of gender and sex in some subfields of education research, despite an established body of academic literature that asserts the different meanings attributed to the two terms (see Butler 1996), namely that gender is conceptualised as a social construct and sex as a biological attribute. Garvey et al. (2019) have identified 'methodological troubles' in research in this area that place both theoretical and analytical work at peril through the use of gender and sex as binary variables. This shows a disregard for a wider representation of gender identities that could have been achieved through a careful operationalisation of gender as a concept that conceals in itself a range of complex meanings. This represents a failure 'to subject ordinary language (...) to a methodological critique [and] entails the risk of mistaking objects pre-constructed in and by ordinary language for data' (Bourdieu, Chamboredon and Passeron 1991, 21). It is in this regard that Rasmussen et al. (2020) remind us of the intrinsic relationship between conceptualisation and operationalisation of research as a critical form of theory application. In other words, research benefits methodologically from theoretical clarity as it moves through the different stages of the research process (see also Glasser and Smith 2016). Theory application then becomes an iterative process.

In sketching out a process of theory application one needs to be flexible and remain open to alternatives that more adequately explain the phenomenon. Having said that, a blueprint can be outlined as a guide for the essential elements of theory application using the principle of *theory as method*.

Figure 2.1 provides a simple and straightforward approach to conducting theory-driven education research and illustrates for us how theory can help shape methodological practice. The role of theory thus is three-fold in that theory can influence methodology via three stages in the research process:

- *Stage 1 theoretical conceptualisation*: Theory operates as a research lens that informs and helps problematise a given research phenomenon. At this stage, theory serves the purpose of contextualisation, helping to devise research problems from a critical standpoint
- *Stage 2 theoretical operationalisation*: The researcher's work on conceptualisation in stage 1 provides the foundation for stage 2, which is focused on the application of theory to the research design, including the development of research instruments that are framed by conceptualisation
- *Stage 3 theoretical interpretation*: This stage sees the research data examined via the lens of the original concepts framing the methodological approach. Here, social theory is used to make sense of the data and to translate the findings into new understandings and conceptual knowledge

As illustrated in Figure 2.1, all three stages are influenced by a strong commitment to reflexivity as a way to hold the researcher to account in all stages of the methodology. Alongside this, the methodology benefits from the dynamic influence of theory hybridisation, which can assist the continuous process of intellectual work, rather than to narrow the understanding of the research phenomenon to a given school of thought or theorist.

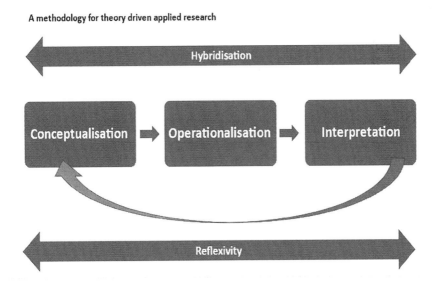

Figure 2.1 A methodology for theory driven applied research

Conclusion

This chapter argues that education researchers should consider more fully the ways in which social theory is utilised in contemporary forms of education research. At the centre of this consideration should be a concern to develop a form of critical research literacy that positions theory as at least the significant other of method in our efforts to advance methodological innovation. The quality of education research, especially in terms of intellectual advancement, would benefit greatly from the further harnessing of social theory and its transformative potential. Our position as detailed in this chapter is that strong forms of theory application require close attention to both the ways in which theory is conceptualised *and* operationalised. But at its best theory application also demands of the researcher the capacity to engage in theory hybridisation as well as to critically reflect on the way they have incorporated theory into their research. These different elements constitute a powerful critical literacy when it comes to research design, one that moves us away from siloised devotion to specific theorists/schools of thought as well as the current pervasive disconnect between theory and method.

If anything, this proposal fits well the legitimate desire for rigour and trust-worthiness to be at the heart of theory-driven education research. An important dimension of any methodology is the energy devoted to being *methodical*, not just in questions of instrument design and data collection but also in the application of theory. The second edition of this collection provides an opportunity to take stock of the methical nature of existing education research and how this can be extended. It is an opportune time to establish theory as a core component of educational research methodology.

Enhancing the position of theory can also contribute to education research, expanding its domain of influence, even outside the field of education itself. Moving away from a devotion to particular theorists and adopting a more critical stance towards theory more generally can help pave the way for education theories that can be useful to other sectors; in this regard one can point to the concepts of Bourdieu, whose work on capital for example (itself a result of conceptual hybridisation) has become a major influence in other academic disciplines.

In the spirit of critical reflexivity, let us add two notes of caution to our proposal. The first is that a greater appreciation and acknowledgement of social theory in research methodology should make efforts to avoid what Habermas has referred to as 'conceptual fetishism' (Habermas 1967/1988, 188). Replacing one form of fetish with another would be an unwelcome and unproductive endeavour and would detract from the ambition to further integrate theory and method. The critical literacy described above is designed to make theory and method communicate more effectively with one another, not to enable theory to adopt a privileged and detached position outside the research process.

Dallmayr offers a useful caveat in this regard when he argues for a conditional and contingent form of theorising that accepts the equal weight afforded to practice. He presents the notion of a conditional, non-systematic mode of theorising; theorising, for Dallmayr, 'does not pretend to systematic epistemic knowledge, but only to an ongoing clarification of its own limitations or conditions of possibility' (Dallmayr 1984, 6). This modest approach to theory is a more logical and reasonable one, which removes theory from its sometimes-vaunted pedestal and allows the user to adopt a more nuanced but also effective attitude to theory. Kumar Gir (2006, 232) puts it succinctly – that theory can be approached as 'our companion rather than as a master, as a moving light house which gives possible direction in the sea of complex reality, rather than as a fixed star.'

The second note of caution relates to what Savage and Burrows (2007) call the 'coming crisis of empirical sociology' and the role of social theory in it. While their seeming association of social theory with teleology is debatable, they make a useful point that social theory will not 'solve' whatever crisis empirical research may or may not be experiencing. Theory is not designed to be a substitute for research data (of whatever kind) and cannot be expected to fill in the gaps of empirical work. As suggested in this chapter, effective research requires theory to engage with forms of practice and to assist us in our efforts to comprehend changing educational dynamics. Making a case for application as a key element in research in its own right will only strengthen this dynamic, not weaken it.

References

Allan, J. 2022. Foucault and his acolytes: Discourse, power and ethics. In *Social theory and educational research: Understanding Foucault, Bourdieu, Habermas and Derrida*, ed. M. Murphy, 47–64. London: Routledge.

Alvesson, M. and K. Sköldberg. 2000. *Reflexive methodology: New vistas for qualitative research*. London: Sage.

Bartlett, L. 1991. The Dialectic between theory and method in critical interpretive research. *British Educational Research Journal* 17, 1: 19–33.

Baur, N. 2017. Process-oriented micro-macro-analysis. Methodological reflections on Elias and Bourdieu. *Historical Social Research/Historische Sozialforschung* 42, 4: 43–74.

Beckman, K., T. Apps, S. Bennett and L. Lockyer. 2018. Conceptualising technology practice in education using Bourdieu's sociology. *Learning, Media and Technology* 43, 2: 197–210. doi:10.1080/17439884.2018.1462205.

Benjamin, J. 2017. *Beyond doer and done to: Recognition theory, intersubjectivity and the third*. London: Routledge.

Berger, P. 2002. Whatever happened to sociology? *First things* (online). Available at: www.firstthings.com/article/2002/10/whatever-happened-to-sociology.

Bourdieu, P., J.-C. Chamboredon and J.-C. Passeron. 1991. *The craft of sociology: Epistemological preliminaries*. Berlin: De Gruyter.

Bourdieu, P. and L. Wacquant. 1992. *An invitation to reflexive sociology*. Chicago, IL: University of Chicago Press.

Brosnan, C. 2013. How and why social science theory can contribute to medical education research. *Medical Education* 47: 3–17.

Burawoy, M. 2005. Provincialising the social science. In *The politics of method in the human sciences: Positivism and its epistemological others*, ed. G. Steinmetz, 508–525. Durham, NC: Duke University Press.

Butler, J. 1996. Gender as performance. In *A critical sense: Interviews with intellectuals*, ed. P. Osborne, 109–125. London: Routledge.

Champagne, P. and J. Duval. 2018. Situating the course on general sociology in the work of Pierre Bourdieu. In *Classification struggles: General sociology*, Volume 1, ed. P. Bourdieu, 134–157. Cambridge: Polity.

Cicourel, A.V. 1964. *Method and measurement in sociology*. Glencoe, IL: Free Press.

Costa, C. 2013. The habitus of digital scholars. *Research in Learning Technology* 21. doi:10.3402/rlt.v21i0.21274.

Costa, C. 2016. Double gamers: Academics between fields. *British Journal of Sociology of Education* 37, 7: 993–1013. doi:10.1080/01425692.2014.982861.

Costa, C., C. Burke and M. Murphy. 2019. Capturing habitus: Theory, method and reflexivity. *International Journal of Research & Method in Education* 42, 1: 19–32. doi:10.1080/1743727X.2017.1420771.

Costa, C. and M. Murphy. eds. 2016. *Bourdieu, habitus and social research: The art of application*. London: Palgrave.

Costa, C., A. Pereira, Y. Taylor and M. Murphy. 2018. Higher education students' experiences of digital learning and (dis)empowerment. *Australasian Journal of Educational Technology* (Early Online). doi:10.14742/ajet.3979.

Dallmayr, F.R. 1984. *Polis and praxis: Exercises in contemporary political theory*. Cambridge, MA and London: MIT Press.

Foucault, M. and G. Deleuze. 1980. Intellectuals and power: A conversation between Michel Foucault and Giles Deleuze. In *Language, counter-memory, practice: Selected essays and interviews by Michel Foucault*, ed. D.F. Bouchard, 205–217. Ithaca, NY: Cornell University Press.

Gale, T. 2018. What's not to like about RCTs in education? In *Mobilising teacher researchers: Challenging educational inequality*, eds. A. Childs and I. Menter, 207–223. Abingdon: Routledge.

Gane, N. 2004. Judith Butler: Reanimating the social. In *The future of social theory*, ed. N. Gane, 47–76. London: Bloomsbury.

Garvey, J.C., J. Hart, A.S. Metcalfe and J. Fellabaum-Toston. 2019. Methodological troubles with gender and sex in higher education survey research. *The Review of Higher Education* 43, 1: 1–24. doi:10.1353/rhe.2019.0088.

Glasser, H.M. and J.P. Smith. 2016. On the vague meaning of 'gender' in education research: The problem, its sources, and recommendations for practice. *Educational Researcher* 37, 6: 343–350. doi:10.3102/0013189X08323718.

Habermas, J. 1967/1988. *On the logic of the social sciences*. Cambridge: Polity Press.

Hall, S. 1997. Cultural identity and diaspora. In *Identity and difference*, ed. K. Woodward, 51–59. London: Sage.

Hope, A. 2022. Retooling school surveillance research. Foucault (post)panopticism. In *Social theory and educational research: Understanding Foucault, Bourdieu, Habermas and Derrida*, ed. M. Murphy, 47–64. London: Routledge.

Kroneberg, C. 2019. Theory development in comparative social research. *Köln Z Soziol* (Suppl 1) 71: 29–51.

Kuhn, T. 1996. *The structure of scientific revolutions*. Chicago, IL: University of Chicago Press.

Kumar Gir, A. 2006. Creative social research: Rethinking theories and methods and the calling of an ontological epistemology of participation. *Dialectical Anthropology* 30: 227–271.

McCarthy, G.E. 2001. *Objectivity and the silence of reason: Weber, Habermas and the methodological disputes in German sociology.* Abingdon: Routledge.

Mills, C.W. 1959. *The sociological imagination.* New York, NY: Oxford University Press.

Murphy, M. 2010. Forms of rationality and public sector reform: Habermas and education in the context of social policy. In *Habermas, critical theory and education*, eds. M. Murphy and T. Fleming, 78–93. New York, NY: Routledge.

Murphy, M. ed. 2017. *Habermas and social research: Between theory and method.* Abingdon: Routledge.

Murphy, M. 2021. *Social theory: A new introduction.* London: Palgrave.

Murphy, M. and C. Costa. eds. 2015. *Theory as method: On Bourdieu, education and society.* Abingdon: Routledge.

Nowicka, M. 2015. Habitus: Its transformation and transfer through cultural encounters in migration. In *Bourdieu, habitus and social research: The art of application*, eds. C. Costa and M. Murphy, 93–110. London: Palgrave.

Oswick, C., P. Fleming and G. Hanlon. 2011. From borrowing to blending: Rethinking the processes of organisational theory. *The Academy of Management Review* 36, 2: 318–337.

Pierre, E.A.S. 2017. Deleuze and Guattari's language for new empirical inquiry. *Educational Philosophy and Theory* 49, 11: 1080–1089. doi:10.1080/00131857.2016.1151761.

Rasmussen, M.L., S. Graefenstein, A. Singleton, A. Halafoff and G. Bouma. 2020. Methodological challenges of designing a survey to capture young people's (non-binary) affiliations in relationship to religion, sexuality and gender. *International Journal of Social Research Methodology* 23, 6: 695–709. doi:10.1080/13645579.2020.1763692.

Rhodes, R. 2017. The hollowing out of the state. In *Network governance and the differentiated polity: Selected Essays*, Vol. 1. R. Rhodes, 1–20. Oxford: Oxford University Press.

Rose, G. 1992. *Broken middle: Out of our ancient society.* Oxford: John Wiley and Sons.

Savage, M. and R. Burrows. 2007. The coming crisis of empirical sociology. *Sociology* 41, 5: 885–899.

Steinmetz, G. 2005. Positivism and its others in the social sciences. In *The politics of method in the human sciences: Positivism and its epistemological others*, ed. G. Steinmetz, 1–56. Durham, NC: Duke University Press.

Swedberg, R. 2014. *The art of social theory.* Princeton, NJ: Princeton University Press.

Wacquant, L. 2014. Putting habitus in its place: Rejoinder to the symposium. *Body & Society* 20, 2: 118–139. doi:10.1177/1357034X14530845.

Part II
Foucault

3 Foucault and his acolytes

Discourse, power and ethics

Julie Allan

Introduction

The ideas of the philosopher Michel Foucault have proved seductive to many researchers in education and his work has 'decisively lived on in academia' (Nealon 2008, 1). This chapter introduces Foucault and traces the development of his ideas, beginning with his archaeologies of knowledge, medicine and madness, followed by a series of genealogies of discipline and sexuality. His later work on ethics, directed towards the self and including the practice of transgression, as well as bioethics and biopolitics, will also be discussed. This tracing of Foucault's thought will be accompanied by a consideration of aspects of his biography and reflection of how some of his own professional and personal experiences may have helped him to develop and refine his ideas. The fascination his work has held for educational researchers, and the way in which it has been applied, with varying degrees of sophistication (or rather levels of engagement with the original concepts), will be examined, as will the dissatisfaction with his ideas expressed by some of his most ardent critics, such as Habermas (1986) and Rorty (1986; 1990). Some critical reflections on the experiences of bridging theory and method, and of bridging theory and practice, will be offered, the latter a bridging only insofar as his ideas are used to *rethink* the challenge of inclusive education. The chapter will conclude with a discussion of whether there is such a thing as a legacy of Foucault and, if so, how this might be constituted.

A fancy for Foucault

> I think I have in fact been situated in most of the squares on the political checkerboard, one after another and sometimes simultaneously: as anarchist, leftist, ostentatious or disguised Marxist, nihilist, explicit or secret anti-Marxist, technocrat in the service of Gaullism, new liberal and so on. An American professor complained that a crypto-Marxist like me was invited in the USA, and I was denounced by the press in Eastern European countries for being an accomplice of the dissidents. None of these descriptions is important by itself; taken together, on the other hand, they mean something. And I must admit that I rather like what they mean.
>
> (Foucault 1997a, 113)

DOI: 10.4324/9781003156550-5

Foucault sought to defy categorisation of himself as one kind of scholar or another. He is indeed something of a contradiction, issuing enjoinders to study power and knowledge at its roots, for example in schools and hospitals, whilst remaining largely at a structural level in his own analysis. Furthermore, as Andersen (2003) points out, his concepts are often many sided and have unintended meanings. They are presented, according to Andersen, in a rather unsystematic way, frequently with repetition of similar ideas. Another difficulty with Foucault's work concerns the considerable epistemological and ontological shifts he made from his beginning work, which he termed archaeology, through to genealogy and finally ending (although this work appears to have been far from concluded) with ethics, including the practice of transgression, bioethics and biopolitics.

Alongside the serious scholars who have produced significant analyses of education there are many more who have presented their work with a Foucauldian *lens* and this prolific *lensification* is intriguing. A lens is either given by particular concepts, for example 'provided by Foucault's concept of knowledge and power' (Rodriguez and Craig 2007, 739), used as a means of 'complicating power relations' (Fenech and Sumeson 2007, 109) or in order to seek alternative educational possibilities (Butin 2002). Curiously, there is such a thing as an optical device, a microscope, that bears the name of Foucault, its optician inventor, but which was developed to counteract the aberrations caused by imaging by lenses at high power. This Foucault (Leon) also developed a 'Foucault test' for evaluating astronomical mirrors, described as 'quick and reliable' (www.telescope-optics.net/foucault_test.htm). It may be unfair to suggest that those adopting a Foucauldian lens have been enticed by a similar apparent simplicity, but the limited use made of Foucault's ideas, with lens in many cases serving as little more than a gloss, may warrant such a suggestion. Each of the phases of Foucault's work, and the man who was shaping them, is outlined below.

Archaeology

Foucault's initial interest was in structures and discourses, and in particular in the way in which discourses produced particular truths. Foucault was appointed as Professor of Psychology at the University of Clermont-Ferrand in 1960, having successfully defended his thesis, *Madness and civilisation*, at the Sorbonne and having had some public success with this text. This was in spite of some questions being raised about whether what he was offering could be considered to be history (Miller 1993). Foucault spent two years, from 1966, in Tunisia, returning to Paris to cement his involvement as a political as well as an intellectual figure, taking part in the events of May 1968, and he became a regular public commentator and participant in demonstrations. At the same time, Foucault was engaging with the French literary world and taking inspiration from the likes of Bataille, Blanchot and Becket.

In his archaeologies of knowledge (Foucault 1972a), of medicine (Foucault 1973a) and of mental illness (Foucault 1967; 1976), Foucault demonstrated deftly how discourses produced the '*restitution* of truth' (Foucault 1967, 197; original emphasis). In the *Birth of the clinic* (Foucault 1973a, 105), Foucault traced the development of medicine, illustrating how the gaze opened up a 'domain of clear visibility' and how the hospital provided a regulated space in which medical knowledge was acquired, recorded and passed on through the rituals of teaching. In his studies of mental illness, *Madness and civilisation* (Foucault 1967), his doctoral thesis at the Sorbonne, and *Mental illness and psychology* (Foucault 1976), he revealed the ways of speaking about mental illness and the way in which psychology made it possible to reveal the conditions of madness, yet was unable to 'tell the truth about madness' (ibid, 74) because he understood that madness itself possesses the truth about psychology.

Foucault, in this early stage of his work, was intensely interested in structuralism and in how it came to be a central force of so many human sciences including psychoanalysis in, for example, the work of Lacan (1982), anthropology (Lévi-Strauss 1996), linguistics (Saussure 1990) and literary criticism (Barthes 1990). Even Marxism developed a strand that was structuralist under the hand of Althusser (1968). In his analysis of the discourses of structuralism, in *The order of things* (Foucault 1973b), he was seeking to refine structuralist principles, having been swept along in the enthusiasm for structuralism within France in the 1970s (Dreyfus and Rabinow 1982). In this work he was seeking to determine the 'possibilities and rights, the conditions and limitations, of a justified formalization' (Foucault 1973b, 382). At the same time, however, the refinement of his archaeological method effectively undermined structuralist principles by attempting to examine the structural rules that governed discourse. Ultimately, Foucault distanced himself from the structuralist project. Foucault's archeological method has been used to examine negligence in the law (Dent 2002), black consciousness ideology in South Africa (Howarth 2002) and the category of 'mental retardation' in 19th- and early 20th-century Paris (Snigurowicz 2008). While finding archaeology useful and revelatory, these authors caution against using it as a stand-alone method.

Rorty (1986) questions whether Foucault's archaeology represents anything close to a new theory of knowledge and concludes that the way Foucault has set his archaeology up makes this impossible. Furthermore, Rorty (1986, 47) argues that Foucault's 'negative maxims' are neither derived from theory nor constitute a method, although he does concede that he offers 'brilliant rediscriptions of the past, supplemented by helpful hints on how to avoid being trapped by old historiographical assumptions' (ibid, 47). Dreyfus and Rabinow (1982, 43) also pronounce Foucault's archaeology, which they dub a 'quasi structuralist theory,' a failure because it runs into the very problems which Foucault had identified in his analyses of the human sciences.

Genealogy

In Foucault's shift from archaeology to genealogy, the focus of his work moved from discourses to institutions such as prisons, schools (Foucault 1977a), and to sexuality (Foucault 1978; 1985; 1986). Foucault's political involvement appeared to inspire much of his writing and in 1971 Foucault announced his leadership, together with his long-term partner, Daniel Defert, of the Prisons Information Group (GIP), which appeared to be less about gathering information and more about political agitation. Foucault did, nevertheless, collect information about conditions within prisons, 'the only place where power is manifested in its naked state and where it is justified as a moral force' (Foucault 1972b, 6). Foucault also made his first visit to the United States in 1975 at a point when he was writing the *History of sexuality*, but, according to Defert, much of what he had already drafted, on masturbation, incest, hysteria, perversion and eugenics, was shelved following his visit to California (Miller 1993).

In his genealogies, Foucault uncovered how knowledge and power were interlinked and constructed individuals as objects of knowledge and as subjects who were controlled, even – and perhaps especially – by themselves. His analyses overturned understandings of modern phenomena, driving home the realisation that where we might think we have greater freedom, we are, in reality, more tightly constrained than ever before. We tolerate this exercise of power only because it is hidden in the everyday. In *Discipline and punish* (Foucault 1977a), a detailed and morbid account of a regicide being hung, drawn and quartered in the 18th century is followed by an equally detailed, but apparently more benign, regime of imprisonment almost a century later. Foucault invites us to consider that the removal of the physical punishment as a spectacle has, in fact, led to a more insidious form of control over individuals' bodies and their souls. His analysis is extended to education and the 'disciplinary regimes' which turn young people into 'docile bodies' (ibid, 138).

Foucault developed a series of constructs about power and knowledge which he offered as a useful 'box of tools' (Foucault 1977a, 208) for understanding how individuals were controlled and constrained. The most important of these is 'the rather shameful art of surveillance' (ibid, 172), a disciplinary technique for ensuring individuals were sorted, regulated, normalised and made to behave in particular ways. Foucault identified three ways in which surveillance was undertaken. First of all, hierarchical observation was a means of making it possible 'for a single gaze to see everything perfectly' (ibid, 173). Physical structures were created, based on Jeremy Bentham's panoptican design, to ensure maximum scrutiny of people:

> to render visible those who are inside it … to act on those it shelters, to provide a hold on their conduct, to carry the effects of power right to them, to make it possible to know them, to alter them.
>
> (ibid, 172)

Hierarchical observation, thus, encompassed a form of supervision of supervisors, with everyone accountable to authority from above. The effectiveness of the supervision was guaranteed by the fact that it was 'absolutely *discreet*, for it functions permanently and largely in silence' (ibid, 177) and since it was impossible to know when one was being watched, it was necessary to behave as if this was the case.

Normalising judgements are also used, according to Foucault, to justify correction and coercion in teaching and promote standardisation and homogeneity. Individuals can be measured in terms of their distance from their norm and once the extent of their deviance from the norm is established, disciplinary techniques can be used to homogenise and normalise and, of course, exclusion can be justified as a means to these ends. Foucault regards normalisation as one of the great instruments of power at the end of the classical age, but alerts us to its continued use:

> It is easy to understand how the power of the norm functions within a system of formal equality, since within a homogeneity that is the rule, the norm introduces, as a useful imperative and as a result of measurement, all the shading of individual differences.
>
> (Foucault 1977a, 184)

Foucault's third dimension of surveillance, the examination, combines hierarchical observation and normalising judgements in a ritualised form which transforms the 'economy of visibility into the exercise of power' (ibid, 187). The examination also introduces individuality in order to fix and capture and makes each individual a 'case', capable of being 'described, judged, measured, compared with others, in his very individuality' (ibid, 191). These mechanisms of surveillance create subjects who are known and marked in particular kinds of ways and who are constrained to carry these knowledge and marks. The kind of power exercised here, Foucault tells us, is not the negative kind which represses, masks or conceals; rather, he argues, it is the kind which produces 'reality; it produces domains of objects and rituals of truth' (ibid, 194) in the shape of individuals and what is known about each of them.

Foucault's genealogies of sexuality, substantially rewritten after his US visit, forced a rethink of existing understandings of our relationship with sex. He developed the notion of a 'perverse implantation' (Foucault 1978, 36), in relation to sexuality, a means of naming deviance (and its distinguishing characteristics) in order to then cure or remove them. He described the emergence of an elaborate set of codes for speaking about so called normal sexuality – between a married couple – and identifying what deviated from this norm. In this 'discursive explosion' (ibid, 38) in the 18th and 19th centuries, scrutiny was exercised over:

> the sexuality of children, mad men and women and criminals; the sensuality of those who did not like the opposite sex; reveries, obsessions, petty manias, or great transports of rage. It was time for all these figures,

scarcely noticed in the past, to step forward and speak, to make the difficult confession of what they were

(ibid, 38)

Foucault's analyses of subjectification, in which he demonstrated so effectively
how individuals were incapable of resistance, have proved seductive to many
who have undertaken their own genealogies of educational contexts (Ball
1990; Blacker 1998; Marshall 1989; Fendler 1998). Baker's (1998) 'history of
the present' (ibid, 118) demonstrates how childhood was produced within the
public school movement in the United States, although what it meant to be a
'child' was not debated. Special needs and disability have also been seen as ripe
for Foucauldian analysis. Tremain's (2005) collection of papers on *Foucault and
the government of disability* contain a wealth of analyses of epistemologies, ontol-
ogies, histories, governmentalities, ethics and politics, which reveal 'some of the
fascism which still runs round in our heads and still plays itself out in our
everyday behavior' (McWhorter 2005, xvii). These studies situate individuals as
impotent, heavily constrained and with dismal prospects. Medical, juridical and
administrative practices construct and demarcate the disabled subject and the
discourses of inclusion are underpinned by a homogenising imperative. In spite
of this, however, we are urged to 'think beyond accepted dogmas' (Tremain
2005, 22) and to do what we can:

The point here, I think, is not to feel bad about the injustice or the suffering in the world … The point is to pull up short before the possibility
that what you thought was true might not be, that what you thought was
normal or natural might be the product of political struggle, and to start –
from just that place – to *think,* which means to question, to critique, to
experiment, to wonder, to imagine, to try.

(McWhorter 2005, xvii)

Foucault (1982) encourages us to read the 'modern state' (ibid, 214) of penal
institutions, education and even sexuality as creating less, rather than more,
freedom and the establishment of governmentality ensures that each person is
both an individual and part of a totality:

I don't think that we should consider the 'modern state' as an entity which
was developed above individuals, ignoring what they are and even their
very existence, but on the contrary as a very sophisticated structure, in
which individuals can be integrated, under one condition: that this individuality would be shaped in a new form, and submitted to a set of very
specific patterns.

(ibid, 214)

Whilst Foucault's critique of the way subjects are disciplined have appealed to so
many scholars, it has also earned him criticisms that his work is overly pessimistic

(Rorty 1990) and did little to encourage individuals to take action (Shumway 1989). Others have argued that Foucault's depiction of 'docile bodies' (Foucault 1977a, 138) denies agency and creates a 'fleshless passive body' (Hughes 2005, 84) which is 'dissolved as causal phenomenon' (Schilling 1993, 80) and with powers which are limited to those invested in them by discourse.

Ethics

Foucault's later work, ethics, or what Han (2002) describes as a history of sub-jectivity, contains a much more sanguine view of agency and depicts individuals as capable of working on themselves to achieve new kinds of existence. His turn to ethics arose from his concern with the self and its capacity for both resistance and transformation. It has already been suggested that his genealogies on sexuality had been profoundly influenced by his visits to the United States and his own experi-ence of liberated gay sex. His development of a framework of ethics surfaced in his later volumes on sexuality and he signalled this shift in what he called a 'genealogy of ethics', declaring himself 'much more interested in problems about techniques of the self and things like that than sex ... sex is boring' (Foucault 1984, 340). Foucault died of complications arising from Aids and, it is suggested, as a result of practising his own 'limit experiences' (Miller 1993, 29).

Foucault's framework of ethics focuses on:

> the forms of relations with the self, on the methods and techniques by which he works them out, on the exercises by which he makes of himself an object to be known, and on the practices that enable him to transform his own mode of being.
>
> (Foucault 1985, 30)

Foucault gave little advice on how one should undertake transformation of this kind in practice (Smart 1998). He mentions the role of the counsellor, friend, guide or master who will tell you the truth about yourself, but does not discuss the nature of the relationships involved. Bernauer (1999, xiv) suggests that Foucault provides an invitation to others 'not to renounce the soul ... but to transgress its borders, to reinvent one's relationship to it.' This invitation enables individuals to see themselves as the main source of transformation, rather than waiting for a more substantial structural or material change. As Veyne (1997) observes, 'the self is the new strategic possibility' (ibid, 231), capable of responding to the dangers which are encountered:

> The ethico-political choice we have to make every day is to determine which is the main danger ... My point is not that everything is bad but that everything is dangerous ... If everything is dangerous, then we always have something to do. So my position leads not to apathy but to a hyper- and pessimistic activism.
>
> (Foucault 1984, 343)

Foucault (1985) regards ethical practice as having four dimensions, which he elaborates upon in relation to Christianity and sexuality. He points out that the four dimensions of ethics will inevitably overlap and cannot be dissociated from one another or from the actions that support them. The four dimensions are:

1   *Determination of the ethical substance*. This dimension involves the identification of 'this or that part of oneself as prime material of his moral conduct' (Foucault 1985, 26). Individuals decide which aspect of the self is to be worked on or changed and in Foucault's example of Christianity, one's beliefs, intentions or desires might be specified as objects for transformation in order to become a better Christian.

2   *The mode of subjection*. The second of the ethical dimensions concerns the way in which the individual recognises how he or she operates in relation to certain rules and to find other ways of observing these rules. Foucault uses the example of fidelity and contends that there are many ways to practise austerity and 'be faithful' (Foucault 1985, 26). An example of the mode of subjection, provided by Blacker (1998), is the Greek aristocrat who fashions his diet according to certain aesthetic criteria.

3   *Self-practice or ethical work*. This aspect involves what one does 'not only in order to bring one's conduct into compliance with a given rule, but to effect transformation of oneself into the ethical subject of one's behaviour' (Foucault 1985, 26). Thus, sexual austerity in Foucault's example can be practised silently through thought or by a much more explicit and 'relentless combat' (ibid, 26). It is a form of 'asceticism' (Blacker 1998, 362) through which individuals transform themselves.

4   *The telos*. The final dimension concerns the ultimate goal which an individual is trying to achieve through ethical work. In Foucault's example, fidelity is identified as part of a journey towards complete self-mastery and he highlights the moral aspect of the transformation of self which is involved. Blacker describes this process as a kind of 'controlled and self-regulated dissemination of the subject into the world, a positive dissolution … not self-absorption, but being absorbed into the world: a "losing-finding" of the self' (Blacker 1998, 362–363; original emphasis).

These practices of the self are not acquired easily but have to be learned through disciplined training and through reading and writing and Foucault (1997b) underlines the importance of writing for oneself and for others:

> No technique, no professional skill can be acquired without exercise; nor can one learn the art of living, the *techne tou biou*, without an *askesis* that must be understood as a training of the self by the self … writing is regularly associated with 'meditation' and with that exercise of thought on itself that reactivates what it knows, that makes present a principle, a rule, or an example, reflects on them, assimilates them, and thus prepares itself to confront the real.
>
> (ibid, 235–236)

Foucault's notion of writing as a form of meditation draws on Seneca and Epictetus and he sees this as proceeding in two different ways. The first is linear, taking the writer from meditation through to the activity of writing and onto *gumnazein*, 'training in a real and taxing situation: work of thought, work through writing, work through reality' (Foucault 1977b, 236). The second is circular, going from meditation through to a rereading of notes which provoke further meditation. The reflexive function of writing, particularly in correspondence with others, is emphasised by Foucault: to write is thus to 'show oneself, make oneself seen, make one's face appear before the other' (ibid, 243). It is a way of 'summoning the gaze of the other' (ibid, 247). Reading is also seen as implied by the practice of the self because 'one cannot draw everything from one's own funds ... As a guide or example, the help of others is necessary' (ibid, 236).

Foucault argues that one should become so accomplished in ethical practice that one engages in it unconsciously:

> You must have learned principles so firmly that when your desires, your appetites or your fears awaken like barking dogs, the logos will speak with the voice of a master who silences the dogs by a single command.
>
> (Foucault 1987, 6)

Foucault's ethical practice is directed towards a kind of sexual austerity, it is also a political, social and philosophical endeavour which is put into practice through a kind of 'curiosity' (Foucault 1988, 321), which he explains:

> evokes the care of what exists and might exist; a sharpened sense of reality, but one that is never immobilized before it; a readiness to find what surrounds us strange and odd; a certain determination to throw off familiar ways of thought and to look at the same things in a different way ... a lack of respect for the traditional hierarchies of what is important and fundamental.
>
> (ibid, 321)

Foucault highlights the necessity of establishing conduct which seeks the rules of acceptable behaviour in relations with others, but foregrounds the self as the principle object of care, and as the means through which care for others can occur. Smart (1998) claims that the contemporary version of caring for oneself, which is characterised by self-determination, self-expression and hedonism, has led to indifference towards the other, but this need not be the case.

Although Foucault's ethics still remains a largely neglected work, it has been directed towards the inclusion of children with special needs (Allan 2005; 2008), strategies for interrupting the exclusion of young people (Youdell 2006) and the work of the academic (Blacker 1998). Establishing an ethical project in response to educational problems enables the work we each have to do on ourselves to be set out in terms of the determination of the ethical substance, mode of subjection, self-practice or ethical work and a telos (Allan 2008).

Transgression

Transgression emerged in Foucault's writings on ethics as a subversive tactic which could enable individuals to transform themselves. Transgression is a form of resistance involving the crossing of limits or boundaries. It is not antagonistic or aggressive, nor does it involve a contest in which there is a victor; rather, transgression is playful and creative. Among disabled people, transgression has been a significant means of challenging limits and disabling barriers. It is possible to recognise both collective transgression and more subtle and indirect transgression by individuals.

The development of the concept of transgression was sparked by Foucault's interest in Kant's critique of limits, but represents a more practical (and political) form of engagement. Foucault saw transgression as distinctively different from transcendence or transformation: He did not envisage individuals as gaining absolute freedom from limits, but instead suggested that individuals, in crossing limits or boundaries, might find moments of freedom or of otherness. Foucault's account of where transgression takes place is somewhat complex. In his *Preface to transgression* (Foucault 1977b), written as an introduction to the work of Bataille, he argues that 'It is likely that transgression has its entire space in the line it crosses' (ibid, 73). This implies a boundary that can only be there by crossing it. The limit and transgression depend on each other, but the relationship is not a simple one; rather, the relationship, according to Foucault, is like a spiral, with moments of crossing of the limit appearing as a flash of lightning in the night which give a darkening intensity to the night it obscures. Foucault also describes the interplay of limits and transgression as being regulated by a simple obstinacy. The act of crossing the limit does not violate it, but simultaneously affirms and weakens it. Foucault regards this as a form of non-positive affirmation, which has to be constantly repeated, and likens it to Blanchot's notion of contestation, which does not imply a generalised negation, but an affirmation that affirms nothing.

Foucault (1977b) acknowledges a difficulty with words which hampers philosophy and sees the absence of a language with which to talk about transgression as inhibiting its practice. Nevertheless, he expresses his hope that one day transgression will be as much a part of our culture as contradiction was for dialectical thought. Bataille also looks forward to the normalisation of transgression whereby silent contemplation would be substituted with language (Foucault 1984). Foucault uses sexuality to illustrate transgression, arguing that since the writings of Sade and, more recently Bataille, sexuality has been a fissure which marks the limit within us and designates us as a limit. Foucault has been criticised extensively for failing to provide empirical examples of his concepts and indeed his discussion of sexuality provides little guidance on the practical pursuit of transgression. His own sexual transgression can hardly be seen as a model for others to follow, given its contribution to his own untimely death (Miller 1993). Transgression has, nevertheless, been viewed as an attractive construct in relation to marginalised and oppressed groups, not least of all because it forces a recognition of exclusion. For those who transgress, according to Boyne (1990, 82), 'otherness lies ahead' and this allows individuals to shape their own identities by subverting the norms which compel them to repeatedly perform as subjects with a particular marginal identity, such as disabled or ethnic minority. They are not required to – and indeed could not – reject these identities entirely, but can vary the way in which they have to repeat these performances.

Relatively few studies have focused directly on transgression, but researchers studying resistance have uncovered strategies which could be read in this way. In Cooper's (1997) study of religious education, for example, resistance served the function of halting change and involved schools selectively incorporating the religious provisions of the English Education Reform Act 1988, while ignoring others. In Bloor and McIntosh's (1990) study of surveillance and concealment, new mothers avoided both breast feeding and the wrath of the health visitors checking up on them and their resistance was regarded as effective because it enabled 'a way of avoiding control without confrontation' (ibid, 176). Sullivan's (2005) study of paraplegics in a spinal unit revealed individuals' 'struggle for control of the body' (ibid, 39). Sullivan found their resistance 'harrowing', but as successful in rejecting the authoritarianism and totalising aspects of control. My own research with disabled students (Allan 1999) highlighted the positive effects of being able to transgress their disabled identities and practise alternative modes of existence.

Biopower and biopolitics

Foucault (2003, 242) names 'biopower' a new type, or technology of power, which differs from the disciplinary power and which is applied not, as in disciplinary power, 'to man-as-body but to the living man, to man-as-living being' (Foucault 2003, 242) or as species. And whereas disciplinary power focused on the regulation of behaviour inside institutions such as the factory or the school, biopower is directed at 'life and lifestyles' (Nealon 2008, 47). The shift in Foucault's work from discipline to biopower is described by Nealon (ibid, 5) as moments of 'intensifications', whereby power becomes increasingly light, efficient and economic. The reach of biopower is also extended through intensification, to encompass larger sections of the population and offers a kind of suturing of an apparent gap between the 'wholesale' and 'retail' Nealon (ibid, 46). This surfaces when something (usually bad, criminal or pathological) has to be understood and accounted for and is achieved through the deployment of the norm. Such behaviour – and the person exhibiting it – is thus understood and explained in terms of its deviation from the norm. As Nealon (ibid) reminds us, the danger of such an intensification is not in its potential to exclude but in its determination to include and account for everything and everyone.

Biopolitics first surfaces in Foucault's first volume of the *History of sexuality* (Foucault 1976), and subsequently in his public lectures at the Collège de

France. For Foucault (2004), biopolitics cannot be grasped without a comprehensive understanding of liberalism and neo-liberalism. Consequently, having expounded during the entirety of his lectures entitled *The birth of politics*, he (merely) demonstrates the 'condition of unintelligibility of biopolitics' (Senellart 2004, 327). This leads Wallenstein (2013) to suggest that Foucault lost interest in biopolitics or at least simply viewed it as an intermediary analytical point marking his transition from discipline to subjectivity. Foucault does, nevertheless, offer a definition of biopolitics as:

> The attempt, starting from the eighteenth century, to rationalise the problems posed to governmental practice by phenomena characteristic of a set of living beings forming a population: health, hygiene, birthrate, life expectancy, race …

> (Foucault 2004, 317)

The political and economic issues that these problems raise create complex problems for governments, especially when taken account of in the context of liberalism. This is because of the presumption of respect for subjects as legal entities with individual freedoms that must be balanced against the state's intervention in the lives of the population. Biopolitics, which as Wallenstein (2013) notes became interchangeable with governmentality, can thus be seen as the navigation between these aspects and, as such, remains a useful concept.

Critical reflections on bridging theory and method

In reflecting on bridging theory and method I feel the need to offer a chronology of my experiences of *finding* Foucault and then of encountering, and remaining with, the later Foucault. My doctoral study of pupils with special educational needs in mainstream schools was so obviously destined to be a Foucauldian analysis as I was interested in how pupils became identified and assessed as having special educational needs. Before collecting the data from teachers, parents and especially the pupils themselves I was aware of constructs such as hierarchical surveillance and the 'gaze', which had come from my reading of Foucault's genealogical works, as likely to have relevance. Most importantly, I was guided by Foucault's understanding of power and knowledge as being imbricated and yet amenable through discourse. This discursive orientation was an important element of the bridging of theory and method and consequently my data collection consisted of fairly formal semi-structured interviews but also included notes of all the conversations with and between participants. The analysis of the data was a further instance of theory/method bridging whereby the data were read with key disciplinary constructs such as hierarchical surveillance (Allan 1996) in mind and indeed these helped with sense-making. However, the data produced some distinct surprises, most notably in the amount of resistance from the pupils. The pupils' identities were indeed being constructed for them through 'special needs knowledge' and this was being done through recognisable disciplinary techniques. Their intensive resistance, however, could not be explained fully and it was at this point that I sought out Foucault's later writings on ethics. This encounter was epiphanic rather than bridging and allowed me both to analyse how and to what extent pupils were able to resist their 'special needs identities' and to begin to frame possibilities for thinking differently about what it means to be disabled (Allan 1999).

The later Foucault's writings on ethics provided the inspiration for a non-empirical analysis of inclusive education and a bridging of theory and practice and this recognised Foucault as one of the 'philosophers of difference', alongside Derrida and Deleuze. *Rethinking inclusive education: The philosophers of difference in practice* (Allan 2008) enabled an extended analysis of the perceived failures to be inclusive and to offer solutions that are reformulations of the inclusion problem. The later Foucault more than held his own in this arena and it was possible to articulate a framework of ethics that set out the work to be done on the selves of teacher educators and beginning (student) teachers to achieve an ethics of inclusion. Teacher educators, first of all, could be encouraged to disrupt the legacy of special education and to seek more inclusive practices. Their determination of the ethical substance, or the part the self to be worked upon might be undertaken by looking at disabled writers' account of the 'damage' done by the practices of special education (Barnes 1996; Oliver 1992; 1996; 1999) and analysing the extent to which these practices exist within the teacher education programme. Identifying the mode of subjection, for teacher educators might involve considering questions of ideology in inclusion and unpacking the rules and discursive regimes which govern conduct within higher education institutions (HEIs). Self-practice or ethical work could be directed at teaching, pursuing inclusiveness in the relationships with student teachers and contributing to debates about inclusive education. The telos, the overall goal, could be considered by those involved in teacher education asking 'What do we want to achieve and why?'

Beginning (student) teachers, engaging in ethical work, might begin by identifying the part of themselves as teachers which they wished to work on (determining the ethical substance). Their mode of subjection could come from examining the rules within their practice schools or within the HEI which create barriers to inclusion. Self-practice or ethical work could be directed towards their professional conduct and their attempts to be inclusive. This might necessitate identifying teaching practices and actions that create barriers to inclusion and modifying these. Lastly, students could be invited to work out the overall goal, the telos, perhaps taking guidance on this from children and young people and their families. They could be asked to articulate the purpose of inclusion, i.e. what it should do for them, and how to recognise good, rather than effective, inclusion. An ethics of inclusion, thus, was proposed as a bridging between theory and practice which encouraged teacher educators and beginning teachers to turn to themselves and to realise the importance of self-care and self-work in enabling them to function as the principal agents of inclusion.

A subsequent piece of work, undertaken with Valerie Harwood (Harwood and Allan 2014), returned to bridging theory and method and focused on a concerning exponential rise in the numbers of children and young people being diagnosed with Attention Deficit Hyperactivity Disorder (ADHD). Suspecting that we may be witnessing a global phenomenon of psychopathology, discourses and practices that lead to children being diagnosed as mentally ill, we drew on the work of Foucault to examine the instrumental role of schools in these processes. We formulated a series of questions that were based on Foucault's notion of intensification and which directed our analysis of each of the 'periods' of schooling: from the cradle to the crèche; the primary years; the high school years; and higher education. We asked: Who is aroused to concern? What are the relations or networks of power? What are the disorders of interest? What are the modes of practice? and, lastly, What are the desired consequences/outcomes in respect of the people who are the focus of concern? Our analysis led to us offering the following key arguments:

1   Within schooling we are passing from an exclusionary technology to an inclusive one and from disciplinary power to biopower and this has led to more children and young people being 'captured' and represented as mentally ill.
2   The diagnosis of mental disorders is an assemblage of desire, vagueness and flexibility.
3   While schools have been a key site for the psychopathologization of children's behaviour, historically, they have also been viewed as a principal *cause* of children's problems.
4   Disadvantage and poverty, as well as other markers of identity such as 'race', disability, and gender, are established as 'risk factors', which become intertwined in interpretations of children's behaviours – to the extent that diagnosis becomes inevitable.
5   An optimism, levelled at young children of nursery and primary age, that their mental illness can be resolved through intervention recedes by the time the young person reaches secondary school and is replaced by concern at the dangerous potential of the young person in higher education.
6   Resistance (from professionals) to psychopathologization generates new forms of recognition of children and young people.

(Harwood and Allan 2014, 11)

The experience of bridging of theory and method was, to us, satisfying and revealing, but surfaced further questions which we will go on to address, using a similar analytical approach, in our next book entitled *On the self: Discourses of health and mental education* (Allan and Harwood forthcoming).

Foucault's legacy: He makes you think

Whatever Foucault's work constitutes, his critics, among them Rorty, Andersen, Dreyfus and Rabinow, appear to agree that it is not a major social theory.

He has become lodged in epistemological *cul-de-sacs* because of the very problems with social theory that he himself identifies in his analyses. We can say, however, that Foucault, by inviting new ways of seeing and asking questions about what we think we know, provides 'unforseen untried possibilities in our history' (Rajchman 1995, 14). We should also recognise that Foucault, particularly in his later work, invites us, indeed encourages us, to 'question what is given to us as necessary to think and do' (Burchell 1996, 32), and those who have charged Foucault with pessimism have missed much. Foucault himself argued that it was always his intention 'to show people that they are freer than they feel' (in Martin et al. 1988, 10–11), but perhaps this point was missed as a consequence of believing that Foucault would help us to abandon the truth. Rather, his work helps us find new ways of living today and to 'invent or contrive new ways of saying the truth' (Burchell 1996, 32). This is not an insubstantial legacy.

References

Allan, J. 1996. Foucault and special educational needs: A 'box of tools' for analysing children's experiences of mainstreaming. *Disability and Society* 1, 2: 219–233.

Allan, J. 1999. *Actively seeking inclusion: Pupils with special educational needs in mainstream schools.* London: Falmer.

Allan, J. 2005. Inclusion as an ethical project. In *Foucault and the government of disability*, ed. S. Tremain, 281–297. Ann Arbor, MI: University of Michigan Press.

Allan, J. 2008. *Rethinking inclusive education: The philosophers of difference in practice.* Dordrecht: Springer.

Allan, J. and V. Harwood. Forthcoming. *On the self: Discourses of health and mental education.* London: Palgrave Macmillan.

Althusser, L. 1968. *Lire le capital.* Paris: François Maspero.

Andersen, N. 2003. *Discursive analytical strategies: Understanding Foucault, Koselleck, Laclau, Luhman.* Bristol: Policy Press.

Baker, B. 1998. 'Childhood' in the emergence and spread of US public schools. In *Foucault's challenge: Discourse, knowledge and power in education.* eds. T. Popkewitz and M. Brennon, 117–143. New York, NY and London: Teachers College Press.

Ball, S. 1990. Management as moral technology: A Luddite analysis. In *Foucault and education: disciplines and knowledge.* ed. S. Ball, 153–166. London: Routledge.

Barnes, C. 1996. Theories of disability and the origins of the oppression of disabled people in Western society. In *Disability and society: Emerging issues and insights.* ed. L. Barton, 43–60. London: Longman.

Barthes, R. 1990. *S/Z.* Oxford: Basil Blackwell Publishers.

Bernauer, J. 1999. Cry of spirit. Foreword to *M Foucault Religion in culture.* ed. J. Carette, xi–xvii. Manchester: Manchester University Press.

Blacker, D. 1998. Intellectuals at work and in power: Towards a Foucaultian research ethic. In *Foucault's challenge: Discourse, knowledge and power in education.* eds. T. Popekewitz and M. Brennan, 348–368. New York, NY: Teachers College Press.

Bloor, M. and J. McIntosh. 1990. Surveillance and concealment: A comparison of techniques of client resistance in therapeutic communities and health visiting. In *Readings in medical sociology.* eds. S. Cunningham-Burley and N. McKeganey, 159–181. London: Routledge.

Boyne, R. 1990. *Foucault and Derrida: The other side of reason*. London: Routledge.

Burchell, G. 1996. Liberal government and techniques of the self. In *Foucault and political reason: Liberalism, neo-liberalism and rationalities of government*. eds. A. Barry, T. Osborne and N. Rose, 19–36. Chicago, IL: University of Chicago Press.

Butin, D. 2002. This ain't talk therapy: Problematizing and extending anti-oppressive education, *Educational Researcher* 31, 3: 14–16.

Cooper, D. 1997. Strategies of power: Legislating worship and religious education. In *The impact of Michel Foucault on the social sciences and humanities*. eds. M. Lloyd and A. Thacker, 147–172. Houndmills: Macmillan Press Ltd.

Dent, C. 2002. Reflecting on continuity and discontinuity in "the law": An application of Foucault's archeological method in a reading of juridical decisions of negligence. Unpublished PhD thesis. Murdoch University.

Dreyfus, H. and P. Rabinow. 1982. *Michel Foucault: Beyond structuralism and hermeneutics*. Brighton: The Harvester Press.

Fendler, L. 1998. What is it impossible to think? A genealogy of the educated subject. In *Foucault's challenge: Discourse, knowledge and power in education*. eds. T. Popekewitz and M. Brennan, 39–63. New York, NY: Teachers College Press.

Fenech, M. and J. Sumeson. 2007. Early childhood teachers and regulation: Complicating power relations using a Foucauldian lens, *Contemporary Issues in Early Childhood* 8, 2: 109–122.

Foucault, M. 1967. *Madness and civilisation*. London: Tavistock.

Foucault, M. 1972a. *The archaeology of knowledge*. London: Tavistock.

Foucault, M. 1972b. 'Les intellectuels et le pouvoir': Entretien de Michel Foucault avec Gilles Deleuze. *L'Arc* 49, 4 Mars 1972. http://1libertaire.free.fr/MFoucault110.html.

Foucault, M. 1973a. *The birth of the clinic*. London: Routledge.

Foucault, M. 1973b. *The order of things: An archaeology of the human sciences*. New York, NY: Vintage/Random House.

Foucault, M. 1976. *Mental illness and psychology*. Berkeley and Los Angeles, CA: University of California Press.

Foucault, M. 1977a. *Discipline and punish: The birth of the prison*. London: Penguin.

Foucault, M. 1977b. A preface to transgression. In *Language, countermemory, practice: Selected essays and interviews by Michel Foucault*. ed. D. Bouchard, 29–52. Oxford: Basil Blackwall.

Foucault, M. 1978. *The history of sexuality: An introduction*. Harmondsworth: Penguin.

Foucault, M. 1982. The subject and power. In *Michel Foucault: beyond structuralism and hermeneutics*. eds. H. Dreyfus and P. Rabinow, 208–226. Chicago, IL: University of Chicago Press.

Foucault, M. 1984. On the genealogy of ethics: An overview of work in progress. In *The Foucault reader*. ed. P. Rabinow, 340–372. New York, NY: Pantheon.

Foucault, M. 1985. *The use of pleasure: The history of sexuality*, 2. Trans R. Hurley. Harmondsworth: Penguin.

Foucault, M. 1986. *The care of the self: The history of sexuality*, 3. Trans R. Hurley. New York, NY: Routledge.

Foucault, M. 1987. The ethic of care for the self as a practice of freedom. Interview in *The final Foucault*. eds. J. Bernaur and D. Rasmussen, 1–20. Cambridge, MA: MIT Press.

Foucault, M. 1988. The masked philosopher. In *Michael Foucault: Politics, philosophy, culture. Interviews and other writings*. ed. L. Kritzman, 323–330. London: Routledge.

Foucault, M. 1997a. Polemics, politics and problematizations. In *Michel Foucault Ethics: Essential works of Foucault 1954–1984*. ed. P. Rabinow, 381–390. London: Penguin.

Foucault, M. 1997b. Writing the self. In *Foucault and his interlocutors.* ed. A. Davidson, 234–248. Chicago, IL: University of Chicago Press.

Foucault, M. 2003. *Society must be defended: Lectures at the College de France, 1975–1976.* New York, NY: Picador.

Foucault, M. 2004. *The birth of biopolitics: Lectures at the College de France, 1978–1979.* New York, NY: Palgrave Macmillan.

Habermas, J. 1986. Taking aim at the heart of the present. In *Foucault: A critical reader.* ed. D. Couzens Hoy, 103–108. Oxford: Basil Blackwell.

Han, B. 2002. *Foucault's critical project: Between the transcendental and the historical.* Stanford, CA: Stanford University Press.

Harwood, V. and J. Allan. 2014. *Psychopathology at school: Theorising mental disorder in education.* Abingdon/New York: Routledge.

Howarth, D. 2002. Evaluating Michel Foucault's explanation and critique of ideology. *Political Studies* 50: 117–135.

Hughes, B. 2005. What can a Foucauldian theory contribute? In *Foucault and the government of disability.* ed. S. Tremain, 78–92. Ann Arbor, MI: University of Michigan Press.

Lacan, J. 1982. *Ecrits.* London: Routledge.

Lévi-Strauss, C. 1996. *The savage mind.* Oxford: Oxford University Press.

Marshall, J. 1989. Foucault and education. *Australian Journal of Education* 33, 2: 99–113.

Martin, L., L. Gutman and P. Hutton. 1988. *Technologies of the self: A seminar with Michel Foucault.* Amherst, MA: University of Massachusetts Press.

McWhorter, L. 2005. Foreword. In *Foucault and the government of disability.* ed. S. Tremain, xiii–xvii. Ann Arbor, MI: University of Michigan Press.

Miller, J. 1993. *The passion of Michel Foucault.* London: HarperCollins.

Nealon, J. 2008. *Foucault beyond Foucault: Power and its intensifications since 1984.* Stanford, CA: Stanford University Press.

Oliver, M. 1992. Intellectual masturbation: A rejoinder to Söder and Booth. *European Journal of Special Needs Education* 7, 1: 20–28.

Oliver, M. 1996. *Understanding disability: From theory to practice.* Houndmills: Macmillan.

Oliver, M. 1999. Final accounts and the parasite people. In *Disability discourse.* eds. M. Corker and S. French, 183–191. Milton Keynes: Open University Press.

Rajchman, J. 1995. Foucault ten years after. *Michel Foucault: J'Accuse. A Journal of Culture/Theory/Politics* 25: 14–20.

Rodriguez, L. and R. Craig. 2007. Assessing international accounting harmonization using Hegelian dialectic, isomorphism and Foucault. *Critical Perspectives in Accounting* 18, 6: 739–767.

Rorty, R. 1986. Foucault and epistemology. In *Foucault: A critical reader.* ed. D. Couzens Hoy, 41–50. Oxford and New York, NY: Basil Blackwell.

Rorty, R. 1990. Foucault, Dewey, Nietzsche. *Raritan* 9: 1–8.

Saussure, F. 1990. *Course in general linguistics.* London: Duckworth.

Schilling, C. 1993. *The body and social theory.* London: Sage.

Senellart, M. ed. 2004. Course context. In M. Foucault, *The birth of biopolitics: Lectures at the College de France, 1978–1979,* 327–331. New York, NY: Palgrave Macmillan.

Shumway, D. 1989. *Michel Foucault.* Charlottesville, VA: University Press of Virginia.

Smart, B. 1998. Foucault, Levinas and the subject of responsibility. In *The later Foucault.* ed. J. Moss, 78–92. London: Sage.

Snigurowicz, D. 2008. The phénomèn's dilemma: Teratology and the policing of human anomalies in nineteenth- and early-twentieth century Paris. In *Foucault and the government of disability*. ed. S. Tremain, 172–188. Ann Arbor, MI: University of Michigan Press.

Sullivan, M. 2005. Subjected bodies: Rehabilitation and the politics of management. In *Foucault and the government of disability*. ed. S. Tremain, 27–44. Ann Arbor, MI: University of Michigan Press.

Tremain, S. ed. 2005. *Foucault and the government of disability*. Ann Arbor, MI: University of Michigan Press.

Veyne, P. 1997. The final Foucault and his critics. In *Foucault and his interlocutors*. ed. A. Davidson, 225–233. Chicago, IL: University of Chicago Press.

Wallenstein, S. 2013. Introduction: Foucault, biopolitics and governmentality. In *Foucault, biopolitics and governmentality*. eds. J. Nillson and S. Wallenstein, 7–34. Södertörn: Södertörn University.

Youdell, D. 2006. *Impossible bodies, impossible selves: Exclusions and student subjectivities*. Dordrecht: Springer.

4   Retooling school surveillance research

Foucault and (post)panopticism

Andrew Hope

Introduction

The panopticon is an architectural design for a prison, which was used by the French social historian Michel Foucault (1977) as an 'ideal type' to explore how discipline was utilised by the state in mid-19th-century France. In this context, an ideal type provides a typification of a phenomenon, constructed by extracting its essential characteristics, and its purpose is to provide a structure against which real examples may be compared. Consequently, the concept of the panopticon has broad appeal to social–cultural researchers exploring surveillance practices, as it offers a theoretical framework that aids in the gathering and analysis of empirical data.

This chapter explores academic writing on panopticism, whilst also considering issues and challenges faced by researchers wishing to use this concept to make sense of the social impact of surveillance technologies within schools. Initially, Foucault's discussion of the panopticon in his influential text *Discipline and punish* (Foucault 1977) is examined, before some contemporary developments of key (post)panoptic ideas are analysed. These insights are then applied as panoptic themes are developed that could aid researchers focusing upon school observational practices. Some of the practical limitations of the panoptic metaphor are discussed as student resistance to school discipline is pondered. Ultimately, it is argued that while panopticism still holds some value for school surveillance researchers, an awareness of the inherent limitations should also encourage them to retool, as and when appropriate, through occasionally abandoning the concept and drawing on other insights.

Foucault's discussion of the panopticon

It has almost become a cliché that any social–cultural work focusing upon surveillance in late-modernity should pay intellectual tribute to the work of Michel Foucault. Since its publication in 1975, Foucault's book *Surveiller et punir: Naissance de la prison*, which was printed in English under the title *Discipline and punish: The birth of the prison* (Foucault 1977), has exerted a strong influence over writings on the social impacts of contemporary surveillance,

DOI: 10.4324/9781003156550-6

both with regard to educational institutions and wider society. Indeed, Simon (2005, 2) asserts that there can be no theorisation of the social aspects of contemporary surveillance without reference to this work.

Foucault (1977) asserts that by the mid-19th century there was a punitive change in France, from physical punishment to regimented incarceration, focusing upon the 'transformation of the soul' rather than the torture of the body, with the intent of creating individuals who policed themselves (Mathiesen 1997). Central to this idea of self-surveillance was Foucault's discussion of the Panopticon, a prison design wherein exposed, backlit prison cells, situated around the periphery of a building, faced inwards towards a central watchtower. As Foucault (1977, 200) noted '[b]y the effect of backlighting, one can observe from the tower, standing out precisely against the light, the small captive shadows in the cells of the periphery'. Yet the central watchtower is darkened and inside of it Venetian blinds and internal partitions are used to avoid the betrayal of movement, so that potential watchers can not be seen by those in the cells. Power is visible in the form of the central watchtower; the inmate is exposed and the potential watcher is hidden.

Samuel Bentham is credited with the original idea of the panopticon (Boyne 2000, 288), although it was his brother the utilitarian philosopher Jeremy Bentham who published the design in 1791, claiming that it would 'invigorate industry', 'reform morals' and 'facilitate education'. Investing power in light, inspection and architecture, the prisoner in Bentham's design is subject to permanent display; 'the object of information, never a subject in communication' (Foucault 1977, 200). Bentham's design disassociates power from particular people, investing it in a configuration of light, inspection and architecture. Individuals, uncertain that they are being watched, yet fearful of the possibility, start to police their own behaviour. In this context, observation comes to be perceived as continuous. Thus, Bentham's innovation was not just to inspect or ensure an asymmetrical gaze, but also to use uncertainty as a means of social control (Lyon 1994, 65). He maintained that this design had a wider application than prisons, subsequently drawing up plans for a circular nursery as well as designing several schools with semi-circular arrangements to facilitate the influence of the teacher (Markus 1993, 68).

Foucault (1977) drew upon this design as a powerful model for social analysis, suggesting that constant surveillance could encourage individuals to monitor and adjust their own behaviour. Nevertheless, as Norris (2003) notes, care must be taken not to over-privilege the visual aspects of the panopticon. It is noteworthy that Bentham's original design of the panopticon also encompassed 'panauralism' by including metal listening tubes to augment the visual surveillance (Markus 1993), so that guards could listen to prisoners. Furthermore, using the example of the birth certificate, Foucault (1977, 216) draws attention to the importance of keeping records as part of the panoptic mechanism.

Indeed, Foucault is equally concerned with procedures that situate individuals in a disciplinary discourse. Thus, he begins his discussion of panopticism by considering measures taken in the 17th century to contain the outbreak of plague (Foucault 1977, 195). This illustrates that for Foucault surveillance is merely one aspect of panopticism, which includes a much wider discourse on 'disciplinary technology', regimes of control, the labelling of individuals, the keeping of records and attempts to influence self-perception.

Haggerty and Ericson (2000, 607) suggest that the 'disciplinary aspect of panoptic observation involves a productive soul training which encourages inmates to reflect upon the minutia of their own behaviour in subtle and ongoing efforts to transform their selves'. In schools the keeping of registers, filing of reports, wearing of standardised uniforms, observance of rules, strict use of timetables, regimented examinations and ostentatious punishments can all be seen as fashioning a panoptical discourse of control. Hence, the visual element of panopticism can be seen as merely one part of a process of 'corrective training'. Indeed Foucault (1977, 170) notes '[t]he chief function of disciplinary power is to "train" … Discipline "makes" individuals; it is the specific technique of a power that regards individuals both as objects and as instruments of its exercise'. Discourse has a central role in such training, encouraging individuals to behave in a prescribed manner, whilst reproducing the means of control through acceptance and the ongoing replication of normalising judgements. In this context, normalisation refers to processes whereby certain standards of behaviour become hegemonically accepted as naturally the ones that should be adhered to in society. Consequently, emergent discursive constructs act as regulatory forces that have productive power, they demarcate, circulate and differentiate. Foucault (1977) suggests that the successful operation of such power lies in the use of simple instruments such as observation, punishment, and normalising discourses. Resultant regimes of control operate discursively through the classification of certain behaviours as 'normal', the labelling of 'miscreant' individuals and attempts to influence self-perception. Consequently, in responding to potential permanent surveillance, individuals may not merely be engaging in self-monitoring, but also in a normalisation process, where they come to accept certain types of behaviour as (in)appropriate. Thus students may accept that certain types of activity are examples of misbehaviour in school, never questioning the application of such a label.

Foucault's vision of a panoptical society highlights how a small number of people can exercise control over a large group of individuals, not merely through 'the few watching the many' (both physically and through records), but via self-surveillance and the observed accepting the normalising discourse embedded in the monitoring process, which suggests the 'appropriate' way to behave.

Panopticism in contemporary society

Although some commentators (Lyon 1994; Boyne 2000) assert that the panopticon provides a compelling metaphor for understanding surveillance in contemporary society, there is a growing critique in surveillance studies of the ideas underpinning this concept (Poster 1990; Norris and Armstrong 1999; Hier 2003; Koskela 2003; Yar 2003). Thus, as Manokha (2018, 219) observes

'the metaphor of the Panopticon, particularly in the field of surveillance studies, is growingly seen as inadequate to understand the impact of the latest
surveillance tools and practices'.

Criticism often coalesces around Foucault's perceived failure to address
contemporary developments in surveillance technologies, focusing instead on
18th- and 19th-century total institutions (Haggerty and Ericson 2000, 607).
Hence, Koskela (2003) suggests that panopticism offers a convincing model
for 'modern' society, but not for late modernity where power and control
have seemingly become more dispersed and fluid. *Surveiller et punir* was first
published in 1975 and Foucault died in 1984. Whilst both events preceded
the creation of the World Wide Web, the widespread utilisation of wireless
digital technologies and the rise of surveillance capitalism, critics still argue
that his failure to consider surveillance technologies operating in the 1960s
and 1970s compromised his analysis. The diversification of media, the subsequent rise of digital databases, internet connectivity and mobile technologies
have led to a recognition that there might be a need to rethink the panoptic
metaphor. This perceived inadequacy has led to numerous attempts to retool
the notion of the panopticon, '[s]o we come across electronic panopticons
and superpanopticons as well as variations such as the synopticon or the
polyopticon' (Bauman and Lyon 2013, 49).

In particular, critics highlight four elements of contemporary monitoring
processes that should be considered in reappraising panopticism. These are the
influence of the mass media, the inter-relational nature of surveillance, the
growing use of databases and advancements made in the simulation of surveillance. Additionally, there is a fifth element that is worth considering, namely
the political economy of panopticism. These will each be considered in turn.

Mathiesen (1997, 219) commenting upon Foucault's failure to mention the
mass media, and in particular television, suggests that '[i]t's more than just an
omission; its inclusion in the analysis would necessarily in a basic way have
changed his whole image of society as far as surveillance goes'. In an attempt to
address this shortcoming, Mathiesen considers the viewer society and the
'synopticon' of the mass media, in which the many watch the few. He points
out that the synopticon has a long history from festivals and theatres through to
films and television. The synopticon 'directs and controls or disciplines our
consciousness' (Mathiesen 1997, 230) through mass media. Twenty-four hour
rolling news reports controlled by powerful media interests, reinforced through
an obsession with 'celebrity' opinions, may unduly influence how individuals in
society think and act. In Foucault's terms this could be seen as part of a normalising mechanism. For example, consider the impact of celebrity chef Jamie
Oliver's television 2005 series *Jamie's School Dinners*, first aired in the United
Kingdom. Criticism within the programme of the unhealthy food consumed
by school children resulted in a change of public opinion, the development of
new government policy, the banning of many 'junk foods' in schools and the
introduction of healthier choices. More recently with the rapid growth in fake
news websites, social media influencers and popular live streamers the

mediascape has become far more complex, but additionally even more pow-erful. Ultimately as Doyle (2011) suggests, the synopticon works in parallel with the panopticon, suggesting an amendment to Foucault's analysis, rather than a rejection or radical restructuring of arguments.

Martin, van Brakel and Bernhard (2009) note that much discussion of the panoptic gaze assumes a two-actor model, in which information flows one way from a single source. Yet, in contemporary society surveillance may be inter-relational in nature, rarely is the observed truly a passive object. Not only do individuals engage in counter-surveillance, but they can also be involved creatively in the construction of their own data identity. Haggerty and Ericson (2000) reject Foucault's concepts, instead drawing upon Deleuze to suggest the existence of a 'surveillant assemblage', a 'multiplicity of het-erogeneous objects' that work together as a functional entity. 'They comprise discrete flows of an essentially limitless range of other phenomena … [are] multiple, unstable and lack discernible boundaries' (Haggerty and Ericson 2000, 608–609). Such analysis draws critical attention to a tendency to treat surveillance technologies discreetly, when the reality is that they often act as dynamic, fluid networks. Such linking of multiple sources of data in schools from a number of different media has been labelled Surveillance 2.0 (Kuehn 2008; Hope 2016), with Kuehn (2008: 87) noting that while the monitoring tools used in schooling are still predominantly Surveillance 1.0, with each practice operating individually, 'one can see all of the pieces coming together that will make it possible to create this totally invasive form of education'.

Whilst, encouraging researchers to think of 'surveillant assemblage' as 'essentially limitless' could encourage the analysis of new forms of social control that might have been disregarded using a more rigid conceptual approach, practical considerations often dictate that social research focuses on a limited element of social reality. This is not to reject the idea of an assemblage, but rather to note that any analysis will inevitably fail to be all-encompassing. Although Foucault's discussion of the panopticon does suggest a two-actor model, it does not preclude a more complex relationship. Importantly, despite complex social dynamics much teacher–student interaction might still be best understood with reference to this simple model.

The continuous and automatic monitoring of individual's everyday lives through digital technologies has resulted in the increased use of classification systems. Lyon (2003, 13) suggests that such social sorting 'highlights the classi-fying drive of contemporary surveillance', wherein '[t]he resulting classifications are designed to influence and to manage populations and persons thus directly and indirectly affecting the choices and chances of the data subjects'. Indeed, according to Poster (1989; 1995) the development of on-line technology and complex data handling systems has led to the emergence of a super-panopticon. Whereas Foucault suggested that subjects in the panopticon were conscious of their own self-determination, Poster (1995, 93) argues that with the super-panopticon 'subject constitution takes an opposing course of objectification, of producing individuals with dispersed identities, identities of which the individuals might not even be aware'. Surveillance in this context has gone beyond Foucault's consideration of panopticism. Individuals may no longer be aware that they are the subject of surveillance; furthermore, they may be unlikely to understand how information held on networked databases is used to construct consumer, worker or citizen profiles. Information derived from mundane activities such as using a store loyalty card when shopping, booking leisure activities with a credit card or even surfing on the internet can be used to construct such personal data profiles. For Poster (1989) this development has led to dissolution of distinctions between public and private spheres and the construction of a range of new disparate 'identities' that, unknown to the individual, may have a very real effect on everyday life. Yet it is questionable whether the creation of 'data doubles' online will have a panoptic impact. After all, if an individual is denied access to resources without been told that this is a consequence of their covertly observed actions, it is unlikely that they will modify their behaviour and engage in self-surveillance.

Bauman (1992) rejects Poster's notion of the super-panopticon arguing that whereas the panopticon was meant to instil discipline, databases merely confirm credibility. Yet as Lyon (2001) notes, Bauman underestimates the power of contemporary classification and social sorting systems, which 'make surveillance automatic across all socio-economic strata' (ibid, 92–93). Thus, publicly accessible databases such as school league tables can impact on students' educational choices and the resources that are subsequently available to schools (Selwyn 2000). While Foucault (1977, 192) recognised the importance of data gathering, the 'turning of real lives into writing ... as a procedure of objectification and subjection', he could hardly be criticised for failing to anticipate the size, scope and speed of such information flow in late modernity. Yet significantly Poster sees this development as an extension of the panoptic metaphor, rather than something radically different.

The growing use of databases has led some commentators to suggest that surveillance in contemporary society is no longer merely about recording information or deterring certain actions but rather is also concerned with prediction. In a classic study of undercover police work in the United States, Gary Marx (1988) noted how 'categorical suspicion' led to pre-emptive surveillance. Computer matching of lists generated categories of likely offenders that could blemish an individual's reputation without due cause. Such surveillance techniques have been introduced into educational establishments, most notably in the form of student violence risk assessment databases. Drawing on the work of Baudrillard on simulation, Bogard (1996, 76) argues that 'the technological enlargement of the field of perceptual control ... has pushed surveillance beyond the very limits of speed towards the purest form of anticipation'. Here Bogard is concerned with the anticipation of the real, aided by forms of diagnostic surveillance. While prediction may add an element to panopticism, simulation of the actual process of surveillance is nothing new. Indeed, Bogard seems to imply that an element of simulation is present in the panopticon, albeit he argues that the perfection of surveillance, through simulation, will lead to the elimination of the panopticon itself. This somewhat misses the point that surveillance has broader outcomes than those met by simulation. Although simulation can encourage social order and self-policing, it cannot hold individuals accountable for acts committed. Nevertheless, the growing body of work around pre-crime highlights the manner in which simulation can be (mis)used for 'charging and prosecuting groups and individuals considered to present a future threat' (McCulloch and Pickering 2010, 32). Although such practices don't currently exist in schools, associations can worryingly be made between pre-crime processes and digital school surveillance technologies in terms of future potential (Hope 2021).

Boyne (2000) argues that contemporary developments in screening and surveillance require the retention of elements of Foucault's (1977) work. Although some of the key ideas surrounding panopticism might be flawed, outdated descriptions of ideal types, this does not mean that they are without value as analytical tools of contemporary surveillance practices. After all, Foucault and Deleuze (1977, 208) note that social theory should not be approached as something to genuflect before but rather as a tool kit that is used selectively depending on the analytical task at hand.

An often-overlooked aspect of the panoptic model is its political economy. Himmelfarb's (1965, 220) criticism of Bentham's panoptic plan recasts it as profit-making technology, for 'Bentham himself actually intended to be the contractor and the governor of the prison' with the intent that prisoners work 14-hour days in the manner he found to be economically most profitable. In a similar light it is unsurprising that Robbins and Webster (1993, 245), see the Panopticon as 'the precursor of [F.W. Taylor's] Scientific Management'. While Foucault (1977, 221) writes that 'the accumulation of men and the accumulation of capital – cannot be separated' this aspect of the Panopticon receives little attention. Yet, through a political economy lens it can be seen that not only does the panoptic plan, if realised, meet the needs of capitalist society it also has potential to generate profit. Unlike the previous criticisms, this final one focuses not on an omission within Foucault's conceptualisation of panopticism, but rather on an aspect that deserves further development.

Having maintained that there remains much of critical value in Foucault's writings on panopticism, some suggestions as to how the concept might be utilised in undertaking research into school surveillance will now be explored.

Panoptic themes and surveillance in schools

Schools have a long history of monitoring students through physical observation, attendance registers, examinations, student progress reports and searches (of desks, lockers, clothes and bags). Such surveillance has been augmented through the introduction into schools of computer databases, internet tracking devices, plagiarism programmes, anti-terrorism protocols, classroom management software, closed-circuit television (CCTV) cameras (inside institutional grounds as well as on school buses), metal detectors, biometrics (iris, fingerprint or face recognition devices), substance screening technologies, pedometers, body cameras, drones and educational robots. Observational practices are rife in contemporary schools, spilling beyond traditional spaces. For example, prosthetic surveillance (Rich and Miah 2009) in schools is becoming increasingly common through the provision of Internet of Things (IoT) devices such as pedometers, fitness video games and high-tech sensors that measure food intake. Such technological incursions focus not only on the body, the 'geography closest in', but also reach far beyond the school environment. Thus, Queensland State Government supplied laptops to students with software control, which reportedly extended surveillance into children's homes (Courier Mail 2012).

Such technologies exert an influence, seeking to 'operate as political agents that produce social relationships … [they] embody rationalities and engender forms of life' (Kupchik and Monahan 2006, 624). Increasingly, students learn to watch and be watched, expecting surveillance and accepting it as a norm, as they become socialised into a 'culture of observation'.

Yet, a degree of wariness should be adopted in suggesting that such new technologies represent a radical change in surveillance practices. For, as Feeley (2003, 118) notes with reference to CCTV, it may 'represent a dramatic increase in situational social control and crime prevention, but they may be functional equivalents of other forms of informal controls that [previously] operated'. Furthermore, it should not be assumed that new observational technologies simply result in the burgeoning of school surveillance. After all, 'technological systems themselves are neither the cause nor the sum of what surveillance is today' (ICO 2006, 9). Rather there is a need to understand how such devices work, how they are used and how they influence individuals in the contexts in which they are embedded. Nevertheless, it can be argued that there has been a quantitative and qualitative expansion in school observational practices in recent years, which signifies not just a 'deepening' of elements of surveillance, but also the emergence of new social processes. Given such changes it is necessary to consider in what manner panopticism can still provide a useful framework for those researching surveillance in schools, through considering observation by others and of the self, discourse and simulation. Focusing on these areas will not only offer further theoretical insights, but will also provide some practical indications as to how social researchers might benefit from drawing upon panopticism in undertaking school-based research.

Observation by others and the self

Traditionally, teachers exercised social control over students through physical observation of presence, behaviour and academic output. Insofar as monitoring was necessary to ensure that students had engaged with and understood key topics, such practices were embedded in the curriculum and not merely part of a disciplinary regime. In considering whether school surveillance can be described as panoptic, Gallagher (2010, 268) notes that 'the teacher's surveillance, as a discontinuous process, could not guarantee the docility of bodies in the classroom … surveillance was a strategy, only ever partially and temporally effective'. Yet new technologies extend both the temporal and spatial reach of teachers' surveillance practices. Casella (2010) describes how some US schools track students outside the institution through radio frequency identification (RFID) chips implanted in identity cards. Furthermore, an increasing number of schools employ the services of private companies to observe their students' use of Facebook, Twitter, Instagram and other social media through software such as Snaptrends, Digital Fly and Ascham (Nation 2016; Sydney Morning Herald 2011; Vaas 2015).

While Foucault (1977, 201) suggests that an 'invisible' observer is a guarantee of order, with the result that 'if they are schoolchildren, there is no copying, no noise, no chatter, no waste of time', this ignores the fact that school surveillance is rarely continuous and ubiquitous, or that students respond in a 'disciplined manner' to potential observation. Yet new surveillance technologies contain the promise of constant, albeit not omnipresent, monitoring. It is this possibility of observation that encourages students to engage in self-surveillance. Students become socialised into a culture of monitoring within schools, encouraging them to behave as a compliant subject. Central to Foucault's discussion of panopticism and power is the potential to encourage people to engage in observation of the self. Fostering the practice of self-surveillance means that external monitoring becomes 'permanent in its effects, even if it is discontinuous in its action' (Foucault 1977, 201). Thus, students who suspect that their actions are being recorded by a CCTV camera stationed in the corner of classroom might reflect upon their own behaviour and modify it appropriately. The motivation to engage in self-surveillance should not be overstated, however. Simon (2005) asserts that for self-policing to occur individuals must comprehend 'the rules', make 'appropriate' judgements and recognise the signs of a possible spectator. The blind, ignorant, irrational or carefree could be immune to the effects of such panoptic power. Thus, the social researcher needs not only to consider how power operates through surveillance, but also its limitations and the opportunities created for resistance.

Surveillance in schools does not merely focus on the body of the student. The development of on-line technology and complex data handling systems has led to an increase in classification systems and social sorting of information, enabling what Clarke (1992) labels as 'dataveillance'. As Selwyn (2011) infers the increasing use of management information systems, attendance databases, online student records and Virtual Learning Environments in schools have extended institutional surveillance capabilities. The extent to which such technologies embody panoptic power is open to question. Bauman (1992) argues that databases merely confirm credibility, rather than instilling discipline. Yet in schools databases are often linked to other disciplinary devices and practices. For example, McCahill and Finn (2010) describe how in some schools an absence in the attendance database triggers an automated text messaging system to notify parents of their child's absence. Indeed, as school databases are often connected to broader disciplinary practices, students will be aware of such monitoring and may consequently engage in self-surveillance, adjusting their behaviour to avoid drawing unwanted attention. Consequently, it can be argued that the panopticon provides a useful metaphor when considering such surveillance via school databases.

Yet, it is not only students who are confronted with this controlling gaze. Teachers are increasingly exposed to new surveillance technologies. Selwyn (2011, 478) notes how senior managers made routine use of online systems to render individual teachers' lesson plans 'open' for 'editing' and 'adjusting' by more experienced and specialised colleagues. Thus, rather than being hidden, watching from a darkened watchtower, teachers are equally on display, subjected to panoptic scrutiny. This suggests that those researching school surveillance should resist the temptation to focus exclusively on students. After all, school staff are also subject to the operation of panoptic power, ranging from student feedback forms to formal school inspections.

With regards to physical surveillance by oneself and others, the panopticon offers educational researchers a useful model in exploring how observation is exercised in schools and its extent. Perhaps more importantly it draws attention to the manner in which self-surveillance can be engendered in institutional settings. Thus, a key issue for those seeking to apply Foucault's ideas would be not merely how students and staff are monitored, but how such processes then encourage individuals to reflect upon and monitor their own behaviour.

Normalising discourses

The panopticon involves more than the possibility of direct supervision in an enclosed institutional setting. Foucault (1977, 195) asserts that any analysis of physical surveillance needs to be equally concerned with procedures that situate individuals in a disciplinary discourse. In schools, the wearing of standardised uniforms, observance of rules, strict use of timetables, regimented examinations and ostentatious punishments can all be seen as part of panopticism, fashioning a discourse of control. Yet, the discourses in which observational tools become embroiled may be complex, contradictory and contested.

Drawing upon panopticism to explore surveillance practices in schools, social researchers might consider the discourses surrounding such activities. In this context discourses can be defined as a collection of related statements that seek to control and channel behaviour. Such discourses might be found in signs, such as those in libraries requesting silence, or within school documents. They may also be aural or embodied in repeated actions, passed from one individual to the next. Focusing upon school lunches, Pike (2008, 419) noted that 'no child could scrape food into the bin and exit the dining room without being subject to surveillance by lunchtime supervisor. Packed lunch eaters were generally required to take their waste food home in their lunchbox so that it might be monitored by parents later in the day'. In this situation, not only are students being subjected to surveillance, but there is also an underlying discourse that children should eat all of the food provided and avoid waste. Thus, surveillance practices can be seen as embedded in broader discourses of appropriate behaviour. Reflecting upon Foucault's work, it is important that educational researchers make such normalising discourses explicit. Only by doing so will the broader social complexities start to be exposed, giving rise to deeper, more critical understanding. Indeed, some discourses may be so deeply enshrined that individuals don't reflect on the choices that led to their acceptance. Thus, with regards to the example of school lunches, it might be asked why leaving food waste is seen as problematic. In some cultures, such actions might be seen as a display of wealth or the exercise of restraint. Yet increasingly in the United Kingdom it has become accepted that schools can regulate what students eat, with teachers often confiscating junk food. Consequently, to gain a deeper understanding of school surveillance practices it is necessary to expose and explore the underlying normalising discourses.

Simulation of surveillance

Within contemporary schools, panoptic simulation of surveillance operates through simulacrum and predictive data systems. Harrington (2005, 328) notes that a simulacra can be broadly defined as a superficial, but untrue, likeness. Thus, fake CCTV cameras in schools can encourage individuals to behave as if the technology is 'real'; at least until the deceit is exposed. At the heart of the panoptic metaphor is the idea of simulated surveillance. Although the underlying suggestion is that actual physical surveillance by others will occur intermittently, much of the power of Bentham's design rests in this uncertainty and the subsequent, at least partial, simulation of surveillance. Subsequently, researchers should consider not just the school surveillance practices that do occur, but also ones whose possibility of occurrence leads to an adjustment in behaviour.

Bogard (1996) suggests that surveillance has been pushed towards simulation, anticipating reality, aided by forms of diagnostic surveillance. Such predictive systems have long existed in schools, albeit relying on teacher intuition and knowledge of students rather than complex databases. Yet, developments in computer technology and data handling software mean that the speed and reach of such systems has greatly increased. At the turn of the century, Staples (2000) noted that the US Federal Bureau of Alcohol, Tobacco and Firearms working in association with a 'threat evaluation' company piloted a program called Mosaic 2000. This software aimed to confidentially vet and rate potentially violent students based on a series of questions drawn from case histories. In effect such predictive processes combine all three elements of panopticism discussed above. In the subsequent decades school threat assessment software for students, such as that developed by Navigate360 and CrisisGo, are far more commonplace. Such technologies include the monitoring of activities/data, privilege the normalising discourse of intervention based solely on the probability of inappropriate behaviour and ultimately seek to simulate a likely reality.

Student resistance to surveillance

Insofar as surveillance has become a characteristic of everyday life in late-modernity, then so too has resistance towards it (De Certeau 2002). While Foucault (1982, 245) argues that regardless of the social system 'there always remain the possibilities of resistance, disobedience and oppositional groupings', his arguments regarding resistance to panopticism are underdeveloped. Consequently, researchers exploring panoptic surveillance practices in schools may be tempted to focus on the institutional exercise of power, ignoring how students seek to resist it. Addressing this shortcoming, this section explores student resistance to observational practices through false conformity, avoidance, counter-surveillance and playful performance. The following discussion is best understood as a development of notions that are central to a critical understanding of panopticism, rather than a rejection of the theory.

As schools breed cultures of resistance that have a purpose in wider society (Willis 1977), resisting school surveillance might be 'integral to the educational process' (Martin, van Brakel and Bernhard 2009, 221), equipping students for future life in a surveillance saturated society. Resistance can take diverse forms, from action that hinders or challenges unequal power relations to moments of relative freedom when the apparently powerless step outside the realities of oppression (Spencer 1996, 489). Although the resultant lack of conceptual consensus might be seen as problematic, certain common properties of resistance can nevertheless be discerned, including its socially constructed nature, its interactional character, the central role of power and its complex dynamic (Hollander and Einwohner 2004, 548). Such considerations suggest that the study of resistance should be situational, contextual and historically specific (Fernandez and Huey 2009, 200).

For the social researcher, intentional feigned conformity is not easy to identify or differentiate from similar responses arising from apathy. Yet, faked compliance might mask resistance to institutional observation, after all 'refusal is a broad term that ... may also involve feigned participation' (Marx 2003, 382). Hence, Bash, Coulby and Jones (1985) argue that it is possible to resist through conformity, suggesting that such an action would be passive rather than active. Moreover, Simon (2005) notes that if individuals perform compliance, surveillance may not be able to distinguish between acceptance and refusal. Panoptic technologies are challenged by feigned conformity and the limitations of observational systems to facilitate social integration exposed (Simon 2005). There exist empirical difficulties in exposing such strategies, particularly if the primary data collection method relies on observation. Thankfully, if anonymity is guaranteed, students may be forthright with researchers in interviews. Nevertheless, the researcher needs to engage with this issue and consider whether what looks like conformity with school surveillance practices is actually feigned compliance.

Avoidance of surveillance in schools might be much easier than it would be in Foucault's model of the panopticon. In educational institutions physical surveillance is unlikely to be universal or constant. Hence certain school spaces may be less monitored, particularly outside lesson times. Yet with the increase of digital surveillance there is a creep towards an all-encompassing reach. From the perspective of a researcher the problem becomes how to note and map, attempts at avoidance of surveillance, particularly when they occur outside educational buildings. Some students may be eager to regale researchers with stories of such experiences, yet it is likely that many will remain silent.

Referring to the growing potential to use new surveillance technologies to observe those in authority, Man, Nolan and Wellman (2003) draw attention to what they refer to as 'sousveillance', the use of observational devices to mirror and confront the monitoring processes undertaken by institutions. This strategy is not concerned with circumventing surveillance but rather directly confronting it through ostentatiously watching the watchers. Websites such as Rate My Teacher provide an online area in which students can post material, potentially exposing staff to a worldwide gaze. Steeves (2010, 94) relates two incidents in Quebec Province, Canada, where students provoked teachers into losing their temper, recorded the occurrence on their mobile phones and uploaded the images onto YouTube. Furthermore, Weiss (2010) draws attention to students writing about their experiences of school surveillance, arguing that such creative practices can work as a vital form of sousveillance. Insofar as such material may be published on Facebook or other social networking sites, it could be argued that observation and online discussion of school staff surveillance activities may become increasingly significant as a form of resistance. In the panopticon the prisoner is merely an object to be surveilled. Yet in schools the observer is often also on display. In this context, the educational researcher should not just focus on the 'controlling gaze' of those in authority but also on students watching staff. This highlights the importance of considering the complex 'surveillant assemblage' in schools and not merely restricting analysis to a simple two-actor model.

While the metaphors of both panopticism and the synopticon are useful in considering contemporary power relations and offer an account of why people are 'surveillance tolerant', they also highlight a purpose of surveillance that is absent from much discussion of Foucault's work. Namely, that surveillance is not just concerned with discipline and control, but also with performance, entertainment and play. Driven by the popularity of reality television programmes there has been a growth in the contemporary culture of surveillance, generating 'a new savvy, even blasé attitude to surveillance, which sees its potential entertainment value' (Bell 2009, 209). Thus, rather than trying to become invisible to surveillance many people are actually seeking to increase their exposure 'playing with, goading and yes, even flirting with surveillance' (Groombridge 2002, 43). Students may playfully confront surveillance in schools, seeking to be seen. Bell (2009) argues that a 'hijacking' of the dominant uses of surveillance is possible, with voyeurism and exhibitionism acting as forms of resistance, raising the possibility of new and varied ways of (re)configuring the 'algebra of surveillance', allowing individuals to perform surveillance in ways that seek to take back control. While surveillance can be playful, so to can the act of resisting it. As Marx (2009, 299) suggests defying observation can be 'a dynamic adversarial social dance involving strategic moves and counter-moves, it has the quality of an endless chess game mixing old and new moves'. Indeed, young people might feel the need to draw attention to and celebrate their inappropriate behaviour, sating their need to flaunt these acts of resistance. Incidents of students 'playing' with school surveillance abound. In one UK secondary school a year 12 male student discovered a friend's internet password, used it to log on to the school network, found an unfiltered pornographic website, printed an explicit image and left it for a member of staff to find, before ultimately confessing to the deception (Hope 2007, 94). In such instances playful public performance becomes more important than avoiding punishment. After all, without the engagement of an audience the whole experience might prove less gratifying. While such acts of resistance may share certain outcomes with risk-taking, namely engendering excitement, fostering identity formation, facilitating skilled performance and traversing boundaries, they might also have a significant symbolic function. Thus, the panoptic gaze may be offered up as an object for critical public contemplation, while existing power relations are mocked. Consequently, educational researchers should consider the entertainment value of both surveillance and resistance to it.

Retooling school surveillance research

Critics suggests that the panopticon has come to exert an oppressive influence as the dominant social–cultural lens through which to examine surveillance. This is incongruous given that Foucault never intended for his insights to become monolithic structures. Indeed as 'Foucault engaged in reinterpretation, self-criticism and the challenging of his own past arguments ... it was never possible to be forced into trying to elucidate a final truth' (Hope 2015, 573). Rather, Foucault described his books as 'little tool boxes' urging others 'to use this sentence or that idea as a screwdriver or spanner' (Foucault 1975, cited in Paton 1979, 115). Consequently, Mills (2003, 6) suggests that Foucault's ideas be used as a way of approaching a subject as opposed to a set of rigid principles.

Nonetheless, it is difficult to escape the feeling that over the years Foucault's discussion of panopticism has been treated less as a collection of tools, more as theoretical edifice, less as post-structural insights, more as the harbinger of some unifying theory. This is not to deny that there remains much that is of value in the concept of panopticism, as has hopefully been shown in this chapter. Yet, when working with panopticism it is also helpful to know when to step away from it. When to put down one set of tools and retool. This is not to suggest the abandonment of panopticism, but rather the use of a more diverse range of tools. While there is a wealth of alternative insights from academic literature and research to draw upon, given that this chapter is focused upon Foucault, some other options from his expansive body of work will be introduced by way of illustration. In particular, the tools to be found in Foucault's writings on 'technologies of the self' and biopower will be briefly considered.

Foucault's later writings on 'technologies of the self' focused on how people constituted themselves within society, being constrained or empowered through different discourses (Hope 2015). Thus, he used this notion to describe people's 'operations on their own bodies and souls, thoughts, conduct and way of being, so as to transform themselves' (Foucault 1988, 18). Drawing upon this tool, 'technologies of the self' could be used to challenge an overly deterministic and homogeneous view of those subjected to surveillance, while facilitating a deeper examination of how people seek to develop their own identities through social media engagement, play and resistance.

For Foucault (2007, 1), biopower was a 'set of mechanisms through which the basic biological features of the human species become the object of a political strategy, of a general strategy of power'. He initially proposed a simple bipolar model of biopower, drawing on notions of discipline and biopolitics. Thus, he argued 'discipline is the technology deployed to make individuals behave, to be efficient and productive workers, biopolitics is deployed to manage population' (Foucault 2004, 242). Not only do such tools refocus attention upon the physical body, they also include a consideration of populations as well as individuals. Furthermore, this addresses Monahan and Torres's (2010, 7) criticism that many surveillance researchers focus on Foucault's discussion of discipline found in his work on panopticism, while neglecting its examination in his other writings. Thus, Foucault's conceptualisation of biopower offers new tools with which to consider school surveillance technologies. It is argued that '[s]uch an approach will become increasingly important as research examines emerging surveillance-related issues, such as students' right to privacy, questions concerning the ownership of data and the social impact of data doubles' (Hope 2016, 899).

These brief *précis* are merely intended to draw attention to the range of other tools available in Foucault's toolbox (a more appropriate metaphor here might be that of a tool shed). At this juncture, it is appropriate to add a word of warning. Given Foucault's apparent disdain for unifying theories, one should probably be extremely wary if thinking of amalgamating these insights in a way that he himself avoided.

Conclusion

As an ideal type panopticism offers numerous insights for educational researchers studying school surveillance practices. It highlights the importance, not merely of the act of watching, but also of self-surveillance, normalising discourses and simulation. Whilst Foucault's discussion of the panopticon is underdeveloped in certain areas, such as on the topic of resistance, it nevertheless provides a convincing analysis of the operation of disciplinary power, which continues to assist and inspire social researchers. At the same time, researchers should not feel enslaved to this conceptual model. Foucault intended his books to be 'little tool boxes', which suggests not only the selective use of some of his ideas, but also a willingness to retool if the current instrument isn't proving helpful or effective. While it has been argued that panopticism has continued value, this does not dictate that it is necessarily the best framework to use. Rather, researchers should feel free to search wider afield, in other writings of Foucault, in other work within surveillance studies, or indeed across other disciplines. In conclusion, while panopticism should be used as deemed appropriate, school surveillance research should also be retooled as required.

Bibliography

Bash, L., D. Coulby and C. Jones. 1985. *Urban schooling: Theory and practice*. London: Holt, Rinehart and Winston.

Bauman, Z. 1992. *Intimations of postmodernity*. London: Routledge.

Bauman, Z. and D. Lyon. 2013. *Liquid surveillance: A conversation*. Cambridge: Polity Press.

Bell, D. 2009. Surveillance is sexy. *Surveillance and Society* 6, 3: 203–212.

Bogard, W. 1996. *The simulation of surveillance*. Cambridge: Cambridge University Press.

Boyne, R. 2000. Post-panopticism. *Economy and Society* 29, 2: 285–307.

Casella, R. 2010. Safety or social control? The security fortification of schools in a capitalist society. In *Schools under surveillance: Cultures of control in public education*. eds. T. Monahan and R. Torres, 73–86. New York, NY: Rutgers University Press.

Clarke, R. 1992. The resistible rise of the national personal data system. *Software Law Journal* 5, 1: 25–59.

Courier Mail. 2012. Screen spy keeps watch on school students' home laptop activity. 17 May. Available at: www.couriermail.com.au/news/queensland/screen-spy-keeps-wa tch-on-students/news-story/9faedc0adcc84027df7da7af9bc1d6ff (accessed 29 November 2021).

De Certeau, M. 2002. *The practice of everyday life*. Berkeley, CA: University of California Press.

Doyle, A. 2011. Revisiting the synopticon: Reconsidering Mathiesen's 'The Viewer Society' in the age of Web 2.0. *Theoretical Criminology* 15, 3: 283–299.

Feeley, M. 2003. Crime, social order and the rise of neo-Conservative politics. *Theoretical Criminology* 7, 1: 111–130.

Fernandez, L.A. and L. Huey. 2009. Is resistance futile? Thoughts on resisting surveillance. *Surveillance & Society* 6, 3: 198–202.

Foucault, M. 1975. Des supplices aux cellules [The punishment cells] (interview with R.-P. Law). *Le Monde*, 21 February, 9363.

Foucault, M. 1977. *Discipline and punish: The birth of the prison*. London: Allen Lane.

Foucault, M. 1982. Space, knowledge and power. In *The Foucault reader: An introduction to Foucault's thought*, ed. P. Rabinow, 239–256. London: Penguin.

Foucault, M. 1988. Technologies of the self. In *Technologies of the self*. eds. L.H. Martin, H. Gutman and P.H. Hutton, 16–49. Amherst, MA: University of Massachusetts Press.

Foucault, M. 2004. *Society must be defended: Lectures at the Collège De France, 1975–1976*. New York, NY: Picador.

Foucault, M. 2007. *Security, territory, population. Lectures at the Collège De France, 1977–1978*. Houndmills: Palgrave Macmillan.

Foucault, M. and G. Deleuze. 1977. Intellectuals & power: A conversation between Michel Foucault and Giles Deleuze. In *Language, counter-memory, practice: Selected essays and interviews by Michel Foucault*. ed. D.F. Bouchard, 205–217. Ithaca, NY: Cornell University Press.

Gallagher, M. 2010. Are schools panoptic? *Surveillance & Society* 7, 3–4: 262–272.

Groombridge, N. 2002. Crime control or crime culture TV? *Surveillance & Society* 1, 1: 30–36.

Haggerty, K.D. and R.V. Ericson. 2000. The surveillant assemblage. *British Journal of Sociology* 51, 4: 605–622.

Harrington, A. ed. 2005. *Modern social theory: An introduction*. Oxford: Oxford University Press.

Hier, S. 2003. Probing the surveillant assemblage; On the dialectics of surveillance practices as processes of social control. *Surveillance & Society* 1, 3: 399–411.

Himmelfarb, G. 1965. The haunted house of Jeremy Bentham. In *Ideas in history*. eds. R. Herr and H. Parker, 199–238. Durham, NC: Duke University Press.

Hope, A. 2007. Risk-taking, boundary-performance and intentional school internet 'misuse'. *Discourse: studies in the cultural politics of education* 28, 1: 87–99.

Hope, A. 2015. Foucault's toolbox: Critical insights for education and technology researchers. *Learning, Media and Technology* 40, 4: 536–549.

Hope, A. 2016. Biopower and school surveillance technologies 2.0. *British Journal of Sociology of Education* 37, 7: 885–904.

Hope, A. 2021. Visions of the pre-criminal student: reimagining school digital surveillance. In *The pre-crime society: Crime, culture, and control in the ultramodern age*. eds. B. Sellers and B. Arrigo, 105–126. Bristol: Policy Press.

Hollander, J.A. and R.L. Einwohner. 2004. Conceptualizing resistance. *Sociological Forum* 19, 4: 533–554.

ICO (Information Commissioners Office). 2006. A report on the surveillance society. Available at: https://ico.org.uk/media/about-the-ico/documents/1042390/surveilla nce-society-full-report-2006.pdf (accessed 29 November 2021).

Koskela, H. 2003. 'Cam era' – The contemporary urban panopticon. *Surveillance & Society* 1, 3: 292–313.

Kuehn, L. 2008. Surveillance 2.0: The 'information panopticon' and education. *Our Schools/Our Selves*. 1 July: 81–91. Available at: www.policyalternatives.ca/sites/defa ult/files/uploads/publications/Our_Schools_Ourselve/10_Kuehn_surveillance_2.pdf (accessed 29 November 2021).

Kupchik, A. and T. Monahan. 2006. The new American school: Preparation for post-industrial discipline. *British Journal of Sociology of Education* 27, 5: 617–631.

Lyon, D. 1994. *The electronic eye: The rise of surveillance society*. Cambridge: Polity Press.

Lyon, D. 2001. *Surveillance society: Monitoring everyday life*. Milton Keynes: Open University Press.

Lyon, D. 2003. Surveillance as social sorting: Computer codes and mobile bodies. In *Surveillance as social sorting. Privacy, risk and digital discrimination*. ed. D. Lyon, 13–30. London: Routledge.

Man, S., J. Nolan and B. Wellman. 2003. Sousveillance: Inventing and using wearable computing devices for data collection in surveillance environments. *Surveillance & Society* 1, 3: 331–355.

Manokha, I. 2018. Surveillance, panopticism, and self-discipline in the digital age. *Surveillance & Society* 16, 2: 219–237.

Markus, T.A. 1993. *Buildings and power*. London: Routledge.

Martin, A.K., R.E. van Brakel and D.J. Bernhard. 2009. Understanding resistance to digital surveillance: Towards a multi-disciplinary, multi-actor framework. *Surveillance & Society* 6, 3: 213–232.

Marx, G. 1988. *Undercover: Police surveillance in America.* Berkeley, CA: University of California Press.

Marx, G. 2003. A tack in the shoe: Neutralising and resisting the new surveillance. *Journal of Social Issues* 59, 2: 369–390.

Marx, G. 2009. A tack in the shoe and taking off the shoe: Neutralization and counter-neutralization dynamics. *Surveillance & Society* 6, 3: 294–306.

Mathiesen, T. 1997. The viewer society. *Theoretical Criminology* 1, 2: 215–234.

McCahill, M. and R. Finn. 2010. The social impact of surveillance in three UK schools: 'Angels', 'devils' and 'teen mums'. *Surveillance & Society* 7, 3–4: 273–289.

McCulloch, J. and S. Pickering. 2010. Future threat: Pre-crime, state terror, and dystopia in the 21st century. *Criminal Justice Matters* 81, 1: 32–33.

Monahan, T. and R. Torres. 2010. Introduction. In *Schools under surveillance: Cultures of control in public education.* eds. T. Monahan and R. Torres, 1–18. New York, NY: Rutgers University Press.

Mills, S. 2003. *Michel Foucault.* Abingdon: Routledge.

Nation. 2016. The school-security industry is cashing in big on public fears of mass shootings. 9 August. Available at: www.thenation.com/article/archive/the-school-security-industry-is-cashing-in-big-on-public-fears-of-mass-shootings/ (accessed 29 November 2021).

Norris, C. 2003. From personal to digital: CCTV, the panopticon, and the technological mediation of suspicion and social control. In *Surveillance as social sorting: Privacy, risk and digital discrimination.* ed. D. Lyon, 249–281. London: Routledge.

Norris, C. and G. Armstrong. 1999. *The maximum surveillance society: The rise of CCTV.* Oxford: Berg.

Paton, P. 1979. Of power and prisons. In *Michel Foucault: Power/truth/strategy*, ed. M. Morris and P. Patton, 109–146. Sydney: Feral.

Pike, J. 2008. Foucault, space and primary school dining rooms. *Children's Geographies* 6, 4: 413–422.

Poster, M. 1989. *Critical theory and poststructuralism: In search of a context.* Ithaca, NY: Cornell University Press.

Poster, M. 1990. *Mode of information: Poststructuralism and social context.* Cambridge: Polity Press.

Poster, M. 1995. *The second media age.* Cambridge: Polity Press.

Rich, E. and A. Miah. 2009. Prosthetic surveillance: The medical governance of healthy bodies in cyberspace. *Surveillance & Society* 6, 2: 163–177.

Robins, K. and F. Webster. 1993. 'I'll be watching you': Comment on Sewell and Wilkinson. *Sociology* 27, 2: 243–252.

Selwyn, N. 2000. The national grid for learning: Panacea or panopticon? *British Journal of Sociology of Education* 21, 2: 243–255.

Selwyn, N. 2011. 'It's all about standardisation' – Exploring the digital (re) configuration of school management and administration. *Cambridge Journal of Education* 41, 4: 473–488.

Simon, B. 2005. The return of panopticism: Supervision, subjection and the new surveillance. *Surveillance & Society* 3, 1: 1–20.

Spencer, J. 1996. Resistance. In *Encyclopedia of social and cultural anthropology*, eds. A. Barnard and J. Spencer, 489. London: Routledge.

Staples, W.G. 2000. *Everyday surveillance: Vigilance and visibility in postmodern life.* Oxford: Rowman & Littlefield Publishers Inc.

Steeves, V. 2010. Online surveillance in Canadian schools. In *Schools under surveillance: Cultures of control in public education.* eds. T. Monahan and R. Torres, 87–103. New York, NY: Rutgers University Press.

Sydney Morning Herald. 2011. Schools use the net to eavesdrop on students. 13 August. Available at: www.smh.com.au/technology/schools-use-the-net-to-eavesdrop-on-students-20110812-1iqx2.html (accessed 29 November 2021).

Vaas, L. 2015. How one school district is monitoring social media of students and teachers. *Naked Security.* Available at: https://nakedsecurity.sophos.com/2015/07/31/.how-one-school-district-is-monitoring-social-media-of-students-and-teachers/ (accessed 29 November 2021).

Weiss, J. 2010. Scan this: Examining student resistance to surveillance. In *Schools under surveillance: Cultures of control in public education.* eds. T. Monahan and R. Torres, 213–229. New York, NY: Rutgers University Press.

Willis, P. 1977. *Learning to labour: How working class kids get working class jobs.* Farnborough: Saxon House.

Yar, M. 2003. Panoptic power and the pathologisation of vision: Critical reflections on the Foucauldian thesis. *Surveillance & Society* 1, 3: 254–271.

5 Using Foucault to examine issues of girls' education in a religiously driven postcolonial security state

Ali Sameer

Introduction

In this chapter, I examine how discourses of 'securitisation' and related discourses of nation building and religion are related to education and the social construction of girls' education in Pakistan. Here securitisation captures the unique historical and cultural development of Pakistan as a postcolonial, security-centric state and the powerful role of the military-mullah nexus to that development. Moreover, the discourse of securitisation is used here to capture the continuing role of religious patriarchy in nation building and the organisation of education systems and forms of gender exclusion.

The data for the chapter is from my PhD research project, which was a qualitative study aimed at exploring the links between securitisation discourses and the social construction of girls' education in Pakistan. To investigate these issues empirically, my PhD involved documentary analyses and interviews with 28 high-ranking state and non-state officials working in Pakistan, including Ministry of Education officers, military officers, religious leaders and scholars, third sector and charity workers and educationists, including school teachers and leaders.

Throughout this chapter the aim is to tackle the Eurocentric blind spots of Foucault – in the past he has been accused of using French evidence to constitute epistemological frameworks to make assumptions about the rest of the world, or to quote Edward Said, 'as if *history* itself took place only among a group of French and German thinkers' (Said 2000, 196–197). This chapter addresses this methodological quandary through an examination of girls' education in the religiously driven postcolonial security state of Pakistan. The chapter suggests that the Foucauldian notion of discourse has definite strengths when attempting to comprehend the way power/knowledge works in a society, but once applied out of its *original Western* context it can exhibit significant limitations. Using Pakistan as a case study, I argue that it is important to reconfigure theoretical and methodological approaches to this issue through a *hybridised approach* to European social theory when applied outside its context. Before I proceed further, it is important to unpack the idea of *hybridisation* that helped me both as a researcher and an academic to shape up my methodological choices.

DOI: 10.4324/9781003156550-7

When examining a contested topic (girls' education) in a contested setting (Pakistan) by a researcher with a contested identity (a man undertaking research on an issue related to girls), a linear theoretical approach might fail to grasp the nuances of the research process. In order to tackle this research quandary, I opted for theoretical *hybridisation* (Murphy 2017). I hybridised the international relations concept of securitisation laid out by the School of Copenhagen (Buzan et al. 1998) and its reading from a Foucauldian discourse perspective to illuminate the security discourse of Pakistan. To cover the gender angle, I opted for Butler's performativity theory on gender (Butler 2010). This theoretical hybridisation, as highlighted by Murphy (2017) not only shaped my theoretical framework for the research study but also assisted in my methodological choices. An empirical example of this was my choice of chosen research method, *elite interviews*, and the selection of research participants.

Additionally, as argued by Murphy (2017), the process of *hybridisation* enables a researcher to challenge the perspective that social theories laid out by thinkers such as Foucault are fixed and unalterable. Therefore, offering an empirical example of this alteration, the chapter ends by elaborating that in a postcolonial Pakistan, the working of discourse(s) has a different rationale compared to European contexts. Consequently, through an exploration of Foucault's discourse theory via the work of postcolonial theorists, along with the research participants' responses, the chapter discerns that there exists *a double discourse on girls' education in Pakistan*. This duality of discourse, on the one hand, involves *visible discourses* on girls' education that not only empower them but also support their educational attainments. However, there are *invisible discourses*, which exist in the shape of *the discourse of hypocrisy* and *the hidden curriculum* that negate such empowerment and educational attainment.

These *invisible* discourses, such as the discourse of hypocrisy and the hidden curriculum, are not restricted to educational institutions but are exhibited by social and state institutions as well. I discern that the unique case of Pakistan's securitisation not only sustains the policies of colonial India, but it still works with the same classification system that constitutes the girls/women as 'the other', with an aim to keep them inside the disciplinary discourses of Pakistani society. I give an empirical example of this *discourse of hypocrisy* by pointing out that men gauge the sexuality of a girl/woman based on her behaviour. For example, it is the relationship status that exists between a man and a girl/woman that sets differentiation parameters between a mother and a temptress. Moreover, the participants used religious dogma to support the idea of girls'/women's education, but when asked to divulge the reasons for the deteriorating situation of girls' education in society, they astonishingly blamed the religious clergy for using religion to promote conservatism in society that results in building intolerant behaviours towards girls' education. This argument, where participants can use the same reason to justify two different social attitudes towards a single issue, tells us a lot about the persistent duality that becomes the hallmark of the gender and educational discourse in Pakistan. Consequently, I have labelled this duality discourse as the *discourse of hypocrisy*.

In regard to *the hidden curriculum*, it is a medium through which girls/ women are given knowledge about their performativity. It is not restricted to pedagogical practices, and educational opportunities, but the construction of the knowledge system that enables the girl to identify her legitimised role in Pakistani society, and willingly fits into it. For instance, the issue is not when girls/women get educated but when, on the basis of that education, they try to negotiate the already established gendered roles. This negotiation is perceived to be a threat to the male hegemonic dominance, where the discourse of securitisation teaches girls/women the gendered roles they are expected to perform to ensure the longevity of the state and the whole community. Therefore, these invisible discourses, in the form of the discourse of hypocrisy and the hidden curriculum, become a converging point for the already existing multiple patriarchal practices to utilise the securitisation discourse to constitute knowledge on gender and education in Pakistan. Keeping this duality of discourses in mind, the chapter concludes that discourses should be studied and explored in the context of their social and cultural relevance and differences.

A brown man saving a brown girl: A moral and *methodological* quandary

Gayatri Spivak criticised Edward Thompson's work in which he aimed to protect a brown woman from brown men. Her claim was that the Western academic production of knowledge used to study colonial subjects was a way of a white man speaking to a white man about the dilemma of a brown woman (Spivak 1994). When I went to interview my first participant for my data collection, it dawned upon me straight away that *I* as a brown man conducting a research at a British university not only would have to interview officials who command immensely powerful positions, but also both the *topic* of my research and my own *identity* would be a matter of concern for the research participants. Ihsan, who heads one of the social science departments at a premier federal university, remarked about this dilemma. As the interview session concluded, and I was about to leave his office, he remarked:

> You have done your masters from Quaid-e-Azam University in Anthropology, I can understand your choice of topic. Most men coming from the anthropology department of that institution are interested in issues such as gender.

During the interview at one point when I questioned him about the security struggles of Pakistan and their impact on the society, in an annoying way he remarked:

> How many brothers and sisters do you have?

I replied:

> I have one sister.

To that he replied:

> Why did your father not let your sister go abroad for higher education? He chose you not her. So would you say the securitisation of Pakistan is stopping him from sending his daughter abroad? No son, it has nothing to do with the army or the security issues of Pakistan, it is a part of our culture, where boys are given preference.
>
> (department head, educationist, male)

Right after my first interview session, I realised that my own identity as a Pakistani man conducting research on the issue of girls' and women's education would be a major point of power contestation. However, soon into the data collection process, it appeared to me that I also had to negotiate the power dynamics of *research relations* (Burgess 2005, 5). During one interview session, a participant kept on saying to me, 'I will only allow you to utilise my information, if you promise that you will not *promote the Western agenda* through your work'. When I inquired from him what he meant by promoting a Western agenda, he replied, 'by highlighting those issues which will put the country or the society in a negative light'. My personal outlook being a male and coming from a British university to conduct research on the issue of gender and education required constant negotiation of approval from the participants, as I was dealing with the people occupying positions of power. On a few occasions, the initial part of the interview sessions resembled a student–teacher interaction. I had to justify my rationale for choosing the topic, and from time to time I was told that there were numerous flaws in my ideas, and I had to be educated from their perspectives so that I could establish a strong command of my topic. One participant went so far as to completely dismiss the idea of my research and stressed that I should go to rural and underdeveloped parts of the country. According to him there were no issues with girls' education in the developed and urban centres of the country, whereas the real problem was in the poverty stricken, security risk and culturally backward areas. He also suggested that he could organise a trip for me to security risk areas near the Afghanistan border with full protection, but only if I had the heart and will to explore the 'real issue'.

Dealing with such ethical dilemmas helped me to understand Bronfenbrenner's (1952) sentiments when he highlighted that such situations can only be avoided by refraining from conducting any sort of research (ibid, 453). However, in such circumstances, the reflective approach of a researcher can help them to understand the complications associated with social and educational research (Burgess 2005, 7). I dealt with this ethical dilemma by using the 'two ideals-about-interviewer-practices', i.e. *rapport* and *neutrality* (Rapley 2008, p. 19). Keeping in mind that interviews are spaces of interactions, and various methodological practices to conduct interviews are under the influence of local norms and values, I tried to utilise both 'neutral facilitation and co-operative self-disclosure' (Rapley 2001, 317–318). I did not confront the opinions that were hurled at me by the participants. Not even once during the course of the interviews did I use forms of deception to exploit particular responses from the participants (see Bryman 2004; Lichtman 2013; Silverman 2015; Ryen 2008). Also, following the local socio-political norms and customs, I refrained from mentioning anything controversial about the institution that the participant was part of. Even in instances where participants tried to patronise me, I did not show any sort of disregard or take it personally. I remember at the end of a very candid and detailed interview with a policy maker who went to a British university, I asked her, 'Do you have any last comments you would like to add?'. She replied, 'just remember, they [the British] do not like smart and strong-headed people. My supervisor tried hard to patronise me, but I resisted that. Make sure you do the same'.

If I apply Foucault's discourse theory, where he argues that within a discourse the constitution of a subject takes place (Foucault 1981), therefore, the process of negotiation that took place between the research participants and I over the course of interviews cannot, in my analysis, be labelled as their prejudice towards me. In order to understand their behaviour, it is crucial to locate the discourse in which those negotiations took place. During the interview, I was not only a brown man or an ordinary citizen of Pakistan, but when I engaged them via the process of interviews, I as a male researcher investigating controversial issues, such as security and gender, who studies at a Western university, acquired a new identity. With an identity that cannot be placed in already existing discourses, therefore, the negotiation and contestation of power during the interviews created a new discourse. For instance, Spivak criticised Thompson because, according to her, it was a white man trying to save a brown woman from a brown man. Likewise, I can be labelled as a brown man trying to save a brown woman from the rest of brown men. Applying Spivak's analysis, it can be argued that I am not offering a solution to the problem because, in a way, I am part of the problem.

If I as a researcher acquire a new identity while conducting research, despite spending more than half of my life in Pakistan, what about applying a foreign theoretical lens to study a local subject or issue? This approach – where I apply Foucault's theory of discourse to study an oriental issue – becomes a methodological quandary of my research. Consequently, in the next section I aim to further explore this dilemma.

Using Foucauldian poststructuralist framework in a postcolonial society

In applying a poststructuralist theoretical framework to study the issue of gender and education in a postcolonial society, I concede that in a way this makes the voice of this research an echo of colonial knowledge production. According to Legg (2007), colonisation was not only a form of territorial invasion but was also a representation of 'epistemic and historiographical violence and domination' (ibid, 265). The emergence of postcolonial and subaltern studies was with the intent to emancipate the colonial subject from this epistemic domination, emanating in the rise of writers such as Edward Said, Gayatri Spivak, Audre Lorde, Homi Bhabha, Sara Suleri, Stuart Hall and Frantz Fanon, along with the wave of postcolonial feminists.

The field of postcolonial and subaltern studies explicitly relied on the Foucauldian vocabulary to academically construct the contours of the postcolonial project (Nichols 2010). However, at the same time, it had to tackle the Eurocentric blindness of Foucault, where he was accused of using French evidence to constitute epistemological frameworks to make assumptions about the rest of the world (Said 2000, 196–197). Hence, he became a victim of his own criticism where he highlighted the hegemonic discourses of the Western power/ knowledge production mechanisms (Foucault 1980). Keeping in mind the repercussions that could stem from relying on the Foucauldian blind spot, which kept the issues of postcolonial subject and feminism out of his sight (Racevskis 2005), I deliberately opt to use Foucault to address the academic gap in the literature on Pakistan. However, in deference to Thompson's (2018) work, it is a brown man speaking to white men and women about the struggles of brown women in a postcolonial society. Hence, in order to make my speech coherent I have chosen to stand on the shoulders of Western theorists such as Foucault and Butler, but that cannot bury the fact that neither Foucault nor Butler, through their work, were able to study a postcolonial subject. Therefore, the application of Foucault's work to study discourses that play a significant role in the constitution of a postcolonial subject could be underlined as a limitation of the study.

That said, the weakness of this limitation becomes the strength of my argument. Given that postcolonial societies suffer from a colonial hangover, any academic effort to decolonise the *White mythologies* and assimilate the *unassimilable excess* that the Third World is (Young 2004), suffers from the Western–colonial academic hangover. The reason for this is the *language*. Although, Said, Spivak, and Bhabha had tried to decolonise and deconstruct the West (ibid), they could not get away from the most potent residue of the imperialism, which is their usage of European language and vocabulary. Phillipson labelled this *linguistic imperialism* (Phillipson 2003), and Said declared it as the inheritance of imperial legacy (Phillipson 1997, 238). Therefore, the struggle to negate the influence of Western theory and the absence of the Third World in their works cannot be addressed until academic expression sets itself free from its reliance on the European languages. But I argue that this limitation can be negotiated by assigning *new* meanings to the imperial and colonial concepts that aim to describe the Third World. Just like Foucault and his utilisation of Nietzschean and Kantian concepts to construct new meanings for the postmodern West (Thiele 1990; Mahon 1992; D'entrèves 1999), Spivak and Said used Foucauldian, Derridean and Marxist concepts to introduce the Third World issues from a non-Western perspective to postmodern Europe, and tackle the Eurocentrism of the Imperial West (Young 2004; Spivak 2010; Alavi 1991;

Racevskis 2005). Thus, the language of the study is a reflection of a colonial hangover, but it does strive to offer a new perspective on older concepts and issues. I believe for academics and researchers from postcolonial societies, studying in Western societies, the real struggle should be to challenge the linguistic imperialism by utilising the Western concepts to offer new meanings both for Western and postcolonial readers. In my case, I have utilised the medium of *hybridisation* to constitute new methodological practices, whether it was reconfiguring my research study's theoretical framework or using hybridised social theories to construct an analytical framework to analyse the research findings, the intrinsic objective was assigning new meanings to old social issues.

Applying Foucauldian discourse theory to a religiously driven postcolonial security–state: At times it works

If a quote can summarise the crisis that is faced by girls' education in Pakistan then I have to settle for an excerpt from an interview conducted with a religious leader, Lateef, who runs a religious school. Taking up a stance that the religious clergy is wrongfully blamed for ruining the country's image and held responsible for creating barriers towards girls' education, he expressed:

> There is a well-planned propaganda against us that we are against girls' education and spreading radicalisation in society. This propaganda is there because the media is in the hands of *kafirs* [infidels] or *munafiqs* [hypocrites]. In order to tackle this propaganda and counter it I have penned by own book. I did my research and found out that for example the whole case of Malala is a propaganda. Basically, Malala is not a Pakistani girl, she is a Caucasian European girl, who was born in Poland in the year 2000 and her real name is Gene. She is a product of Christian machinery and implanted here to show that Taliban are against girls' education. This is what we call propaganda, and by using this propaganda through this candle-mafia and NGOs, they are creating their own set of knowledge and truth.
>
> (Religious scholar, educationist, male)

The significance of the quote is not in its content but who uttered it. A religious person making such a statement in the West might not get a serious response but if a religious scholar says something of this sort, it has a certain weight in the context of Pakistan. Foucault (1980) argues that the workings of power in a society are handicapped without the discourses of truth as power 'operates through and on the basis of this association' (ibid, 93). According to him (ibid), the functioning of our societies seeks the forced production of truth for its functioning, moreover, exercise of power and production of truth are intertwined, which rely emphatically on each other for the workability of both. He further argues that power is in a constant struggle to institutionalise and professionalise the production of truth. Thus, we are subjected to the production of truth because it is truth that makes laws, carves out discourses and people's existence is the reflection of those discourses, which in return are marked by specific effects of power. Consequentially, the specific relationships between power, right and truth are organised in particular ways in our societies, thus leading to an interchange between the exercise of power and the production of truth (ibid, 93–94). Further building on his argument, Foucault (2002) highlights the ways in which power relations and knowledge production takes places within discourses. He reasons that:

> The important thing here, I believe, is that truth isn't outside power, or lacking in power: contrary to a myth whose history and function would repay further study, truth isn't the reward of free spirits, the child of protracted solitude, nor the privilege of those who have succeeded in liberating themselves. Truth is a thing of this world: it is produced only by virtue of multiple forms of constraint. And it induces regular effects of power. Each society has its regime of truth, its 'general politics' of truth: that is, the types of discourse which it accepts and makes function as true; the mechanisms and instances which enable one to distinguish true and false statements, the means by which each is sanctioned; the techniques and procedures accorded value in the acquisition of truth; the status of those who are charged with saying what counts as true.
>
> (ibid, 131)

Hence, summarising Foucault's main postulates of power, right and truth, it is evident that power relations through the production of truth constitute knowledge within the realm of discourses. Therefore, it is the performance of power within discourses that determines what we are and how we are to live and behave (Foucault 1980). But the most important factor, which he highlights in the above quote is the idea of 'every society having its own system of truth production'. Hence, the system of production of truth in Pakistan is heavily determined by the army and its religious clergy. Consequently, if an influential religious leader says that the whole story of Malala is a propaganda and points fingers towards foreign forces, the issue of girls' education becomes a non-starter and it is seen as some sort of threat. This is where the actual strength of Foucault's discourse theory lies: It helps us to understand the impact of the securitisation discourse on girls' education in Pakistan.

At the same time, much of the academic literature on Pakistan has severely criticised the role of the military–mullah nexus for sabotaging the socio-political structures of Pakistani society (Alavi 1988; Cohen 2004; Haqqani 2010; Samad 2011). Contrary to this, I suggest that rather than eyeing the authority of the military–mullah nexus as a forceful compulsion on the people, the main point of interest should be to understand the acceptance by people of this hegemonic rule. It is the willing participation of the people in the discourse of securitisation that becomes a crucial aspect to inspect.

Accordingly, this leads to an inquiry into the voluntary participation of people in the securitisation discourse, in order to comprehend the way the securitisation discourse achieves this voluntary participation. While talking about the production of discourse in his lecture, *Orders of discourses*, Foucault illustrated three tiers of exclusion mechanism that contribute towards the generation of the dominant discourse in society. According to him the most significant aspect of this exclusion mechanism is the distinction between true and false (Foucault 1981; Mills 2003b). Foucault argues that this distinction is 'historically constituted'. This historical division for him constructed our 'will to know'. It is this will to know that determines the position of 'knowing subject' to interpret knowledge. And this 'will to truth, like other systems of exclusions, rest on institutional support: it is both reinforced and renewed by whole strata of practices' (Foucault 1981, 54–55). The reason the people believe in the voice of security actors, such as the army or a religious person, in regard to the securitisation discourse as legitimate voices is because it has to be spoken by an authority that has the expertise to utter that truth (Mills 2003b, 58). In the case of Pakistan, the military and mullahs are deemed experts by the people to utter the truth regarding the securitisation discourse.

Understanding this knowledge production in Pakistan requires a comprehension of the foundations on which the state is erected. A brief glimpse of this can be seen from the opinions expressed by Sana, arguing the nation-state case of Pakistan, who commented:

> The other crucial important point we need to understand is that we are not a Westphalian state, we were a nation before a state. So, the mere fact that Pakistan exists as a state is a modern phenomenon, but the fact that we existed as a nation for more than a thousand years is a historical reality. And we existed as a Muslim nation for thousands of years. Our identity is Islam and due to this identity people gave all these sacrifices. Muslims and Hindus lived together for thousands of years but the Hindu–Muslim riots of 1935 securitised this relationship.
>
> (Educationist, policy maker, female)

This notion of a Muslim nation looking for a secured Muslim state paved the way for the emergence of the *indivisible trinity*, i.e. Islam, Pakistan and the army (Ahmad 1996, 382). Looking at the history of Pakistan, using Islam as a legitimacy agent by the various military and civilian governments to justify their authority is nothing new (Ahmed 2007; Ahmad 1996). Whether it was the slogan of the Islamic socialism by the civilian democratic government of Zulfiqar Ali Bhutto in 1970s, the wave of conservative Islamisation during the cold war era by the military regime of Zia, or the exploitation of mystical Islam in the name of *modern enlightenment* by the military government of President Musharraf in 2000s, Islam has been the mainstay of their authority (Nasr 2004; Haqqani 2004; Mezzera and Aftab 2009). This legitimacy factor was further elaborated by Sana, who mentioned:

First and foremost is to understand that Pakistan is an ideological state. We are an ideological state, that means Islam plays a central role in Pakistan's strategic culture. It cannot be replaced with anything else. This is something which Quaid-e-Azam [the title given to the founding father of Pakistan Muhammad Ali Jinnah] recognised, this is something which everyone, every political leader and every military leader in Pakistan has understood and applied. A different nuance. This is something where power is actually flowing in the country.

(Educationist, policy maker, female)

In this regard, the identification of power hubs holds the key to initiate the process to configure the securitisation of Pakistan. Based on the points highlighted above, it could be argued that Islam becomes the primary legitimacy factor for the power structures in Pakistan to justify their authority. It is through the legitimacy of religion that the power structures negotiate power and 'reduce the tension between power holders and subordinates' (Coicaud 2013, 40). This legitimacy exists both at the state level and at the public level. For instance, Iffat described the legitimacy of religion at the state level. According to her:

In our case our own state is religious, it says we are the Islamic Republic of Pakistan, our state has a religion.

(Third sector official, educationist, former policy maker, female)

Whereas Sadia illustrated the impact religion has on an ordinary Pakistani. She remarked:

See our ABC is about religion, people even comment for instance that it should be A for Allah not A for apple. All of our things revolve around religion because religion has a very rigid framework in our society, it is not dynamic it is not evolving, it is not changing with our days and nights and that's why we fear it, there is the element of fear and because of that we do not want to question it.

(Educationist, third sector official, female)

As a result, this force of legitimacy not only empowers the guardianship of the army, but it also creates further power structures, such as the religious elite, i.e. the mullahs. Although the army and the religious forces strengthen each other, there exists friction as well. Talking about the wave of radicalisation that crippled society after the incidents of 9/11, Tabish, a provincial education secretary who heads the Punjab curriculum board, underlined the might of the religious forces. He stated:

Even the 2008 anti-radicalisation slogan which was led by the military regime of that time to bring religious moderation failed because your mullahs hold a strong influence on our society. Although we do not elect them to Parliament, still they command a very strong street power, they come onto the roads and say this is against Islam, and by doing this they bring out the masses onto the roads. We cannot deny that but, yes, they do have street power.

(Civil servant, policy maker,
curriculum board director, male)

This depicts the might of religion in Pakistani society. It not only works at the macro level, where it defines the stature of Pakistani state, but also at the micro level, where it has the ability to bring out people from their houses onto the roads. The legitimising characteristics of religion influence both the state and its socio-cultural practices. This impact on the construction of reality can be assessed from the opinions expressed by Iffat:

Due to the reason that the state has a religion there is a constant fight and struggle between various sections of the society. The mullah gets the authority to define the Islamic state, and he tells a woman to dress up in burkas, asks to domesticate them, and don't provide them with education. On the contrary, the state of Pakistan, the Parliament, says women should go to school and get educated. However, we should not give them tickets to run in the elections so that they don't come into the Parliament. Therefore, it is the state which has created this conflict within the state where the state has proclaimed that it has a religion.

(Third sector official, policy maker, educationist, female)

Interestingly, it is not the power structures that can be blamed for exploiting the discourse of legitimacy. Even it becomes a deterrent for ordinary citizens to fend off accountability. As an example of empirical evidence, Sohail discerned the ways through which accountability is dodged by exploiting this legitimacy factor. Criticising the competency issues of school teachers, he said that accountability is only for those who are either poor or do not have any socio-political contacts. However, to ensure their survival, according to him, such people use religion as a shield to avoid accountability. When I asked him to narrate an example from his own experience as an education secretary, he said:

What I am going to tell you is highly unofficial. I know many female teachers, who are friends or relatives. For example, I know a lady who is a maths teacher and she is pro-religious; she goes to the class and teaches students to recite *Kalmas* [religious texts], she teaches them how to pray, which is the job of an Islamic studies teacher. She won't teach them maths, if you ask her why she is doing this, she replies it is because they are not literate about religious stuff. I will see if anyone tries to terminate her from her job. Anyone who tries to terminate her would be reprimanded.

(Bureaucrat, education policy maker, male)

When I asked the education secretary why he could not penalise a lower grade employee for failing to meet her official duties, he said:

> The reason is the society grills/trains you. Imagine if I don't say my Friday prayers, whether it is right or wrong and obviously it is wrong, my staff even ask me why I missed my Friday prayers. When society is in this frame of mind, what can you talk about?
>
> (Bureaucrat, education policy maker, male)

Therefore, this means that the discourse of legitimacy not only ensures an individual's survival but also enables that individual to assert their authority over others by claiming to be part of that discourse. In other words, as described by Foucault, 'discourse is not simply that which manifests (or hides) desire – it is also the object of desire … discourse is the power which is to be seized' (Foucault 1981, 52–53). In the above example, a subordinate, by becoming a part of the discourse of legitimacy not only is able to challenge the authority of their boss but also achieves the ability to create a system of parallel power mechanism. If we take this example then we can understand the working of discourses in society, which according to Hekman (1986) is the ability of a discourse to 'not only create knowledge but also power' (ibid, 174). So far, the case study of Pakistan lends itself well to Foucauldian discourse theory, as it helps to understand the link between the securitisation of Pakistan and how it constitutes a system of knowledge production that has a significant impact on the overall society. However, a deeper look into the case of Pakistan shows that, although at times Foucauldian discourse theory exhibits explanatory power in a postcolonial state such as Pakistan, the way discourses operate in reality in a religiously driven postcolonial security state deviate from a strictly Foucauldian approach to Western discourses.

Foucauldian discourse theory and its application in a religiously driven postcolonial security state: At times it requires *hybridisation*

Foucault (1980) says, 'sovereignty and disciplinary mechanisms are two abso-lutely integral constituents of the general mechanism of power in our society' (ibid, 108). His idea of *our society*, however, cannot be applied wholesale to a postcolonial society. The reason, I argue, is that the idea of the state which Foucault presents is based on European societies, where the sovereign power of a monarch was gradually overtaken by power apparatuses such as courts, prison, army and schools, which disseminated power through various discourses that reproduced regulatory practices, and led to the creation of subjects (Rouse 1999). In the Foucauldian world, the state derives legitimacy through the pro-cess of *normalisation*. In the process of normalisation, the state constitutes laws that appear to be normal for its citizens, and the acceptance of these laws by the citizens ensures the legitimacy and authority of the state, which results in the discourse of discipline (Foucault 2009; Astore 2016). But, as in the case of postcolonial states, the colonial powers and their institutions did not seek legitimacy from the natives to rule them; it was a reign of oppression by the colonials over the natives (Memmi 2003), where the rule of law was colonial *difference* that aimed to preserve the 'alienness of the ruling group' (Chatterjee 1993, 10).

However, when the colonials left, the power structures, which colonials used to govern the local population, for example army and bureaucracy, were over-developed in comparison to society (Alavi 1973). Consequently, in postcolonial societies, the new successors of power used 'the rhetoric of nationalism' based on religion, tribal and territorial differences to establish their rules, which replicated the ambitions and policies of the former colonisers, and created the *colonial legacy* (Wiener 2013, 5–7). It can be suggested that in postcolonial societies the state inherits an over-developed apparatus, which uses institutional practices to control the indigenous population, as argued by Alavi (1973). However, this *control* is not achieved through oppressive practices nor by the *normalisation approach*, but these colonial residues strengthen their authority by gaining the support of people through the discourse of legitimacy, as highlighted in the previous section.

Similarly, if the Foucauldian idea of *our society* cannot be entirely applied to a postcolonial society then it would be interesting to see the working of discourses. Throughout each interview, the participants vehemently advocated for girls' education. This I have labelled the *visible discourse* on girls' education. Contrary to this, the participants opposed the idea of girls' education without saying anything directly towards it. This dual side to the visible discourse is labelled as the *invisible discourse* on girls' education. It is outside the scope of this chapter to list all those examples, but below are some dichotomous responses from the participants that depict the duality of discourses on girls' education in Pakistan.

On the question of providing education to women in an Islamic society such as Pakistan, Shabbir argued that Islam provides equal opportunities to a woman to achieve education or establish a business. Besides, he claimed that daughters are blessings of God, and in an Islamic society there should be equal opportunities for both men and women, there should not be any concept that one system is for the elites of the society and the other system for the general masses. But at the same time, he warned about the dire effects a woman has on a man. He remarked that she is a *fitna* (strife, temptation), and the intelligence agencies around the world employ the concept of three Ws, wine, women and wealth, to manipulate people. According to him, if a person visits a psychiatrist then he would tell him that, for centuries, women have been used to lure men and get secrets from them. In short, a woman is a temptress and can cause havoc to men.

Interestingly, after saying this, he felt the need to turn this evil temptress into a pure and holy being. Therefore, immediately in the next line, he *legitimised* her status by placing her in a relationship with a man. He said:

But at the same time our religion was telling something different regarding a woman. It was said to seek knowledge from the lap of your mother to your grave. So, the lap of a mother was considered the first educational institution in Islam. It has bestowed such a big honour on a woman. Take the example of Hajj where women and men are performing the tawaf [one of the Islamic rituals of pilgrimage] together. It is about the purity of spirits not about the body, purity which comes from hearts.

(Educationist, religious scholar, male)

In an instant, a woman can be classified as a temptress or a conflict, and cause havoc for men. But the lap of a mother is considered holy and equivalent to an educational institution. If seen through the discourse of colonialism, this *vulnerable temptress* idea was projected by colonial masters as well. An ideal situation to explore the patriarchal thinking of the white colonial male could be seen in the case of European barmaids in colonial Calcutta and Rangoon. In the 1920s, Lord Curzon, the viceroy of the Sub-Continent, banned European barmaids from working in those parts of western India because their 'presence in the morally ambiguous space of the bar posed a threat to British prestige' (Wright 2017, 22). Also, the presence of white women serving non-European brown native men meant 'an inversion of the desired colonial hierarchy' (ibid, 22). Contrarily, for the same colonial masters, the repressed sexuality of native Muslim women made them an exotic fantasy (Ramusack 2004), and the unveiling of oriental women were deemed as unravelling the hidden secrets (Yeğenoğlu 2003). A similar pattern can be seen in today's postcolonial South Asia, where men compete for their masculine superiority in the patriarchal discourse on their ability to protect their mothers (Silva 1997).

Hence, it is not the agenda of women's suppression and liberation that is on the mind of men, whether colonial or postcolonial, but the negotiation of male space, which is played out by controlling women's bodies. When I asked the participants to define the role of a woman in Pakistani society, an overarching majority used male companionship as a point of reference to describe a woman's role. Even the question of women's rights in society received an answer in the context of the male companionship reference. It was as though a girl or a woman on her own does not possess any rights, but has to be a well-guarded and respected woman. According to Mehdi (religious, scholar, educationist, male), in the daily matters of life, women are given rights as a mother, wife, daughter and sister. Further, he stated that the financial responsibilities are 'not placed on the shoulders of women, I think in an Islamic society, a woman is given a *respectable status*, and this is the case in Pakistan as well. People in Pakistan, who have a religious education, and are well educated, they treat their women in a just and dignified manner'.

An interesting issue that he highlighted in his comment was an empirical example of the invisible discourse. Here *he* (religious scholar), who as a legitimate power to constitute truth in the context of Pakistan because he is an authority on religion, subtly defined a 'well-educated' and 'religious' person.

According, to him, a person is eligible to fall into this category if they provide a respectable status to their women, and that respectable status is equated with a woman who is looked after by her husband and does not bear any financial responsibilities. Therefore, this is an empirical example of the visible discourse on the social construction of gender, which is openly expressed. However, if a man allows a woman in her family to work, that signifies that he is not giving her a respectable status and, at the same time, is not a religious and well-educated man. This production of a regime of truths, *which is not said but implied*, I argue, becomes *the invisible discourse*, such as the discourse of gendered hypocrisy and the hidden curriculum that produce legitimate knowledge about the issue of girls' education in Pakistan.

The agenda of liberation is stapled to her relationship to a man, that is the reason the majority of the participants kept on associating a girl's education as a rite of passage for her to become a good mother. Moreover, as she is a constant source of temptation, and labelled as *fitna* (temptation) (Khoja-Moolji 2018; Mernissi 2003), as remarked by a few participants, her uncontrolled sexual needs demand a constant check. In an example, during one of the interview sessions, Sadia (educationist, third sector official, female) underlined that this notion of constant protection defines a girl's educational choices both in urban and rural settings. She stressed that subjects that deal with the domains of business, hotel management and hospitality are looked at in a sceptical way. She believed that if a girl decides to study these subjects, men related to her, such as her father or brother who are responsible for her security, do not allow her to opt for them. For them, she would get exposed to a treacherous environment, which could lead to her moral corruption.

Further explaining her point, she discerned that the male mind-set identifies a woman as his wife, sister or daughter but not an individual. The idea that women are weak, insecure and need male companionship for them to avoid danger, inculcates a mind-set in the society, where men believe it is their responsibility to make choices on behalf of their women. On another occasion, Nisar, who works at the National Parliament in Pakistan through his reply depicted the double standards at work in the discourse of girls'/women's education in Pakistan. His reply unveiled the practical manifestation of the discourse of hypocrisy and the hidden curriculum on the issue of girls' education. He disputed:

> For the last three days, we were stuck in that meeting trying to debate women's rights. A woman is produced for a man, what more to be discussed about it. A woman is produced to fulfil your needs and for your service, and beyond that she has no rights. The basic issue is our education process is not in sync, the upper-class education is different from the lower-class education. They are removing Islamisation and including Westernisation. What they are trying to do is include some form of the

upper class's education element in the lower-class education, at least by diminishing the religious aspect from it.

When I asked him whether girls'/women's education in Pakistan begets a different treatment as compared to the boys'/men's education in Pakistan he argued:

> You need to understand something highly significant first. We all say, including the government, the Parliament, the state and the political structures, that girls should get education, there is no conflict about it. *But they must not be in practice* [he uttered this line in English in an asserting tone]. When a woman opts to practice her educational learning, and she talks about equal rights this causes *raulay* [problems, conflicts, and issues].
>
> (Civil servant, male)

Consequently, I suggest that the whole discourse on girls' education in Pakistan is centred on her sexuality, hence, it becomes a means for the men to control and discipline her, which again takes us back to the Foucauldian understanding that institutions play a role in the creation of subjects that could be controlled and disciplined (Foucault 1995). Just like the colonial space was represented by the domination of the British white male (Mills 2003a), in the case of postcolonial Pakistan, the vacant space was occupied by its male predecessor. The prime example of continuation of this colonial domination through the colonial residual could be seen in the policies that were initiated by the military regimes of Pakistan, which aimed the majority of its policies towards the female body, whether it was the conservative Islamisation by General Zia-ul-Haq during the 1980s (Alavi 1991; Cook 2001; Suleri 2009), or the modern enlightenment by General Musharraf in the 2000s (Akhtar and Métraux 2013; Khattak 2010). The former used the Islamic legal system to substitute the Anglo-Saxon postcolonial jurisprudence system (Suleri 2009), whereas the latter exploited the moderate mystic Islamic values to appease the Western countries in the post-9/11 world (Zia 2009).

If I look at the arguments presented by the participants and analyse the academic literature, I would suggest that nothing much has changed in relation to the *Muslim* women of the Sub-continent. During the colonial days, they were under threat and needed liberation; also, in today's Pakistan they are perceived as weak and vulnerable beings that are under constant threat. In the same way that the British felt that they had to save brown subaltern women from the oppressing brown men (Spivak 1994), Pakistani men want to shield women from other men, either local or foreign. And the one way to ensure women's *pious* survival is to bring them into the realm of family-hood (Mernissi 2003; Khoja-Moolji 2018). However, analysing the way discourses operate in a postcolonial society cannot be performed by solely relying on Foucauldian discourse theory. The *hybridisation* approach to social theory, where I have addressed the blind spots of Foucauldian approach by bringing in the work of postcolonial academics, enabled me to understand the working of discourses in a postcolonial society. This duality of discourses, where the visible discourse promotes girls' education but the invisible discourse discourages it, offers not only a diverse exploration of the issue but also a unique analysis on how discourses operate in postcolonial societies.

Conclusion

The chapter argues that the social construction of girls' education in Pakistan cannot be addressed without understanding the security struggles and colonial past of the country. It is the amalgamation of this colonial past and security dilemmas that led to the formation of *the visible* and *invisible* discourses on girls' education in Pakistan. Moreover, the chapter illustrates that the examination of a social issue in a postcolonial society cannot be fully explored by relying on European theoretical frameworks, but it requires a hybridisation of diverse social theory concepts to address issues in a society that is quite distinct from Western societies, both in its social and political demeanours. If one says that a postcolonial theorist can grasp the working of discourses in a postcolonial society without taking help from Foucauldian concepts, then that would be an over-simplification. Thus, in such complex and contested social scenarios, *hybridisation* can enable researchers to create unique methodological choices and assign new meanings to current social issues. Taking the example of Pakistan, the chapter highlights that the Foucauldian concepts have definite strengths to address social issues in a postcolonial society. However, the Eurocentric blind spots of the Foucauldian approach requires support from postcolonial academics to counter such methodological quandaries.

As mentioned above, when conducting research on a contested topic in a contested society, established theoretical approaches might offer limitations. The complexity of my topic pushed me to approach theories that help me understand the intricacies of gender and education in a religiously driven postcolonial security state. In my case, the journey started with Foucault's power/ knowledge theory, which guided me towards his concept on discourse. However, the Eurocentrism of Foucauldian thought made me realise that if I relied solely on a single theoretical framework, I might restrict my research approach to a descriptive analysis. A synthesis of diverse theories, such as Foucauldian discourse theory and postcolonialism, offered me a chance to assign new meanings to old and current social issues and move from a descriptive understanding of girls' issues in Pakistan to an analytical one.

Moreover, as argued in this chapter the working of power mechanisms is embedded in the socio-cultural context of discourses. Likewise, the emergence and maintenance of discourses cannot be fixed either. Therefore, keeping this in mind, the historical and cultural, convergence and progression of discourses can play a significant role for policy makers, educational researchers and academics to investigate social issues in a constantly evolving world. As famously uttered by Said (1983), theories travel, both through time and in their contextualisation (Legg 2007). Hence, there is always a way forward in understanding the power/knowledge and discourse nexus, in a different realm, with a new approach.

References

Ahmad, M. 1996. The crescent and the sword: Islam, the military, and political legitimacy in Pakistan, 1977–1985. *The Middle East Journal* 50: 372–386.

Ahmed, M. 2007. Legitimacy crises in Pakistan (A comparative study of political behavior). *Journal of Political Studies* 12: 7–14.

Akhtar, N. and D.A. Métraux. 2013. Pakistan is a dangerous and insecure place for women. *International Journal on World Peace* 30: 35–70.

Alavi, H. 1973. The state in post-colonial societies: Pakistan and Bangladesh. *New Left Review* 74: 344–373.

Alavi, H. 1988. Pakistan and Islam: Ethnicity and ideology. In *State and Ideology in the Middle East and Pakistan*. eds. F. Halliday and H. Alavi, 64–111. Houndmills: Macmillan Education.

Alavi, H. 1991. Pakistani women in a changing society. In *Economy and culture in Pakistan: Migrants and cities in a Muslim society*. eds. H. Donnan and P. Werbner, 124–142. London: Palgrave Macmillan.

Astore, R.A. 2016. Defining the legitimacy and power of the state through Weber and Foucault. *Inquiries Journal/Student Pulse* (Online) 8. Available at: www.inquiriesjournal.com/a?id=1410 (accessed 10 December 2018).

Bronfenbrenner, U. 1952. Principles of professional ethics: Cornell studies in social growth. *American Psychologist* 7: 452–455.

Bryman, A. 2004. *Social research methods*. Oxford: Oxford University Press.

Burgess, R. G. 2005. Ethics and educational research: An introduction. In *The ethics of educational research*. ed. R.G. Burgess, 1–10. Philadelphia, PA: The Falmer Press.

Butler, J. 2010. *Gender trouble: Feminism and the subversion of identity*. New York, NY: Routledge.

Buzan, B., O. Wæver and J. De Wilde. 1998. *Security: A new framework for analysis*. London: Lynne Rienner Publishers.

Chatterjee, P. 1993. *The nation and its fragments: Colonial and postcolonial histories*. Princeton, NJ: Princeton University Press.

Cohen, S.P. 2004. *The idea of Pakistan*, Washington, DC: Brookings Institution Press.

Coicaud, J.-M. 2013. Crime, justice, and legitimacy: A brief theoretical inquiry. In *Legitimacy and criminal justice: An international exploration*. eds. J. Tankebe and A. Liebling, 37–59. Oxford: Oxford University Press.

Cook, N. 2001. The discursive constitution of Pakistani women: The articulation of gender, nation, and Islam. *Atlantis: Critical Studies in Gender, Culture and Social Justice* 25: 31–41.

D'entrèves, M.P. 1999. Between Nietzsche and Kant: Michel Foucault's reading of 'What is Enlightenment?'. *History of Political Thought* 20: 337–356.

Foucault, M. 1980. *Power/knowledge: Selected interviews and other writings, 1972–1977*. New York, NY: Vintage.

Foucault, M. 1981. The order of discourses. In *Untying the text: A post-structuralist reader*. ed. R. Young, 48–51. London: Routledge & Kegan Paul.

Foucault, M. 1995. *Discipline and punish: The birth of the prison*. New York, NY: Vintage Books.

Foucault, M. 2002. Truth and power. In *Power*. ed. J.D. Faubion, 111–153. London: Penguin Books.

Foucault, M. 2009. *Security, territory, population: Lectures at the Collège de France, 1977–78*. New York, NY: Palgrave Macmillan.

Haqqani, H. 2004. The role of Islam in Pakistan's future. *The Washington Quarterly* 28: 83–96.

Haqqani, H. 2010. *Pakistan: Between mosque and military*. Washington, DC: Carnegie Endowment.

Hekman, S.J. 1986. *Hermeneutics and the sociology of knowledge*. Cambridge: Polity Press.

Khattak, S.G. 2010. Women in local government: The Pakistan experience. *IDS Bulletin* 41: 52–61.

Khoja-Moolji, S. 2018. *Forging the ideal educated girl: The production of desirable subjects in Muslim South Asia*. Oakland, CA: University of California Press.

Legg, S. 2007. Beyond the European province: Foucault and postcolonialism. In *Space, knowledge and power: Foucault and geography*. eds. J. Crampton and S. Elden, 265–289. Burlington, VT: Ashgate.

Lichtman, M. 2013. *Qualitative Research for the Social Sciences*. London: Sage Publications.

Mahon, M. 1992. *Foucault's Nietzschean genealogy: Truth, power, and the subject*. New York, NY: State University of New York Press.

Memmi, A. 2003. *The colonizer and the colonized*. London: Earthscan.

Mernissi, F. 2003. The meaning of spatial boundaries. In *Feminist postcolonial theory: A reader*. eds. R. Lewis and S. Mills, 489–501. Edinburgh: Edinburgh University Press.

Mezzera, M. and S. Aftab. 2009. Country case study: Pakistan State-Society Analysis. Available at: www.clingendael.org/sites/default/files/pdfs/20090300_cru_pakistan_mezzera.pdf (accessed 11 March 2018).

Mills, S. 2003a. Gender and colonial space. In *Feminist postcolonial theory: A reader*. eds. R. Lewis and S. Mills, 692–719. Edinburgh: Edinburgh University Press.

Mills, S. 2003b. *Michel Foucault*, London: Routledge.

Murphy, M. 2017. *Habermas and social research: Between theory and method*. Abingdon: Routledge.

Nasr, V. 2004. Military rule, Islamism and democracy in Pakistan. *Middle East Journal* 58: 195–209.

Nichols, R. 2010. Postcolonial studies and the discourse of Foucault: Survey of a field of problematization. *Foucault Studies*: 111–144.

Phillipson, R. 1997. Realities and myths of linguistic imperialism. *Journal of Multilingual and Multicultural Development* 18: 238–248.

Phillipson, R. 2003. *Linguistic imperialism*. Oxford: Oxford University Press.

Racevskis, K. 2005. Edward Said and Michel Foucault: Affinities and dissonances. *Research in African Literatures* 36: 83–97.

Ramusack, B.N. 2004. *The Indian princes and their states*. Cambridge: Cambridge University Press.

Rapley, T. 2008. Interviews. In *Qualitative research practice*. eds. C. Seale, G. Gobo, J.F. Gubrium and D. Silverman, 15–33. London: Sage Publications.

Rapley, T.J. 2001. The art(fulness) of open-ended interviewing: Some considerations on analysing interviews. *Qualitative Research* 1: 303–323.

Rouse, J. 1999. Power/knowledge. In *The Cambridge companion to Foucault*. ed. G. Gutting, 92–114. Cambridge: Cambridge University Press.

Ryen, A. 2008. Ethical issues. In *Qualitative Research Practice*. eds. C. Seale, G. Gobo, J.F. Gubrium and D. Silverman, 218–235. London: Sage Publications.

Said, E.W. 1983. *The world, the text, and the critic*. Cambridge, MA: Harvard University Press.

Said, E.W. 2000. *Reflections on exile and other essays*. Cambridge, MA: Harvard University Press.

Samad, Y. 2011. *The Pakistan–US conundrum: Jihadists, the military and the people: The struggle for control*. El Paso, TX: Cinco Puntos Press.

Silva, N. 1997. 'Mothers, daughters and "whores" of the nation': Nationalism and female stereotypes in post-colonial Sri Lankan drama in English. *Journal of Gender Studies* 6: 269–276.

Silverman, D. 2015. *Interpreting qualitative data*. London: Sage Publications.

Spivak, G. 2010. *The Spivak reader: Selected works of Gayati Chakravorty Spivak*. New York, NY: Routledge.

Spivak, G.C. 1994. Can the subaltern speak? In *Colonial discourse and post-colonial theory: A reader*. eds. P. Williams and L. Chrisman, 90–105. Bodmin: Harvester Wheatsheaf.

Suleri, S. 2009. Woman skin deep: Feminism and the postcolonial condition. In *The post-colonial studies reader*. eds. B. Ashcroft, G. Griffiths and H. Tiffin, 756–769. New York, NY: Routledge.

Thiele, L.P. 1990. The agony of politics: The Nietzschean roots of Foucault's thought. *The American Political Science Review* 84: 907–925.

Thompson, E.J. 2018. *Revival: Suttee (1928): A historical and philosophical enquiry into the Hindu rite of widow-burning*. Abingdon: Routledge.

Wiener, M.J. 2013. The idea of 'colonial legacy' and the historiography of empire. *Journal of the Historical Society* 13: 1–32.

Wright, A. 2017. Maintaining the bar: Regulating European barmaids in colonial Calcutta and Rangoon. *The Journal of Imperial and Commonwealth History* 45: 22–45.

Yeğenoğlu, M. 2003. Veiled fantasies: Cultural and sexual difference in the discourse of Orientalism. In *Feminist postcolonial theory: A reader*. eds. R. Lewis and S. Mills, 542–566. Edinburgh: Edinburgh University Press.

Young, R. 2004. *White mythologies: Writing history and the west*. Abingdon: Routledge.

Zia, A.S. 2009. Faith-based politics, enlightened moderation and the Pakistani women's movement. *Journal of International Women's Studies* 11: 225–245.

Part III

Habermas

6 Jürgen Habermas

Education's increasingly recognised hero

Terence Lovat

Introduction

Despite not being conceived with educational research in mind, Habermas' theories of knowing and communicative action have potential to deepen research understandings in education. In his theory of knowing, beyond the well-worn *techne* of learning, Habermas conceives of more authentic ways of knowing through critical reflection and engagement, or *praxis*, conceptions of learning with potential to challenge the dominant notions of the role of the teacher and efficacious pedagogy. Furthermore, in his theory of communicative action, Habermas posits the self-reflective knower as one who comes to see their own lifeworld relative to those of others. Through this way of knowing, the knower develops communicative capacity and ultimately communicative action, knowing with potential to transform the learning experience. The chapter will provide a summary of the lifeworld of Habermas himself, expound on Habermasian theory and illustrate its pertinence to educational research through several contemporary applications concerning schools and higher education. It will conclude with examples of unanticipated and unexpected applications of Habermasian thought to other educational fields.

Habermas's own lifeworld

Jürgen Habermas, born in 1929 in Dusseldorf, Germany, is widely referred to as a sociologist and philosopher and younger member of the so-called 'Frankfurt School', a group of social theorists and philosophers associated with the Institute for Social Research at Frankfurt University, including names such as Horkheimer, Marcuse, Adorno, Fromm and Apel. The Frankfurt School is particularly associated with neo-Marxist postwar reconstruction theory and, among a number of key theoretical positions for which its leadership is acknowledged, the set of perspectives broadly known as 'critical theory' – a radically interdisciplinary field designed to ensure that the best thoughts of scholarship are applied to solving real-life issues. From the mid-1960s until his retirement in 1993, Habermas played a leading role in developing, refining and furthering critical theory and making applications to multiple fields.

DOI: 10.4324/9781003156550-9

For Habermas, critical theory represented a way of repairing what he came to understand increasingly as the corrupt regime of Nazism, a thoroughly shameful moment in German history, as he saw it. For one who grew up in a marginally pro-Nazi family, who joined the Hitler youth (compulsorily) and, at 15 years of age, was sent to fortify the western defences as the Third Reich was crumbling, the sense of shame seems to have been personalised to the extent that it came to drive his critical theory with a particular passion. The passion is around ensuring that, in future, personal, social and political action is so informed with norms of reason and compassion that there could never again be a Third Reich. Arguably, Habermas' single most enduring influence has been in his epistemological work, a theory of knowing that impels the kind of reasoned and compassionate reflection and self-reflectivity that issues in benevolent action. Granted that his entire platform of thought rests on a theory of knowing, there would seem to be much for educationists to consider. While, on self-admission, Habermas has paid little attention to the details and niceties of formal education and its paraphernalia, he nonetheless presents as the reluctant hero of education for the power of his epistemology to depict authentic learning as being considerably beyond the *techne* if the goal of learning is to be one befitting being human.

Placing Habermas in the knowing debate

Habermas' perspective on the unity of knowledge is part of the heritage of modern work dating at least to Dewey (1922; 1956a; 1956b) and the attempt to identify the standard patterns that underpin knowing, learning and instruction. Ayer's (1936) logical positivism had tried to ground all authentic knowing in the rational or empirically observable/measurable. In turn, Tyler (1949) generated from this conceptual identification a virtual science around assessment regimes, and Bloom and associates (Bloom 1956; Krathwohl et al. 1964) built further on it in the form of the taxonomies of educational objectives.

Meanwhile, Ferre (1982) had begun the dismantling of the apparatus of logical positivism in declaring that 'facts are never given in isolation from the minds that receive them' (ibid, 761). Ferre implied that the things we call 'facts' are really theories, and hence less observable/measurable than in the ways that logical positivists held to be determinative. Such a rejoinder was further reinforced by Lakatos (1974) and Kuhn (1970), who coined the notions of 'touchstone' and 'paradigm', respectively, to connote the true basis of claims to know. In a word, knowing is not linear, it is complex; nor is it objective in any simple observable or measurable sense because it is infused with the subjectivity of the person doing the knowing. Quine (1953) went on to show just how subjective were the assertions of those claiming to be objective and Feyerabend (1975) launched highly critical attacks on education systems for the ways in which they had prioritised certain forms of knowledge over others, on the purported basis that they offered surer knowing (read 'rational or observable/

measurable knowing'), while other ways of knowing were relegated to the margins of education.

The response from educationists was to take recourse in various 'forms of knowledge' arguments in order to counter the veritable domination of logical positivism in practical systems of education. Phenix (1964) wrote that curriculum comprises 'realms of meaning', rather than a single realm and that each realm (read 'discipline') needed to be understood and dealt with according to its own terms of meaning. Hirst and Peters (1970) agreed, stating that 'in the recent past, education had been conceived … too much in terms of a set stock of information, simple skills and static conformity to a code' (ibid, 37).

The Hirst and Peters 'forms thesis' held that there were certain forms of knowledge which underlay any claim to know. The seven forms comprised Mathematics and Logic, Physical Sciences, Human Sciences, Literature and Fine Arts, History, Philosophy and Religion. Each of these forms had an appropriate procedure, or methodology, which suited gathering knowledge within its domain. Hence, while empirical observation and measurement might well be appropriate for dealing with forms of knowledge in the physical sciences, the human sciences required a closer, more subjective approach on the part of the one wishing to know, and knowing in the fine arts and religion required something different again. From this perspective, the great error in logical positivism was in supposing that one or two of the forms of knowledge constituted all knowledge.

It is within the terms of this historical moment that Habermas' work comes to have most meaning, including for education. In a sense, Habermas (1972; 1974) constructed his own forms thesis but laid it on firmer epistemological and cognitive grounds, seeing it resting not on partitioned knowledge sets as ontological reifications but rather on the ways in which the mind works in constructing reality. As an early aside, this construct of knowing, a rare combination of philosophy and science, might yet have greater potential than has been realised so far for conversation with the emerging neurosciences. Habermas' explanation for apparent divisions in knowledge derives from his belief that knowing is impelled by a series of cognitive interests, interests that are part and parcel of the way the human mind works. These interests are three-fold. First, there is an interest in technical control which impels an 'empirical analytic' type of knowing. Second, the interest in understanding meanings gives rise to an 'historical hermeneutic' way of knowing, or communicative knowing (the knowing that results from engagement, inter-relationship and dialogue with others). Third, there is an interest in being emancipated, a free agent as it were, which issues in a 'critical/self-reflective' way of knowing, a way of knowing that ultimately entails knowing oneself. 'There is no knowing without knowing the one doing the knowing', we might say.

As far as Habermas is concerned, all three cognitive interests are operative regardless of the discipline area. Whatever the subject matter, our interest in technical control will lead us to want to know all the facts and figures associated with the subject at hand; this is where the quest for empirical–analytic knowing originates and is of use in the total quest to know. Similarly, our interest in understanding the meaning behind an event will lead us to explore the inner dimensions, to try to relate one factor to another and to negotiate interpretations with other interested stakeholders; this impels an historical/hermeneutic type of knowing that serves to extend our understanding and the totality of our knowing. Lastly, the cognitive interest in emancipation, that which ensures our autonomy as a knower, will make us reflect critically on our subject matter, our sources and ultimately ourselves as agents of knowing. This is the preserve of critical/self-reflective knowing and where, according to Habermas, the only truly assured, totally comprehensive and authentic human knowing occurs.

At the heart of Habermas' thesis is the notion that the cognitive interest to be free in our knowing impels an intensive critique of all of the assumptions and sources of our knowing up to that point in time. Among the assumptions and sources are those of both the external and internal world. Externally, one confronts one's enculturated past, one's corporate beliefs and community values, one's family, school, political and religious heritage. Internally, one confronts oneself. Through critical/self-reflective knowing, one is challenged to let go of much of the past and to embrace new futures. The end of critical/self-reflective knowing is found in *praxis*, practical action for change. One cannot remain in the same place once one has confronted one's past and oneself. In a sense, the ultimate point of the learning game is to be found in knowing oneself and the consequent change of belief and behaviour that inevitably follows. Habermas saw this process as cleansing and purifying one's intentions and actions in ways that were lacking in the germination of the Third Reich and its many followers. It is here that some of his passion to ensure that the Third Reich could never happen again can be seen.

In Habermas' (1984; 1987) later theory of communicative action, he builds on the theory of knowing, describing the development of 'communicative capacity' as the initial outgrowth of the self-reflective knower and then, moreover, of 'communicative action'. Communicative capacity is when the self-reflective knower comes to see his or her lifeworld as one of many, all of them needing to function in a myriad of life-worlds, and so comes to possess communicative capacity. It is in a sense the fully flourished result of the historical–hermeneutical, or communicative, way of knowing when infused with the critical/self-reflective way of knowing, a veritable formula for the modern, globally competent, intercultural communicator.

Beyond this is the notion of communicative action, an action orientation beyond that which can be impelled by historical–hermeneutical knowing, requiring instead the more profound knowing that comes from self-reflectivity. Herein, the self-reflective knower takes a step beyond mere tolerance of other life-worlds to take a stand to defend the right of all legitimate life-worlds to exist and be accommodated within the human community. The stand is both for justice and for oneself because one's newfound self, one's own integrity, is at stake. This is a concept about personal commitment, reliability and trust-worthiness that impels and demands practical action that makes a difference. It is a refinement and sharpening of the outpouring of authentic knowing, namely *praxis*, as conceived of in Habermas' theory of knowing, the kind of committed action that can only come from the wellspring enshrined in the notion of self-reflectivity, from one who knows who they are, values the integrity of being authentic and commits oneself to establishing the kinds of caring and trusting relationships that bear the best fruits of human interactivity. Again, Habermas' passion to correct the wrongs of the past, especially around German Christian anti-Semitism, and to ensure such travesties can never happen again, can be seen in the way this theory is constructed.

In his clear conjoining of knowing with doing, Habermas' fundamental Aristotelian reliance becomes apparent. In being caught between the rational-ism of his teacher, Plato, and the pragmatism that always allured him, Aristotle finally settled on a way of knowing that relied on, yet was beyond, both rationalism and pragmatism in their simpler senses. This was a way of knowing that arose partly from the human need to be guided by one's intellect (as in rationalism) and partly from the need to be guided by one's common sense and intuition (as in pragmatism) but, above all, by one's need to be authentic in what one claimed to know. *Eudaemonia* is Aristotle's supreme good, but it is not a good that can be pursued merely by being known or merely by being experienced. It is a good that must be lived. The kind of judgment essential to the pursuit of *eudaemonia* is what Aristotle finally described as a practical jud-gement, a judgement that leads to practical action, or *praxis* in Habermasian terms.

The Aristotelian connection helps us to see how far Habermas has taken us from the postulations of the logical positivists for whom knowing was entirely locked in to the empirical–analytic domain. The potential for Habermasian theory to inform modern quests to 'think outside the square' across a spectrum of fields seems limitless (Miller 2011; Koller and Hiebaum 2016). Among these fields is educational research. Considerable important educational research has been expended in making application of Habermasian theory to a range of issues relevant to educational theory and practice (Van Manen 1977; Young 1989; Doll 1993) and Habermas (2001) acknowledges the validity of this con-nection in some of his later work. I will focus below on two main species of educational research, in which I have been a participant, to illustrate the perti-nence and usefulness of Habermasian theory to these projects. I will then briefly elaborate on other projects with which I have been involved that, less expectedly, were enlightened and guided by a Habermasian application.

Curricular and pedagogical research in schools and higher education

In earlier work (Lovat and Smith 2003; Lovat et al. 2005), it was proposed that the Habermasian theory of knowing could be used to analyse different moments in the teacher–learner relationship, and the power thereof, so to clarify and sometimes contest the assumptions that sit behind certain curriculum approaches and forms of pedagogy. In that work, empirical/analytic knowing was said to lead naturally to a relationship where the teacher is cast as 'expert' and the learner as the novice. The teacher is there to teach and the learner to learn in top–down, linear fashion. In other words, all power is with the teacher with little to none on the part of the learner. As such, this schema offers epistemic justification for a high order didactic approach to pedagogy. For a learning task concerned with a skill that the teacher clearly possesses, and the learner does not, didactic pedagogy might well be the most efficient way to close the gap, whereas learning focused on historical or sociological understandings and interpretations could render such pedagogy obstructive. Of course, if the learning exercise is encased in a mandatory testing regime wherein it is considered there is only one licit interpretation, then the issue becomes one not so much about the appropriateness of the pedagogy as the ethics of the entire teaching learning exercise.

Historical/hermeneutic knowing tends more obviously to a conception of the teacher–learner relationship as one of partnership, communicating about meanings and negotiating about understandings; power is shared to an extent. This would impel naturally a more democratic pedagogy, one that allows and indeed encourages a measure of free thought and speech, including to speculate beyond the hard evidence and/or even to make mistakes as part of the learning process. Such pedagogy would seem more appropriate to interpretive learning about meanings and understandings in the humanities and social sciences.

When dealing with knowing of critical/self-reflectivity, impelled by the cognitive interest in being free to think one's own thoughts, so to engage in *praxis*, the relationship between teacher and learner has potential to attain that measure of symmetry, even power sharing, beyond that which is obtained through historical/hermeneutic knowing. Herein, there is a relegation of power by the teacher to the learner as the learner is endowed with the confidence and the power of being in control of their own knowing. This can even result in roles being reversed, with the teacher, in a sense, sitting at the feet of the structural learner in the role of the veritable learner, or 'listener'. If the listener wishes to know what the learner has learned, and even more so if the listener wants to know what the learner now knows, then they will be dependent upon the learner sharing what is known and taking seriously the learner's greater knowledge in a particular field. For an example of this, see the reference below under 'Unexpected educational applications of Habermas', where I note two PhD projects where I, as supervisor, learned much from the greater knowledge in two particular fields – medical decision-making and diplomatic training – of my students.

The challenge for traditional understandings of how teaching/learning functions relates to the obvious truth that learners might often 'know' in ways that are outside the knowing of the teacher. This will be especially the case in the context of higher education research but might well apply at any level of education. In the epistemic world that sits behind empirical–analytic knowing and the resultant didactic pedagogy, it would be intolerable that the learner might be said to know more than the teacher. In the epistemic world of historical–hermeneutic knowing, this is tolerable and able to be negotiated, although not necessarily to be expected. In dealing with critical/self-reflective knowing, however, it is to be expected and indeed celebrated that new knowing, quite beyond the first-hand knowledge of the teacher, has evolved.

Van Manen (1977) captures the relationship between the teacher and the learner that is being proffered herein when he says the following of the type of learning he sees ensuing from critical/self-reflective knowing:

> The norm is a distortion-free model of a communication situation … [where] there exists no repressive dominance, no asymmetry or inequality among the participants of the educational process.
>
> (ibid, 227)

For Van Manen, like Habermas, it is at this point alone that education becomes distinctively ethical, characterised by a sense of justice, equality and the freedom of individuals to follow their instincts of knowing wherever they might lead. It is also the way of knowing which, it is said, is a necessary precursor to the stretching of the boundaries of knowledge, to genuinely new knowing taking place. If one were to take Van Manen's 'no asymmetry' thesis seriously, one would surmise that the only form of testing and measuring that could do justice to, or perhaps even detect, evolving knowledge of this type would be one which was conducted largely in self-reflective mode.

In other earlier work (Lovat et al. 2008), this thinking was applied to an analysis of doctoral examination reports and it was noted that there were few instances where reports went beyond the didactic pedagogical mode of correction and little evidence of examiners acknowledging the level of 'original contribution' (supposedly the benchmark criterion for doctoral success), even though the majority of the theses in question were successful. It was therefore speculated on whether this indicated that the expectations placed on the doctorate were in fact not being met or whether it was indicative of the incapacity of the university teachers, serving as examiners, to break out of didactic pedagogy and the empirical–analytic assumptions sitting behind it, even when dealing with learners at the alleged zenith point of learning.

Of the 2,121 examiner reports under analysis, there was only one that seemed clearly to reveal text indicative of an examiner functioning in critical/self-reflective mode. It began with the words, 'There are those pleasant occasions when one is asked to review a paper or examine a thesis and you wish that you had written it. I believe that this is one of those experiences' (Lovat et al. 2008, 71). This comment re-positioned the examiner's relationship with the student away from one of expertise-to-subject, or even of shared negotiability. The relationship established was at least symmetrical and could even be argued to have turned the traditional relationship on its head to become one of awe on the part of the examiner towards the student's original contribution, one which the examiner admitted that they had not themselves made. In that sense, the student had exceeded the expertise of the examiner and, in a rare display, this examiner was prepared to admit it. The teacher had become the learner.

In this example, the Habermasian theory of knowing allowed for critical gaze to be applied to an area of educational research with potential to assist in unravelling the learning assumptions that sat behind an arguably unhelpful pedagogy, or one at least demanding critical analysis and review, and so to re-conceive how a particular educational regime might function better. In this case, the findings received wide dissemination and have been cited in a variety of academic and policy sites at the international level (cf. Park 2007; Carter and Whittaker 2009). Moreover, the ramifications of such appraisal have potential to go beyond the particular regime being targeted. A wider concern about rigidity of pedagogy was present in the observation that if those responsible for assessment at the PhD level are locked into 'gate-keeping' pedagogy, then what hope for more authentic pedagogy when applied to undergraduate and school levels of learning? Work around these matters has continued (Lovat et al. 2015; 2021; Clement et al. 2015; Holbrook et al. 2017; Starfield et al. 2017; Kiley et al. 2018; Dally et al. 2019; 2020), including being cited in the journal, *Nature* (Gould 2016). Invariably, the work has utilised Habermasian perspectives in interpreting findings.

An application to holistic learning and student wellbeing

A persistent concern of education is with the notion of student achievement and whether this is best served for the majority through regular instrumentalist approaches to learning and assessment (e.g. direct instruction, standardised curricula and norm-referenced testing, etc.) or whether student achievement is so enmeshed in broader issues of wellbeing that more holistic approaches to learning are required. Amidst this debate comes an array of updated evidence that points to the influence of values education on student wellbeing, including academic diligence and improvement (cf. Noddings 2002; Arthur 2003; Rowe 2004; Campbell et al. 2004; Benninga et al. 2006; Carr 2006; Nucci and Narvaez 2008; Lovat and Toomey 2009; Arthur 2010; Lovat 2010a; 2012a; 2012b; 2017a; 2017b; 2018; 2019a; 2019b; 2020a; 2020b; Lovat and Clement 2008a; 2008b; 2008c; 2014; 2016; Lovat and Dally 2018; Lovat et al. 2009; 2010a; 2010b; 2010c; 2011a; 2011b; 2011c; 2011d).

Values education research and practice is not considered by most educational systems to be a regular instrumentalist approach to learning, normally considered to be marginal to the mainstream agenda of academic content and assessment, and even arguably to be a little oppositional to it through its focus on 'beyond the academic curriculum'. Neither is values education organised in a way that would allow it to be an *ipso facto* device for mainstream academic content, not being characterised by a firm set of guidelines so much as a loose alliance of approaches with the common focus of creating, in learning sites, values-rich environments through relationships, modelling and ambience, and inserting values discourse into the overt curriculum. It is therefore not principally concerned with matters of academic development per se, but rather with student wellbeing as a whole. This makes the above research findings all the more interesting. It seems undeniable now that approaches to learning that de-emphasise academic content and assessment, concentrating rather on creating supportive environments of learning and richer and more personalised discourse, impact positively on student behaviour and classroom calm and, in turn, lead to students being more attentive to their academic work. This would seem to indicate that, in all likelihood, all dimensions of student wellbeing, including academic learning, might be better served through holistic approaches to learning.

A variety of philosophical and empirical work has been proffered in recent times to explain the inherent connections between the various dimensions of student wellbeing and so to justify more holistic approaches being taken to learning. For example, Carr (2006) has revived the philosophical case of John Dewey and Richard S. Peters in arguing that there can be no adequate and effective learning without teachers who model integrity and practise their profession in a way that entails sound relationships and moral interchange with their students. It is for him principally a matter of informal logic that teachers who go about their business in a fully professional and ethical way, with all the attachments of more secure environments and richer classroom talk and interchange, will produce better results of all kinds. In a sense, coming at the same issue from a different standpoint are the psychologists and neuroscientists. Ainley (2006) illustrated clearly that student motivation to learn can only be fully engaged when the emotional context is conducive. Damasio's (2003) work in the neurosciences has gone even further in findings that show that the seat of cognition in the brain is not separable from the seats of affect and sociality. Hence, it is not surprising that the environment characterised by healthier relationships and greater affirmation, together with more challenging discourse, will be the one where students are motivated to learn and attend better to their work.

Newmann and associates' (1996) work on the 'pedagogical dynamics' required for quality teaching also provides a clue in that several of the dynamics concern relationships and the ambience of learning. For instance, 'catering for diversity' referred to the centrality of the respectful and sensitive relationship between teacher and student, so ensuring an ambience where the student feels accepted, understood and valued. Similarly, 'school coherence' was of the school that is committed unswervingly to the good of the student, a values-rich concept connoting dedication, responsibility, generosity and integrity on the part of all stakeholders. Meanwhile, the ultimate pedagogical dynamic of the 'trustful, supportive ambience' was deemed to be so indispensable that it would render all teaching ineffective if not attended to.

Osterman (2010) speaks in a sense to all the above conclusions in providing evidence of the greater learning capacity instilled by environments where students feel they belong and therefore experience strengthened emotional wellbeing. Furthermore, she illustrates in this evidence the integral connection between teacher relationship and support and the nature of the pedagogy provided by the teacher. It is neither the teacher who merely provides a supportive ambience nor the one who merely instructs well whose practice enhances academic diligence. It is the teacher whose pedagogy is characterised by the integrity of a supportive relationship and best practice pedagogy as one action, rather than two, who brings students to new levels of academic enhancement.

The role that Habermas has played in providing an epistemological explanation and justification for these insights into the holistic nature of learning has been inestimable. While essentially a philosophical perspective, Habermas's insights have rare potential to straddle the various disciplines that are informing the debate. His theories of knowing and communicative action offer, between them, particularly powerful tools for analysing the capacity of values education to transform people's beliefs and behaviours in ways that conform to the evidence. For one thing, they render the notion of values neutrality in education non-viable and therefore challenge the authenticity of any education conceived of solely in instrumentalist terms (Lovat 2020b). In contrast, they lead naturally to the notion that any legitimate education requires a values-laden approach, in terms of both ambience and discourse. Hence, they help to explain why it is that values education's priority in saturating the learning experience with both a values-filled environment and explicit teaching that engages in discourse about values-related content tends towards such holistic effects as have been uncovered in the research. Furthermore, the Habermasian notion that critical/self-reflective knowing issues in emancipation and empowerment, so spawning communicative capacity and communicative action, both justifies and explains the effects of an approach to learning that prioritises the transaction of values.

Habermasian epistemology therefore is able to be used to justify philosophically and explain the practical effects of an approach to learning that is aimed at the full range of developmental measures in the interests of holistic student learning and wellbeing. Rather than connoting a mere moral or, least of all, religious option, values education is able to be constructed philosophically and pedagogically as an effective way in which learning can proceed in any school setting (Habermas 1990). Hence, we find Habermas regularly cited among scholars engaged in values education research (cf. Crawford 2010; Crotty 2010; Gellel 2010; Henderson 2010; Lovat 2020a; Lovat et al. 2010a; 2011a).

Crotty (2010), for instance, employs a Habermasian perspective to make sense of the improved academic focus that he saw so clearly demonstrated in the participants in the case studies he observed of values education leading to effective social engagement and greater success. This perspective enabled him to name the effect as 'enhanced higher order thinking leading to emancipatory knowledge':

> This knowledge-guiding interest concerns the human capacity to be self-reflective and self-determining. The knowledge that is produced by interaction with the interest informs human responsibility. The self-reflection

makes the individual aware of those ideologies that influence humans and it offers a way for the individual to deal with them. It seems obvious to me that in the four clusters this particular mode of knowledge is shared by teachers and students.

(ibid, 635)

Crotty goes on to apply this thinking to the effects he observed in each of four case studies. He concludes, 'In short, habits of self-reflection have been fostered, ideologies have been recognized and higher order thinking has been taking place' (ibid, 636).

The programmes that Crotty was observing involved social engagement, or service learning, as a component of the values education intervention. The work of Billig (2002) shows that service learning is a particularly powerful form of values education. Its reputation is of being the form of values education with some of the most tangible effects on improved academic performance (Lovat and Clement 2016). Again, Habermasian theory has been utilised in trying to understand why this is the case:

> The frame of reference emanates from Habermas's 'Ways of Knowing' and 'Communicative Action' theories. In a word, it is the one who knows not only empirically analytically and historically hermeneutically, but self-reflectively who is capable of the just and empowering relationships implied in the notion of communicative action. In a sense, one finally comes truly to know when one knows oneself, and authentic knowing of self can only come through action for others, the practical action for change and betterment implied by *praxis*. Habermas provides the conceptual foundation for a values education that transforms educational practice, its actors in students and teachers, and the role of the school towards holistic social agency, the school that is not merely a disjoined receptacle for isolated academic activity, but one whose purpose is to serve and enrich the lives not only of its immediate inhabitants but of its community.
>
> (Lovat et al. 2010a, 616)

In other words, Habermas rests his notion of effective social action (namely, *praxis*) on people reaching the most sophisticated levels of knowing. In this respect, and in contrast with more dated thinking about values formation and the role (or lack thereof) of the teacher and formal schooling in such formation, the Habermasian emphasis on knowing as the key to values formation suggests that effective social and moral citizenship is not only educable, but also that there is an inherent educational component in it. Furthermore, it helps to clarify why it is that attaining such a level of knowing and then committing to concomitant action would logically have an impact on one's powers of knowing generally and so issue in enhanced academic performance.

In a word, Habermasian thought has potential to deepen profoundly not only our understanding of the full human developmental capacities that are implied in effective learning but, moreover, to help us in developing the kinds of pedagogies needed to give them effect. The employment of Habermas in the context of values education leading to social engagement, in the way illustrated above, serves as a case in point. Herein, we see a line of convergence opening up between his theoretical world and the pedagogy required to produce the kind of values education that leads to effective social engagement, such that new knowing results from the deeper learning that occurs. In effect, the Habermasian theories constitute an epistemological template for social engagement that is informed by authentic human knowing, at one end, and, at the other end, impelling altruistic action.

In a word, Habermasian theory determines that effective education can never be focused solely on 'the basics' of technical learning (the *techne*) if it is seriously looking to the good of its clients and society at large. In a Habermasian schema, social engagement that is aimed at developing *praxis* and communicative action is not an added extra or marginal nicety. It is at the heart of what an authentic school will be about, namely, embracing a wide-ranging social agency both for the wellbeing of its students and for the betterment of society as a whole. In contrast to instrumentalist notions of schooling (Lovat 2020b), a Habermasian notion will impel educational charters that deal with the intellectual, social, emotional, moral and spiritual good of their clientele. This is an educational intention directed towards teachers and schools playing a role in the forming of individuals who understand integrity and apply it to their practical decision-making, and furthermore assist in the cohering of those individuals into functional and beneficent societies.

An implication of this education intention is around the removal of any artificial division between knowing and values since all knowing has an ethical component and is related in some way to human action. With this understanding, Habermas challenges contemporary education to deal with the essentials rather than mere basics of learning. He offers an epistemology that impels holistic and comprehensive pedagogy that engages with the full array of real-life issues. In a specific application, I have shown how a 'Habermasian pedagogy' can be applied to the very real contemporary life issue of how schools deal with the topic of Islam and Muslim students by setting up curricular and pedagogical structures to ensure incorporation into the school of a topic that is at risk of being demonised and a population at increasing risk of being marginalised (Lovat 2010b; 2019b; Lovat et al. 2011).

Unexpected educational applications of Habermas

Most of my own utilisation of Habermas has been in the school and higher education fields, as indicated above. Nonetheless, I have found his thinking to be useful across a range of other fields, sometimes in ways I had not anticipated. For example, I wrote a paper (Lovat 2004) where I used his ways of knowing theory to delineate different ways in which ethical decision-making might proceed. The paper became one of the bases for a PhD project by a medical practitioner whose line of work often entailed life and death decision-making for pre-natal and neo-natal infants. The practitioner also taught in the medical education programme and was particularly interested in how trainee doctors might be better prepared for these kinds of decisions. The completed project was titled, *An examination of moral decision-making in medicine, informed by a Habermasian paradigmatic approach: Implications for medical education* (Walker 2015). After completion, the project resulted in several publications (Walker and Lovat 2016a; 2016b; 2017a; 2017b; 2018a; 2018b; 2019) that made significant use of Habermas in a range of applications. The centrepiece of the project revolved around the notion of 'dialogic consensus', using a combination of Habermas's ways of knowing and communicative action theories to construct the kind of practical decision-making protocols that could allow a diverse group of stake-holders (parents, medical specialists, social workers, pastors, etc.) to come to a reasonable life and death decision. This was an application I had not envisaged until, as ever, the PhD student became the teacher and the supervisor the learner (Lovat et al. 2005).

The other unusual application came through another PhD project, *A Habermasian analysis of Arab–West Inter-governmental and inter-ambassadorial relations: Implications for Western diplomatic training* (Al-Jararwah 2017). In this case, the candidate worked in the diplomatic corps of a Middle East Embassy and was concerned to improve the training arm to better prepare future diplomatic workers with elevated understanding of the complexities they were dealing with. In this task, the candidate utilised the same combination of Habermasian theories as the medical education thesis just described. Its objectives were outlined in the following way:

> … to provide elucidations on how political Islam is observed … when Jürgen Habermas's descriptive, interpretive and critically self-reflective methods of analysis are applied to it; to provide a holistic analysis of the historical factors that influence political Islam among Arab Muslims; to explore how these factors diverge from existing assumptions about political Islam in the Western setting; and, to pinpoint and elaborate upon extant hindrances in Western inter-governmental and inter-ambassadorial discussions. The findings revealed numerous shortcomings in current approaches to political Islam … findings also identified apprehensions towards Islamic thought in the Western setting and pinpointed effective political and educational notions through the application of Habermas's critical theory and theory of communicative action. Finally, the dissertation outlined the rationale for a diplomatic training program for Western diplomats and politicians.
>
> (ibid, v–vi)

In another set of projects, I was involved with a colleague in making application of Habermasian thought to social work training and practice (Gray and Lovat 2007; 2008; Lovat and Gray 2008). These examples serve simply to amplify the many ways in which Habermas' rare, innovative epistemic work can be exploited to assist those in life-worlds grappling with profoundly important issues to develop communicative protocols that stretch our thinking, improve our practice and, importantly, enhance education in those life-worlds.

Conclusion

One can see the importance of Habermas to educational thought and practice at almost any level at which one wishes to consider it. This chapter has provided merely a handful of some of the more worked-over applications. One senses with Habermas that his influence will continue to be felt for generations. Like the ancient Greeks, Aquinas, Descartes, Voltaire and Dewey, among many others, his insights represent a paradigm shift, promising to shape new futures while, at the same time, to ground us in our heritage. His balanced appraisal of the most sophisticated knowing being one that relies as much on human communication and knowing of self as it does on empirical facts and figures is, as demonstrated above, reminiscent of the moderation of Aristotelian thought about human virtue, whereby one knew what was right, cared about one's fellows and knew how to translate this knowing and feeling into practical action. So, to be introduced to Habermas is to be introduced to Aristotle and, through this, to all of the foundations of thought relevant to any agency of human service where knowledge assumptions are transacted and applied to educational regimes. In a word, and partly on the basis of my own experience, I believe Habermas is in for the long term as a hero of education, one now increasingly recognised as such.

References

Ainley, M. 2006. Connecting with learning: Motivation, affect and cognition in interest processes. *Educational Psychology Review* 18: 391–405.

Al-Jararwah, M. 2017. A Habermasian analysis of Arab–West inter-governmental and inter-ambassadorial relations: Implications for Western diplomatic training. Unpublished PhD. The University of Newcastle, Australia.

Arthur, J. 2003. *Education with character: The moral economy of schooling*. London: Routledge.

Arthur, J. 2010. *Of good character: Exploration of virtues and values in 3–25 year-olds*. Exeter: Imprint Academic.

Ayer, A.J. 1936. *Language, truth and logic*. London: Victor Gollancz.

Benninga, J., M. Berkowitz, P. Kuehn and K. Smith. 2006. Character and academics: What good schools do. *Phi Delta Kappan* 87: 448–452.

Billig, S.H. 2002. Support for K-12 service-learning practice: A brief review of the research. *Educational Horizons* Summer: 184–189.

Bloom, B. 1956. ed. *Taxonomy of educational objectives: Book 1 cognitive domain*. London: Longman.

Campbell, R.J., L. Kyriakides, R.D. Muijs and W. Robinson. 2004. Effective teaching and values: Some implications for research and teacher appraisal. *Oxford Review of Education* 30: 451–465.

Carr, D. 2006. Professional and personal values and virtues in education and teaching. *Oxford Review of Education* 32: 171–183.

Carter, B. and K. Whittaker. 2009. Examining the British PhD viva: Opening new doors or scarring for life. *Advances in Contemporary Nurse Education* 32: 169–178.

Clement, N., T. Lovat, A. Holbrook, M. Kiley, S. Bourke, B. Paltridge, S. Starfield, H. Fairbairn and D. McInerney. 2015. Theory and method in higher education research: Exploring doctoral examiner judgements through the lens of Habermas and epistemic cognition. In *Theory and Method in Higher Education Research*. Vol. 3. eds. J. Huisman and M. Tight, 213–234. London: Emerald.

Crawford, K. 2010. Active citizenship education and critical pedagogy. In *International research handbook on values education and student wellbeing*. eds. T. Lovat, R. Toomey and N. Clement, 811–824. Dordrecht: Springer.

Crotty, R. 2010. Values education as an ethical dilemma about sociability. In *International research handbook on values education and student wellbeing*. eds. T. Lovat, R. Toomey and N. Clement, 631–644. Dordrecht: Springer.

Dally, K., A. Holbrook, T. Lovat, and J. Budd. 2019. Examiner feedback and Australian doctoral examination processes. *Australian Universities Review* 61, 2: 31–41.

Dally, K., A. Holbrook, T. Lovat and H. Fairbairn. 2020. Supervisor perspectives on the 'end-stage' of the doctoral examination process. *Higher Education Research & Development*. doi:10.1080/07294360.2020.1847049.

Damasio, A. 2003. Feelings of emotion and the self. *Annals of the New York Academy of Sciences* 1001, 1: 253–261.

Dewey, J. 1922. *Human nature and conduct: An introduction to social psychology*. New York, NY: Modern Library.

Dewey, J. 1956a. *The child and the curriculum*. Chicago, IL: University of Chicago Press.

Dewey, J. 1956b. *The school and society*. Chicago, IL: University of Chicago Press.

Doll, W. 1993. *A post-modern perspective on curriculum*. New York, NY: Teachers College Press.

Ferre, F. 1982. *Language, logic and god*. New York, NY: Harper & Row.

Feyerabend, P. 1975. *Against method: Outline of an anarchistic theory of knowledge*. London: Humanities Press.

Gellel, A. 2010. Teachers as key players in values education: Implications for teacher formation. In *International research handbook on values education and student wellbeing*. eds. T. Lovat, R. Toomey and N. Clement, 163–178. Dordrecht: Springer.

Gould, J. 2016. What's the point of the PhD thesis? *Nature* 535: 26–28.

Gray, M. and T. Lovat. 2007. Horse and carriage: Why Habermas's discourse ethics gives virtue a praxis in social work. *Ethics and Social Welfare* 1: 310–328.

Gray, M. and T. Lovat. 2008. Practical mysticism, Habermas and social work praxis. *Journal of Social Work* 8: 149–162.

Habermas, J. 1972. *Knowledge and human interests*. Trans. J. Shapiro. London: Heinemann.

Habermas, J. 1974. *Theory and practice*. Trans. J. Viertal. London: Heinemann.

Habermas, J. 1984. *Theory of communicative action*. Trans. T. McCarthy. Vol. I. Boston, MA: Beacon Press.

Habermas, J. 1987. *Theory of communicative action*. Trans. T. McCarthy. Vol. II. Boston, MA: Beacon Press.

Habermas, J. 1990. *Moral consciousness and communicative action*. Trans. C. Lenhardt and S. Nicholson. Cambridge, MA: MIT Press.

Habermas, J. 2001. *The liberating power of symbols: Philosophical essays.* Cambridge: Polity Press.

Henderson, D. 2010. Values, wellness and the social sciences curriculum. In *International research handbook on values education and student wellbeing.* eds. T. Lovat, R. Toomey and N. Clement, 273–290. Dordrecht: Springer.

Hirst, P. and R.S. Peters. 1970. *The logic of education.* London: Routledge & Kegan Paul.

Holbrook, A., K. Dally, C. Avery, T. Lovat and H. Fairbairn. 2017. Research ethics in the assessment of PhD theses: Footprint or footnote? *Journal of Academic Ethics* 15: 321–340.

Kiley, M., A. Holbrook, T. Lovat, H. Fairbairn, S. Starfield and B. Paltridge. 2018. An oral component in PhD examination in Australia. Issues and considerations. *Australian Universities Review* 60, 1: 25–34.

Koller, P. and C. Hiebaum. 2016. *Jürgen Habermas: Faktizität und Geltung.* Berlin: Walter de Gruyter.

Krathwohl, D., B. Bloom and B. Masia. 1964. *Taxonomy of educational objectives. Handbook II affective domain.* New York, NY: McKay.

Kuhn, T. 1970. *The structure of scientific revolutions.* Chicago, IL: Chicago University Press.

Lakatos, I. 1974. Falsification and the methodology of scientific research programs. In *Criticism and the growth of knowledge.* eds. I. Lakatos and A. Musgrave, 91–196. Cambridge: Cambridge University Press.

Lovat, T. 2004. Aristotelian ethics and Habermasian critical theory: A conjoined force for proportionism in ethical discourse and Roman Catholic moral theology. *Australian E-Journal of Theology* 3. Available at: www.researchgate.net/publication/265111707_Aristotelian_Ethics_and_Habermasian_Critical_Theory_A_Conjoined_Force_for_Proportionism_in_Ethical_Discourse_and_Roman_Catholic_Moral_Theology (accessed 25 November 2021).

Lovat, T. 2010a. Synergies and balance between values education and quality teaching. *Educational Philosophy and Theory* 42, 4: 489–500.

Lovat, T. 2010b. Improving relations with Islam through religious and values education. In *International handbook of inter-religious education.* eds. K. Engebretson, M. de Souza, G. Durka and L. Gearon, 695–708. New York, NY: Springer.

Lovat, T. 2011. Values education and holistic learning: Updated research perspectives. *International Journal of Educational Research* 50, 3: 148–152.

Lovat, T. 2012a. Service learning in the Australian values education program. In *Service learning and educating in challenging contexts: International perspectives.* eds. T. Murphy and J. Tan, 199–215. London: Continuum.

Lovat, T. 2012b. Values education. In *The Routledge companion to education.* eds. J. Arthur and A. Peterson, 380–388. London: Routledge.

Lovat, T. 2013. Values education programs. In *International guide to student achievement.* eds. J. Hattie and E. Anderman, 279–281. New York, NY: Routledge.

Lovat, T. 2017a. Values education as good practice pedagogy: Evidence from Australian empirical research. *Journal of Moral Education* 46: 88–96.

Lovat, T. 2017b. No surprise in the 'surprise effect' of values pedagogy: An edusemiotic analysis. In *Edusemiotics: A handbook.* ed. I. Semetsky, 93–106. Dordrecht: Springer.

Lovat, T. 2018. Vasiyl Sukhomlinsky's inspiration and guidance in the Australian Values Education Program. In *Academic notes series: Pedagogical sciences.* Edition 172. ed. O. Sukhomlinska, 15–22. Kiev: Ministry of Education and Science of Ukraine State Pedagogical University.

Lovat, T. 2019a. *The art and heart of good teaching: Values as the pedagogy.* Singapore: Springer Nature.

Lovat, T. 2019b. Values education, efficacious learning and the Islamic connection: An Australian case study. In *Encyclopedia of teacher education.* ed. K. Tirri, Dordrecht, 1-6. Springer Nature. Available at: https://link.springer.com/referenceworkentry/10. 1007%2F978-981-13-1179-6_186-1 (accessed 25 November 2021).

Lovat, T. 2020a. Enhancing teacher practice and student wellbeing through moral education: Analysing the effects of the Australian Values Education Program. In *Professional ethics and the moral work of teaching: Western contemporary research.* eds. E. Campbell and H. Wang, 146–165. Hong Kong: Fujian Education Press.

Lovat, T. 2020b. Values as the pedagogy: Countering instrumentalism. In *Pedagogy and pedagogical challenges.* ed. K. Tirri, 15–28. London: IntechOpen. Available at: www. intechopen.com/online-first/values-as-the-pedagogy-countering-instrumentalism (accessed 25 November 2021).

Lovat, T. and N. Clement. 2008a. The pedagogical imperative of values education. *Journal of Beliefs and Values* 29, 3: 273–285.

Lovat, T. and N. Clement. 2008b. Quality teaching and values education: Coalescing for effective learning. *Journal of Moral Education* 37, 1: 1–16.

Lovat, T. and N. Clement. 2008c. Values education: Bridging the religious and secular divide. *Journal of Religious Education* 56, 3: 40–49.

Lovat, T. and N. Clement. 2014. So who has the values? Challenges for faith-based schools in an era of values pedagogy. In *International handbook of learning, teaching and leading in faith-based schools.* eds. J. Chapman, S. McNamara, M. Reiss and Y. Waghid, 567–582. Dordrecht: Springer.

Lovat, T. and N. Clement. 2016. Service learning as holistic values pedagogy. *Journal of Experiential Education* 39, 2: 115–129.

Lovat, T., N. Clement, K. Dally and R. Toomey. 2010b. Addressing issues of religious difference through values education: An Islam instance. *Cambridge Journal of Education* 40, 3: 213–227.

Lovat, T., N. Clement, K. Dally and R. Toomey. 2010c. Values education as holistic development for all sectors: Researching for effective pedagogy. *Oxford Review of Education* 36: 1–17.

Lovat, T., N. Clement, K. Dally and R. Toomey. 2011c. The impact of values education on school ambience and academic diligence. *International Journal of Educational Research* 50, 3: 166–171.

Lovat, T. and K. Dally. 2018. Testing and measuring the impact of character education on the learning environment and its outcomes. *Journal of Character Education* 14, 2: 1–22.

Lovat, T., K. Dally, N. Clement and R. Toomey. 2011a. *Values pedagogy and student achievement: Contemporary research evidence.* Dordrecht: Springer.

Lovat, T., K. Dally, N. Clement and R. Toomey. 2011d. Values pedagogy and teacher education: Re-conceiving the foundations. *Australian Journal of Teacher Education* 36, 7: 30–44.

Lovat, T., K. Dally, A. Holbrook and H. Fairbairn. 2021. Oral defence as a feedback mechanism in doctoral development and examination. *Australian Education Researcher* 48. doi:10.1007/s13384-021-00456-6.

Lovat, T. and M. Gray. 2008. Towards a proportionist social work ethics: A Habermasian perspective. *The British Journal of Social Work* 38, 6: 1100–1114.

Lovat, T., A. Holbrook and S. Bourke. 2008. Ways of knowing in doctoral examination: How well is the doctoral regime? *Educational Research Review* 3: 66–76.

Lovat, T., A. Holbrook, S. Bourke, H. Fairbairn, M. Kiley, B. Paltridge and S. Starfield. 2015. Examining doctoral examination and the question of the Viva. *Higher Education Review* 47, 3: 5–23.

Lovat, T., M. Monfries and K. Morrison, 2005. Ways of knowing and power discourse in doctoral examination. *International Journal of Educational Research* 41, 2: 163–177.

Lovat, T. and D. Smith. 2003. *Curriculum: Action on reflection.* 4th edn. Melbourne: Thomson.

Lovat, T. and R. Toomey. eds. 2009. *Values education and quality teaching: The double helix effect.* Dordrecht: Springer.

Lovat, T., R. Toomey and N. Clement. eds. 2010a. *International research handbook on values education and student wellbeing.* Dordrecht: Springer.

Miller, G.D. 2011. *Mimesis and reason: Habermas's political philosophy.* New York, NY: SUNY Press.

Newmann, F. and Associates. 1996. *Authentic achievement: Restructuring schools for intellectual quality.* San Francisco, CA: Jossey Bass.

Noddings, N. 2002. *Educating moral people: A caring alternative to character education.* New York, NY: Teachers College Press.

Nucci, L. and D. Narvaez. eds. 2008. *Handbook of moral and character education.* New York, NY: Routledge.

Osterman, K. 2010. Teacher practice and students' sense of belonging. In *International research handbook on values education and student wellbeing.* eds. T. Lovat, R. Toomey and N. Clement, 239–260. Dordrecht: Springer.

Park, C. 2007. *Redefining the doctorate.* London: Higher Education Academy. Available at: https://s3.eu-west-2.amazonaws.com/assets.creode.advancehe-document-manager/documents/hea/private/redefining_the_doctorate_1568036860.pdf (accessed 25 November 2021).

Phenix, P. 1964. *Realms of meaning: Curriculum and methods in education.* New York, NY: McGraw-Hill.

Quine, W.V. 1953. *From a logical point of view.* Oxford: Oxford University Press.

Rowe, K.J. 2004. In good hands? The importance of teacher quality. *Educare News* 149: 4–14.

Starfield, S., B. Paltridge, A. Holbrook, T. Lovat and M. Kiley. 2017. Evaluation and instruction in PhD examiners' reports: How grammatical choices construe examiner roles. *Linguistics and Education* 42: 53–64.

Tyler, R. 1949. *Basic principles of curriculum and instruction.* Chicago. IL: University of Chicago Press.

Van Manen, M. 1977. Linking ways of knowing with ways of being practical. *Curriculum Inquiry* 6: 205–228.

Walker, P. 2015. An examination of moral decision-making in medicine, informed by a Habermasian paradigmatic approach: Implications for medical education. Unpublished PhD. The University of Newcastle, Australia.

Walker, P. and T. Lovat. 2016a. Towards a proportionist approach to moral decision-making in medicine. *Ethics & Medicine: An International Journal of Bioethics* 32, 3: 153–161.

Walker, P. and T. Lovat. 2016b. Dialogic consensus in clinical decision-making. *Journal of Bioethical Inquiry* 13, 4: 571–580.

Walker, P. and T. Lovat. 2017a. *Life and death decisions in the clinical setting: Moral decision-making through discourse consensus*. Singapore: Springer.

Walker, P. and T. Lovat. 2017b. Should we be talking about ethics or about morals? *Ethics and Behaviour* 27, 5: 436–444.

Walker, P. and T. Lovat. 2018a. Dialogic consensus in medicine: A justification claim. *The Journal of Medicine and Philosophy: A Forum for Bioethics and Philosophy of Medicine* 43, 7: 1–14.

Walker, P. and T. Lovat. 2018b. In a world characterized by moral pluralism, is dialogic consensus a way to establish moral truth? *Review of Contemporary Philosophy* 17: 43–55.

Walker, P. and T. Lovat. 2019. The moral authority of consensus: A justification claim. *The Journal of Medicine and Philosophy: A Forum for Bioethics and Philosophy of Medicine* 44, 1: 71–84.

Young, R. 1989. *A critical theory of education: Habermas and our children's future*. New York, NY: Harvester Wheatsheaf.

7 Between the state and the street

Habermas and education governance

Mark Murphy

Introduction

This chapter explores the contribution of Jürgen Habermas to the field of education governance. The theoretical lens through which educational governance is viewed makes a crucial difference to that which is witnessed. This is a truism that is often overlooked in the overemphasis on method and method training in education research. The conceptual language deployed in research is both a product of a researcher's overall methodological stance while also a major factor in the production of the eventual research results and analysis. Habermas, as a key figure in the Frankfurt School of Critical Theory, brings to the table a distinct set of concerns that by themselves constitute a novel lens on education governance. His debt to other theorists such as Max Weber, Emile Durkheim and Talcott Parsons alongside the intersubjective and linguistic worldview of G.H. Mead and pragmatism more generally, produces a perspectivist lens peculiar to second generation critical theory – one of communication distortion, lifeworld disruption, relational dysfunction, all spin offs of Habermas' own concerns with an unforgiving capitalist world order and the damage done to whatever is left of social solidarity.

In my own work, I have aimed to make explicit connections between theory and practice through this Habermasian lens. My collection *Habermas and social research: Between theory and method* (Murphy 2017) was designed to do just this, but across sectors and disciplines, including migration, education, health and urban planning. This list illustrates the myriad possibilities when it comes to translating Habermasian ideas into real life issues, which, contrary to myth, is not that difficult. Elsewhere, I have expanded on some of these themes across a range of publications (Murphy and Skillen 2015; 2018; Murphy 2010; 2018; 2019) that detail the ways in which Habermas and his concepts can be put to work in education and public policy settings.

The concepts themselves act as gatekeepers of what is considered acceptable social investigation, of what counts as really useful knowledge in education and social research. This is true of any influential thinker and there is no harm in this. But a closer look at this worldview reveals omissions and oversights and stones wholly unturned – emotions and the body for example are conspicuous

DOI: 10.4324/9781003156550-10

in their absence from the Habermas canon. What is also absent from Habermas' otherwise impressive conceptual toolbox is a focus on the level of the professional practitioner, or what Lipsky (1980) calls the 'street-level bureaucrat'. The level of the street offers a different perspectivist lens through which to approach the problems of education governance and provide a telling counterpoint to the dual lifeworld-system model that Habermas developed in his more sociological writings.

In this chapter I will explore this relation between the levels of the state and the street in the context of bureaucracy and accountability, while teasing out some of the strengths and limitations of Habermas' work when applied to the education field.

Bureaucracy, democracy and the problem of education governance

When problems of education governance become intractable, as they often do, the 'go-to' solution is often increased accountability. Demanding a greater level of accountability from educational institutions and professions is viewed as the rightful approach to such problems, whether they be related to issues of justice and equity, malpractice and institutional neglect or financial malfeasance and corruption. And for good reason: As Michael Lipsky argued in *Street-level bureaucracy* (1980), accountability in public service and political life is necessary and legitimate, as it serves as the link between bureaucracy and democracy (Lipsky 1980, 160). In the 21st century, however, the evidence for such a link is increasingly tenuous. A large quantity of research highlights the fact that accountability is often a weak link in the state armoury and can create more problems than it solves. Increased accountability, while on paper acting as an honest broker between bureaucracy and democracy, has instead produced a set of 'perverse effects' (De Bruijn and Van Helden 2006, 406) including de-professionalisation, increased workload (Franco-Santos et al. 2012, 42) and damage to the quality of front-line services (Murphy and Skillen 2015). The widespread introduction of performance indicators and other quality assurance mechanisms have been accused of encouraging 'corrosive' practices into the university sector (Schwier 2012; Shore 2008), and in some cases for having the opposite effect to that for which they are intended (West 2010). Arguably even more problematic, accountability has been blamed for encouraging institutional regimes of 'symbolic compliance and impression management' (Visser 2016, 79), leading to what Hood calls sets of 'assurance behaviours' (Hood 2011, 127), behaviours that can be used by organisations and individuals 'in their efforts to fend off blame' (ibid, 129).

These perverse and pathological side effects of bureaucratic interventions in issues of justice and legitimacy provide an ideal testing ground for the critical approach of social theory, no more so than in the work of Habermas. This chapter addresses this issue by exploring these pathologies via Habermas and his theory of lifeworld colonisation (Habermas 1984; 1987). Briefly put, this theory suggests that the negative consequences of modernisation, ushered in by a one-sided process of (instrumental) rationalisation, manifest themselves in distorted relations that valorise measurable outcomes over the process of mutual understanding and communicative reason. Effectively, for Habermas, bureaucratic mechanisms of accountability are 'tricky' (Barberis 1998, 451) because they have a tendency to overstep their limits, the red tape of political bureaucracy stifling the imperatives of an intersubjective world in which its remit does not govern.

The chapter explores the value of this colonisation thesis to modern day issues associated with the 'regulatory state', that form of state governance with surveillance and enforcement strategies at its core (Majone 1997; Moran 2007; Glaeser and Shleifer 2003). Specifically, the chapter will explore Habermas' potential contribution to debates over the consequences of the regulatory state in the guise of education accountability regimes, consequences that have previously tended to focus on issues such as impression management and risk avoidance without necessarily situating these consequences in a broader theory of societal change. Habermas' theory of colonisation is well placed to provide such a theory of societal change and this theory is used in this chapter to detail one set of consequences around what I call 'distorted relations'. The focus on relations in the regulatory state illustrates the damage such an approach to governance inflicts on what Habermas called 'communicative' rationality.

At the same time, it is accepted that there are limitations of the colonisation thesis as an explanatory device, and in this chapter I argue that not all the consequences of accountability can be considered illustrative of a damaged communicative intersubjectivity. Specifically, the chapter turns to the concept of *street-level bureaucracy* for further refinement of Habermas' ideas around governance and its relevance to theories of the regulatory state.

The problem of bureaucracy in the regulatory state

The fraught relation between democratic principles and the *real politik* of bureaucratic governance has been a key focus of attention in the field of public administration (Meier and O'Toole 2006), a field that unfortunately has only a tangential connection to the field of education studies. This is a field heavily influenced by the work of Max Weber (1968), who positioned bureaucracy as a necessary component of any modern democracy. Bureaucracy for Weber underpinned a strong state, as well as providing a coherent foundation for the spread of modern capitalism. The rationality of efficiency and organisation offered by bureaucratic modes of government ensured that the potential for economic and social progress is maximised. The characteristics of bureaucracy such as office hierarchy, rigid rules and norms, precision, accuracy, clarity – these all made important contributions to the efficiency and organisation demanded in 20th-century political and economic life.

These achievements, however, come at a price, and that price is the loss of institutional and professional autonomy. Weber once famously remarked that bureaucracies 'can serve any master' (Weber 1954), meaning that bureaucracy can dominate or liberate, depending on who holds the reins of bureaucracy. It is often the case that the administering of bureaucracy encourages practices of domination: 'every domination expresses itself and functions though administration. Every administration, on the other hand, need domination, because it is always necessary that some powers of command be in the hands of somebody' (Weber 1954, 109).

This controlling aspect of bureaucracy meant that Weber was faced with a paradox: He appreciated the need for systems of formal rationality, i.e. for characteristics such as calculability, predictability, efficiency, control and their institutionalisation in bureaucratic modes of governance. All are vital in managing the complexity of modern societies. Weber considered formal rationality as 'superior to any other form in precision, in stability, in the stringency of its discipline and in its reliability' (Weber 1968, 337). But he also saw this as the curse of modernity – the valorisation of efficiency and calculability sucked much of the freedom and meaning out of social life and left society in what he poetically referred to as the 'polar night of icy darkness' (Weber 2001, 123). This led him to characterise rationalisation more broadly as an 'iron cage'.

Weber first talked about the 'iron cage' in his book *The Protestant ethic and the spirit of capitalism*. Iron cage is a translation of the phrase *stahlhartes Gehäuse*, a literal translation of which is 'housing hard as steel'. It was Talcott Parsons who devised the English phrase 'iron cage' in his translation of Weber's book. The housing or cage was a by-product of the Protestant ethic that created a belief system to underpin the spread of capitalist modernisation. This belief system resulted in values such as efficiency and calculation that themselves produced modern systems of bureaucracy, effectively outliving their roots in ascetic Calvinist theology. According to Weber, this by-product of religion became an iron cage, imprisoning modern society into bureaucratic systems of governance that diminish people's capacity for freedom.

Public administration research has tended to focus on this pessimistic and decidedly gloomy portrayal of bureaucracy, in which bureaucratic procedures and system are 'considered a conspiracy against the public' (Meier and O'Toole 2006, 7). From this perspective, bureaucracy is 'synonymous with inefficient business administration, pettifogging legalism, and red tape' (Clegg 2011, 207). This is also the case for what Travers (2007) calls the new bureaucracy of quality assurance, the mechanisms of accountability that have mushroomed in the era of the regulatory state. The research on accountability suggests that the iron cage of Weber's nightmares has descended once again via the proliferation of auditing, evaluations, inspections and performance indicators (Diefenbach 2009; Papadopoulos 2010).

Such downsides of modern systems of bureaucracy are well documented in the literature, but for some reason this has not resulted in a revisiting of Weber's dilemma in the context of accountability regimes. Instead, the academic literature has devoted its energies to describing and classifying the workings of the regulatory state, particularly in the shape of new public management (Christenensen, Lie and Laegeid 2007). This analysis has its place in discussions of accountability, but they would seriously benefit from a more socio-theoretical approach to the topic of education governance. This is where Habermas enters the equation, not least because he offers a viable reconstruction of Weber's approach to modernity and bureaucracy.

From commodification to colonisation

Habermas' analysis of bureaucratic governance reflects his intellectual lineage, not only that of Weber and the Frankfurt School, but also Karl Marx. Marx's critical approach to social analysis aimed to identify the pathologies generated by capitalist modernisation, an approach adopted by the Frankfurt School in its efforts to develop a critical theory of society. Two key pathologies identified by Marx were alienation and commodification (Marx 1959). Theodor Adorno and Max Horkheimer, key figures in the work of the early Frankfurt School, developed their own pathology in the shape of the 'totally administered society' (Adorno and Horkheimer 1972) – an idea of an over-bearing reason that combined the worst effects of alienation, commodification as well as Weber's iron cage.

Habermas appropriated aspects of these approaches for his own work, but his analysis of the dysfunctions of capitalist modernisation manages to both update and also transform understandings of capitalism and state governance. In devising his own conceptual apparatus Habermas tended not to engage with the dominant Marxist critiques of the state that were fashionable at the time. When he was developing these ideas, in the 1960s and 1970s, debates over the capitalist nature of the state were dominant in the critical sociology and political science literature. Marxist theorists such as Ralph Miliband and Nikos Poulantzas were prominent in these debates, seeking sophisticated analyses of the relation between the state and market – echoes of these ideas can still be found in contemporary Marxist political economy, a field that devotes much of its energy to assessing the impact of multinational corporations on nation state forms of democracy (Jessop 2015).

While Habermas shared with Marx a concern over the unjust distribution effects of capitalism (Müller-Doohm 2010, 449), he was also concerned to avoid a form of analytical conflation when it came to the state–economy nexus. Habermas' conceptual aim was to ensure that the political and economic realms retained their unique and distinct character while also crafting theoretical space for action-oriented approaches to political economy. To assist his aim, he developed a theory of 'steering media', key amongst which are power and money. The introduction of this robust functionalist element allows Habermas to deliver a reconstructed Marxist historical materialism, which provides him with a welcome escape route away from deterministic approaches to theory.

This reconfiguration also helped Habermas in its efforts to grapple with 20th-century problems of public administration. This was especially true in his analysis of the welfare state compromise, an analysis developed with one of the key Marxist questions in mind: How did the capitalist system manage to avoid a working class revolution? As a partial response to this question, Habermas suggests that the welfare state compromise, one aimed at managing capitalist exploitation while alleviating its worst effects, went some way to quelling revolutionary favour among the working class. At the same, he envisaged significant problems with this compromise when it comes to the legitimacy of the state to govern. In his book *Legitimation crisis*, Habermas (1976) theorises that legitimation crises result from nation states overstepping their limits. The greater responsibility states adopt over welfare services as well as consumption, the more likely it is that crises of social integration will take place in the lifeworld. As a result, the state, if it cannot somehow adequately confront the pathologies of capitalist modernisation, ends up paying a price, and the 'price for this failure is withdrawal of legitimation' (ibid, 69).

The lifeworld, part of Habermas' new two-level conception of society, was the site of this legitimation withdrawal. This conception afforded Habermas the opportunity to deliver an action-theoretic as well as a systems-theoretic analysis of the process of societal rationalisation. He uses the term lifeworld to signify the background consensus of everyday lives, which includes the taken-for-granted understandings of social life that guide people's lives, while the system refers to the world in which political and market imperatives dominate; i.e. the state administrative apparatus (steered by power) and the economy (steered by money). This two-level concept of society provides Habermas with the tools to examine the increasing autonomy of what he calls 'systematically integrated action contexts' from socially integrated lifeworlds (Habermas 1987, 305).

This dual-perspective methodological reconstruction provided Habermas with the framework to tackle the core issue at the heart of Weber's theory – bureaucratisation and the iron cage of modern public administration. While Habermas relies heavily on Weber's analysis of societal rationalisation and its troubling side-effects (Habermas 1987, 301), at the same time he takes Weber to task for equating capitalist modernisation to societal rationalisation. Key to this critique is the fact that Weber's take on the iron cage was guided by the restricted idea of purposive rationality.

According to Habermas, Weber's reliance on the model of the purposive-rational actor leads Weber to provide an inaccurate diagnosis of the times. To present what Habermas considers to be a more effective diagnosis, it is necessary to provide a substantial restructuring of Weber's theory. This re-structuring was based on two grounds: First, Weber emphasised the idea of purposive rationality to the exclusion of other forms of rationality; and, second, he confused action theoretic and system theoretic concepts. To counter the first problem, Habermas proposes the introduction of the concept of communicative rationality 'tailored to the lifeworld concept of society and to the developmental perspective of lifeworld structures' (Habermas 1987, 305).

The second problem was resolved by Habermas via his two-level concept of society – system and lifeworld; this offered an analysis of the process of societal rationalisation via both an action-theoretic and a systems-theoretic perspective. This dual perspective offered up a wholly new way of understanding bureaucratisation: While for Weber, bureaucratisation represented the institutionalisation of purposive-rational action, Habermas argued that bureaucratisation 'should be regarded as the sign of a new level of system differentiation' (Habermas 1987, 307). Bureaucratisation for Habermas was the anchoring of the steering mechanisms of the economy and the state – money and power, respectively – in the structures of the lifeworld.

Habermas reconfigured this bureaucratisation thesis in terms of a conflict between social and system integration, a distinction that highlighted the co-existence of two sets of relationships, one between actors and one between parts of the system. The conflict between these sets of integrative relations has implications for state governance and its effects on lifeworld contexts. It means that, because sets of actions are no longer socially integrated, but rather take their cues from the system, social relations become divorced from actor's identities. Increasing bureaucratisation has resulted in a heightened separation between social relations and the identities of actors in the lifeworld (Habermas 1987, 311).

Weber understood the trend towards bureaucratisation in action-theoretic terms. For him, the paradox of societal rationality lay in the relations between two different types of action orientations; i.e. value-rational action and purposive-rational action orientations. Habermas, however, argues that bureaucratisation and the paradoxes that arise from it should instead be understood in terms of a relation between two different types of societal integration, namely social and system integration.

Phenomena related to the iron cage now count as 'effects of the uncoupling of system and lifeworld' (Habermas 1987, 318). As the media of money and power function independently of language, they are not connected to the communicative structures of the lifeworld, which are dependent on language as the means of reaching understanding. As a consequence, these media allow the uncoupling of formally organised domains of action from the structures of the lifeworld, which in turn unleash their functionalist reason of system maintenance onto the lifeworld structures. It is this pathological side-effect of societal rationalisation that Habermas refers to as the 'colonization of the lifeworld'.

Alongside this analysis, Habermas takes care to emphasise the role of bureaucratisation as an ordinary and to some extent legitimate component of modernisation processes (Habermas 1987, 318). He thus makes a distinction between functional and dysfunctional forms of bureaucratisation, as he needs to distinguish the normal mediatisation of the lifeworld from the pathological colonisation of the lifeworld. For Habermas, it is only when the economic and political system, via the media of money and power, attempts to reify the symbolic structures of the lifeworld that pathologies occur. Only actions that align well with economic and political imperatives can be adopted by the steering media of money and power. These media, however, are out of place – dysfunctional – in areas such as cultural reproduction, social integration and socialisation – the work of the lifeworld. Imperatives associated with money and power cannot transplant themselves onto these forms of symbolic reproduction with 'without pathological side-effects' (ibid, 322–323).

It is this 'systematically induced reification' (Habermas 1987, 327) of the symbolic structures of the lifeworld that Habermas views as constituting colonisation – his 'malignancy thesis' as White (2016, 195) calls it. The capacity to act communicatively and to fulfil the symbolic reproductive function of the lifeworld is under threat from systemic imperatives, which, via the media of money and power, reify those structures of the lifeworld that are based on communicative action. Habermas (1987, 326) terms this reification of everyday communicative practice a 'one-sided rationalisation', a restricted rationality ushered in by the process of capitalist modernisation. This is a process with origins in 'the growing autonomy of media-steered subsystems, which not only get objectified into a norm-free sociality beyond the horizon of the lifeworld, but whose imperatives also penetrate into the core domains of the lifeworld' (ibid, 327).

Relational distortion and the regulatory state

This reformulation of the bureaucracy question allows for a more nuanced take on bureaucracy. Education regulation in the form of accountability mechanisms can now be assessed from two different angles – one in which the instrumental rationality of value for money must share space alongside the ability of this form of steering to offer communicative value. The significance of transparency and surveillance as a form of public answerability needs to be assessed alongside its capacity to damage forms of intersubjective communication – orientations to mutual understanding as opposed to means-end calculations.

Applying this thesis of a one-sided rationality run amok to the field of education regulation, one can start to make claims as to its relevance – does evidence of colonisation exist? In what situations does dysfunctional bureaucracy come to the surface? One area to highlight in this regard is the intersubjective communicative aspects of the education sector – the manner in which these damaging effects get played out in the key educational *relations*. More specifically, this would entail a study of the relations between professionals and end users – for example relations between teacher and student.

This issue provides an effective link between the complex grand theory of Habermas and the day-to-day concerns of professionals across the sector. While the nature of professionalism is of course a topic of much debate, one of the key elements of professional life, at least in the education sector, is the relationship between the professional and the non-professional. Unlike much of the literature on professionalism, however, which tends to focus more on interprofessional relations or relations between professionals and institutions/government, the Habermas-inspired work focuses on the key relations between educator and student. In the field of education, concern has been raised over the encroachment of accountability demands into this relationship. Aper (2002,

13) in a critique of accountability in US schools, utilises Habermas' framework to explain that, while student achievement is a rational goal of schools, 'when intense emphasis is placed on limited measures of this objective at the expense of the intersubjective lifeworlds of schools, serious distortion of the system and lifeworld occur' (ibid).

This theme is developed by Lee in a case study of standardised testing and literacy education (Lee 2014). Here, the colonisation thesis is used to identify the damaging effects of instrumental rationality on both the capacity of teachers to teach and the ability of students to learn skills such as critical thinking. Using the example of DIBELS (Dynamic Indicators of Basic Early Literacy Skills), Lee argues that this form of education governance has pathological effects on both sides of the relationship:

> DIBELS decouples itself from the lifeworld domain and becomes a systemic force that comes back to encroach on or colonize the lifeworld by replacing communicative rationality with instrumental rationality … It facilitates and dictates how reading should be taught [and learnt].
>
> (ibid, 91–92)

Such a view arguably reflects those of a significant proportion of education professionals, and their attitudes towards the dysfunctionality of hyper-instrumentalist logic applied to education, particularly via testing (West 2010).

Viewed through the prism of the colonisation thesis, these findings can be understood as the result of an over-bearing instrumental reason narrowing the space and opportunity for communicative practices to emerge. The damage done to relations of trust resulting from new bureaucratic methods of governance, is compounded by the effects new bureaucratic modes of regulation have on the moral agency of street-level bureaucrats such as teachers (Murphy 2020). This is the focus of Zacka's (2017) study *When the state meets the street: Public service and moral agency*, in which he details how the 'moral lives' of teachers are reconstituted as a result of increased regulatory frameworks. Zacka argues that frontline workers are faced with 'impossible situations' (ibid, 200) with competing claims to their authority and expertise weaving their way into procedures, regulations, protocols but also into forms of tacit knowledge and professional practice. This has potent side-effects which help corrode the moral integrity of public services. Teachers for example become indifferent or hostile to their students in the face of competing demands and what appear as attacks on their professional integrity. When faced with bureaucratic pressures, these street-level bureaucrats end up adopting unsatisfactory conceptions of their own professional responsibilities.

These impossible situations represent a 'performative self-contradiction' (Zacka 2017, 227), one that teachers face when trying to reconcile their own sense of professional identity in the face of contradictory pressures. The impossibility arises when teachers struggle to retain their moral identity and integrity 'while continuing to systematically and consciously perform actions that are contrary to it' (ibid, 227–228). He summarises it thus:

You cannot expect me, as a teacher, to keep doing what I need to do to meet the accountability requirements. As a teacher, (according to how I understand this term and myself), it is impossible for me to do so. Of course, I, as an individual, could still perform the actions that you require of me. But I would effectively no longer be a teacher in my own eyes. What I cannot do is hold on to the identity and to the actions at the same time.

(quoted in ibid, 228)

This collapse of moral agency at the front-line has major implications for state legitimacy. The quality of front-line of public services, where state and street-level forms of bureaucracy intersect, is a significant indicator of the state's duty of care to its citizens. The state's capacity to protect its citizens find its litmus test in this moral integrity. Front-line services are also important from a conceptual point of view as they offer a street-level approach to understanding bureaucracy, governance and democratic life, a ground-up approach that illustrates how fluid and complex governance is in the lives of both professional services such as education and those ordinary citizens who avail of them.

Given that the dominant focus across these studies is on the colonising tendency of instrumental rationality, it is worth pausing to consider the alternative theory – colonisation via communicative reason, especially as it has implications for how one understands the perceived benefits of accountability. Although untested and lacking adequate empirical support, it could be the case that such an alternative theory could be built off the back of the colonisation thesis. Habermas (1996) himself recognises this potential in *Between facts and norms*, in which he suggests that communicative reason can also overstep the mark and dominate in areas without recognising its own limitations. He was acutely aware of the 'anarchist consequences' (Gregoratto 2015, 539) of his theory of communicative action, of a reason that failed to acknowledge societal complexity and institutional reality.

This argument can be applied to the communicative aspect of much of the accountability agenda and the desire for justification and answerability – i.e. transparency. There is an exaggerated search for transparency in public sector governance – a trend visible for example in the health care sector internationally – where there is a great demand for new forms of audit, control, and reporting systems which 'reveal and visualise health care processes and outcomes' (Blomgen and Sahlin 2007, 155). This desire to reveal and make visible processes of legitimation and justification may constitute pathological consequences in themselves, of a dysfunctional communicative element in the structures of governance.

Bringing the street-level in

Habermas' thesis of lifeworld colonisation thesis provides real conceptual power in efforts to assess the downsides of accountability. It has a number of advantages in this regard: It offers a higher degree of scrutiny of the pathologies of modernisation; it updates Weber in relation to new forms of bureaucratisation;

and it brings a critique of political economy into the analysis. But while this application of Habermas is an important contribution to the theory of education governance, it is an application that comes with strings attached. The theory of lifeworld colonisation is quite abstract and is built on a complex conceptual apparatus of communicative action – its relation to forms of education practice cannot be easily applied to distinct education contexts and policy reforms. Also, Habermas developed his theory to account for pathologies in the context of lifeworld activities, such as damage to cultural reproduction and socialisation: pathologies of education governance can only be inferred indirectly.

Habermas' concern with issues such as cultural reproduction never translated into an interest in the lifeworld of professionals working in education bureaucracies. This is a missed opportunity, as this shift in perspective can provide an alternative view of bureaucracy as mediated by *professionals* – by those who interact with the public and deliver public services. From this perspective, one can take a more detailed look at bureaucratic and regulatory governance as they are practiced at the level of the 'street' – as detailed by Lipsky in *Street-level bureaucracy*. Street-level professionals such as teachers are in a position to 'make policy' through their ability to use discretion when dealing with their pupils. Working at the street level offers teachers and other education professionals with an important mediating function when it comes to the demands of state-level bureaucracy, providing them with a priceless autonomy over how they implement policy directives in their interactions with those in their care.

Lipsky viewed this intersubjective dimension – the relations and communications that occur between people – as a key component of the work of street-level bureaucrats. It is also a dimension at the heart of Habermas' theory of communicative action. The essence of street-level bureaucracy is that it requires professionals to 'make decisions about other people' (Lipsky 1980, 161), a requirement that positions professionals as producers of policy (Hupe and Hill 2007, 280). This conception of policy production at the level of the 'street' provides an alternative to more traditional systems-level approaches to government regulation and control – much of the discussion of education policy tends to overlook this capacity completely in favour of narrow state-level understandings of governance. Alongside this, a theory of street-level bureaucracy creates a conceptual space in which to detail how professionals such as teachers manipulate official policy in the context of their relationships with pupils – an aspect ignored by Habermas. Although Lipsky was aware that street-level bureaucrats operated within the context of significant external constraints, their position at the level of the street affords them a position of real influence.

The inclusion of the street-level into the analysis of bureaucratic governance also brings to the fore the existence of other regulatory mechanisms that operate alongside the colonising tendencies of the state and the market. One of these is law – a field of significant interest for Habermas (Murphy 2005). Recent decades have seen the spread of a litigation culture in countries such as the United States and the United Kingdom, with members of the public increasingly seeking recourse to the law to appeal or complain, or to achieve compensation (Allsop and Jones 2008). The increasing tendency of people to resort to litigation suggests that recourse to the law is seen as a more immediate form of taking public services to account. Numerous aspects of public-sector work have been affected by the spread of a litigation culture, with sectors such as education seeing steady rises in the number of lawsuits (Furedi and Bristow 2012).

This increase in forms of legal accountability could be a function of a broader legitimation crisis, a crisis that pits the state against its own citizens. Whether or not this is the case, it is evident that this development has implications for education work. The author's own work examines the prevalence of legal forms of accountability in the public sector and their impact on professional work (Murphy and Skillen 2018). The evidence indicates that the mechanisms of quality assurance, designed to document and measure quality, can also work as mechanisms of legal exposure for professionals such as teachers. The findings evidence the conflicting effects of evidential exposure, with the evidential requirements of accountability constituting a double-edged sword: evidence providing a platform for calling individuals and institutions to account, while also opening up professionals to liability exposure. The evidential nature of accountability mechanisms, as Power previously argued, increases exposure to legal risk (Power 1997).

An unintended consequence of accountability is that it tends to magnify legal risk in education professions, as evidential exposure uncovers incompetence and lays the blame at unchecked professional discretion and judgement. This form of bureaucracy brings with it a culture of suspicion, and this culture, as well as the strategies of containment it encourages among institutions, is difficult to disengage from once established. The magnification of legal risk compounds this culture, one in which the capacity to cover one's tracks and avoid legal risk become all important.

Concerns over this form of overregulation, as well as the role of professional discretion, illustrate the importance of incorporating the professional level into our understandings of accountability. They also offer a useful way of addressing limitations in Habermas' conceptual apparatus and the incapacity of the colonisation thesis to include the professional sector into the theory of system-level steering. This indicates that the dual methodological approach favoured by Habermas works only in certain scenarios and needs further refinement to better represent modern forms of political governance. After all, the debate over accountability and its consequences is, to a great extent, a product of boundary disputes – who gets to make professional decisions, where do judgement and discretion lie and to what extent should they be deployed? Regulatory oversight seeks to discipline and manage professional autonomy but there needs to be a greater understanding of the consequences of this oversight as well as the numerous ways in which policy can be made at the level of the street.

Conclusion

This chapter has explored the application of Habermas' ideas to the field of education governance and specifically educational accountability. This application illustrates that there are real advantages through delving into the deep intellectual well of second-generation critical theory, not least that it allows for a more nuanced analysis of bureaucracy than is sometimes the case. Bureaucratic forms of regulation have their benefits and these should not be ignored in the rush to classify bureaucracy purely as 'red tape' – a classification that is common when it comes to fields such as education and the public sector. This was not the intention of Weber, and the same can be said for Habermas. There are useful and practical elements of bureaucracy that have become indispensable in the modern world, and it is wise to remember that bureaucracy provides an efficient answer to increasing societal complexity via an organisational form 'premised on the ethical values of universalism and meritocracy' (Clegg 2011, 206). It is also important to consider the tensions that exist between bureaucracy and democratic imperatives, and the work of Habermas has helped to illuminate these tensions in a way that does justice to the early work of Weber. His work also points us away from the minutiae of performance criteria and efficiency savings and towards a focus on the more urgent question: How do we manage modernity (Clegg 2011)?

Habermas does not have the last word on the pathologies of bureaucracy and accountability, and in this chapter I have highlighted one of the blind spots in his conceptual arsenal, that of the world of street-level bureaucrat. The identification of gaps in ideas is important, as it helps to construct conceptual bridges between sets of ideas – this helps to assess the accuracy and value of abstract theory in practical contexts, a process Habermas himself would no doubt agree with. He is after all a master of hybridisation, an intellectual strength which is no more evident than in the two volumes of *The theory of communicative action*. Here he expertly weaved together a complex theory via measured critiques of Durkheim, Weber, Marx and Mead, among others (Murphy 2017, 13).

As evident elsewhere in the current collection, extolling the virtues of hybridisation is an important activity when it comes to the theory–method relationship, as too often researchers approach theories as if they represent the final say on social issues. This form of theoretical fetishism is to be avoided, as the most effective research applications of theory adopt a critical stance, opening theory to critique while combining it with other socio-theoretical concepts. At their best they also aim to 'test' theory against practice: The examples included in this chapter illustrate the utility of Habermas to analysis of education reform agendas, but also suggest that no one theory (no matter how comprehensive) can manage to explain in full the complexity of changing forms of education policy and professional practice.

References

Adorno, T. and M. Horkheimer. 1972. *Dialectic of enlightenment*. London: Continuum.
Allsop, J. and K. Jones. 2008. Withering the citizen, managing the consumer: Complaints in healthcare settings. *Social Policy and Society* 7, 2: 233–243.
Aper, J. 2002. Steerage from a distance: Can mandated accountability systems really improve schools? *Journal of Educational Thought* 36, 1: 7–26.
Barberis, P. 1998. The new public management and a new accountability. *Public Administration* 76: 451–470.

Blomgen, M. and K. Sahlin. 2007. Quests for transparency: Signs of a new institutional era in the health care field. In *Transcending new public management: The transformation of public sector relations*. eds. T. Christenensen and P. Laegeid, 155–178. Aldershot: Ashgate.

Christenensen, T., A. Lie and P. Laegeid. 2007. Still fragmented government or reassertion of the centre? In *Transcending new public management: The transformation of public sector relations*. eds. T. Christenensen and P. Laegeid, 17–42. Aldershot: Ashgate.

Clegg, S. 2011. Under reconstruction: Modern bureaucracies. In *Managing modernity: Beyond bureaucracy?* eds. S. Clegg, S.M. Harris and H. Höpfl, 202–229. Oxford: Oxford University Press.

De Bruijn, J.A. and G.J. Van Helden. 2006. A plea for dialogue driven performance-based management systems: Evidence from the Dutch public sector. *Financial Accountability & Management* 22, 4: 405–423.

Diefenbach, T. 2009. New public management in public sector organizations: The dark sides of managerialistic 'enlightenment'. *Public Administration* 87, 4: 892–909.

Franco-Santos, M., L. Lucianetti and M. Bourne. 2012. Contemporary performance measurement systems: A review of their consequences and a framework for research. *Management Accounting Research* 23, 1: 79–119.

Furedi, F. and J. Bristow. 2012. *The social cost of litigation*. London: Centre for Policy Studies.

Glaeser, E. and A. Shleifer. 2003. The rise of the regulatory state. *Journal of Economic Literature* XLI: 401–425.

Gregoratto, F. 2015. Political power and its pathologies: An attempt to reconsider Habermas' critical theory of democracy. *Constellations* 22, 4: 533–542.

Habermas, J. 1976. *Legitimation crisis*. Oxford: Blackwell Press.

Habermas, J. 1984. *The theory of communicative action*. Vol. 1: *Reason and the rationalization of society*. Boston, MA: Beacon Press.

Habermas, J. 1987. *The theory of communicative action*. Vol. 2: *Lifeworld and system: A critique of functionalist reason*. Boston, MA: Beacon Press.

Habermas, J. 1996. *Between facts and norms*. Cambridge, MA: MIT Press.

Hood, C. 2011. *The blame game: Spin, bureaucracy, and self-preservation in government*. Princeton, NJ: Princeton University Press.

Hupe, P. and M. Hill. 2007. Street level bureaucracy and public accountability. *Public Administration* 85, 2: 279–299.

Jessop, B. 2015. *The state: Past, present, future*. Cambridge: Polity Press.

Lee, C.G. 2014. Systemic colonization of the educational lifeworld: An example in literacy education. *Educational Philosophy and Theory* 46, 1: 87–99.

Lipsky, M. 1980. *Street-level bureaucracy: Dilemmas of the individual in public services*. New York, NY: Russell Sage Foundation.

Majone, G. 1997. From the positive to the regulatory state: Causes and consequences of changes in the mode of governance. *Journal of Public Policy* 17: 139–167.

Marx, K. 1959. *Economic and philosophic manuscripts of 1844*. Moscow: Progress Publishers.

Meier, K. and L. O'Toole. 2006. *Bureaucracy in a modern state: A governance perspective*. Baltimore, MD: John Hopkins University Press.

Müller-Doohm, S. 2010. Nation state, capitalism, democracy: Philosophical and political motives in the thought of Jürgen Habermas. *European Journal of Social Theory* 13, 4: 443–457.

Moran, M. 2007. *The British regulatory state: High modernism and hyper-innovation*. Oxford: Oxford University Press.

Murphy, M. 2005. Between facts, norms and a post-national constellation: Habermas, law and European social policy. *Journal of European Public Policy* 12, 1: 143–156.

Murphy, M. 2010. Forms of rationality and public sector reform: Habermas and education in the context of social policy. In *Habermas, critical theory and education*. eds. M. Murphy and T. Fleming, 78–93. New York, NY: Routledge.

Murphy, M. 2017. Introduction: Putting Habermas to work in social research. In *Habermas and social research: Between theory and method*. ed. M. Murphy, 1–18. Abingdon: Routledge.

Murphy, M. 2018. Ever greater scrutiny: Researching the bureaucracy of educational accountability. In *Education governance and social theory: Interdisciplinary approaches to research*, eds. A. Wilkins and A. Olmedo, 193–207. London: Bloomsbury.

Murphy, M. 2019. Public sector accountability and the contradictions of the regulatory state. *Administrative Theory & Praxis* 42, 4: 517–530.

Murphy, M. 2020a. Governing universities: Power, prestige and performance. In *Social theory and the politics of higher education: Critical perspectives on institutional research*. eds. M. Murphy, C. Burke, C. Costa and R. Raaper, 17–26. London: Bloomsbury.

Murphy, M. 2020b. Taking education to account? The limits of law in institutional and professional practice. *Journal of Education Policy* (Online First). doi:10.1080/02680939.2020.1770337.

Murphy, M. and P. Skillen. 2015. The politics of time on the front line: street level bureaucracy, professional judgement and public accountability. *International Journal of Public Administration* 38, 9: 632–641.

Murphy, M. and P. Skillen. 2018. Exposure to the law: Accountability and its impact on street level bureaucracy. *Social Policy and Society* 17, 1: 35–46.

Papadopoulos, Y. 2010. Accountability and multi-level governance: More accountability, less democracy? *West European Politics* 33, 5: 1030–1049.

Power, M. 1997. *Audit cultures: Rituals of verification*. Oxford: Oxford University Press.

Schwier, R. 2012. The corrosive influence of competition, growth, and accountability on institutions of higher education. *Journal of Computing in Higher Education* 24: 96–103.

Shore, C. 2008. Audit culture and illiberal governance: Universities and the politics of accountability. *Anthropological Theory* 8, 3: 278–298.

Travers, M. 2007. *The new bureaucracy: Quality assurance and its critics*. Bristol: Policy Press.

Visser, M. 2016. Management control, accountability, and learning in public sector organizations: A critical analysis. *Governance and performance in public and non-profit organizations. Studies in Public and Non-Profit Governance* 5: 75–93.

Weber, M. 1954. *On law in economy and society*. New York, NY: Free Press.

Weber, M. 1968. *Economy and society*. eds. G. Roth and C. Wittich. New York, NY: Bedminster Press.

Weber, M. 2001. *The protestant ethic and the spirit of capitalism*. London: Routledge.

West, A. 2010. High stakes testing, accountability, incentives and consequences in English schools. *Policy & Politics* 38, 1: 23–39.

White, S. 2016. Continental and analytic lenses in relation to the communicative action paradigm: Reconstructive thoughts. *European Journal of Political Theory* 15, 2: 189–204.

Zacka, B. 2017. *When the state meets the street: Public service and moral agency*. Cambridge, MA: Harvard University Press.

8   Applying Habermas' theory of communicative action in an analysis of recognition of prior learning

Fredrik Sandberg

Introduction

This chapter draws on a research project exploring a process of recognition of prior learning (RPL) in the health care sector, for which Habermas' theory of communicative action was used as an analytical framework. Habermas' critical social theory has been of interest to scholars and researchers in education (Ewert 1991), and recent educational literature drawing on Habermas suggest that this interest is ongoing (Murphy and Fleming 2010). Just as it is possible to divide Habermas' intellectual career into different periods, educational scholars draw from different periods in his career, for instance: Earlier writings on knowledge and human interests (Habermas 1971) to communicative action (Habermas 1984; 1987) and the more recent focus on deliberative democracy (Habermas 1996). Habermas' most significant contribution to social theory is, nevertheless, probably associated with his famous turn to language and the attendant construction of the theory of communicative action (Habermas 1984; 1987).

The focus in this chapter is on the process of RPL. RPL can be been defined as a practice that reviews, evaluates and acknowledges skills and knowledge that adults gained through experiential, formal or self-directed learning and formal education (Thomas 2000). In Sweden, RPL was defined as a process of structured assessment, evaluation, documentation recognition of knowledge and competences regardless of where this has been acquired (Ministry of Education 2003). Such general and various definitions do not immediately apply to all contexts of RPL. In this chapter, an RPL process for accreditation of prior work experiential learning to qualify for course credits is explored. The context is an RPL process in an in-service training programme at the upper secondary level in Sweden. The purpose of the programme is to provide an opportunity for health care assistants to become licensed practical nurses through RPL and education. Fourteen female health care assistants attended the in-service programme. Most of the assistants work in the elderly care sector. The in-service training programme is at the upper secondary level and lasts for approximately one and a half years. The participants continue to work 80 per cent of the time and invest 20 per cent of their time in coursework. An empirical analysis based

DOI: 10.4324/9781003156550-11

on the theory of communicative action brings to the fore, for instance: (1) questions of how different kinds of actions and communication influence students learning and understanding in RPL; and (2) although not primarily focused in this chapter, how the tension between the system and the lifeworld influence RPL, education and learning. By rationally reconstructing the RPL process it is, for instance, possible to criticise actions that facilitate the systems colonisation or assimilation of the lifeworld. However, as will be shown here it can also be fruitful to reconstruct learning processes to see how they fit the norms of communicative action to advance, in this case, RPL practice.

Methodological issues concerning the bridge between theory and research methods are further discussed. For the breadth of this chapter a closer look pertaining to such issues in relation to (critical) ethnography and interviews are debated in relation to Habermas' theorisations.

In the next section the main concepts in the theory of communicative action are illuminated.

The theory of communicative action

Educational research began to draw on the work of Habermas at the start of the 1970s (Ewert 1991), and recent work tells us that his work is still gainfully employed in the sector (Murphy and Fleming 2010; Moran and Murphy 2012; Fleming 2012). The work of Habermas has informed several discussions within educational research. In adult educational research, of most relevance here, Mezirow (1981) introduced Habermas when constructing his transformative learning theory. Since then, several researchers in adult education have continued to use Habermas to confer about the purposes of education and learning (e.g. Brookfield 2005; Welton 1995). Even though some relatively recent articles draw on Habermas to explore RPL (Houlbrook 2011; Sandberg 2010; 2011; Sandberg and Andersson 2011), the work of Habermas has rarely been used to explore this phenomenon.

At a macro level, Habermas argues for the need to separate society into system and lifeworld in order to better understand the pathologies of modernity. The system can be viewed as: (1) a bureaucracy, where the steering media is power; and (2) the market or economy, where the steering media is money. Systems can be located in areas in which social integration and language are not the main media for reproduction (i.e. bureaucracies, economical institutions, etc.). In the contexts of family and education, social integration is necessary to reproduce the lifeworld. Habermas' lifeworld forms a horizon of interpretative patterns that are implicitly used when people communicate to generate mutual understanding. However, even though education may be observed as part of the lifeworld and as a context in which social integration occurs, education is also a system. Education must therefore be reproduced as both a system and a lifeworld, but the two must be distinctly separate. For instance, the steering media of money and power could colonise the lifeworld within the area of education by focusing on regulation through tests, grades (Sandberg and

Andersson 2011) and administrative or judicial oversight (Habermas 1987). Habermas argues that '[...] the overbureaucratization of the educational system can be explained as a "misuse" of the media of money and power' (ibid, 293–294). When education is formalised through the power of bureaucracy and legal interventions, relationships between students and teacher and student in education are also at risk of becoming formalised. One main conclusion that Habermas makes is that, just as the lifeworld of the family in late modernity has been formalised, one can also witness a similar development in education ('School') (ibid.). These issues become salient in RPL for accreditation because RPL processes often focus on assessment and grades as the means–end goal of education, rather than on learning in a social context (Briton et al. 1998). These processes could force the education system to focus on coordinating RPL through grades and administrative control to ensure quality in assessment. Thus, the system might assimilate the lifeworld-grounded work experiences of participants in RPL and re-order them in instrumental ways so that they fit the grades/curricula of the institution. Or, as Habermas puts it, 'Autonomous sub-systems make their way into the lifeworld from the outside – like colonial masters coming into tribal society – and force a process of assimilation upon it' (Habermas 1987, 355).

Although the macro-level concepts of the system and lifeworld are useful for a more general analysis, the concepts that structure communicative action must also be explained before it can be used to analyse the empirical data. In his work, Habermas coins several concepts related to communicative action (Habermas 1984; 1987). Such an idea is the formal world concept. In communication individuals can refer to exactly three worlds. First, when someone raises a truth claim, they are referring to something in the objective world. Second, when someone raises a claim to normative rightness, they are referring to something in the social world. Third, when someone claims to be truthful or sincere, they are referring to something in their subjective world. At the same time, an individual can also behave in different ways in different worlds. Goal-oriented actions take place in the objective world, normatively regulated actions take place in the social world and dramaturgical actions take place in the subjective world. In communicative action, actors harmonise their individual goals through consensus (Habermas 1984). By raising truth claims and claims to normative rightness and truthfulness – thus referring to the objective, social and subjective worlds – individuals can successfully harmonise their plans for action (Habermas 1987). They thus attempt to reach a mutual understanding of the goals of the process (means-end rationality), to determine how to act in a manner that is normatively correct (normative rationality) and to depict their subjective worlds through dramaturgical action (expressive rationality). Two of the more important features of communicative action are its teleological and communicative aspects. The goals of the ego are linked with those of other individuals, and goals are pursued cooperatively based on a shared definition of the situation. The concepts presented above can be used to analyse, or as will be the focus in the next section, rationally reconstruct data on educational processes.

Habermas and methodology: Virtual participation, rational reconstruction and critical reflections on bridging the divide between theory and research methods

Within Habermas' work, and especially in the theory of communicative action, it is possible to trace a methodology. In this section, two concepts will be described: Virtual participation and rational reconstruction. Virtual participation is a concept that can describe how a researcher can act when collecting data. Habermas argues that researchers must engage themselves in the communicative structures of the context explored, to understand the meaning of utterances, but this must be done without an involvement in the goal-oriented actions undertaken by actors in the practice system. Habermas' method of rational reconstruction can be seen as an alternative to the approaches found in the empirical-analytical and hermeneutic traditions. Historically, the development of this method progresses as Habermas makes his famous turn to communication and language. It is located somewhere between a transcendental and empirical approach. In a nutshell, it allows a researcher to rationally reconstruct learning processes against the norms of communicative action.

Virtual participation

Before moving into a discussion of how to analyse RPL as communicative action via rational reconstruction, ideas concerning the role of the social researcher as a virtual participant are considered. Researchers must involve themselves in the communicative structures to understand the meaning in a communicative discourse, but without involving themselves in the goal-oriented actions of the practice system explored: thus, they have to become a 'virtual participant'. A researcher that:

> [...] participates in processes of reaching understanding and not for the sake of an end that requires coordinating the goal-oriented actions of those immediately involved. The action system in which the social scientist moves as an actor lies on a different plane [...] the social scientist does not pursue any aims of his own within the observed context [i.e., act goal-oriented] [...] the social scientist has to participate virtually in the interactions whose meaning he wants to understand ...
>
> (Habermas 1984, 114–120)

When it comes to communication, Habermas distinguishes between three validity claims, i.e. truth, normative rightness and sincerity/truthfulness, that in turn connect to three worlds, i.e. objective, social and subjective (Habermas 1984).

When a researcher takes on the role of a virtual actor, they must engage with a performative attitude and thus take a virtual stand on validity claims that are raised in, for instance participatory observations or interviews. The main purpose of this enterprise would be to reach mutual understanding with the participants in the research process. For instance, if an interviewee raises a truth claim or a claim to normative rightness that is not understood by the researcher, the interviewee may be asked to clarify their position. Or if an interviewee engages in a subjective way to explain something truthfully, these expressions may become blurred for a researcher, who might have to ask for further explanations of the subject's experiences. These ideas were adopted when collecting data. Thus, acting virtually is to act communicatively, without passing the fine line of acting-goal oriented within the context explored. These suggestions were used when gathering data. In the next section, Habermas' method of rational reconstruction is explored, a method that inspired the analysis of the RPL process in the current research.

Rational reconstruction

Even though Habermas' theories have been deployed to a great extent in education and the social sciences in general, his method of rational reconstruction has unexpectedly not been deployed to the same extent (Pedersen 2008; 2009; 2011). It can be viewed as a method that focuses on an analysis that is theoretical, critical and non-relativistic at the same time. Its aim is to be descriptive and normative, as well as interpretative and explanatory. A concern is that Habermas' method is developed as a way to describe how his own theoretical work emerges. Thus, the theory of communicative action, in itself, is the result of rational reconstruction. Habermas' use of the concept of 'empirical science' and traditional 'empirical analytical research' are, of course, quite different, and Habermas has been the recipient of some criticism on this issue. Concepts used by Habermas are not specified empirically. The hypotheses derived by Habermas are not always empirical, instead sometimes based on traditional philosophical methods, such as critical explorations of literature, analyses of concepts and more personal reflections. Even though empirical examples are not absent in its entirety, examples and clarification of concepts are continuously not dealt with in satisfactory ways (Pedersen 2009).[1] Of even greater concern, according to Pedersen, is that [...] 'the hypotheses arrived at through rational reconstruction are empirical hypotheses but cannot be tested by empirical means' (ibid, 383).

However, (if we side-step this rather philosophical dilemma) it is still possible to propose a design of how to make use of Habermas' method for empirical explorations (Pedersen 2009). Empirical sources that may be used for reconstructions could include ethnography, document analysis, observations and interviews. Analyses of documents engaging in observations of participants make it possible to get information and knowledge that can be used to construct interview guides – ideas that were adopted in the research project analysed in this chapter. Such methodological concerns are further discussed below focusing on ethnography and qualitative interviews. It is important to note that Pedersen's proposal focuses on empirical investigations in political science. A main difference between Pedersen's use of rational reconstruction and the focus of this chapter is thus that he focuses on 'deliberative democracy'. The focus for the analysis of RPL here is on the possibility for mutual understanding. The following questions drawn from communicative action were used to reconstruct the RPL process:

Theme 1: Reconstruct the students' understanding of the assessment interview as communicative action
Questions posed: What consequences do certain actions have for the RPL process and its outcome focusing on the participant's view of the assessment interview? How can the validity claims inform the process? How can the rationalities inform the process?
Theme 2: Reflexively reconstruct the possibilities of communicative action for advancing RPL focusing on the RPL-placement
Questions posed: By which actions does the RPL placement progress? What does a focus on validity claims reveal?

This type of reconstruction can be used to: (1) critically appraise processes that do not realise the potential for communicative action; (2) reconstruct examples of processes that are more in tandem with the norms of communicative action; (3) highlight the consequences of lack of mutual understanding and communication and the resentment, confusion and fragmentation that individuals may feel when the conditions for proper communication is scarce; and (4) look for examples that show potential for changes in practice.

The above debate about the researcher role and analysis only partially discuss research methods; a more in-depth consideration on the issues are presented below.

Critical reflections on bridging the divide between theory and research methods

I will not lie. The interest in theory marked the beginning and starting point for pursuing a career within academia. Critical social theory and especially the work of Jürgen Habermas came first, and, a bit later, the work of Axel Honneth, Habermas' former student. Habermas' focus on communication and mutual understanding laid out above changed into a focus on Axel Honneth's theory of recognition – a theoretical discussion on the necessity for humans to experience mutual recognition. The relationship between these different critical social theories and how to bridge the gap between them represents a story in itself, which I will return to at the end of this chapter. Let's first further continue with the connection between theory and research methods.

As discussed above, there are ideas within Habermas' theoretical work that can be taken to be accounted for in relation to social theoretical analysis. Beyond this discussion concerned with the role of the researcher as a virtual participant and rational reconstructive analysis, there are possibilities for expanding the discussions into research methods. In this section, further critical discussions on interviewing and critical ethnography will be elaborated in relation to the theory of communicative action.

It took some time to discover that theoretical analyses considering empirical data should not be left to laissez faire methodology – even though that may well be the case sometimes. All researchers, qualitative researchers included, must be able to show how they gathered their data and critically reflect on the issues of such methods as, for instance, ethnographies and interviews. Questions about social theories' impact on construing research questions, doing interviews or choices made in ethnographical field work are important to understand. I will address two themes where these issues became vivid in the research project discussed in this chapter: conducting an ethnographical inspired field study and qualitative interviewing.

Researchers must scrutinise the knowledge we produce when using the interview to collect data, yet: where is the limit to how close we can intervene into an interviewee's lifeworld (in a phenomenological sense)? For a Habermasian-inspired critical social theoretical point of view it takes a distinctive scrutiny: how can mutual understanding be shaped in interviews?

Interviews should at least try to meet the criteria of mutual understanding between interviewer and interviewee. Thus, avoiding seeing the subject as merely an object of phenomenological solipsism. That is because of the dangers involved in the solitary reflection of a subject, as a subject, in an act of self-reflection, can mislead itself (Kember 2000), because a subject must be split into internal intersubjectivity. Thus, in line with Habermas, there has to be a focus on dialogue including a shared definition of the situation (Smyth 2006), and the social scientist must participate in the language processes of the interview he wishes to comprehend.

In critical ethnographic research (Forester 2003), a potential was found to meet the theoretical issues in Habermas' theory of communicative action. Though problems at a theoretical level can be identified for such an endeavour, imminent problems should not restrict the effort to employ the theory of communicative action in empirical research. Fieldwork approached from a Habermasian perspective would allow a researcher to analyse the following, where Forester (2003) enthused the argument, summarised as follows:

- 'The practical accomplishments of relations of power' (ibid, 62)
- 'Participants statements to truth and truthfulness that serve several and 'contingent variable ends' (ibid, 62)
- How normative claims created in practice affect assertions, form agreement, identity, esteem and thus shape future activities
- The communicative practices that, through beliefs, attention, truth and consensus form relationships
- The applied level of speech and interaction

This helps to understand how critical ethnographical-inspired research can be formed in line with Habermas' theorisations. These critical ethnographical claims are also very much in line with the ideas found in virtual participation: To become a participant in the language processes that is under scrutiny.

Thus, interviewing and ethnographical inspired field studies has been, and can be, presented with ideas on how to bridge the divide between theory and research methods. For instance, interviewing would, in the case presented, be about adopting a specific style that focuses the interview towards reaching mutual understanding with the interviewee. Next, the result of the study actualised in this chapter is presented.

A rational reconstruction of a process of recognition of prior learning in the health care sector

In a research project exploring RPL, the theory of communicative action was used for analysis (Sandberg 2010; 2012; Sandberg and Andersson 2011). Many of the procedures in the RPL process included various forms of assessment. Two processes will be focused on in this chapter: (1) the assessment interview where the teachers assess the participants' prior learning more generally against courses in the health care programme; and (2) a six-week placement in which the participant's prior learning was evaluated in a practical setting. Based on this project the focus will be on reconstructing the RPL process as communicative action within two broader themes: (1) conferring about the consequences of a lack of mutual understanding in the assessment interview; and (2) reflexively reconstructing the possibilities of communicative action for developing RPL drawing on data from a six-week RPL placement. Within the first theme, the assessment interview was focused upon an interview that teachers conducted to be able to map and assess the participants' prior learning against several courses in the health care programme. In the second theme, the focus was on a six-week placement where the participants were assessed in practice by a tutor. During the placement, the health care assistants worked under the supervision of a licensed practical nurse. During the RPL placement, the participants and tutors also engaged in discussions concerning the participants' prior learning. In some cases, these discussions lasted several hours each week, and a form with questions drawn from the health care programme curriculum was completed based on these discussions. These forms were then collected by the teachers and used to assess the more practical content from the curricula of several courses within the health care programme. The data used here was based on interviews with the students, conducted after the RPL process was finalised. The interview guide was constructed based on prior observations of the RPL process.

The consequences of a lack of mutual understanding

The first theme explored is based on a reconstruction of the participants' understanding of the assessment interview. It was quite obvious that these interviews were often not based on mutual understanding. Participants are confused about how the assessment is conducted, how the teachers document their answers and many of them also report a feeling of being blocked during the interview. Mia spent quite some time thinking about how it was possible for the teachers to document her prior learning:

> It must be amazingly hard to take notes and get it out. And we said that several times when we talked afterwards in the group [with the other students], that it is totally amazing that they were able to get what they needed.

In this quote Edith reflects on how the teachers documented her answers and is astonished at how the teachers were able to receive enough information based on her answers. However, she never understood this process. Rose, feels the same way and raises several questions:

> What is written down? Is she quoting me correctly? But I guess they write when they have to. It is actually they who are responsible. So you get a true assessment when you step out.

Rose asks herself if the teachers have actually understood her appropriately and documented her prior experiences accurately – i.e. if the process is actually based on a mutual understanding of her prior learning. It is evident that both Mia and Rose do not understand how this assessment process works. The teachers document what they think is true in relation to the curriculum of the courses. Thus, the teachers are aware of claims that are true in relation to the curriculum, but this is not communicated to the students during the process. This process does not seem to be based on mutual understanding and thus the participants try to answer the questions posed by the teachers in a subjective and truthful way and the teachers assimilate the knowledge they consider to be true to the system.

This lack of mutual understanding produces a feeling of 'being blocked'. Here one fundamental issue in communicative action is raised: The lack of mutual definitions concerning the purpose of the assessment interview (means-end rationality). Maria presents the following statements about her experiences of the assessment interview:

> Well, during that conversation [assessment interview] I was totally blocked [...] I don't know why but I know we sat down afterwards and talked about it. And if you had been prepared a little it might have turned out differently.

Maria suggests that she felt blocked during the interview. Her suggestion is that she did not reach a mutual definition of the assessment situation with the teachers. If they had reached a mutual definition, she would have been able to perform differently. Juli also felt blocked during her interview:

> Throughout I thought: What was that? Because you thought that you had to prove something here. In a way you probably did, but all the time I was thinking: What is it they want? What are they looking for? You were a bit blocked there, I felt.

Juli wants to prove something in the interview, but it was not clear to her what this was. This shows that the means-end results of the RPL process and pre-scribed norms of how to act are not mutually defined. Only the teachers know the rationale of the process. This raises concerns about the mutual under-standing of what is normatively right; the students should be able to know how to act in relation to the questions given by the teachers. However, this feeling of being blocked also seems to have other consequences for the students. What seems to take place is that the students have not reached a mutual definition of the purpose of the assessment interview or a mutual understanding with the teachers during the interview. It thus becomes unclear what the focus of the process is. One conclusion is that this process is primarily oriented towards the teacher's success in strategically receiving the 'right' answers to questions they ask. At same time as the students are trying to respond to the teacher's ques-tions, they are trying to understand what is really going on. Sandy discusses this as:

> That phenomenon that arose [during the assessment interview]: At the same time as you answered questions, you frantically reflected and tried to find the knowledge [internally].

Thus, at the same time as Sandy has a conversation with the teachers externally; she is also having a conversation internally. She is trying to figure out what the purpose is. She seems to be alienated.

Many of the students also had problems understanding how their prior learning was supposed to be assessed. When Juli is asked to describe how the teachers assessed her prior learning, she posed several questions internally:

> [...] how could they get anything out of the answers I gave them? But, ok [they said]: We are pleased now. But, what have I said that you [they] can touch upon [grasp]? I thought after these conversations [assessment interviews].

It seems that Juli is trying to understand if and how her answers are true. But this was never communicated to her. It is unclear how her answers were helpful to the teachers. Mandy also felt that the interview was unclear:

> Well, there were quick switches between this and that − from one subject to another. So, alright, was that ok now? If you only started [replying] to the questions, it solved itself. You sat down and talked for an hour. So, alright, an hour has already passed?

For Mandy, the interview did not seem to have a clear thread. Instead, it seemed to jump between different subjects. Like Juli, Mandy also posed questions internally during the interview and accepts that she does not really understand what is going on.

From a Habermasian perspective, the problems raised here reflect the teacher's goal-oriented and strategic actions. The lack of mutual definitions concerning the purpose of the assessment interview and the lack of mutual understanding during the interview seems to have several consequences for the students' understanding of the process. First, the students do not know what the means-end goal of the assessment interview is (or what is true). Second, they do not know how to behave in relation to the prescribed norms in the assessment interview (claim of normative rightness). Because of this, the students are forced to carry on internal conversations. Instead of being a process based on communication between teacher and student, the assessment interview forces the students into internal conversations. These processes also highlight issues concerning the tension between lifeworld and system. It could be seen as a process where the system, through the teacher's goal-oriented and strategic actions, assimilates such experiences that fit the system (curricula). However, this rather instrumental process of the assessment interview that was reconstructed here, does not speak for the entire RPL process. In the next section the focus will be on the RPL placement explained above, a process more in tandem with the norms of communicative action.

Reconstructing the possibilities of communicative action for developing RPL

Another core feature of the RPL process was the six-week placement. In contrast to the rather instrumental process of the assessment interview, the processes taking place in the placements seemed to be more in tandem with the norms of communicative action. It was especially apparent among participants and tutors, who shared similar subjective experiences of caring practice. However, these experiences of the students and tutors were not always the same, and this tended to obstruct engagement between them. Several participants describe their relationships with the tutors as positive. Anna, a participant, reported a positive experience:

> It was so heavenly good, and we connected at once. So, right away it was more like interacting with an ordinary colleague.

Mallory also highlights the collegial character of her relationship with her tutor: 'It was almost like working with a colleague you worked with before. It was really good'. One conclusion that we can draw based on these comments is that because these and other participants and tutors share the immediate lifeworld of caring practice, they also already share a horizon of interpretative patterns, which makes it possible for them to enter into interpersonal relationships and develop mutual understanding of the objective, social and subjective premises of caring practice. However, these individuals may not always agree on the truths, norms and personal experiences associated with working within the field of care work. For example, they may agree that there are normatively correct ways of performing an aspect of care work – but even though they agree that such norms exist, they may disagree that this is the correct way to perform.

The RPL placement and the tutor–student relationship were experienced as positive under certain circumstances. There seem to be two main reasons why this relationship works in terms of communicative action. First, as previously stated, the tutor and candidate share a mutual social context or lifeworld as care workers. They understand each other's context and subjective experience. Second, the tutors on the placement are well informed about its purpose and third managers are able to construct a schedule allowing for conversations between tutor and candidate. Ingrid found that she and her tutor could relate to one another because of their common experiences and interests and that they had plenty of time for dialogue:

> My tutor and I cooperated well. We talked a lot. We reflected very much and talked very much. 'What do you think about that?' I think like this. 'Aha, but how do you think?' But I think like this and that. We were able to have a dialogue [...] Then, we talked a lot about other things around care work and our situation [...] Both me and her were interested in union work, and we talked a lot about that – How to raise our salaries, questions of care ethic and care work in general.

It seems as though the process Ingrid describes is based on mutual understanding and that the cooperative work that she and her tutor completed was successful. This quotation can be linked to two of the more important features of communicative action mentioned above – the goal-oriented and communicative aspects: That ego's goals are linked with those of other individuals, and the cooperating parties pursue their goals through a shared understanding of the situation (Habermas 1984). Even though the primary focus of the conversations was to complete a form handed out by the teachers, the dialogue transcended the boundaries of this formal assessment process to include more developmental discussions of the current status of caring practice.

It is important to note that not all students experienced the type of successful conversations and cooperation. Lena, with 25 years of experience with care work, felt very different:

> Ehh, well, it went all right, but she [the tutor] felt that here I am, tutoring you and I have been working here for two years as a licensed practical nurse, and you have been working in health care since 1985 [...]. We worked – I was there as manual labour. I guess we took some time to sit down and talk, but she did not really understand what it was all about.

This experience draws attention to the problems that arise when the student and tutor are not sharing experiences and an immediate lifeworld and when they are not able to reach a mutual understanding. When the conditions for reaching mutual understanding are not fulfilled, it may be difficult to develop mutual understanding and thus to cooperate to fulfil the goals of the RPL placement. It also shows the importance of reaching consensus of the goal of the process – something that is not possible because of the tutor's lack of knowledge concerning this, according to Lena. In some cases, it is easier to reach a mutual understanding of the situation because the tutor and the student can agree on what is true and normatively right, while considering each other's expressions to be truthful and sincere. In such cases, the student and tutor may almost immediately begin working toward the goals of the placement through a shared understanding of the situation. However, the process also showed potential for making use of prior learning in a critical fashion.

Critical discussions in the social world of caring practice

From a Habermasian perspective, the critical discussions in the placement could be seen as occurring primarily within the normative dimension of care work, where the prescribed norms of caring practice are critically discussed. In some cases, the participants directly address critical issues with care workers at the placement. Many of these issues are raised during the conversations with the tutors. Astrid describes a situation where she reacted to an issue she thought was normatively incorrect:

> There were clients who sat in their wheelchairs a lot. And I was a bit against that because they could walk. So I got my tutor to agree that was wrong. [...] She thought that was good but that she had not thought about it. She thought that we were different [had different views] but that she thought it [my idea] was very good.

Astrid describes a situation in which she thought the staff at the placement acted in a manner that was normatively incorrect. She raises this claim in a conversation with her tutor and offers another claim she considers to be a normatively correct of acting in this situation. The tutor agrees that the staff did not address the situation appropriately and agrees with this claim to normative correctness. When norms are mutually justified in this way, the norm becomes 'true' in the sense that the tutor and the participant can now agree that the right norm has been objectively satisfied. Astrid found that the individuals at her placement were behaving in ways that were normatively incorrect. She also communicated her criticism to her tutor. The participant raises concerns regarding how a norm has been violated. This norm also applies to the tutor as an actor in the same context as the student and can thus be further discussed and objectively accepted as true once the two individuals have reached a consensus. Thus, the norm also has the potential to change. Here, the participants thus show that they can use their prior experiences and learning for critical thinking. These types of critical discussions show potential for change, which will be explored next.

Communication and the possibility of change through RPL

There seem to be potential for change of caring practice, when participants make critical use of their prior learning. Thus, the RPL placement opens up a possibility to question norms that seem to be unjustified. Lisa discusses this:

> I think that there is a need to do that [change the work place] because you become 'home blind'. You have done this for 20 years, and you are supposed to do this for another 20 years. You have to be open-minded when younger people start working and question. You do not have to take it as criticism; instead try out what they say – because they see it from another view.

Lisa suggests that changing one's workplace can be helpful because it can open the mind to other ways of engaging in caring practice. The RPL placements makes it possible to challenge the status quo that often comes with routinised care work. Lisa promotes the idea that health care assistants would benefit from the experience of changing to another workplace. Seeing things from another viewpoint is a positive outcome when, as in Lisa's example, younger people enter the workplace, and it is also something that seems to happen quite often when the participants enter 'new' workplaces for their RPL placements.

For these individuals, engaging in discussions with tutors and other workers facilitate two change processes: (1) participants are able to use their prior learning to think critically about caring practice, in particular thinking about how to perform care work in normatively correct ways. They question and critically use prior experiences and learning to argue for normatively correct ways to perform caring practice; and (2) they also experience other ways of approaching caring practice, experiences they bring back to their normal workplaces and which have potential to change these circumstances as well.

Concluding discussion

The objective of this chapter has been to analyse RPL as a form of communicative action. First, a summary and discussion of this analysis is outlined. Second, a discussion of the challenges of rationally reconstructing the RPL process as communicative action is discussed.

At a more general level, the process analysed above could be seen as a procedure where the education system is focused on coordinating the participants' prior experiences and learning through grades and administrative control. Thus, the system might assimilate the lifeworld-grounded work experiences of the participants and re-order them in instrumental ways so that they fit the grades/

curricula of the institution. However, by a rational reconstruction against the norms of communicative action, two more broad themes were developed. Within the first theme it is possible to return to the three forms of rationalities. What is the goal of the assessment interview (means-end rationality)? How are students' actions supposed to be oriented in relation to the prescribed norms of the RPL process (normative rationality)? How can the participants present a truthful picture of their prior learning and experiences (expressive rationality)? Based on these three forms of rationalities it seems as though the participants: (1) do not know how the assessment is conducted or what the goal of the assessment interview is; (2) do not know how to orient their actions towards the normatively prescribed norms in the process (What does it mean to be a participant in the process? How are the participants supposed to reflect so their prior learning can be made visible for the teachers?; and (3) do not know how to present themselves truthfully. It seems difficult for the students to describe their subjective experiences, when they do not know how to describe these experiences. The reconstruction thus draws attention to the problems when mutual definitions of a situation are not reached through consensus and when mutual understanding is not the focus in general.

Within the second theme a rational reconstruction of the RPL-placement as communicative action seemed to provide helpful insights into the development of RPL: (1) mutual understanding was important so tutors and participants can reach a mutual definition of their situation so that they can cooperate towards the goals of the process; (2) the students and tutors must agree on the goal(s) of the process and cooperate towards these goals; and (3) they must try to understand each other's subjective experiences and act truthfully towards each other. When these conditions were not met, it was hard for the participants to fulfil the goals of the six-week placement. When assessing prior learning in practice, it is vital to try to match the tutor and participant in terms of their work experiences and work context. If not, the placement may become an aggravating process where the tutor and participant fruitlessly try to develop a mutual understanding. Then it becomes unmanageable for the participants to act based on consensus, which have a bearing on learning and development through RPL. The results based on the rational reconstruction presented here included examples where the participants and tutors seemed to expand their views through communication. It seems that when prior learning is used critically, there is a potential for action and thus both learning and changes in practice can possibly occur. Such outcomes would not have been achievable if the tutors and participants had not reached a mutual definition of their situation. Although modestly argued, it seems that critical discussions or discourse was made possible when tutors and participants entered into mutually trusting relationships.

Certainly, there are challenges in rationally reconstructing RPL against the norms of communicative action. Four (but certainly not the only) challenges will be highlighted here: (1) find a balance between the empirical data and the theory; (2) the problem of focusing on the subjective experiences of the participants; (3) communicative action is a normative critical social theory that the participants do not know anything about; and (4) the challenges of presenting a normative analysis to those involved in the study.

The first issue raises a problem concerning how to perform an analysis. Should it be a process where the theory is shoehorned into the data? At first, it could be interpreted that a rational reconstruction is merely about taking the theory and making it 'fit' with the available data. However, this would not be something promoted by Habermas. Instead, communicative action is an interpretative framework and the aim of a rational reconstruction is to be descriptive and normative (i.e. critical), on the one hand, and interpretative and explanatory, on the other hand. However, it is a challenge to balance these issues.

The second issue here is connected to the data used for the analysis. Habermas' main focus is to develop a theory that moves away from the individualistic and ego focus of phenomenology to a focus on an intersubjective dimension. Thus, the lifeworld is for Habermas a collective horizon that reproduces meaning. It might thus at first seem to be a bit problematic to use interviews when conducting a Habermasian analysis. However, as discussed before, it has been promoted that an analysis based on the theory of communicative action can be used to highlight the resentment that individuals feel when they are denied access to proper communication. Even though this is a challenge, the interview guide used in the analysis in this chapter was structured based on observations of processes in real time. When conducting interviews there is also a need to engage as a virtual participant and based on this role reach mutual understanding with interviewees.

The third issue draws attention to power issues between a researcher and those persons involved in the study. It could even be seen as elitist to reconstruct a process against norms that individuals in the study know little or nothing about. However, as the fourth issue points out, presenting the final results to those involved in the study could partly redeem this problem. However, if the reconstruction focused on critically appraising the process, this could become a tough experience for both researcher and participants partaking in the study.

Using Habermas' theory of communicative action to rational reconstruct RPL also shows potential for how critical social theory in general can analyse educational processes. In more recent work I have turned more and more to the work of Axel Honneth, but then previous assertions considered in light of using Habermas' theories had to be examined. It became clear that they both share many assumptions, but the differences must be considered.

Even though a hybridisation (Murphy and Costa 2022) between concepts in their works could be problematic, they could also form new concepts or at least change their connotations. Such a concept is the lifeworld. While Habermas for long maintained a strict view of the lifeworld, Honneth considered it problematic to draw a clear-cut line between them. For instance, work was seen by Habermas as a goal-oriented and systemic activity, beyond the lifeworld-oriented activities taking place in the family and educational settings. Honneth's critique was that work is also a place for processes of recognition and solidarity between individuals, ideally creating the means for individual's self-realisation. These processes in work thus also seem to reproduce the lifeworld. For me these hybridisable discussions led to a critique of both Habermas and Honneth, as it is evident that work most probably pertains to both system and lifeworld.

Hybridisations could also concern methodological issues. Habermas' idea of rational reconstruction (his own method as social theorist) could, as discussed earlier in the chapter, be used to analyse empirical data. Honneth is no stranger to these ideas, but instead talks about normative reconstruction. Even though these ideas of rational and normative reconstruction share similarities, they must be considered and reflected upon. Specifically, if merging Habermas and Honneth's theories in analysis, hybridisation (Murphy and Costa 2022) may then not only depict strict theoretical issues, but also issues focused on methodology.

Note

1 Although Habermas draws on research that is empirical.

References

Briton, D., W. Gereluk and B. Spencer. 1998. *Prior learning, assessment and recognition: Issues for adult educators*. Paper presented at the CASAE Conference Proceedings, University of Ottawa, Ontario, Canada.

Brookfield, S. 2005. Learning democratic reason: The adult education project of Jürgen Habermas. *Teachers College Record* 107, 6: 1127–1168.

Ewert, D.G. 1991. Habermas and education: A comprehensive overview of the influence of Habermas in educational literature. *Review of Educational Research* 61, 3: 345–378.

Fleming, T. 2012. Fromm and Habermas: Allies for adult education and democracy. *Studies in Philosophy and Education* 31, 2: 123–136.

Forester, J. 2003. On fieldwork in a Habermasian way: Critical ethnography and the extraordinary character of ordinary professional work. In *Studying management critically*. eds. M. Alvesson and H. Willmott, 46–65. London: Sage.

Habermas, J. 1971. *Knowledge and human interests*. Boston, MA: Beacon Press.

Habermas, J. 1984. *The theory of communicative action*. Vol. 1. *Reason and the rationalization of society*. Cambridge: Polity.

Habermas, J. 1987. *The theory of communicative action*. Vol. 2. *Lifeworld and system: A critique of functionalist reason*. Cambridge: Polity.

Habermas, J. 1996. *Between facts and norms: Contributions to a discourse theory of law and democracy*. London: Polity.

Houlbrook, M.C. 2012. RPL practice and student disposition – Insights from the lifeworld. *Journal of Education and Work* 25, 5: 555–570.

Kember, D. 2000. *Action learning and action research. Improving the quality of teaching and learning*. London: Kogan Page.

Mezirow, J. 1981. A critical theory of adult learning and education. *Adult Education Quarterly* 32: 3–27.

Ministry of Education. 2003. *Validering m.m. – fortsatt utveckling av vuxnas lärande.* Stockholm: Utbildningsdepartementet.

Moran, P. and M. Murphy. 2012. Habermas, pupil voice, rationalism and their meeting with Lacan's objekt petit A. *Studies in Philosophy and Education* 31, 2: 171–181.

Murphy, M. and C. Costa. 2022. Social theory and methodology in education research: From conceptualisation to operationalisation. In *Social theory and education research. Understanding Foucault, Habermas, Bourdieu and Derrida.* 2nd edn. ed. M. Murphy, 24–43. Abingdon: Routledge.

Murphy, M. and T. Fleming. eds. 2010. *Habermas, critical theory and education.* New York, NY: Routledge.

Pedersen, J. 2008. Habermas method: Rational reconstruction. *Philosophy of the Social Sciences* 38, 4: 457–485.

Pedersen, J. 2009. Habermas and the political sciences: The relationship between theory and practice. *Philosophy of the Social Sciences* 39, 3: 381–407.

Pedersen, J. 2011. *Habermas' method: Rational reconstruction. Dissertation.* Bergen: University of Bergen.

Sandberg, F. 2010. Recognising health care assistants' prior learning through a caring ideology. *Vocations and Learning* 3, 2: 99–115.

Sandberg, F. 2012. A Habermasian analysis of a process of recognition of prior learning for health care assistants. *Adult Education Quarterly* 62, 4: 351–370.

Sandberg, F. and P. Andersson. 2011. RPL for accreditation in higher education: As a process of mutual understanding or merely lifeworld colonisation? *Assessment and Evaluation in Higher Education* 36, 7: 767–780.

Smyth, R. 2006. Exploring congruence between Habermasian philosophy, mixed-method research, and managing data using NVivo. *International Journal of Qualitative Methods* 5, 2: 131–145.

Thomas, A. 2000. Prior learning assessment: The quiet revolution. In *Handbook of adult and continuing education.* eds. A. Wilson and E. Hayes, 508–522. San Francisco, CA: Jossey-Bass.

Welton, M.R. 1995. In defense of the lifeworld: A Habermasian approach to adult learning. In *In defense of the lifeworld: Critical perspectives on adult learning.* ed. M.R. Welton, 127–156. Albany, NY: State University of New York Press.

Part IV
Bourdieu

9 Bourdieu and educational research

Thinking tools, relational thinking, beyond epistemological innocence

Shaun Rawolle and Bob Lingard

Introduction

The French sociologist Pierre Bourdieu (1930–2002) was perhaps the pre-eminent sociologist of the late 20th century. The impact of his work is evident in social theory, sociology of art, culture and the media, sociology of education and in respect of important issues of research methodology and epistemology in the social sciences.[1] It is interesting that Bourdieu's sociology has remained very relevant across the 21st century; for example, many articles in the *British Journal of Sociology of Education* across the first two decades of this century continue to use Bourdieu's theoretical framework (see Gale and Lingard 2015). There is also new work which applies Bourdieu's work to different kinds of society from France and colonial Algeria where the theory was generated; for example, there is a lot of work on Chinese schooling now utilising his work (e.g. Mu, Dooley and Luke 2019). As we will demonstrate, it is the very nature of Bourdieu's theoretical and methodological/empirical approaches which have ensured their on-going relevance.

In this chapter we consider Bourdieu's *oeuvre* and draw implications for education researchers today. Specifically, Bourdieu's work seeks a way through some of the central conundrums facing all social science researchers and we are thinking of educational research here as framed within social science research. Bourdieu's work also provides a way through a range of sticking points that present themselves in the form of conceptual dualisms, such as the structure and agency relationship, and micro and macro binaries. At a broader level, Bourdieu presents a social science that rejects 'theoreticism' (theory not informed closely enough by empirical data and not open to challenge) and 'methodologism' (a narrow concern with methods and techniques to the neglect of epistemological and ontological issues about data collection and knowledge claims) (Bourdieu and Wacquant 1992). In practice, Bourdieu emphasised the necessity of putting both theory and data to work together, and his accounts emphasise the social world as being the product of social constructions, yet also more than such constructions. The effects of social science were, for Bourdieu, located both within the relative autonomy of the academic field, and more broadly within the polity, including other social fields such as education, journalism and

DOI: 10.4324/9781003156550-13

politics. Bourdieu also rejected what might be seen as a *substantialist* account of social phenomena that were the focus of social science research; as such, he rejects individualism and holism. Instead, Bourdieu recognised the *relational* workings of the social arrangement, seeing all social phenomena in relation to their location in a given field and in relation to others in the field.

It is interesting in this respect to consider *Sketch for self-analysis* (2004) in which Bourdieu applies his thinking tools to his own life. Bourdieu (2004c) states emphatically in a front note to the book that 'this is *not* an autobiography', and that he is interested in understanding his own habitus and dispositions in terms of the times and places in which he lived. Bourdieu's account mirrors C. Wright Mills' 'sociological imagination', which stresses the need to understand the interweaving of individual agency with structure through time.[2] An element of potential human agency against structural determinism for Bourdieu is the possibility we as human beings have for what he calls 'socioanalysis', our capacity for reflecting on what has made us who we are; the capacity to reflect upon, and to be reflexive about, our habitus in Bourdieu's terms. It is just such a set of dispositions or habitus that Bourdieu sees as necessary for good sociological research (see Brubacker 1993; Grenfell 2008a; 2008b). We view such a research habitus as central to good research in the sociology of education; this is a research habitus which is able to reflexively understand the positioning of the researcher in respect of what is being researched and in relation to the intellectual field in which the research is located. Reflexive consideration of researcher positionality is central to Bourdieu's research methodologies.

The main aim of this chapter then is to provide an introduction to the theoretical work of Pierre Bourdieu, and to outline different ways that Bourdieu's work is influential and has been engaged with in education research and to suggest implicitly the usefulness of this work for educational researchers. In order to do this, we draw on a range of Bourdieu's own writing published singly or with colleagues, emphasising in particular his engagements with education. Part of our treatment also deals with his wider writing that has subsequently been influential for education researchers, and in particular Bourdieu's anthropological writing and account of practice (Bourdieu 1990b), his approach to social class and cultural issues, his account of the judgement of taste and distinctions (Bourdieu 1984), and his later politically focussed writing (Bourdieu 1989/1996; 2003; 2004a; 2005a). We also note here two important collections of his Collège de France lectures published posthumously that deal respectively with habitus and field (Bourdieu 2020) and the work of the state (Bourdieu 2015).

Running through the account presented is an overarching argument that Bourdieu's work has developed a global influence, utility and continued importance to educational research. There is a case to be made, as Santoro (2009) has argued, for 'putting Bourdieu in a global field' (ibid, 1). In this chapter, we expand on this account to argue a pluri-scalar case in relation to education research: That Bourdieu's theories are important for understanding a global field of education research, different national fields of education research, and cross-field effects between these two scales of fields. Here we are recognising the necessity of understanding the impact on his work of the national field of research in which it was produced, but also stress the need to understand its playing out and cascading effects in different national fields of consumption. This reciprocal looping shares a family resemblance with Giddens' (1987) concept of a *double hermeneutic*, that recognises both the fields of production and fields of consumption. Such recognition is necessary for understanding the impact of Bourdieu's work (Wacquant 1993, 235).

Bourdieu's theoretical work can be understood as the complementary development of three interlinked foci, each of which has been developed, tested and honed through empirical work. It is these three foci that will be explored in the remainder of this chapter. *First* is the focus of Bourdieu's research on specific empirical cases, to which he returned with different elaborations and theorisations at various stages of his writing. These include his writing on Algeria, on education and on art and cultural production. Our focus will be Bourdieu's writing about education in its various forms. This work on education is linked specifically to understanding both social reproduction and change in societies. Wacquant (1993, 235) argues that Bourdieu's *oeuvre* can be seen as 'a generative anthropology of power with special emphasis on its symbolic dimension', especially the misrecognitions involved in the workings of power in social and cultural reproduction. We also note the ways in which Bourdieu returned throughout his research career to some earlier foci and in this reprise conceptualised things differently, as indicative of the reflexivity of his account and the openness of his concepts to re-interrogation via the empirical. *Second* is the development of intellectual resources such as specific conceptual tools (Bourdieu's 'thinking tools') that were developed over the course of his work and tested and applied between different empirical cases. This is considered separately in that as these tools were products of the practice of Bourdieu's intellectual work that were generated over time, they did not emerge as fully formed and complete conceptual tools at the beginning of his career. For example, Bourdieu's (1958/1962) earliest works on Algeria present no direct account of practice or *habitus*, or fields, yet do present an initial account of capital in ways consistent with later work, though not differentiated into forms. *Third* is the development of theoretical resources that elaborate methodological, epistemological and researcher approaches and stances to the study and research of the social world.

In education research, these three broad foci have been engaged to differing degrees, with a variety of commitments to these kinds of theoretical resources. We use this basic analytic distinction as a way of structuring the next sections, but note that this distinction is a specific device designed to add some focus for understanding both the different reception of Bourdieu's work and also the differential potential that his work and theoretical approach hold for educational researchers.

The production, consumption and reception of Bourdieu's research on education

This section is structured as an account of the reception (or 'consumption') of Bourdieu's works about one specific area of study, education. Our central argument in this section is that the utility of Bourdieu's work lies in the multi-faceted theorising of all aspects of research, which therefore provide a range of connections with different elements of research in education.

Engagements with education

> ... a truly rational pedagogy, that is, one based on a sociology of cultural inequalities, would, no doubt, help to reduce inequalities in education and cul-ture, but it would not be able to become a reality unless all the conditions for a true democratization of the recruitment of teachers and students were fulfilled, the first of which would be the setting up of a truly rational pedagogy.
>
> (Bourdieu and Passeron 1964/1979, 76)

The main contribution of Bourdieu's initial works in education lay in the development of a broad theory to explain the reproduction of cultural and social inequalities through education, and the legitimation of these inequalities through misrecognition. For Bourdieu, education acted as a sorting institution that functioned to divide group primarily through the valuing of cultural capi-tal. This cultural capital was implicit in school curricula and pedagogy, and was aligned with, embodied, assumed and possessed by certain classes. This implicit cultural capital became the mechanism of selection, which, with pedagogic action, helped to reproduce inequalities and led to the misrecognition of these cultural differences as differences in individual ability. What was largely con-tentious about this account was the implication that the reproduction of such inequalities was inherently embedded in the structure and functioning of insti-tutions of education, in their curricula and pedagogies, and that such repro-duction occurred largely in spite of the (good) intentions of teachers. Theories in the 1970s premised the identification of education as a major site of change and reform of broader social institutions and for providing equality of oppor-tunity for all, irrespective of social class and possession of certain capitals. It is therefore understandable that Bourdieu's contributions, particularly as outlined in the publication of *Reproduction in education, society and culture* (Bourdieu and Passeron 1970/1977) and *The inheritors* (Bourdieu and Passeron 1964/1979), were viewed with some suspicion by progressive educators and researchers.

At the time of the publication of these books, Bourdieu's argument was heavily criticised as either being conservative or implying the need for a revo-lution to challenge such reproduction. On that very point Bourdieu later noted:

> The paradox I have to recall is that it's precisely the law of gravity that enables us to fly: that is what I always said, from *The Inheritors* onwards,

particularly in the conclusion on 'rational pedagogy', which some people saw as reformist (see quote above). It is by knowing the laws of reproduction that we can have a chance, however small, of minimizing the reproductive effect of the educational institution.

(Bourdieu 2008, 52–53)

Despite this suspicion, initially by those of all political persuasions, Bourdieu's and colleagues' contributions to reproduction theories of education have been influential and have continued salience to a range of researchers in education.

The consumption and reception of Bourdieu's work

There is, in looking at Bourdieu's engagements with education,[3] a significant challenge that we need to signal, as it bears relevance to the potential of Bourdieu's work and to the engagements with his work on education in different nation-states. In essence, the reception of Bourdieu in different education research traditions reveals a range of different national variations.[4] There is not one single univocal narrative that can be told about Bourdieu's influence, in part because of issues of the timing of translation of his work, but also because of the significance and reception of his specific arguments in national debates about education issues, and the question of how dominant scholars in each national education research field at the time of their emergence engaged with these arguments. Robbins (2004), for example, has written about the reception of Bourdieu's work in Britain in relation to the sociology of education, demonstrating the relationship between this reception and the chronology of the translation of Bourdieu's work into English and the significance of his reproduction account in this reception. There are also questions of the specific disciplinary paths through which Bourdieu's theories have been adapted and influential in education research, and the flows of intellectuals between nation-states whose work references Bourdieu's.

We note, for example, that in Australian education research, the initial links between Bourdieu's work and Australian education researchers follow people such as one of Bourdieu's translators, Richard Teese, whose translation of Bourdieu's work first appeared in *Melbourne Studies* (Bourdieu 1980), and the writing of Richard Bates, an Australian scholar linking Bourdieu's theories to education administration (Bates 1980).[5] Yet the subsequent pick up of Bourdieu's ideas in education appeared somewhat curtailed through the reception of dominant Australian sociologists such as Connell, whose then position on education in Australia (argued with colleagues), though theoretically similar, was marked by a sharp refusal of Bourdieu's central arguments about the mechanisms of reproduction through education, and her view that Bourdieu and Passeron presented a static model of education (Connell et al. 1982). This view was presented in *Making the difference* (Connell et al. 1982), but also in Connell's broader critique of reproduction theory (Connell 1983), where she argued that a focus on practice, as opposed to structure, leads to an emphasis on change, rather than structural reproduction. In recounting the uptake of Bourdieu in Australian sociology, Woodward and Emmison (2009) talk about this opposition in stark terms: '(t)here appeared to be no place in Connell's *oeuvre* on class for Bourdieu' (ibid, 4).[6]

In contrast, the initial engagement with Bourdieu's work in England can be traced to a conference of the British Sociological Association (BSA) in Durham. At this conference a range of concerns were raised about reproduction and how the 'taken-for-granteds' of pedagogy and curriculum helped to reproduce the class structure, class codes and class relations through schooling. Discussions at this BSA conference led to collaboration on an edited book, *Knowledge and control* (Young 1971), which illustrated a broad engagement with, and alignment between, Bourdieu and English-speaking scholars such as Basil Bernstein and Michael Young. This book heralded what was to be referred to as the *new sociology of education*. The authors of this book were soon to become dominant scholars within an emerging research concentration bringing together different critical, philosophical and sociological traditions to bear on education. Through this book, Bourdieu's writing on education was to become central to scholarship and research on education in the United Kingdom. The work of Bourdieu and of Bourdieu and Passeron also aligned with the reproduction theories that were heavily influenced by Marxist and neo-Marxist scholarship (Bowles and Gintis 1976). Bourdieu's (1977, published in French in 1970) book with Passeron, *Reproduction in education, society and culture*, was central to the take-up of his work in the sociology of education. It may appear a little odd in a book devoted to education theory to raise two small historical vignettes related to the international circulation of ideas, and in this case, Bourdieu's ideas. However, it is in the links between these two aspects of Bourdieu's work that his theories hold relevance for particular scholars positioned in different national fields.

Theoretical and generative resources: Bourdieu's '*thinking tools*'

Alongside theoretical understandings of specific social/empirical cases, Bourdieu developed a set of what Wacquant (1989) described as 'thinking tools'. Each of these tools was adapted from other scholarship, from philosophy, sociology and anthropology, but reworked to have a specific location and purpose in Bourdieu's work. We separate these theoretical resources from Bourdieu's theorisation of specific empirical cases to illustrate the development of a cumulative framework of specific tools to understand the social world. Hence, while some scholars may disagree with specific theorisations of social cases offered in Bourdieu's work, the thinking tools themselves may have some utility in broader applications to research. The extensibility of this framework was tested in a variety of different research projects, and over the course of Bourdieu's writing there were shifts in the emphasis and use of these tools to suit specific research purposes. These tools serve multiple purposes and help to create a break with the pre-conceived objects of the social world,[7] and to create a distancing that allowed the examination of specific kinds of relationships that are often overlooked.

While we have previously suggested that these tools form a 'theoretical triad' (Rawolle and Lingard 2008), here we group two conceptual couplets from Bourdieu's thinking tools, namely habitus/practice and forms of capitals/social fields. These are grouped primarily for theoretical congruence and the reasonableness of their combination. We arrange these families largely according to their chronological emergence in Bourdieu's work, as the specific couplets discussed are supplemented by subsequent thinking tools, rather than being completely replaced.

Theory of practice: Practice and habitus

The first couplet important to Bourdieu as a way of breaking with common sense views of activity was that of *practice* and *habitus*. These two concepts were developed as part of a project of developing a coherent yet open theory of practice, exemplified in two major works, *Outline of a theory of practice* (Bourdieu 1977) and *Logic of practice* (Bourdieu 1990b), both based on anthropological research in Algeria. The broad theory of practice was developed as a way to understand a number of specific anthropological research interests in Algeria (Bourdieu 1977). Bourdieu refused to approach research in France in ways that completely differed from his research in Algeria and this led to the gradual adaptation of his (broadly) anthropological theory to sociological studies in later works (Bourdieu 1984). Consequently, *practice/habitus* is an important couplet in Bourdieu's work, in that it signifies one of the fundamental conceptual breaks that led to a distinctive approach to sociology, noting an ontological complicity between the two.

Marked by a sharp refusal to offer a definition of practice,[8] Bourdieu's account of practice was characterised by attentiveness to the logic, flow and contest of practical activities and their connections in time. Practice was, in many respects, the core element of social life that required explanation, and it was in the process and carrying out of practice that other aspects of social life, such as the exclusions and exclusivities, classifications and struggles, were located. Within practice, Bourdieu saw the patterned development and flow of social energy, associated with patterns of meaning, and in their carrying out, a reinforcement of selections of those meanings. The other part of this couplet, habitus, was a collection of the sets of dispositions that allowed individual agents and groups of agents to engage with and make meaningful contributions to practice. Elsewhere we have described this as a kind of socio-genetic relationship: That habitus is required as a prior condition for producing practice, and for consuming practice. However, the contribution to practice is dependent on other things in the environment, as well as considerations of strategy and tactics.

The concept of *habitus* was borrowed by Bourdieu from philosophical thought that can be traced to Aristotle. However, Bourdieu's conceptualisation of *habitus* was an original contribution, which he defended against multiple charges.[9] Perhaps the most urgent task that Bourdieu saw for the development and application of *habitus* in both his earliest and late works lay in a reconciliation of two separated features of social science, that of explanations in sociology and economics. In a posthumously published book on the construction of a housing market, *The social structures of the economy* (Bourdieu 2005b), this application was located specifically as an alternative account to the abstractions of *homo economicus*, the human being as rational utility maximiser. There Bourdieu argued for a specifically considered economic *habitus*, stating that …

> … (i)nsofar as he or she is endowed with a habitus, the social agent is *a collective individual or a collective individuated by the fact of embodying objective structures*. The individual, the subjective, is social and collective. The *habitus* is socialised subjectivity, a historical transcendental, whose schemes of perception and appreciation (systems of appreciation, tastes, etc.) are the product of collective and individual history. Reason (or rationality) is 'bounded' not only, as Herbert Simon believes, because the human mind is generically bounded … but because it is socially structured and determined, and, as a consequence, limited.
>
> (Bourdieu 2005b, 211)

Habitus then is the basis for apprehending practice, for noticing differences and being aware of the subtleties of practice, through an alignment borne of collective experiences and histories that are carried in the body. *Habitus* also provides the basis for mis-matches between practice moves and the flow of practice in a field, where collective individuals have moved or been taken out of the collective and individual histories that provided an innate feel for the flow and logic of practice, a 'feel for the game'. The symbolic violence of such mismatches between the habitus of collective individuals and changes in objective conditions was also the focus of one of the first contributions that Bourdieu made from his research in Algeria, in the sustained focus on the imposition of a market economy on traditional agricultural workers (Bourdieu 1958/1962; 2004b). Such an explanation could also be tested in relation to the effects of rapid education policy changes.

Bourdieu's approach to field theory: Forms of capital, social fields

As intimated in the discussion of the practice/habitus couplet, for Bourdieu the major locations in which practice is produced in capitalist societies are different social fields. Bourdieu thought of the social arrangement as consisting of multiple fields with varying degrees of autonomy (more or less autonomous or heteronomous) from an overarching field of power (and in his later work masculine domination (Bourdieu 2001) an overarching field of gender). In some ways, in this social conception Bourdieu was working across Marxist and Weberian approaches. When Bourdieu returned to France from Algeria and continued research, an additional conceptual couplet was added as a way to explain different kinds of social arrangements. This couplet drew on the concept of field, borrowed primarily through the application of relations between elements evident in field theory in physics (although versions of the concept of social fields can be found in the much earlier and unconnected work of Kurt Lewin (1939): see Martin 2003 and Rawolle 2008 for discussion). For Bourdieu, social fields are spaces of competition, in which there are inequities in access to the stakes (capitals) of that competition, and the form in which this competition is carried out is through practice.[10] As a non-substantialist concept, social fields are comprised of an organisation of social forces, with the producers of these field forces being individual agents and collections of agents, located in the relations between these agents. It is through the movement and practice of agents that such fields continue and change. What is crucial to field analysis is locating specific properties that allow the description of relations between agents, and the locating of groups of agents relative to one another. This is the relationality central to Bourdieu's social theorising.

In order to understand the structuring of social fields, and the stakes around which fields were oriented, Bourdieu developed a multi-dimensional view of capital, which provided a variety of different forms of capital with which to discuss the stakes of competition within fields, and differences between different kinds of fields. There were two overlapping ways that Bourdieu theorised capital. On the one hand, Bourdieu argued that each distinct field provides a unique form of capital located within the field, and that practice was largely oriented as a kind of competition for this unique form of capital. Hence, Bourdieu would argue for scientific capital (Bourdieu 2004b), educational capital (Bourdieu 2005b) and journalistic capital (Bourdieu 1998), as ways to point to the specific forms located in particular corresponding fields that were irreducible to the stakes of other fields.

Such field specific capital was accumulated through an investment in the field, and its distinctive forms of practice, with some agents being more successful in their strategies of accumulation and understanding of the rules of the games associated with these practices. However, Bourdieu (1986) would also argue that these kinds of field specific capital could be analysed into a number of elementary forms, which were described as social capital, cultural capital, economic capital and symbolic capital.[11] Each field-specific capital could then be described according to its composition of a ratio of social, cultural, economic and symbolic capital. Hence, as these forms of capital were a kind of trans-substantiated bundle of social energy, there were elementary and compound forms of this energy with the potential to be converted to economic capital. These different forms of capital could be converted by specifically located agents under specific circumstances, and with different exchange rates, dependent on the relations between the relevant social fields, and the gatekeepers and dominant agents located within each field (Bourdieu 1984). Though the language used in relation to this couplet held a specific heritage from the physical sciences and from economics, Bourdieu's was not a mechanistic account of the social world.

An unfinished project: A general theory of fields

Bourdieu's successive studies of different kinds of social fields raised a broader question about how different fields relate. In short, this raised the possibility of a general theory of fields that would help to understand the patterns of relations between fields, movements of fields relative to one another, points of overlap or disconnect between fields, or whether parts of social space exist within which field like relations are not present (see Hilgers and Mangez 2015). While there has been some exploration of this incomplete theory of fields elsewhere (Couldry 2003a; 2003b; Kauppi 2002; Lingard, Rawolle and Taylor 2005; Rawolle 2005), at this point we will emphasise some of the kinds of linkages that Bourdieu raised about this meta-theorising of fields. This general theory of fields was explicitly discussed in one major location ('Some properties of fields', in Bourdieu 1993), and discussed intermittently in other locations, as a way to understand the effects of specific fields on other fields, the relations between fields or the emergence of fields. The first aspect of interest in this general theory of fields explored by Bourdieu related to a question: What quasi-taxonomic differences could be stated about different fields? While there were a number of different divisions offered, one key division expressed was between fields associated primarily with different kinds of social production and those fields associated primarily with different kinds of social consumption. One of the later points of exploration by Bourdieu related to a systematic understanding of ways that specific fields, such as journalism and the economic field, have come to threaten the autonomy and logic of practice of different fields. In this point of exploration, Bourdieu directly dealt with processes such as globalisation and mediatisation, processes in which some fields gradually come to influence the patterns and functioning of other fields, and the principles of hierarchisation of these fields. In this process, these affected fields become less autonomous and more heteronomous in character.

The incompleteness of this general theory of fields presents a number of points for further exploration for researchers (Hilgers and Mangez 2015). Questions remain about how to understand the time-frames over which field-like relations develop and continue, and ways that practice leads to the accumulation of different kinds of capital (see Rawolle's 2005 account of temporary social fields), or ways to group and connect different kinds of effects between fields. Thus, homologies between fields present one kind of explanation, but there may be other kinds of effects that deserve further attention (see Lingard and Rawolle 2004; Rawolle and Lingard 2008 for a conceptual and empirical elaboration of 'cross-field effects'). Such effects may be based, for example, on the connections or interactions between practices, or the products of practice, such as policy texts or performance on specific indicators (Rawolle 2010a). Such effects may also relate to the kinds of autonomy available within a field, and how positions of domination within a field are established (see Maton 2005 in relation to higher education). Bourdieu's inchoate outlines of global fields also present an opportunity for further development and exploration (see

Lingard and Rawolle 2010; 2011; Lingard, Rawolle and Taylor 2005; Marginson 2010). Fields in Bourdieu's work refer to social relations, not necessarily geographic and spatial ones. This is productive for consideration of fields and globalisation. We have written about an 'emergent global education policy field', for example, which has effects (cross-field effects) in national education policy fields and how these effects to some extent are borne by the habitus of international and national policy makers (Lingard and Rawolle 2010; 2011; Lingard, Sellar and Baroutsis 2015). This brings us to the major point we would want to make about Bourdieu and educational research. His thinking tools that we have considered briefly here are generative ones, which can be reflexively utilised to research various topics in education. We turn in the next section to consider the necessary research habitus, according to Bourdieu, for utilising his work in education.

Methodological approaches and researcher stances: Beyond epistemological innocence

> ... how artificial the ordinary oppositions between theory and research, between quantitative and qualitative methods, between statistical recording and ethnographic observation, between the grasping of structures and the construction of individuals ... These alternatives have no function other than to provide a justification for the vacuous and resounding abstractions of theoreticism and for the falsely rigorous observations of positivism, or, as the divisions between economists, anthropologists, historians and sociologists, to legitimise the limits of *competency*: that is to say that they function in the manner of *social censorship,* liable to forbid us to grasp a truth which resides precisely in the relations between realms of practice arbitrarily separated.
>
> (Bourdieu and de Saint Martin 1978, 7, cited in
> Bourdieu and Wacquant 1992, 27–28)

In this section, we will look at Bourdieu's contribution to methodology in the social sciences. The quote above well encapsulates the challenges Bourdieu offers in respect of methodology in terms of many of the arid binaries, both theoretical and methodological, that surround and legitimate research practice and theorising in the social sciences. We are thinking in particular of the now old divisions between quantitative and qualitative approaches and note Bourdieu's use of both; this usage is determined by appropriateness to research topic. Bourdieu's eclectic, but principled, approach to methodology, has made a significant contribution to the social sciences, particularly in respect of what we might see as necessary researcher disposition or habitus. We will outline the core elements of Bourdieu's contribution here.

Bourdieu (1990b) has referred to his research methodology as 'fieldwork in philosophy', while Jenkins (2002), in his quite critical account of Bourdieu's contribution to sociology and social science methodology, describes Bourdieu's work as 'experiments in epistemology'. Indeed, Jenkins (ibid, 46) argues that one of Bourdieu's greatest contributions to sociology is 'that he never lost sight of the practicality of epistemological issues (or of their importance)': issues, as he puts it, that are concerned with how we know something (the evidence or data associated with that knowing), how we are able to say we 'know' something and the status of our claims (ibid, 46). This methodology has useful application in educational research, particularly in the sociology of education and in what has been referred to as 'policy sociology' in education (see Lingard 2021).

What Bourdieu has argued for in his accounts of research and data collection and analysis is the application of his thinking tools (habitus and practice, fields and capitals) to the researcher and researcher's location in both the academic field and in the research field. Indeed, he argued that this reflexive positioning was absolutely necessary, noting that many intellectuals and particularly positivist social scientists most often denied or neglected this reality. For Bourdieu, such a self- or socio-analysis will ensure a better social science. He thus sees the necessity of vigilant reflexivity in the research process, but also regards this vigilance as being central to an appropriate research habitus within the social sciences for producing good research and theory. This is what connotative descriptors such as research as 'fieldwork in philosophy', 'experiments in epistemology' and 'epistemological reflexivity' are trying to capture in relation to Bourdieu's contribution to theory and methodology. This is an important contribution, supporting a reflexive researcher disposition, but in the cause of better social science, not as a reflection of an epistemological anarchy of a relativist 'anything goes stance'. We note here as well Bourdieu's use of quantitative data, but not within a positivist framework, and also note his use of qualitative data, also not within a positivist framework.

Bourdieu argues the necessity of reflexivity of the researcher in recognition of this dual reality, mirroring Durkheim's conception of 'social facts' in social science as both social constructions, but also having an empirical reality. This recognition, of the 'constructedness' of social science generally and in research necessitates, according to Bourdieu (1999, 608), a rejection of 'epistemological innocence'. We think that this rejection of epistemological innocence is central to understanding Bourdieu's approach and contribution to research methodology. Here Bourdieu observes,

> The positivist dream of an epistemological state of perfect innocence papers over the fact that the crucial difference is not between a science that effects a construction and one that does not, but between a science that does this without knowing it and one that, being aware of work of construction, strives to discover and master as completely as possible the nature of its inevitable acts of construction and the equally inevitable effects those acts produce.

> (Bourdieu 1999, 608)

Bourdieu (2004b) reflects on this rejection of epistemological innocence further in his *Science of science and reflexivity*. Here he notes,

Casting an ironic gaze on the social world, a gaze which unveils, unmasks, brings to light what is hidden, it cannot avoid casting this gaze on itself – with the intention not of destroying sociology but rather of serving it, using the sociology of sociology in order to make a better sociology.

(ibid, 4)

This means that reflexivity is central to good social science research and to researcher habitus. We have to be aware of our own positioning in relation to data collection: We like the concept of 'positionality' (our word, not Bourdieu's) and the need to continually recognise and acknowledge our role in data collection as a way towards better social science.[12] It is such matters that Bourdieu argues must be reflected upon and laid bare in the conduct of good social science research. Yet others have attempted to extend the concept of positionality in research as a necessary component part of researcher habitus or disposition. Rizvi and Lingard (2010) in doing policy sociology on education in the context of globalisation argue that policy analysis needs to consider the location of the researcher in relation to the focus of analysis, explicate the theoretical and political stance adopted, and reflect upon the significance of the spatial location of the researcher to the analysis. Bourdieu's addition to such considerations of researcher positionality was to stress the need as well to locate oneself reflexively as researcher within the academic field.

It is important to note here that Bourdieu wrote about the need to reject epistemological innocence in a methodological reflection on research interviews conducted for the study of the impact of neo-liberal politics on the lives of 'ordinary' French people: *The weight of the world: Social suffering in contemporary society* (Bourdieu et al. 1999). In that reflection on methodology he has some interesting things to say about conducting research interviews, a most common mode of data collection in the social sciences and in education research. Thus he notes, the risk of shocking both the 'rigorous methodologist' and 'inspired hermeneutic scholar', that 'the interview can be considered a sort of *spiritual exercise* that, through *forgetfulness of self*, aims at a true *conversion of the way we look* at other people in the ordinary circumstances of life' (Bourdieu 1999, 614). He continues,

The welcoming disposition, which leads one to make the respondent's problems one's own, the capacity to take that person and understand them just as they are in their distinctive necessity, is a sort of *intellectual love: a gaze that consents to necessity in the manner of the 'intellectual love of god'*, that is, of the natural order, which Spinoza held to be the supreme form of knowledge.

(ibid, 614)

This observation indicates something of the centrality in Bourdieu's work of thinking about data collection in the field well beyond technical issues, utilising a necessary and ever-present epistemic reflexivity.

Another important aspect of Bourdieu's work on methodology is his rejection of a dichotomy between theory and data, between theory and methodology; instead, he recognises the necessary relationship between the two and the impact that each has on the other, recognising an ontological complicity here. In keeping all theory open to empirical challenge, he is rejecting the doxa associated with certain accounts of the empirical and of the theoretical. As Wacquant (1992, 35) notes, 'Bourdieu maintains that every act of research is simultaneously empirical (it confronts the world of observable phenomena) and theoretical (it necessarily engages hypotheses about the underlying structure of relations that observations are designed to capture)'. In our words, we see Bourdieu emphasising the epistemological issues associated with both and the need for alignment across the onto-epistemologies of both theory and methodology. Furthermore, we can see talk of his concepts, dealt with earlier in this chapter, as 'thinking tools' also grasping this provisionality of concepts and theory. In focusing on the on-going imbrications of theory and data, we might see Bourdieu's approach as 'abductive', simultaneously applying both deductive (theory to data) and inductive (data to theory) approaches to analysis.

For Bourdieu, reflexivity is also central to the dissemination of research. The rejection of epistemological innocence and acknowledgement that all research is simultaneously empirical and theoretical, as well as practical, demands, Bourdieu suggests, an openness and vulnerability, indeed honesty, in the presentation of our research in both oral and written genres. In talking about handing down the trade of doing social science research, Bourdieu says this about research presentations:

> A research presentation is in every respect the very opposite of an exhibition, of a *show* in which you seek to show off and to impress others. It is a discourse in which you *expose yourself*, you take risks. ... The more you expose yourself, the greater your chances of benefiting from the discussion and the more constructive and good-willed, I am sure, the criticisms and advice you will receive.
>
> (Bourdieu and Wacquant 1992, 219)

As Bourdieu (1992, 219) noted, 'Homo academicus relishes the finished', but this should not disavow us of the reality of the practical and mundane elements of conducting research, the pragmatic decisions that need to be made about definitions of social objects and their operationalisation, what data to collect, who to interview, the *cul-de-sacs* and practicalities of data collection, and so on. Yet while these are pragmatic choices, at the same time 'the most 'empirical' technical choices cannot be disentangled from the most 'theoretical' choices' (ibid, 225).

Bourdieu is also eclectic in respect of theoretical and methodological traditions to frame our research, but principled not anarchistic in this eclecticism. Thus he observes,

The long and short of it is, social research is something much too serious and too difficult for us to allow ourselves to mistake scientific *rigidity*, which is the nemesis of intelligence and invention, for scientific *rigour*, and thus to deprive ourselves of this or that resource available in the full panoply of intellectual traditions of our discipline and of the sister disciplines of anthropology, economics, history etc.

(Bourdieu 1992, 227)

He takes a similar stance in respect of quantitative and qualitative methodologies, using one or the other or both, depending on the object of the research. This is the point we made earlier about the need to align the onto-epistemologies of theory and methodology and also with the focus of research. Bourdieu's choices of statistical methods to use in research reflect his relational account (this asserts the primacy of relations between things, rather than things in and of themselves) of the social and commitment to field analysis to ensure such alignment.

Grenfell (2008b, 219–227) has outlined what he sees as the methodological principles deriving from Bourdieu's work. We will consider these briefly here, but note at the outset that these principles should not be seen as stages in a process, rather these principles continually interact in the conduct of research working with a Bourdieusian approach to methodology. The three principles are firstly, the deconstruction of the research object, challenging every day, taken-for-granted construction of the research topic. In many ways, this is akin to the distinction some in the social sciences have made between the 'making' and 'taking' of research problems; Bourdieu operationalises a 'making' of research problems and of concepts in the social world. What Bourdieu is suggesting is the necessity to deconstruct the prefigured. This deconstruction focuses on 'unthought categories of thought which delimit the thinkable and predetermine the thought' (Bourdieu 1990a, 178). The second element of Bourdieu's methodological principles, according to Grenfell, entails a 'three-level approach to study the field of the object of research' (Grenfell 2008b, 220). This principle requires analysis of the position of the field being studied in relation to the overarching field of power, the mapping of the positioning of agents within the field and an analysis of the habitus and dispositions of these agents. The third and final principle is that of reflexivity to challenge what Bourdieu saw as three possible aspects of bias or distortion in social science research. The first potential form of bias derives from the positioning of the researcher in the social space, the second from the doxa or orthodoxies of the field and the researcher's positioning within it, and the third from the fact that researchers actually have the time to do such research, outside the necessity of other actions in the world (ibid, 226).

In Bourdieu's earlier work that gave more emphasis to the autonomy of fields, academic work and research were seen to be operating and functioning within different fields with different logics of practice from that of politics. In his later work, however, when he became more directly political in the context of what he saw as the damaging consequences of the dominance of neo-liberal approaches and a performative representation of globalisation, Bourdieu reflected on the role of the intellectual in the public sphere. His posthumously published *Political interventions: Social science and political action* (Bourdieu 2008) contains many of Bourdieu's political interventions across his career. In his reflections on the social science/political interventions relationship, he went beyond Sartre's conception of the 'total intellectual' who had something to say on everything, beyond the 'organic intellectual' of Gramsci serving the political interests of a class or other grouping, beyond the 'specific intellectual' of Foucault, where there were more micro-political engagements with social movements to what he referred to as a 'collective intellectual'. The use of 'collective' here was a way of recognising the collective aspects of the development of theory and the conduct of research, as with the way habitus attempted to capture the cultural, historical, structural embodied in the individual, so the collective intellectual recognised the impact and contribution of the academic field and colleagues to the production of knowledge. The idea of the 'collective intellectual' was also to grasp the need for an 'interdisciplinary and international' strategy in association with progressive social movements, particularly in the context of neo-liberal globalisation (Bourdieu 2004b, 387). In this context, Bourdieu argued the necessity of academics becoming collective intellectuals functioning *in* the field of politics, as well as in their academic fields. However, importantly, this did not mean they functioned *as* politicians. Here he was seeking to overcome a tension, a dichotomy between scholarship (and its logics of practice) and political commitment (and its logics of practice). He put it this way:

> The object was to overcome the opposition, particularly strong in English-speaking countries, between scholarship and commitment and restore with full force the French tradition of the intellectual, in other words the person who intervenes in the world of politics but without thereby becoming a politician, with the competence and authority associated with their membership of the world of science or literature, as well as in the name of the values inscribed in the exercise of their profession, as values of truth and disinterest.
>
> (Bourdieu 2008, 387)

So for Bourdieu, scholarship and commitment go together, but in terms of the researcher participating in political struggles, he argued, 'the most valuable contribution a researcher can make to the political struggles is to work, with all the weapons that science offers at the moment in question, to produce and promote the truth' (Bourdieu 2010, 271). Related, Bourdieu was also very critical of those academics who had become 'media stars' as a step in the dissemination of their work; these, he argued, most often had less academic capitals in the academic field than those academics who eschewed media participation; indeed, these media academics only had capitals in the journalist field and as such their 'science' was distorted through the logics of practice of the journalistic field, which emphasised 'structural amnesia' and the necessity for things to be ever new. Both these logics of practice sit in stark contrast to the disposition or habitus of the good social science researcher, who acknowledges their positioning in the academic field and the collective contributions to their research habitus. The mediatisation of academic work most often ensures the antithesis of what Bourdieu meant by the necessity of the political commitment of the scholar, researcher and intellectual. Such mediatisation has also distorted or shaped politics and education policy making, with policies now resorting to aphorism with greater emphasis on the discursive representation of policy than on its actual implementation into practice (Lingard and Rawolle 2004).

Conclusion

In this chapter, we have attempted to depict and characterise the central contributions of the work of Bourdieu, including outlining his generative thinking tools of practice and habitus, capitals and fields, as well as his work on education and reproduction, and his contribution more generally to considerations of methodology in the social sciences and the necessity of rejecting epistemological innocence and for being ever reflexive. In our own work we have found these thinking tools, his educational research and theorising, and his account of the features of the elements of a suitable researcher habitus to be very helpful. His insistence on the practicality of good research practice we have also found to be energising. Bourdieu assists us in managing the theoretical, political and methodological conundrums that confront those doing research in education framed as social science. His insistence on research and scholarship with commitment is attractive to us, as is his account of how researchers can be political without succumbing to the distorting logics of practice of the field of politics and the field of journalism. Drawing on Bourdieu, we also acknowledge here the ontological complicity between theory and the empirical, between structure and agency. It is the generative open-endedness of his work across those domains which we find most productive. His contributions to the social sciences generally and educational research more specifically must not function as straight-jackets, but rather be enabling, generative, productive and open to ongoing empirical challenges and to present and immanent social change. Herein lies the worth and contribution of Bourdieu's extensive *oeuvre*.

Notes

1 For good introductions to Bourdieu's life and contributions to the social sciences, see Lane (2000), Webb et al. (2002), Grenfell (2004; 2008a; 2008b) and Reed-Danahay (2005).
2 Bourdieu and colleagues directly include C. Wright Mills in an account of referent points for sociological work in Bourdieu, Chamberedon and Passeron's (1991) *The craft of sociology: Epistemological preliminaries* (Bourdieu et al. 1968/1991).

3 The collection *Political interventions social science and political action* (Bourdieu, 2008) provides specific instances of Bourdieu's direct interventions into education policy (see Parts 2 and 6).

4 This point mirrors a range of papers focussed on the international circulation of Bourdieu's ideas in sociological work, which consider both the global reception, as well as individual national case studies that illustrate the way that the global picture obscures the rather more difficult path of Bourdieuian ideas within specific national sociological traditions. See Santoro (2009) for an overview of these contributions.

5 These examples are used for illustrative purposes to highlight how movement of ideas was congruent with movement and location of scholars.

6 For overviews of these debates, see Teese (1982), and see Kenway (1983) for an overarching critique.

7 In a sense, Bourdieu saw pre-conceived concepts taken directly from the social world without careful examination as a 'epistemological obstacle' to social science, in that their social history and strategic use, signifying social position within specific fields, tended to be obscured (e.g. the use of the words 'choice', or 'quality' in education). The idea of an epistemological obstacle can be traced to Gaston Bachelard, a French philosopher of science.

8 Elsewhere, we have borrowed from Warde's work to argue that 'when Bourdieu talks of practice, he indicates three interconnected associations (Rawolle and Lingard 2008, 730):

   '• practice is the carrying out of an activity, for example, running a policy review …
   • practice is the nominalisation of a process, or the formal naming of an activity that gives it social organisation, points of harmonisation and boundaries, such as the naming and instituting of specific policy reviews.
   • practice is differentiated from theories about practice, and is circumscribed by shorter cycles of time that give it structure, limits and meaning.'

   Rawolle (2010b) argues for the inclusion of a *fourth* association, in the products of practice such as policy texts. For a further exploration of Bourdieu's account of practice in education research, see the 2010 special issue of *Critical Studies in Education*: Vol. 51, issue 1, and Heimans (2011).

9 For Bourdieu 'Habitus provides the connection between agents and practices through "systems of dispositions", which are bodily incorporations of social history. Habitus provides predispositions towards and capacities for practice for agents, which are transposable to different contexts' (Bourdieu 1990, 116).

10 As Rawolle (2005, 708) argues:

   'Formally, Bourdieu (1993) suggested a number of properties … they:
   • are structured spaces of positions;
   • have general laws or logics that guide interactions and the stakes towards which practices are oriented;
   • contain social struggles for the stakes and the forms of capital valued and conversion rates between different forms of capital;
   • require a socialized body endowed with a habitus … that orients the dispositions of agents to the stakes, and so to the continuation of that social field;
   • are structured by a state of power relations at a given point in time;
   • produce distinctive patterns of strategies adopted by different agents relative to their own position and trajectory; (and)
   • function analogous to a game.'

11 For clear definitions of each of these forms of capital, see Bourdieu (1986).

12 Others, of course, have written about similar concepts. For example, in *Orientalism*, Said (2003, 20) speaks of '*strategic location*', which encapsulates the author's positioning in a text and of '*strategic formation*' to refer to the relationship between a particular text and others in the field. Said also spoke of the need to 'world' texts, i. e. to understand texts in context(s).

References

Bates, R. 1980. Educational administration, the sociology of science, and the management of knowledge, *Educational Administration Quarterly* 16, 2: 1–20.

Bourdieu, P. 1958/1962. *The Algerians*. Boston, MA: Beacon Press.

Bourdicu, P. 1977. *Outline of a theory of practice*. Cambridge: Cambridge University Press.

Bourdieu, P. 1980. Language and pedagogical situation. Trans. Richard Teese. In *Melbourne Working Papers 1980*. eds. David McCallum and Uldis Ozolins, S. 36–77. Melbourne: University of Melbourne.

Bourdieu, P. 1984. *Distinction*. Cambridge, MA: Harvard University Press.

Bourdieu, P. 1986. The forms of capital. In *Handbook of theory and research for the sociology of education*. ed. J. Richardson, 241–258. Westport, CT: Greenwood.

Bourdieu, P. 1989/1996. *The state nobility: Elite schools in the field of power*. Cambridge: Polity Press.

Bourdieu, P. 1990a. *In other words. Essays towards a reflexive sociology*. Stanford, CA: Stanford University Press and Cambridge: Polity Press.

Bourdieu, P. 1990b. *The logic of practice*. Stanford, CA: Stanford University Press.

Bourdieu, P. 1992. *An invitation to reflexive sociology*. With Loic J.D. Wacquant. Cambridge: Polity Press.

Bourdieu, P. 1993. *Sociology in question*. London: Sage.

Bourdieu, P. 1998. *On television and journalism*. London: Pluto Press.

Bourdieu, P. 1999. Understanding. In The weight of the world: Social suffering in contemporary society. eds. P. Bourdieu, A. Accardo, G. Balazs, S. Beaud, F. Bonvin, L. Bourdieu, P. Borgois, S. Broccolichi, P. Champagne, R. Christin, J.-P. Faguer, S. Garcia, R. Lenoir, F. Oevrard, M. Pialoux, L. Pinto, D. Podalydes, A. Sayad, C. Soulie and L.J.D. Wacquant, 607–626. Cambridge: Polity Press.

Bourdieu, P. 2001. *Masculine domination*. Cambridge: Polity Press.

Bourdieu, P. 2003. *Firing back: Against the tyranny of the market*. London: Verso.

Bourdieu, P. 2004a. From the King's house to the reason of state: A model of the genesis of the bureaucratic field. *Constellations* 11: 16–36.

Bourdieu, P. 2004b. *Science of science and reflexivity*. Chicago, IL: University of Chicago Press.

Bourdieu, P. 2004c. *Sketch for self-analysis*. Cambridge: Polity Press.

Bourdieu, P. 2005a. The political field, the social science field, and the journalistic field. In *Bourdieu and the journalistic field*. eds. R. Benson and E. Neveu, 29–47. Cambridge, UK and Malden, MA: Polity Press.

Bourdieu, P. 2005b. *The social structures of the economy*. Cambridge: Polity Press.

Bourdieu, P. 2008. *Political interventions: Social science and political action*, Cambridge: Polity Press.

Bourdieu, P. 2010. A sociologist in the world. In *Sociology is a martial art: Political writings by Pierre Bourdieu*. ed. G. Sapiro, 261–278. New York, NY: The New Press.

Bourdieu, P. 2015. *On the state: Lectures at the College de France, 1989–1992*. London: Wiley.

Bourdieu, P. 2020. *Habitus and field, General sociology, Volume 2 (1982–1983)*. London: Wiley.

Bourdieu, P., A. Accardo, G. Balazs, S. Beaud, F. Bonvin, L. Bourdieu, P. Borgois, S. Broccolichi, P. Champagne, R. Christin, J.-P. Faguer, S. Garcia, R. Lenoir, F. Oevrard, M. Pialoux, L. Pinto, D. Podalydes, A. Sayad, C. Soulie and L.J.D. Wacquant. 1999. *The weight of the world: Social suffering in contemporary society*. Cambridge: Polity Press.

Bourdieu, P., J.-C. Chamberedon and J.-C. Passeron. 1968/1991. *The craft of sociology: Epistemological preliminaries*. Berlin: Walter DeGruyter & Co.

Bourdieu, P. and J.C. Passeron. 1964/1979. *The inheritors: French students and their relations to culture*. Chicago, IL: University of Chicago Press.

Bourdieu, P. and J.C. Passeron. 1970/1977. *Reproduction in education, society and culture*. London: Sage.

Bourdieu, P. and L. Wacquant. 1992. *An introduction to reflexive sociology*. Chicago, IL: University of Chicago Press.

Bowles, S. and H. Gintis. 1976. *Schooling in capitalist America*. New York, NY: Routledge.

Brubacker, R. 1993. Social theory as habitus. In *Bourdieu: Critical perspectives*. eds. C. Calhoun, E. LiPuma and M. Postone, 212–234. Cambridge: Polity Press.

Connell, R.W. 1983. *Which way is up? Essays on class, sex and culture*. Sydney: Allen & Unwin.

Connell, R.W., D.J. Ashenden, S. Kessler and G.W. Dowsett. 1982. *Making the difference: Schools, families and social divisions*. Sydney: Allen & Unwin.

Couldry, N. 2003a. Media meta-capital: Extending the range of Bourdieu's field theory. *Theory and Society* 32: 653–677.

Couldry, N. 2003b. Media, symbolic power and the limits of Bourdieu's field theory. MEDIA@ LSE Electronic Working Papers. London: LSE.

Gale, T. and B. Lingard. 2015. Evoking and provoking Bourdieu in educational research. *Cambridge Journal of Education* 45, 1: 1–8.

Giddens, A. 1987. *Social theory and modern sociology*. Stanford, CA: Stanford University Press.

Grenfell, M. 2004. *Pierre Bourdieu: Agent provocateur*. London: Continuum.

Grenfell, M. ed. 2008a. *Bourdieu: Key concepts*. Stocksfield: Acumen.

Grenfell, M. 2008b. Postscript: methodological principles. In *Bourdieu: Key concepts*. ed. M. Grenfell, 219–227. Stocksfield: Acumen.

Heimans, S. 2011. Coming to matter in practice: enacting education policy. *Discourse: Studies in the Cultural Politics of Education* 33, 2: 313–326.

Hilgers, M. and E. Mangez. eds. 2015. *Bourdieu's theory of social fields: Concepts and applications*. London: Routledge.

Jenkins, R. 2002. *Pierre Bourdieu*. 2nd edn. London: Routledge.

Kauppi, N. 2002. Elements for a structural constructivist theory of politics and of European integration. Centre for European Studies Working Paper Series #104. Harvard, MA: Minda de Gunzburg Center for European Studies, Harvard University.

Kenway, J. 1983. Marking a difference to whom and to what? *Australian Journal of Cultural Studies* 1, 2: 212–221.

Lane, J. 2000. *Pierre Bourdieu: A critical introduction*. London: Pluto Press.

Lewin, K. 1939. Field theory and experiment in social psychology: concepts and methods. *The American Journal of Sociology* 44: 868–896.

Lingard, B. ed. 2021. *Globalisation and education*. London: Routledge.

Lingard, B. and S. Rawolle. 2004. Mediatizing educational policy: The journalistic field, science policy, and cross-field effects. *Journal of Education Policy* 19, 3: 361–380.

Lingard, B. and S. Rawolle. 2010. Globalization and the rescaling of education politics and policy: implications for comparative education. In *New thinking in comparative education: Honouring R. Cowen*. ed. Marianne A. Larsen, 33–52. Rotterdam: Sense Publishers.

Lingard, B. and S. Rawolle. 2011. New scalar politics: Implications for education policy. *Comparative Education* 47, 4: 489–502.

Lingard, B., S. Rawolle and S. Taylor. 2005. Globalizing policy sociology in education: Working with Bourdieu. *Journal of Education Policy* 20, 6: 759–777.

Lingard, B., S. Sellar and A. Baroutsis. 2015. Researching the habitus of global policy actors. *Cambridge Journal of Education* 45, 1: 25–42.

Marginson, S. 2010. Global field and global imagining: Bourdieu and worldwide higher education. *British Journal of Sociology of Education* 29, 3: 303–315.

Martin, J.L. 2003. What is field theory? *American Journal of Sociology* 109: 1–49.

Maton, K. 2005. A question of autonomy: Bourdieu's field approach and higher education policy. *Journal of Education Policy* 20: 687–704.

Mu, M., K. Dooley and A. Luke. eds. 2019. *Bourdieu and Chinese education: Inequality, competition, and change.* London: Routledge.

Rawolle, S. 2005. Cross-field effects and temporary social fields: A case study of the mediatization of recent Australian knowledge economy policies. *Journal of Education Policy* 20, 6: 705–724.

Rawolle, S. 2008. When the knowledge economy became the chance to change: Mediatization, cross-field effects and temporary social fields. Unpublished PhD thesis. University of Queensland, Australia.

Rawolle, S. 2010a. Practice chains of production and consumption: Mediatized practices across social fields. *Discourse: Studies in the Cultural Politics of Education* 31, 1: 121–135.

Rawolle, S. 2010b. Understanding the mediatisation of educational policy as practice, *Critical Studies in Education* 51, 1: 21–39.

Rawolle, S. and B. Lingard. 2008. The sociology of Pierre Bourdieu and researching education policy. *Journal of Education Policy* 23, 6: 729–741.

Reed-Danahay, D. 2005. *Locating Bourdieu.* Bloomington, IN: Indiana University Press.

Rizvi, F. and B. Lingard. 2010. *Globalizing education policy.* London: Routledge.

Robbins, D. 2004. The transcultural transferability of Bourdieu's sociology of education. *British Journal of Sociology of Education* 25, 4: 415–430.

Said, E. 2003. *Orientalism.* London: Penguin.

Santoro, M. 2009. Putting Bourdieu in the global field: Introduction to the symposium. *Sociologica* 2: 1–31.

Teese, R. 1982. Review of *Making the Difference. Thesis Eleven* 5–6, 1: 328–331.

Wacquant, L. 1989. Towards a reflexive sociology: A workshop with Pierre Bourdieu. *Sociological Theory* 7, 1: 26–63.

Wacquant, L. 1992. Toward a social praxeology: The structure and logic of Bourdieu's sociology. In P. Bourdieu and L. Wacquant, *An invitation of reflexive sociology,* 1–60. Chicago, IL: University of Chicago Press.

Wacquant, L. 1993. Bourdieu in America: Notes on the Transatlantic importation of social theory. In *Bourdieu: Critical Perspectives.* eds. C. Calhoun, E. LiPuma and M. Postone, 235–262. Cambridge: Polity Press.

Webb, J., T. Schirato and G. Danaher. 2002. *Understanding Bourdieu.* London: Sage.

Woodward, I. and M. Emmison. 2009. The intellectual reception of Bourdieu in Australian social science and humanities. *Sociologica* 2–3: 1–121.

Young, M.F.D. ed. 1971. *Knowledge and control: New directions for the sociology of education.* London: Collier Macmillan.

10 Research in Christian Academies

Perspectives from Bourdieu

Elizabeth Green

Introduction

I first encountered Bourdieu on an MA Education degree course. When I enrolled for the degree I was a secondary school teacher in England and my intention was to get an edge in the promotions game and not to get hooked on research, although that is ultimately what happened. Unwittingly in that decision I was enacting one of Bourdieu's critical concepts: Cultural capital. Education conferred on me a distinction or a material advantage; the MA opened the door to a PhD and the rest as they say 'is history'. In fact, Bourdieu (1986) would say that the whole of the social world is 'accumulated history' (ibid, 46). This means that there is no way out of the cultural assumptions and habits which we have inherited and which we will reproduce in the ways we interact with society. This chapter will argue that Bourdieu's theory of education, reproduction and distinction is a powerful tool for the analysis of education, particularly in faith-based settings, which is the context in which I work.

Bourdieu's writings are complex; first encounters with his work are stretching and sometimes off-putting for new researchers. The first thing by Bourdieu which I read was *The forms of capital* reprinted in A.H. Halsey et al.'s (2001) edited collection called *Education: Culture, economy and society*. I was drawn to Bourdieu's analysis of the social world and won over by his determination not to reduce it to a series of mechanical interactions between people, groups and social structures.

> The social world is accumulated history, and if it is not to be reduced to a discontinued series of instantaneous mechanical equilibria between agents, who are treated as interchangeable particles, one must reintroduce into it the notion of capital and with it, accumulation and all its effects.
>
> (Bourdieu 1986, 46)

This quotation illustrates why it is sometimes necessary to persevere with Bourdieu. I did not on first reading understand everything in *The forms of capital*, but I got a sense of the scale of Bourdieu's contribution to the theory and practice of sociology and of his commitment to critical and systematic empirical

DOI: 10.4324/9781003156550-14

research. The second section of this chapter will explore the nature of that contribution in the context of Bourdieu's own history by introducing him as an academic and sketching in the trajectory of his research. I will introduce four key concepts which underpin Bourdieu's work: Field, habitus, symbolic violence and cultural capital. Bourdieu remains a controversial figure and the section will conclude with a brief summary of some of the main criticisms of his theoretical work.

In order to get a handle on Bourdieu I find it helpful to read empirical research which applies his concepts to education. My MA introduced me to the work of Grace (1978; 2002), who applies Bourdieu's concepts to urban education and to Catholic education. I read avidly the work of Ball (2003) and Reay (1998), who draw on Bourdieu to analyse education reform and school choice in relation to class and to gender. This experience has led me to conclude that one of the most effective ways to introduce Bourdieu's theory and method to a new audience is through a case-study of research. In UK sociology of education research Bourdieu has chiefly been applied to the study of social class. My work broadens this to study the impact of religious faith in education. In the third section of this chapter I present a case study from my own research carried out in English Academies sponsored by a Christian foundation. In the fourth section I illustrate how I've built on Bourdieu's theory by integrating concepts from other thinkers into my research designs. This will illustrate what Bourdieu's work offers to education researchers. The chapter will conclude that the loose definitions, the evolution of concepts and their application make Bourdieu's social theory a very adaptable tool for analysing contemporary religious culture and the impact of faith-based education.

Bourdieu and his concepts

In *Sketch for a self analysis*, Bourdieu (2007) wrote that 'to understand is first to understand the field with which and against which one has been formed' (ibid, 4). The aim of this section is to introduce some of the primary concepts in Bourdieu's work set against the backdrop of Bourdieu's own formative experiences and early career history. *Sketch for a self analysis* was born out of the final lecture which Bourdieu gave at the Collège de France. Bourdieu was adamant that the text was not an auto-biography but rather an attempt to analyse himself 'from the point of view of sociology' (Bourdieu 2007, 1). By analysing himself as the sociological object Bourdieu was putting into practice what is, arguably, one of his most important legacies for research: The exercise of reflexivity.

Throughout his work Bourdieu consistently challenged the assumption that the production of academic knowledge was a neutral activity. Bourdieu insisted that the researcher needed to submit themselves to the same rigorous critique that they would apply to the object of their research. This would include reflecting on things like their own history and academic formation and requires a kind of 'double-distancing' which Bourdieu termed 'objectification of objectification' (Jenkins 2002, xvi). Objectification of objectification requires two steps. Most of us will be familiar with the first step and it represents stepping back or distancing ourselves from the object of our research. For example, when researching classroom interaction many researchers would initially assume a position of distance so that they can observe and analyse the interaction. Bourdieu calls that 'objectifying' and advocates that the researcher needs to go further than this and reflect on the nature of the distance they have created. The second step is to put under the same reflective microscope the relationship that the researcher has to the researched when they are carrying out fieldwork. In the case of our example this would mean 'objectifying' the relationship that the researcher has to the class and to the classroom interaction. Bourdieu was an active empirical researcher himself, he essentially provides the researcher with a toolkit of concepts to support their reflexive analysis of the social world. These concepts are both theoretical and analytical but they are also allied closely to the practice of research, in other words they are also methodological. My argument is that these concepts are highly practical and of direct relevance to the daily practice of fieldwork; thus it is worth persisting through Bourdieu's dense and at times verbose articulation of how they work. I am going to use the history of Bourdieu's own academic formation to introduce the following key concepts: Habitus, field, symbolic violence and cultural capital.

Bourdieu was born in 1930; he grew up in Béarn, a rural village in South-Eastern France. His grandfather had been a peasant sharecropper, but his mother came from a wealthier peasant family and his father was a minor civil servant. Bourdieu describes himself as separated from his classmates at primary school because of his father's white collar education and separated from his peers at the boarding school he subsequently attended because of his rural accent and provincial ways. One of the things that characterises Bourdieu's early education is a feeling of not belonging and an awareness that his relationship with his peer group didn't match the lofty ideals proclaimed in the rhetoric of the classroom. He described this acute awareness of social difference as 'a terrible education in social realism' (Bourdieu, 2007, 91). When Bourdieu died in 2002 he held the high honour of a Chair at the Collège de France and was a famous public intellectual. There may well be an element of mythologising in the story of the peasant boy made good but as Bourdieu reflects on his early experiences in *Sketch for self analysis*, he illustrates how attitudes, assumptions and dispositions are unconsciously formed; in this he is offering an explanation of what habitus is and how it can be applied in research.

The concept of habitus dates back to the time of Aristotle, it was a moral concept associated with virtue ethics. This is the belief that good or virtuous dispositions can be acquired which will form moral character and regulate our actions through good practice or 'habit'. Bourdieu uses habitus to refer to the deeply rooted assumptions, not explicitly reflected upon but held almost subconsciously, which we all inherit. These assumptions regulate both individual and collective action in the social world. Bourdieu (2007) wrote that his history and cultural formation in Béarn shaped his habitus giving him 'a marked taste for disputation' (ibid, 89). Robbins (2000) writes that Bourdieu first applied the concept in relation to dancing when in 1962 he published an account of peasant life in Béarn. Bourdieu described the country dances held in the village as being 'occasions of a clash of civilisation' between rural and urban habitus (Robbins 2000, 28). Bourdieu was also trying to get away from the separation of mind and body, or of theory and practice, in his understanding of the social world. For Bourdieu habitus isn't something which happens just in the mind but is physical, for example in the dancing; it isn't something which people consciously reflect on but nor is it simply mechanical, nor was Bourdieu saying that habitus is identical for all people. Bourdieu took seriously the fact that society is comprised of people, classes and groups who occupy positions relative to each other and to society as a whole. This way of conceptualising society is called structuralism. Structuralism was very popular when Bourdieu took up his academic posts in the late 1950s. After Bourdieu had graduated and taught for a year in a provincial school he was conscripted into the army and served two years in Algeria (1956–1958). His fieldwork during the time of revolution and agricultural crisis in Algeria was to prove formative. He produced a structuralist analysis of the culture of the Kabyle, the largest cultural and linguistic community in Algeria (Bourdieu 1979). Bourdieu's study of this group led him to reject one of structuralism's key assumptions which is that different societies adopt intrinsically different functions, this is referred to as functionalism. Bourdieu found that *within* the Kabyle people constructed differences and took up different positions and roles regulated by the habitus. Later in his work he accounted for the nature and impact of position taking using the concepts of symbolic violence and cultural capital. We will consider these concepts after first picking up the thread of Bourdieu's history in order to get a handle on his concept of field.

In 1960, Bourdieu returned to France to take up a position as assistant at the Faculty of Arts at the University of Paris. The dominant intellectual discipline of the Université de Paris had been philosophy. Bourdieu was well acquainted with the legacy of Jean-Paul Sartre whose existentialism he rejected. Jenkins (2002) writes that Bourdieu believed there was more to the social life 'than the subjective consciousness' of the individuals 'who move within it and produce it' (ibid, 17). Bourdieu argued that there was a real or objective social world beyond the interaction and self-awareness of individuals. Field is a concept used to define the dimensions of this social space. So for example when Bourdieu joined the Faculty of Arts the field of philosophy was being threatened by the rise in popularity of the field of social sciences. This also helps to illustrates Bourdieu's argument that habitus can only operate 'in relation to the social field' (Jenkins 2002, 82). Bourdieu believed that different groups compete for recognition or cultural validation within a social field and thus it is always an arena of struggle and competition. Bourdieu experienced this struggle first hand. In 1968, the same year in which he became the Director of the Centre de Sociologie Européenne, there were violent student protests in Paris. Bourdieu (2007) interpreted the student movement as a reaction to the threat that the rise of the social sciences represented to the traditional dominance of philosophy. The late 1960s marked the beginning of a prolific period of research and publications, Bourdieu turned education itself into the object of his sociological analysis. By investigating the habitus of students (see Bourdieu and Passeron 1979, *The inheritors*) and exploring where power lay within the structure of the university field, he called into question its apparent meritocratic values and the dominance of particular disciplines. Bourdieu concluded that education is one of the key ways in which social reproduction takes place.

It is primarily within the field of education that Bourdieu developed his theory of social reproduction. The key text which sets out this theory is *Reproduction in education, society and culture* (Bourdieu and Passerson 1970/1977) first published by Bourdieu and Passeron in 1970. *Reproduction*, as I'll refer to it for short, is probably one of the best known and well used of Bourdieu's texts in sociology of education. Its arguments underpin the work done on school choice, class and gender that I mentioned in the introduction to this chapter. Unfortunately, it is also one of the least accessible texts in terms of language and construction partly because Bourdieu presents his theory as a series of propositions and glosses. This is a stylistic device in which a proposition is a statement proposing a definition or thesis and a gloss provides further explanation or description for clarity. A central concept in *Reproduction* is symbolic violence. This refers to the way in which culture is imposed upon people or groups, this is experienced by society as legitimate, but Bourdieu argued that it conceals the power relationships which make it possible.

> O. Every power to exert symbolic violence, i.e. every power which manages to impose meanings and to impose them as legitimate by concealing the power relations which are the basis of its force, adds its own specifically symbolic force to those power relations.
>
> (ibid, 4)

Symbolic violence is often exercised via social structures such as education or religion. The concept of symbolic violence can be used to track the exercise of power and explore how particular cultural practices, for example passing an examination or submitting a thesis, are recognised and legitimated to validate and preserve control in the social field. As a form of protest, Bourdieu refused to submit a thesis when he graduated from the École normale supérieure in Paris. If you share the habitus of the dominant cultural elite; so in Bourdieu's context if you are a philosopher and a sophisticated Parisian intellectual, you will inherit and reproduce a set of cultural assumptions and expectations which will preserve the existing social order and the dominance of Parisian intellectuals. Similarly, if you are a rural peasant from Béarn, your cultural assumptions and expectations stem from a cultural habitus, one which is not recognised in the elite French university, but which reproduces the cultural practices of rural life in South-East France. While one or two bright exceptions might become French public intellectuals, the exercise of symbolic violence means that one cannot do so without participating and, therefore, reproducing the cultural practices of the dominant social group. There are clearly some problems with this theory, not least the very real criticism to which Bourdieu's work is often subjected that this is a deterministic view of culture which does not take into account individual action or agency. Criticisms of Bourdieu's concepts will be discussed at the end of this section; there is one more key concept to explore first, that of cultural capital.

Bourdieu posited his concept of cultural capital directly against the philosopher Kant's notion that the pursuit of the aesthetic is pure and somehow morally neutral, or at least disinterested (Jenkins 2002). The title of Bourdieu's (1984) publication *Distinction: A social critique of the judgement of taste* is a direct reference to Kant, who published *The critique of judgement* in 1790 (Kant 1790/ 2007). Bourdieu (1984) challenged the notion that 'culture' had an intrinsic value and that the appreciation and the quest for culture was thus untainted by such base extrinsic rewards as economic value. With the concept of cultural capital Bourdieu extended the meaning of 'capital' beyond its typical use in economic exchange theory where it primarily denotes monetary profit (Moore 2004). Bourdieu argued that the acquisition of cultural capital primarily through the social institution of education can confer distinction upon an individual and therefore material advantage (Bourdieu and Passeron 1977, proposition 3.1.3., 35). In his introduction to the first edition of *Distinction*, Bourdieu (1984) writes that sociology endeavours to understand how culture and cultural tastes are produced. He argues, however, that cultural practices such as the appreciation of fine art or music, can't be fully understood unless they are situated back into the wider context of social relationships, particularly class, and then analysed. Jenkins (2002) writes that Bourdieu is applying reflexivity here; the double distancing or 'objectification of objectification' which insists that we reflect both on culture as a product and on our definition of culture as a process. Bourdieu is reminding us to ask this question: what has produced the classifications which we use to define art or music etc. as 'culture'? He argues strongly in *Distinction* that all cultural practices are linked to educational level and social origin, in other words cultural taste functions as 'a marker of class' (Bourdieu 1984, xxv).

There are a series of critiques of Bourdieu's work not least of which is that he fell short of the overarching grand sociological theory he sought to produce. As a public intellectual in his later career, Bourdieu extended his 'objectification of objectification' to comment on French politics, society and culture. His critics point out that he never really dealt with the question of what makes the sociological perspective authoritative in its account of the social world, as opposed to the philosophical and structuralist perspectives which Bourdieu sought to refute. Indeed, Bourdieu's theory remained heavily influenced by structuralism as he sought a more 'scientific' account of socialisation and social reproduction. This leads us to perhaps the major criticism of Bourdieu's work, which is that his theory is essentially deterministic. Critics argue that Bourdieu's assertion that there is 'no way out of the game of culture' suggests 'a self perpetuating and mechanical model of society' (Jenkins 2002, 118). Bourdieu pays little attention to the capacity of individuals to act in the world; this is referred to in philosophy and sociology as agency. Connell (1983) argues that Bourdieu does not really explain what habitus is or how it interacts with agency and that he is vague about how institutions work. He also argues that Bourdieu's theory doesn't account for the way institutions and social systems change, especially over a period of time. Despite these significant flaws, many of Bourdieu's critics do accept that his theoretical work has made a significant contribution to our understanding of the social world and has equipped research with 'a way of talking about what living in the world is really like' (Connell 1983, 153).

Applying Bourdieu's concepts to research

In this section of the chapter I intend to illustrate how I applied Bourdieu's concepts of field, habitus, symbolic violence and cultural capital to my own research in an Academy sponsored by a Christian foundation. As I indicated in my introduction, one of the ways to get a handle on Bourdieu's social theory is to see it applied in practice. I begin by setting the scene and contextualising the 'field' of Academies as well as explaining how central the interaction between theory and methodology was for my research design. I take Bourdieu's concepts in turn, demonstrating how they were applied and giving examples of what kinds of things they revealed in my data. I have found that Bourdieu's concepts provide a helpful framework in which to analyse the impact of religion on school culture. This is important because, as Grace (2004) has argued, religion, as opposed to class, race and gender, is often left out when researchers in the West analyse education.

The Academies policy

To set the scene it is important to outline the history of the policy before I explain why I conceptualised Academies as a field within my own research. Academies are 'publicly-funded independent schools' freed up from local education authority control (DfE 2012). Under successive governments their number has increased dramatically; at the time of writing, Academies and their newer counter-part Free Schools make up 32 per cent of primary schools and 75 per cent of secondary schools in England accounting for an enrolment of over 4.1. million pupils (DfE 2019).

Academies were originally a central part of the New Labour Government's education policy. The initiative extended a Conservative government policy of the 1980s which had established City Technology Colleges (CTC) in areas of urban deprivation. My research was carried out in a CTC and two Academies sponsored by a Christian Foundation that has been a provider throughout all the various iterations of the policy. CTCs, Academies and Free Schools have greater freedom to set their own curriculum, pay and conditions because they are free from local education authority control. Under New Labour the Academies had to have a sponsor, these were drawn from business, private philanthropists, Christian churches and Christian charitable foundations. About a quarter of the first wave of Academies had a Christian sponsor (these are referred to as 'sponsored Academies'). The Academies Act 2010, passed by the Liberal Conservative Coalition Government actively encouraged schools previously maintained by local authorities to convert to Academy status (these are referred to as 'converter Academies'). In 2016, the Conservative Government declared its intent to ensure all state-funded government schools converted to Academy status by 2022 (DfE 2016a). The creation of Multi Academy Trusts (MATs) have become the preferred model of governance and a key factor in accelerating the growth of Academies (DfE 2016b). MATs contract separately with the Secretary of State for Education to run groups of Academies, and in 2019 there were 1,170 MATs in England managing at least two Academies. The Church of England is the biggest sponsor of Academies in England with 250 sponsored Academies and over 650 convertor Academies (The Church of England 2020). This means, in effect, that all iterations of the Academy policy have supported the influence of Christian faith in the provision of publicly funded education in England.

Research design

The overall aim of my research was to undertake an ethnographic study. In contradiction to the way research methods are often taught, I did not identify a site, create research questions and subsequently choose a methodology that would best answer them. The ethnographic nature of the study was a central part of the theoretical rationale for the entire project. In this section, I define ethnography and explain why Bourdieu's theoretical concepts can be deployed as methodological tools within it. I provide examples of the interaction between theory and methodology in my research design before taking each of Bourdieu's concepts in turn and illustrating how they were deployed in the research.

Bourdieu argued that most research accounts are remote; separate to what is really going on in the social world. He therefore saw his familiarity with the rural settings in which he carried out his early work as an aid to reflexivity because he was not positioned entirely outside the field. I, too, am familiar with my research setting. Although I had no prior association with the CTC or Academies where I did my fieldwork, I attended an independent Christian school up until the age of 16 and I taught history in Church of England and Roman Catholic secondary schools before commencing my research. As with Bourdieu's early fieldwork, my study was an ethnography. I came to this research topic as a person of religious faith and a teacher with practical experience of teaching in faith schools. In other words, I was a partial insider of the faith school culture I wanted to investigate.

I was aware that separating theory from method is artificial; so, too, is failing to take account of the philosophical assumptions that interact with research design. Ethnography is a research method closely associated with anthropology. It is essentially a study of culture in which the researcher is a participant in the social world asking questions with a view to explaining it to the outsider and clarifying it for the insider (Green 2009a). Bourdieu was an ethnographer, his account of the interaction between structure, practice and agency is designed to be applied to the social world. His key concepts of field, habitus, symbolic violence and cultural capital are as much methodological tools as they are analytic and theoretical.

Framing analytical questions is a key technique in my research methodology and analysis. I have modelled this approach on Grace's (2002) work in Catholic education. Grace conceptualised Catholic education as a field and framed a set of questions using Bourdieu's concepts to trace the nature and impact of power and cultural assumptions in the field; this is a form of reflexivity. The practice of research always starts with a question and mine was: How does the Christian ethos of the sponsor show itself in the social and academic experiences of the students and staff? Following Grace (2002), I developed a whole suite of questions built around Bourdieu's key concepts of field, habitus, symbolic violence and cultural capital, these are explored below. Arriving at these questions didn't follow a nice neat sequential pattern. Nor did the questions remain 'formal research questions' to be investigated as per an experimental research design. Some questions became observation or interview prompts when I was collecting data. Other questions became categories and codes in my processes of data analysis and some were the subject of personal reflections. I wrote reflective memos alongside my field notes to keep track of my mood and motivation throughout the research. I found that new questions arose from data collection, analysis and/or reflection. In some cases, questions which had seemed important at the start of my research became less of a priority or got dropped all together. Research in the real world is messy and I found that I needed to take account of this in my research design.

I attempted to build the kind of 'objectification of objectification' that Bourdieu described into my research design by dividing my field work into three- and four-week blocks. In total, I spent six months at my research site. When I was at the school I carried out ethnographic observations of formal and informal settings, conducting a series of in-depth interviews with a purposive sample of 18 members of staff in key roles and 30 year ten (15 and 16 years old) students and doing documentary analysis. I was typically on site five days a week from eight am to five pm and I also attended after school events and meetings during the evenings and weekends. The pattern of blocking time this way turned out to be very significant for my use of theory in the research design. During the blocks when I was away from the site, I revisited my analytical questions and invited others to explore them with me. Critical friends challenged me to expand and develop my use of Bourdieu's concepts. My early field notes and descriptive accounts held rather slavishly to the definitions of Bourdieu's concepts I had found in the literature. This produced a very clinical rendering of the culture I was analysing. You could argue that my early research was falling prey to the same determinism of which Bourdieu is accused. Data that didn't fit my *a priori* theoretical categories was in danger of going unexplained or omitted completely. I revised my approach and made space for noticing empirical questions. In this regard the practice of the objectification of objectification served my research design well.

Field

In my research I conceptualise the Academies sector as a field. Bourdieu's use of field denotes a site of competing interests where there is struggle for recognition. I applied the concept to Academies for two main reasons. First, at policy level the creation and expansion of the Academies has generated fierce debate. The existence of Academies outside local authority provision initiates a set of questions about equity, funding and competition in relation to existing state provision in common schools (for a more in-depth discussion of this, see Gorard 2005; 2014). The sponsorship of Academies by businesses, philanthropists and religious organisations sets up a second set of questions about the ideologies and/or religious beliefs gaining influence within the education system as a whole (for a more in-depth discussion of this, see Ball 2007; Ball and Junemann 2011). I applied the concept of field in my research as a way to keep me mindful of the wider context in which Academies are located. Reflecting back on this enabled me to relate my data to the ongoing emergence of Academies as the new 'norm' in institutional provision. When I began my fieldwork in 2007, Academies were still fairly new, now they are ubiquitous. Bourdieu's concept of field helps researchers to reflect on the nature of the model for education that became dominant in the social world. Bourdieu prompts us to ask what kind of knowledge is valued in the field, what groups hold power in the system and what do they assume education is for? This leads to the second reason I applied the concept of field in my research. I wanted to focus in particular on the impact of a Christian sponsor competing for recognition in the field. The types of analytical questions I reflected on included: Was the sponsor a powerful influence, what kind of knowledge did they value and what did they believe about the purpose of education?

Habitus

The CTC and Academies in which I carried out my research were non-denominational and it was not necessary to be a Christian either to work there or attend as a student. Unlike many church-sponsored Academies, no places were reserved for the children of Christian families. Nevertheless, I did find that the sponsors and the senior staff shared a set of religious beliefs and assumptions which I conceptualised in my research as a habitus. A key finding of the research was that the habitus was embedded in institutional structures such as the order of the school day, assemblies and tutor times. I concluded that the habitus did regulate certain aspects of cultural practice. The sponsors and members of the senior team attended the same local churches and often met to pray and study the Bible together during their leisure time. The exceptions to this were three members of senior staff at the Academies recruited from predecessor schools who did not identify as Christians. In theological terms the shared religious beliefs are best described as reformed or conservative Protestant Christian. Evidence from interviews with the sponsors and senior staff, analysis of policy documents and observation of meetings and assemblies conducted by senior staff demonstrated a highly unified and regulated Christian discourse (Green 2012). My research found that this was characterised by a high view of the authority of the Bible, a belief in the physical death and resurrection of Jesus, personal conversion, an emphasis on personal morality and an imperative to teach and proclaim the 'gospel' or good news about Jesus in the world (Green 2012).

Habitus was a central tool in my analysis because it enabled me to explore the extent to which the sponsor and senior team's habitus influenced practice in the Academy even though Christian beliefs were not universally shared by the rest of the staff and students. In his essay 'Genesis and structure of the religious field', Bourdieu (1971) conceptualised religion as a field within the social world; he argued that religious habitus imposes particular practices and meanings which regulate the structures of society. He had observed this in his earlier fieldwork and he wrote about the significance of Islam for Algerian culture and of Puritanism for European culture in his first book *Sociologie de l'Algérie* (Bourdieu 1958). The problem with Bourdieu's account of religious habitus is that he seems unwilling to allow that it might contribute anything good and he doesn't really acknowledge that spiritual and/or mystical encounters are widespread in human experience (Rey 2007). This is another example of Bourdieu's tendency towards determinism. Cannell (2006) has argued that religion should be taken seriously as a cultural fact; she believes that it is often marginalised in ethnographic accounts as if the religious experience of others can always be explained away by other structures such as politics or the economy. Bourdieu did, however, criticise religious scholars for not paying enough attention to the ways in which religious assumptions and practice are physically embodied in the social world (Rey 2007). I believe this is why sociologists and students of religion persist in using his concepts. They offer a set of tools which are flexible enough to probe the complex relationship between institutional structures, religious practices and individual agency. This is where legitimate questions about the nature and impact of religious faith and experiences are located. I wanted to take seriously the religious beliefs of my research participants; I also wanted to acknowledge that they were not held by everybody in the institution and to be realistic about where power and influence lay. To that end I will provide a brief example of one way in which the religious habitus impacted organisational structure, in this case the physical ordering of the school day (this is discussed in more depth elsewhere, see Green 2009b). This example will lead into a discussion of the concept of symbolic violence and its application in my research.

In the CTC and Academies, every day began with an act of collective worship, either in the form of an assembly or during tutor time, which was known as tutor prayers. Such occasions were deliberately formal. Quiet movement around the building, an emphasis on correct uniform and high standards of conduct and behaviour were all features for which the Foundation has received both praise and criticism (see Green 2009a). The CTC and Academies were deliberately modelled on a traditional educational pedagogy such as one might associate with post-war grammar school education in England. The approach is also driven by the habitus of the sponsors whose objective is to provide a 'Christian religious education with a daily Christian Assembly and the teaching of biblical values and morality' (Emmanuel Schools Foundation 2007). The sponsors fear that society is becoming increasingly more secularised and that as a consequence a sense of public morality and familiarity with the Bible's teaching may be lost. Students attended three assemblies a week and two tutor prayer sessions. I found that assemblies and tutor prayers were key motifs in school life for the religious habitus and its expression in corporate identity. Themes for assemblies and tutor prayers were all planned on a rolling cycle to provide students with an overview of the Bible's narrative. This would encompass what conservative Protestants regard as the key 'turning points' of the narrative, namely the stories of creation, fall, Old Testament history, the incarnation, death and resurrection of Jesus (Carson 2008, 44). There was less emphasis on teaching about corporate holiness or social justice as one might find within Catholic theology, for example. Worship was structured around the written word of the Bible rather than around meditation or reflection, which are practices one might associate with other Christian or alternate faith traditions. During assemblies and in tutor time students kept silent as a passage from the Bible was read. In the assemblies an explanation of the passage was given in the form of an address or short sermon and a Christian hymn would be sung. During tutor prayers students were given comprehension questions about the passage to discuss. Students had all been given a copy of the Bible, which they were expected to have with them as part of their basic school equipment. Bibles were bound in corporate colours identical to the students' uniform and stored in classrooms on specially constructed shelving. The impact of these routines and practices on staff and students will be considered in the next sections as I reflect on Bourdieu's concepts of symbolic violence and cultural capital. For the moment, this example serves as an illustration of how belief in the authority of the Bible impacted the physical ordering of the school day. I argued in my research that the formal presentation of 'Christian ethos' within the CTC and Academies rested upon a particular biblical interpretation which could be conceptualised as the religious habitus of the sponsors and senior staff. This habitus ensured that biblical teaching and the presentation of Christian ethos in the institutions stemmed from a consistent framework which staff and students primarily encountered as form of 'symbolic violence'.

Symbolic violence

One of the key findings of the study was that teaching the Bible was a high status activity. Only those who shared the religious habitus of the sponsors taught the Bible in religious education (RE) and in assemblies. These staff members were therefore much more visible in the formal or public life of the CTC and Academies. This placed them in a symbolically powerful relationship to the Bible because they were seen as the spokespersons authorised to interpret the text; they embodied the Christian ethos of the school and as such they regulated it. Bourdieu (1992) described symbolic violence as the 'the power to constitute the given by stating it' (ibid, 1478). In *Language and symbolic power*, Bourdieu uses the Catholic Church in France as an example of how sacred rites, routines and practices carried out by the clergy could regulate assumptions in society. In his example the clergy embodied in their practice a message about what kind of relationships between groups in society were legitimate and what kind of behaviours were approved and which were not. In so doing, Bourdieu argued that the clergy imposed and preserved their own status and hierarchy which he described as a form of symbolic violence. I used the concept of symbolic violence in my research to delineate which groups were powerful in the CTC and Academies. I found that a kind of theological hierarchy had emerged within staff culture. The hierarchy ranged from those who shared the religious habitus at the top, through to those who identified as Christians but were members of other church denominations, down to those of other faiths and those who identified with no religious faith at the bottom of the hierarchy. There were, therefore, a whole range of voices absent from the formal occasions and structures that I had identified as 'key motifs' for the religious habitus and its expression in corporate identity.

The theological hierarchy is well illustrated through the tutor prayer system. Most members of the teaching staff were form tutors and thus required to deliver tutor prayers whether or not they identified as Christians, so this example very effectively demonstrates two key elements of symbolic violence. First, it demonstrates how an authorised interpretation of biblical text was secured and, second, it demonstrates a gap between the perceived effectiveness of those staff members who shared the religious habitus compared to those who did not. A tutor prayers booklet had been prepared by a senior teacher and was used by all of the tutor groups at the CTC and Academies. The booklet specified the Bible reading for the day, together with some comprehension style questions and provided background context for the passage to prompt tutors who were not familiar with the Bible. Tutors who did not identify as Christians lacked confidence in taking tutor prayers. One form tutor said to me that it was like having to teach history at advanced level when your specialism was in languages (Interview transcript, 2 May 2007). Another said that she sometimes felt under additional pressure to push a particular moral or theological perspective which she may not personally agree with, such as a conservative view of marriage (Interview transcript, 3 May 2007). This contrasted with my observations of the tutors who shared the religious habitus. Having prior knowledge of the Bible and an experience of its teaching in their churches meant that these tutors were far more familiar with the biblical content included in the tutor prayer programme and how to situate and teach Bible passages. The students also gave me the impression that, even if they ultimately considered tutor prayers to be boring and irrelevant, it was the Christian tutors who did them 'correctly'. One of the conclusions of the research was that being able to teach the Bible together with possessing a good level of biblical literacy functioned as a form of cultural capital. The concept of cultural capital helped me to answer two key questions. First, what were the assumptions and practices legitimated through symbolic violence? And, second, How effectively did they shape student culture?

Cultural capital

Applying the concept of cultural capital to my data helped to account for one of the most significant findings of the research. I found that the religious habitus of the sponsors did have an impact upon student culture but that it was limited, and I found that the values and assumptions of the habitus had been re-appropriated by the students in ways that were quite different to the sponsors' intentions. Bourdieu's concept of habitus encompasses the idea that assumptions can be appropriated and re-appropriated, hence old beliefs can persist and continue to have currency, or cultural capital, in alternate settings where you might not expect them to be widely shared (Robbins 2000). Students did value being knowledgeable about religion and they were biblically literate, these were forms of cultural capital. Being able to discuss, affirm or refute biblical claims was seen by them as one of the marks of being a good and successful student; but within student culture this was not dependent on sharing the religious habitus of the sponsors. As Julie, aged 15 explained it to me:

> I think some people who are atheists just say they don't believe but they don't know what they don't believe … I know what I don't believe.
>
> (Interview transcript, 29 March 2007)

Julie is rehearsing here one of the key assumptions of the sponsors' habitus which is that the students should be presented with the Bible's narrative so that they can decide for themselves whether or not its claims about Jesus are true. This assumption had been re-enforced for students by their daily encounter with Bible teaching in an approved format regulated through symbolic violence. I argued in my research that in weighing up the claims of the Bible and deciding whether to accept or, as in most cases, reject them, students were doing precisely what was being asked of them. I found in my research that, with the exception of RE, the religious habitus of the sponsors had no discernible impact on the curriculum or on teaching and learning. The students only encountered the Bible and the religious habitus of the sponsors in tightly regulated spaces in the life of the CTC and Academies. I concluded that this served to re-enforce the commonly held view that religion was not really relevant to the rest of their lives. This stands in opposition to the sponsors' desire to counter the marginalisation of religion in an increasingly secular society. This finding also highlights an important point which Bourdieu's social theory does not address fully. It suggests that the habitus of the dominant cultural group does not by definition render other groups in the culture passive and without agency.

Building on Bourdieu: Related theoretical concepts for research design in faith-based education

I have noticed a greater awareness and appreciation for social theory and community of practice methodology in the fields of educational sociology and faith-based pedagogy. This may reflect a desire on the part of educational researchers to counter the dominance of scientific rationalism and neo-liberal policy trends in education. When evidence of learning or of educational attainment is equated solely with quantitative data, we are left with accounts of human and educational experience which feel woefully small. Ethnographic methodologies are an attempt to grapple with the human person suspended, as Geertz (1973) would put it, within 'webs of significance' (ibid, 5). In opposition to scientific rationalism these approaches rest on constructivist philosophical assumptions. As Cooling (2016) explains this is a contest over the status of different forms of knowledge. This would be familiar territory to Bourdieu. In this section I will briefly illustrate how I built on Bourdieu's theory using related concepts drawn from the work of Charles Taylor, Jean Lave and Étienne Wenger and J.K.A. Smith.

Intrigued by my finding that the religious habitus of the Academies I researched had limited impact on the culture of pupils, I joined a team of researchers at Canterbury Christ Church University, UK who were interested in church school pedagogy (Cooling et al. 2016). Our questions were about the teaching and learning happening in church schools in England. To put the research question into the language of Bourdieu: Did religious habitus form the practice of teaching and learning in distinctive ways in church schools?

I designed the methodology for a multiple-case study project researching the influence of Christian ethos on teaching and learning with 14 teachers in three English church schools (Cooling et al. 2016). Language as a signifier of our assumptions about the status of knowledge and the nature of influence became important in this project. When I shared my first draft of the methodology with a critical friend they commented on the mismatch between our theoretical assumptions and the language I had used in the design about measuring impact. I was much more interested in the interaction between teachers' own beliefs, the church school ethos and practice in the classroom than empirically measuring the impact of religious ethos. Tightening up my conceptual language enabled us to frame the research as a conversation with teachers about the shared imagination around teaching and learning in a church school.

The language of imagination as we used it in our research design comes from the philosophical work of Charles Taylor. He uses the concept of the 'social imaginary' to explain the shared sets of virtues, symbols, laws and institutions that make up the social world (Taylor 2004). As with 'habitus' the 'social imaginary' conceptualises the formation of assumptions, beliefs and practices at the pre-conscious level. I find it to be a more expansive concept than Bourdieu's habitus because of its relationship to time and to the transcendent. Taylor locates the 'social imaginary' in the contemporary western reality of multiple forms of secularism. Taylor also traces in his work the historical echoes of a time when meaning and significance operated in relation to belief in the transcendent, or God; Taylor refers to this as 'higher time' (Taylor 2004). It is not my perspective that faith-based education is an anachronism left over from 'higher time'. I have consistently found in my research that Christian Academies and church schools are products of their 'secular time' influenced by the shared contemporary social imaginary and competing interests in the field. In this sense, Taylor's concepts neatly fit with Bourdieu's conceptual tools: Habitus, field, symbolic violence and cultural capital.

Our question in the church school project was whether it was possible to be intentional about framing teaching and learning with a distinctively Christian social imaginary. The practical consequences of this framing can be seen in the decision to make individual teachers the cases in our research, to ask them to keep reflective journals and to work with the research team to design, teach, watch and re-evaluate sequences of lessons designed using a pedagogical approach called *What if learning* (Cooling et al. 2016).

What If Learning (WIL; What If Learning 2020) was developed to help teachers make connections between Christian faith and teaching and learning in the classroom. It is not a curricular scheme, nor is it a bible course, WIL is a pedagogical approach that can be applied to all subjects and grade levels. WIL assumes that we learn with our minds and our bodies as we participate in the cultural practices of our classrooms. Lave and Wenger (1991) would conceptualise this as participation in a community of practice and J.K.A. Smith describes the rituals and symbols in which we all participate as cultural liturgies (Smith 2009).

Lave and Wenger (1991) explored how people learn in communities of practice by studying situated learning in apprenticeships. One of their key contributions is a model of how shared habits and routines become reified into practices that are authoritative and meaningful for participants (Wenger 1999). Traditional institutions such as the church which were associated with Taylor's 'higher time' are losing their influence and authority to adjudicate and impose cultural meaning in secular societies. Smith (2009) explicitly weaves together Lave and Wenger's model with Bourdieu's concepts to argue that our participation in alternate communities of practice such as consumer choice, political and identity groups form our imaginary in powerful ways. In other words, it is not only the church that has liturgies.

My experience of working with the concepts of social imaginary, communities of practice and cultural liturgies is that they round out the more clinical and deterministic characteristics of Bourdieu's concepts. This has important consequences for research design since it widens the scope for accounting for individual agency whilst still recognising symbolic violence as it manifests in community and cultural practice. These concepts also build on Bourdieu's argument that context always matters in research design because culture is not a neutral or innate background against which religious faith, education policy, pedagogy and curriculum play out. Theoretical and methodological tools which can grapple with nuance, with our bodies, mind and spirit, with individual agency and with community participation are needed in educational research.

Conclusion

Bourdieu's concepts are applied extensively in UK education research often to analyse the impact of class on social reproduction. I have argued in this chapter that a significant legacy of Bourdieu's work is his development of a set of conceptual tools capable of integrating theory and analysis with methodology. By setting the development of Bourdieu's social theory against the backdrop of his biography, I have exemplified another significant contribution of Bourdieu's work, which is reflexivity. Bourdieu challenges us to take account of the relationship of the researcher to the researched and to the social world. I have argued that his tools equip the researcher with practical ways in which to do this. In my research I apply Bourdieu's concepts of habitus, field, symbolic violence and cultural capital to the study of religion in Christian Academies and church schools. Within this chapter I've used the examples from my research to do three things. First, I have illustrated a way of applying Bourdieu's theory in a real research setting. Reading how other researchers make use of Bourdieu's conceptual tools is a helpful way for new researchers to access Bourdieu's writings. Second, I have illustrated how current research is broadening the traditional application of Bourdieu's social theory beyond the study of class, in this case to the analysis of religion. Third, I have illustrated how other theoretical concepts interact helpfully with Bourdieu to enhance research in the field of faith-based education and pedagogy. The flexibility of such concepts and their application make Bourdieu's social theory a very adaptable tool for analysing contemporary culture and education. New researchers should be encouraged to take on the vigorous debate that surrounds Bourdieu's work and make his tools for analysis their own.

References

Ball, S.J. 2003. *Class strategies and the education market: The middle classes and social advantage*. London: Routledge.

Ball, S.J. 2007. *Education plc: Understanding private sector participation in public sector education*. London: Routledge.

Ball, S. and Junemann, C. 2011. Education policy and philanthropy: The changing landscape of English educational governance. *International Journal of Public Administration* 34: 646–661.

Bourdieu, P. 1958. *Sociologie de l'Algérie*. Paris: Presses Universitaires de France.

Bourdieu, P. 1971. Genèse et structure du champ religieux. *Revue française de sociologie* XII, 3: 295–334.

Bourdieu, P. 1979. *Algeria 1960*. Cambridge: Cambridge University Press.

Bourdieu, P. 1984. *Distinction: A social critique of the judgement of taste*. London: Routledge Kegan Paul.

Bourdieu, P. 1986. The forms of capital. In *Education: Culture, economy and society*. 2001. ed. A.H. Halsey, H. Lauder, P. Brown and A. Stuart Wells, 46–58. Oxford: Oxford University Press.

Bourdieu, P. 1992. *Language & symbolic power*. Cambridge: Polity Press.

Bourdieu, P. 2007. *Sketch for a self analysis*. Cambridge: Polity Press.

Bourdieu, P. and J.C. Passeron. 1970. *La reproduction. Éléments pour une théorie du système d'enseignement*. Paris: Éditions de Minuit.

Bourdieu, P. and J.C. Passeron. 1970/1977. *Reproduction in education, society and culture*. London: Sage.

Bourdieu, P. and J.C. Passeron. 1979. *The inheritors: French students and their relation to culture*. Chicago, IL: University of Chicago Press.

Cannell, F. ed. 2006. *The anthropology of Christianity*. London: Duke University Press.

Carson, D. 2008. *Christ and culture revisited*. Nottingham: Apollos.

Connell, R.W. 1983. *Which way is up?* Sydney: George Allen & Unwin.

Cooling, T. 2016. Who was the brain in that jar? Sometimes all good teaching needs is the right framing. *Comment Magazine*, 26 September. Available at: www.cardus.ca/comment/article/who-was-the-brain-in-that-jar/ (accessed 30 December 2020).

Cooling, T., B. Green, A. Morris and L. Revell. 2016. *Christian faith in English church schools: Research conversations with classroom teachers*. Oxford: Peter Lang.

DfE (Department for Education). 2012. About academies. Available at: https://webarchive.nationalarchives.gov.uk/ukgwa/20120421023523/https://www.education.gov.uk/schools/leadership/typesofschools/academies/b0061252/about-academies (accessed 11 April 2012).

DfE (Department for Education). 2016a. White paper: Educational excellence everywhere. Available at: www.gov.uk/government/publications/educational-excellence-everywhere (accessed 28 December 2020).

DfE (Department for Education). 2016b. Multi-academy trusts: Establishing and developing your trust. Available at: www.gov.uk/government/publications/multi-academy-trusts-establishing-and-developing-your-trust (accessed 28 December 2020).

DfE (Department for Education). 2019. Schools, pupils and their characteristics. Available at: www.gov.uk/government/statistics/schools-pupils-and-their-characteristics-january-2019 (accessed 28 December 2020).

Emmanuel Schools Foundation. 2007. *Mission Statement*. Durham: Emmanuel Schools Foundation.

Geertz, C. 1973. *The interpretation of cultures*. New York, NY: Basic Books.

Gorard, S. 2005. Academies as the 'future of schooling': Is this an evidence-based policy? *Journal of Education Policy* 3, 20: 369–377.

Gorard, S. 2014. The link between Academies in England, pupil outcomes and local patterns of socio-economic segregation between schools. *Research papers in education* 29, 3: 268–284.

Grace, G. 1978. *Teachers, ideology and control: A study in urban education*. London: Routledge and Kegan Paul.

Grace, G. 2002. *Catholic schools: Missions, markets and morality*. London: RoutledgeFalmer.

Grace, G. 2004. Making connections for future directions: Taking religion seriously in the sociology of education. *International Studies in Sociology of Education* 14, 1: 47–56.

Green, E.H. 2009a. An ethnographic study of a city technology college with a bible-based ethos. Unpublished DPhil Thesis. University of Oxford.

Green, E.H. 2009b. Speaking in parables: The responses of students to a bible-based ethos in a Christian city technology college. *Cambridge Journal of Education* 39, 4: 443–456.

Green, E.H. 2012. Analysing religion and education in Christian academies. *British Journal of Sociology of Education*: 1–17 (iFirst article). doi:10.1080/01425692.2012.659456 (accessed 11 April 2012).

Halsey, A.H., H. Lauder, P. Brown and A. Stuart Wells. 2001. *Education: Culture, economy and society*. Oxford: Oxford University Press.

Jenkins, R. 2002. *Pierre Bourdieu*. Revised edn. London: Routledge.

Kant, I. 1790/2007. *The critique of judgement*. Trans. James Creed Meredith. Oxford: Oxford University Press.

Lave, J. and E. Wenger. 1991. *Situated learning: Legitimate peripheral participation*. Cambridge: Cambridge University Press.

Moore, R. 2004. Cultural capital: Objective probability and the cultural arbitrary. *British Journal of Sociology of Education* 25, 4: 445–456.

Reay, D. 1998. *Class work: Mothers' involvement in children's schooling*. London: University College Press.

Rey, T. 2007. *Bourdieu on religion: Imposing faith and legitimacy*. London: Equinox Publishing.

Robbins, D. 2000. *Bourdieu and culture*. London: Sage.

Smith, J.K.A. 2009. *Desiring the kingdom: Worship, worldview and cultural formation*. Grand Rapids, MI: Baker Academic.

Taylor, C. 2004. *Modern social imaginaries*. Durham, NC and London: Duke University Press.

The Church of England. 2020. Church schools and academies. Available at: www.churchofengland.org/about/education-and-schools/church-schools-and-academies (accessed 28 December 2020).

Wenger, E. 1999. *Communities of practice: Learning meaning and identity*. Cambridge: Cambridge University Press.

What If Learning. 2020. Available at: www.whatiflearning.com/ (accessed 30 December 2020).

11 Bourdieu applied

Exploring perceived parental influence on adolescent students' educational choices for studies in higher education

Irene Kleanthous

Introduction

The concepts of habitus and cultural capital, suggested by Bourdieu and Passeron (1990), have become prominent for investigating and understanding inequalities between social groups and for understanding parents' practices and their involvement in various educational contexts (Levine-Rasky 2009). Reay (1998a) pointed out that parents' engagement with their children's primary school differed in ways attributable to differences in habitus and the different kinds of capital held by the family. Brooks (2003) argues that various studies of educational choice have outlined what have been called the 'class strategies of middle-class parents: Attempts to achieve a class fit between the habitus of home and institution' (ibid, 86). Brooks (ibid) also notes considerable differences in the extent to which families were involved in the decision-making process and in their knowledge about HE, generally, and the relative status of institutions and subjects, more specifically.

By the same token, Reay et al. (2001) argue that there are class inequalities involved in making decisions about HE. According to Reay et al. (ibid), the inequalities arise from lack of information and general perplexity and confusion about post-compulsory education among working class families. They note that 'while more working-class and minority students are entering university, for the most part they are entering different universities to their middle-class counterparts' (ibid, 858). The role of parents as holders of crucial information on the educational system, what Bourdieu refers to as 'informational capital' (Bourdieu and Wacquant 1992) might explain the differences noted between different social groups.

Interestingly, Lareau and Weininger (2004) provide a review of the literature on cultural capital and refer to its different operationalisations by various researchers. For example, they cite McDonough, who used the concept of parental cultural capital in a qualitative study of influences on students' college choices:

> For McDonough cultural capital comprises the 'first-hand' knowledge that parents have of the college admission process, particularly knowledge that

DOI: 10.4324/9781003156550-15

they do not get from schools (e.g. detailed understanding of the significance of SAT scores, the possibility of raising SAT scores through tutoring […] as well as the initiative to secure private tutors).

(ibid, 121)

This informational capital that parents possess on the educational system has arguably been accumulated through parents' interaction with the educational field.

Cultural context of the study

This chapter discusses some data from a PhD study (Kleanthous 2012), which explored perceived parental influence amongst adolescent students in Cyprus, who were about to make their choices for future studies in HE. The analysis and interpretation of the data relied heavily on Bourdieu's theoretical framework. In particular, I utilised his concepts of practice, field, habitus and capital (economic, social and cultural) to explore parental influence on students' dispositions towards studying in HE. I conceptualised students' dispositions to study in HE as part of their habitus and I sought to explore how these dispositions might have been inculcated by their family.

Bourdieu's notion of 'symbolic violence' was also used to suggest how students misrecognise their parents' influence on their dispositions and their decision-making for studies in HE. Bourdieu defines symbolic violence as 'the violence which is exercised upon a social agent with his or her complicity […] I call *misrecognition* the fact of recognizing a violence which is wielded precisely inasmuch as one does not perceive it as such' (Bourdieu and Wacquant 1992, 167–168). These theoretical tools, 'symbolic violence' and 'misrecognition', were used to interpret the 'denial' of parental influence by adolescent students and some of their parents.

Previous studies conducted in the cultural context of Cyprus have used Bourdieu's theory to interpret their findings. In a study of parental involvement in primary schools in Cyprus, Symeou (2007) argues that families' knowledge of the educational system and their ability to work it to the advantage of their children varies according to social class but also within classes. Professional–managerial families seem more able to mobilise goods, status and social connections in order to advance their children's education. On the other hand, working-class families are usually intimidated by the educational system and feel neither competent to criticise the school nor capable to help their children with their school homework. 'Therefore, working-class parents tend to blame themselves or their children for school problems and to find the school difficult to challenge, whereas upper-class and middle-class parents are more apt to blame the school and to challenge it, and to buy educational services from outside experts if necessary' (ibid, 475).

A qualitative study by Green and Vryonides (2005) regarding the educational choices of modern Greek Cypriot parents, points out that parents consider it to be their duty to provide children with as much support for education as possible, expecting better life opportunities for them than themselves, and perceived costs being outweighed by expectations of the future benefits of educational achievement. Nevertheless, they argue that social capital is an important factor affecting educational choice-making practices. The main finding of their study was that families from lower social classes lack effective social capital and set low aspirations for their children's education. 'For some parents the lack of social capital seems to entail making compromises on the level of education that their children might aim for' (ibid, 336).

An overview of Bourdieu's theoretical framework

Bourdieu and Wacquant (1992) argue that class habitus is 'the structural affinity of habituses belonging to the same class, capable of generating practices that are convergent and objectively orchestrated outside of any collective "intention" or consciousness' (ibid, 125). They also argue that 'habitus is the product of a particular economic condition, defined by the possession of the minimum economic and cultural capital necessary actually to perceive and seize the "potential opportunities" formally offered to all' (ibid, 124). Thus, it could be argued that in the educational field, seizing the 'potential opportunities' for studies in HE relies on students' habitus and arguably middle-class students are pre-disposed to pursue studies in HE. Bourdieu and Passeron (1990) outline how middle-class students' habitus is inculcated by their family and their parents' social class and how their middle-class habitus aligns with the educational system:

> the disposition which middle-class students or middle-rank teachers, and a fortiori, students whose fathers are middle rank teachers, manifest toward education – e.g. cultural willingness or esteem for hard work – cannot be understood unless the system of scholastic values is brought into relation with the middle class ethos, the principle of the value the middle classes set on scholastic values.
>
> (ibid, 192)

Apart from habitus, another important element of Bourdieu's theory is capital in its various forms (economic, social and cultural). Bourdieu (1986) calls capital those resources whose distributions define the social structure, and whose deployment figures centrally in the reproduction of that structure. Such resources are not just economic, but also social and cultural. Economic capital consists of financial stock and income and may be institutionalised in forms of inheritance. Social capital includes social networks and identities of individuals as member of social groups, which provide 'connections' as assets. Cultural capital consists of a large number of types of cultural knowledge and possessions including educational credentials and informational capital. Bourdieu (1998) elaborates on intergenerational transmission of informational capital:

It is difficult to anticipate fluctuations on the stock exchange of scholastic value, and those who have the benefit, through family, parents, brothers, sisters, acquaintances, and so on, of information about the formation circuits and their actual or potential differential profit can make better educational investments and earn maximum returns on their cultural capital.

(ibid, 25)

Bourdieu's theory of social reproduction posits that the acquisition of cultural capital and consequent educational success depend on the cultural capital passed down by the family, which in turn is largely dependent on social class. Bourdieu and Passeron (1990) argue that middle-class students' habitus aligns with the requirements of the educational system because they have acquired more cultural capital from their families than their working-class counterparts. Moreover, they argue that middle-class students are 'equipped with the linguistic and cultural capital and the capacity to invest it profitably, which the system presupposes and consecrates without ever expressly demanding it and without methodically transmitting it' (ibid, 99). Bourdieu (1973) writes:

The educational system demands of everyone alike that they have what it does not give. This consists mainly of linguistic and cultural competence and that relationship of familiarity with culture which can only be produced by family upbringing when it transmits the dominant culture.

(ibid, 80)

Bourdieu on family and symbolic violence

Bourdieu (1996) argues that family 'functions, in habitus, as a classificatory scheme and a principle of the constructions of the social world' (ibid, 21). Bourdieu (ibid) also considers belonging to a 'normal family' a privilege, and this is one of the major conditions of the accumulation and transmission of economic and cultural capital.

The family plays a decisive role in the maintenance of the social order, through social as well as biological reproduction, i.e. reproduction of the structure of the social space and social conditions. It is one of the key sites of the accumulation of capital in its different forms and its transmission between the generations.

(ibid, 23)

The mobilisation of capital from middle-class parents to enhance their children's educational choices is well documented in the literature (e.g. Reay 1998a; 1998b; Symeou 2007). Nevertheless, this chapter problematises Bourdieu's theoretical tool of capital and whether it is adequate for theorising parental influence. I now turn to discuss Bourdieu's view on the family and how parental influence can be conceptualised as a form of symbolic violence.

According to Bourdieu (1980), symbolic violence is at the heart of every social relation and it is present in a gift exchange economy:

> debts and gifts, the overtly economic obligations imposed by the usurer, or the moral obligations and emotional attachments created and maintained by the generous gift, in short, overt violence or symbolic violence, censored, euphemised, that is misrecognizable, recognized violence
>
> (ibid, 126)

I suggest that parental influence might be a form of 'symbolic violence' and the denial of parental influence – whether by students or their parents – serves as a 'misrecognition'. This argument is exemplified with some data indicating how parents invest time and money in their children's education and how this creates a 'debt' for their children. Moreover, I argue that parents have more power in the family field because of the capital they possess and this asymmetry of power relations enables 'symbolic violence' to be exerted on their children. Bourdieu (1998) claims that family tends to function as a field: 'with its physical, economic and, above all, symbolic power relations (linked, for example, to the volume and structure of the capital possessed by each member) and its struggles to hold on to and transform these power relations' (ibid, 69). This study adopted Bourdieu's view that family functions as a field, which inculcates students' habitus, and some alternative conceptualisations of parental influence such as 'familial habitus' (Reay 1998b; 2010) and 'familial doxa' (Atkinson 2011) are discussed later in the chapter.

Methodology

In this chapter, I draw on six in-depth interviews I conducted with adolescent students, who were attending public upper secondary schools (*lyceums*) in Cyprus at the end of the process of completing their university entrance application form. The six case study students were accessed from a larger sample of 563 students who completed a survey for the same study (Kleanthous 2012); each student provided their parents' contact details and hence I was able to interview one of their parents as well. Students were interviewed twice, over a period of one year in order to explore their perceptions of parental influence on their choices for future studies in HE. Students' perceptions were then triangulated against their parents' interviews; this provided a basis for grounding the interpretation of students' 'misrecognition' of parental influence and enabled me to explore how parental influence is mediated by familial capital.

The design of the interview schedule, for both students and their parents, was informed by Bourdieu's theory. The utilisation of the three forms of familial capital (economic, social and cultural) was investigated through the interviews, due to its visibility. However, the interviews provided insights into 'invisible' parental influence, thus I turned to 'symbolic violence' and 'misrecognition' from Bourdieu's theoretical toolkit to interpret the denial of parental influence by adolescent students and their parents. This was a post hoc adaptation of Bourdieu's theoretical tools while analysing and interpreting the data of the study. Costa, Burke and Murphy (2019) argue that putting Bourdieu's theoretical concepts to work involve methodological decisions and development of data collection instruments, but it also 'encompass[es] the process through which the researcher approaches and conceives the research phenomenon under focus' (ibid, 21).

Sample description

The parents' educational level and occupation varies across the sample but these six family case studies are considered to be middle-class families in the Greek–Cypriot cultural context. Although most of the parents were not university degree holders, apart from one parent who was a secondary school teacher, they all have a middle-class status because of their occupation as most of them are public servants (see Table 11.1). It should be noted that in the Greek–Cypriot cultural context, parents' occupation is often used as an indicator of a family's socio-economic status rather than the educational level of the parents.[1] In this sample of parents, only one father had studied at university (i.e. Socrates[2]) but all six families are considered to be middle-class families because most parents have a 'middle-class status' occupation, apart from one mother who is a cleaner (i.e. Georgia).

Findings from students' interviews on familial capital

The data indicated that students 'misrecognise' their parents' influence on their dispositions for future studies in HE. The majority of students who participated in this study claim '*It's my choice*' and deny their parents' influence on their dispositions and decision-making; nevertheless, they assert that they draw on their parents' capital before they make their choices for future studies in HE.

Table 11.1 Demographic information on students' parents

Name	Gender	HE qualification	Occupation
Andreas	Male	No	Semi-government position
Maria	Female	No	Private employee (medical visitor)
Helen	Female	No	Public servant (Ministry of Public Constructions)
Socrates	Male	Yes (Master's)	Secondary school teacher (physical education)
Georgia	Female	No	Cleaner
Monica	Female	No	Public servant (Ministry of Employment)

They often benefit from expensive private tutorials (economic capital) and may access their parents' workplace or work colleagues' expertise before making their career choice (social capital). Most of them are positively disposed towards studying at university and are preparing for university admission by acquiring educational credentials, for example GCEs (cultural capital). I argue that these are instances of the economic, social and cultural capital of the family utilised for enhancing students' education. For the rest of this chapter, I will draw on the six case studies of students and their parents' interviews to illustrate my findings.

As far as finances are concerned, some students are thinking to study abroad, thus drawing significantly on the *economic capital* of the family:

CHRIS: I think if I want to go to England they will help me financially. Or if I go to Greece, they won't tell me stay in Cyprus because of finances. I think they will let me do what I want.

CHRISTINA: They let me free if I want to go abroad, they will support me there is no problem. This helps me because I don't have to think that I might 'overcharge' them financially. They let me free.

Notably, when they were uncertain about their choices for future studies, students turned to their parents' *social capital* and networks such as colleagues from work, or members of the extended family for advice.

INTERVIEWER: Who said that it is good to combine law with chartered accountant?

CHRISTINA: Lots of people from my mum's work. And two cousins of mine who are both working as chartered accountants. They heard at the office that it's very 'strong'.

Interestingly, most students seem to accumulate *cultural capital* by attending private tutorials in order to obtain educational credentials, which will give them access to HE. This is what Bourdieu (1986) calls 'conversions between capitals', buying educational credentials is one way of investing familial economic capital which then converts to cultural capital. Access to university was the most common reason given by students for accumulating educational credentials such as GCE:

CHRIS: It depends, if I didn't have the GCE I would do something else. Either go to England for a year and then get in the university or …

INTERVIEWER: You mean for a foundation year?

CHRIS: Yeah if I didn't have the GCE. But now I can get into any British university.

Although most of these students are the first from their family background to go to university, they seem to have adequate *informational capital* and have chosen elite universities for their studies. One of the students elaborates on his choice of university by referring to the league tables indicating he has a good 'feel for the game' as Bourdieu (1980) calls it:

CHRIS: Yeah I saw a few. I will put Imperial first and then some lower [rank-ing] universities. I think Imperial is the first.
INTERVIEWER: Imperial? Yeah it's one of the best universities in the UK.
CHRIS: I think it's the third, but in these courses it is the first.

Denial of parental influence from adolescent students

Bourdieu's (1980) notion of symbolic violence is used to discuss the 'misrecognition' of parental influence in students' interviews and a glimpse of the data is provided here. I argue that parental influence can be conceptualised as a form of 'symbolic violence' that parents exert on their children (Kleanthous 2012). For example, par-ents pay for their children's private tutorials to try to improve their grades and their children feel their consequent debt, and a moral obligation to try harder at school and to pursue studies in HE. Arguably, parental influence is a: 'gentle invisible form of violence, which is never recognized as such, and is not so much undergone as chosen' (Bourdieu 1977, 192). I argue that in the family field parents possess more power and capital than their children, thus parents can exert symbolic violence to their children by investing familial capital for their education; familial capital then becomes a 'gift' their children need to return in a gift-exchange economy (Bourdieu 1980) by pursuing studies in HE.

Bourdieu (1980) also argues that symbolic violence creates a bond between persons and 'masks the asymmetry of the relationship *by symbolically denying it*' (ibid, 127, my emphasis) thus symbolic violence is misrecognised. As I examined the data, it became clear that these adolescent students 'denied' their parents' influence on their educational choices for future studies in HE. Here I provide some quotes from three students who shared the view that they are not influenced by their parents regarding their decision making for future studies in HE.

CHRIS: She [my mum] *lets me choose* on my own but she will tell me her opinion. Or I might tell her about my choices and she will say "yeah, that's good".
INTERVIEWER: Did she try to encourage you, or guide you towards a certain direction?
CHRIS: No, no. I took my own initiative so she didn't.

INTERVIEWER: Do you think that your parents have high expectations of you to study at university?
CATHERINE: Oh yes they do. They want me to go to university. But it is always what I want. I feel that *they let me choose*.

INTERVIEWER: Do they [your parents] agree with your choices?
CHRISTINA: Yes they agree, *they gave me the freedom* to decide what I want.

This discourse was common across the whole dataset and all students implied that their parents are the ones with more power in the family field who 'let' their children make their own choices. A point I illustrate with examples from fieldwork is that parental influence is unconscious for adolescent students and even their parents, because it relies on the asymmetry of power relations in the family field. Bourdieu (1998) argues that intergenerational relations are driven by 'the logic of debt'.

> But in order for intergenerational exchanges to continue despite every-thing, the logic of debt as recognition must also intervene and a feeling of obligation or gratitude must be constituted. Relations between generations are one of the sites par excellence of the transfiguration of the recognition of debt into recognition, filial devotion, love.
>
> (ibid, 109)

Thus parents 'give' students 'freedom of choice' by making familial capital available to them and indeed students articulated in their interviews they draw on familial capital before they make their choices for HE, although they denied parental influence on their decision-making. I argue that symbolic violence in the family field is mediated by familial capital, which in a gift-exchange economy makes the students feel indebted to their parents.

Misrecognition of parental influence from parents

Although parental influence on students' dispositions towards studying in HE seemed mainly unconscious for the students, their parents appear to be more aware of their parenting practices and the utilisation of their economic, social and cultural capital for the enhancement of their children's education. They explicitly refer to financial support of their children's future studies in HE (economic capital), asking people they know (social capital) about certain courses and providing cultural goods to their children drawing on their own cultural capital. Most parents refer quite explicitly to the utilisation of the economic capital of the family for financially supporting their children's studies:

HELEN: I told him he can go anywhere he wants. Chris was a bit sceptical about England because of the cost but I told him don't worry about it. For me either you go to England or Greece it's the same [cost].

Some parents also seemed to draw on their 'connections', their social capital as Bourdieu (1986) calls it, to help their children make up their mind for future studies in HE. Their social capital consists of either members of the extended family, or professional career advisors. A father, who did not have the infor-mational capital to advise his daughter about her school subjects, turned to professional career advisors for his daughter:

ANDREAS: Sure. What we did was, the teachers we knew who advise about choosing subjects …

INTERVIEWER: Career advisors?

ANDREAS: Yeah career advisors, we talked to a lady we knew. We didn't talk to her, we took Christina to this lady and they talked about some questions she had. And at school, she talked to the career advisor at school about some questions she had. So it's her decision.

Another father's account draws a picture of a parent who transmitted his cultural capital to his daughter by buying cultural goods such as books. This was an incident where the mobilisation of familial capital might have influenced the decision making of the student for studies in HE.

INTERVIEWER: Her specific choice of studies in archaeology, is that something you agree with?

SOCRATES: I do agree with this, although I know in terms of finding a job she might face some difficulties. Because I also like archaeology, and you can see here because I also like archaeology I don't influence her in a negative way. On the contrary, I am positive about it.

INTERVIEWER: Right. Is that a dream she had from a very young age, becoming an archaeologist? Is that something she used to say to you earlier on or did she just decided?

SOCRATES: Yes, yes, way back. And from the tendency that I could see, when she was in primary school I used to buy archaeology books for her.

However, the parents also 'misrecognised' their influence on their children's final decision-making about future studies in HE, claiming that it was the student's 'autonomous' decision:

INTERVIEWER: How come he has decided to study civil engineering? Whose idea was it?

HELEN: His own. It wasn't …

INTERVIEWER: He likes it?

HELEN: Yeah he likes it, because Chris is inclined towards mathematics a lot, he likes these subjects rather than theoretical subjects. He just told us, and we said there is no problem, he can follow any studies he wants.

A number of parents shared the view that they 'plant the idea' of studying at university in their children's head. Arguably, this reflects the inculcation of students' habitus in the family field, which predisposes them to go to university:

INTERVIEWER: You had these expectations since they were young?

MONICA: Yes, since they were babies. *I put this in their head*, they have to study. It's final, it's final they have to study. Even if she becomes a hairdresser or works at a beauty treatment saloon, she has to study at university.

One of the parents' case studies illustrates how she 'plant this idea' in her children's head.

INTERVIEWER: I guess you wanted him to study at university?

HELEN: Definitely.

INTERVIEWER: Did you tell him that when he was younger?

HELEN: At a very young age (laughs). […] I believe that every parent wants, if possible, to see his kid educated, with a good job. *I 'plant' this to my kids* at a very young age. And because we are many here, one was influenced by the other.

INTERVIEWER: Many cousins?

HELEN: Yeah, when my sister's kids went to university, they [my kids] were influenced. They would say 'I will study too, why shouldn't I study as well?' And then his brother studied, for example Chris, he will say 'My brother studied, why shouldn't I study as well?' They are influenced. I believe it's the environment you live in, the family.

A strong family tradition is evident in the data, that of going to university is 'what people like us do'. These last two quotes exemplify how 'symbolic violence' is exerted by parents on their children, by convincing their children of the value of studying at university. A widely-shared theme in parents' interviews, and one I return to later in this chapter, is the unconscious beliefs that family members share and the inculcation of students' habitus in the family field in a way that predisposes students to study in HE. Whether these shared unconscious beliefs could be conceptualised as familial habitus (Reay 1998b; Reay 2010) or familial doxa (Atkinson 2011) is discussed in the next section.

Discussion of findings on parental influence

This study attempted to understand perceived parental influence on HE choice by drawing on six case studies of students and their parents engaged in the choice process. Bourdieu's theoretical tools were deployed in order to understand the practice of HE decision making amongst these adolescent students. Bourdieu's tools of economic, social and cultural capital, symbolic violence and misrecognition were used as theoretical tools to analyse the data. I found that parental influence is subtle and often 'denied' by students and their parents but students 'admit' drawing on their parents' capital to make their choices for future studies in HE, thus I argue that familial capital mediates parental influence.

The 'denial' of parental influence and its unconscious effect on students' habitus led me to conceptualise parental influence as 'symbolic violence', which is 'misrecognised'. Bourdieu (1980) argues that symbolic violence is at the heart of every social relationship. Arguably, if symbolic violence is at the heart of every social relation it must be present in intergenerational relations as well. In his writings Bourdieu (1998) clarifies that 'symbolic violence is the transfiguration of relations of domination and submission into affective relations [...] which can extend to affection or love, as can be seen particularly well in relations between generations' (ibid, 102). According to Bourdieu (ibid), 'they are relations of symbolic violence which can only be established with the complicity of those who suffer from it, like intradomestic relations. The dominated collaborate in their own exploitation through affection or admiration' (ibid, 111). Thus 'symbolic violence' could describe the affective relationship between parents and their children, but it is not, by all means, a consciously violent exertion of power. Bourdieu and Wacquant (1992) argue that 'symbolic violence accomplishes itself through an act of cognition and of misrecognition that lies beyond – or beneath – the controls of consciousness and will' (ibid, 172).

The interview data presented here suggest that there is denial of parental influence from adolescent students regarding their choices for studies in HE but, on the other hand, their parents argue they 'plant the idea' of studying in HE in their children's head. Thus, I argue that students' educational choices for future studies in HE are not wholly independent choices as they assert, because they arise from a habitus inculcated by their family as a result of the pedagogic work of the family (Bourdieu and Passeron 1990). Taken for granted, students do not need to articulate their parents' influence on their educational choices to study at HE because going to university is what 'people like us do'. Reay (2010) also highlights how within middle-class families going to university is simply 'what people like us do', and often too obvious to articulate.

There is a debate in the literature whether shared beliefs and dispositions amongst family members could be conceptualised as 'familial habitus' (Reay 2010) or 'familial doxa' (Atkinson 2011). Reay (2010) stresses that Bourdieu sees habitus as a product of early childhood experience and in particular socialisation within the family. 'Such a view provides the genesis for a conceptualisation of familial habitus' (ibid, 76). Furthermore, she points out that familial habitus – the deeply ingrained system of perspectives, experiences and predispositions family members share (Reay 1998b) helps researchers to make better sense of gendered and intra-class as well as inter-class differences in both secondary school and HE choice practices. Reay (2010) argues that an important aspect of familial habitus is the complicated compilation of values, attitudes and knowledge base that families possess in relation to the field of education. 'It is profoundly influenced by the educational experiences of parents' (ibid, 77).

On the contrary, Atkinson (2011) criticises Reay's notion of 'familial habitus' and argues that we should call these shared beliefs amongst family members 'familial doxa'. Atkinson (2011) claims the family 'shapes the tacit perceptions of the possible and verbalised projections of those implicated in it, and as it is inevitably shaped by the available (pooled) capital stocks and the consecutive trajectories of the generations [...] we should call these beliefs the family-specific doxa' (ibid, 340). For example, attendance at university (especially Oxbridge) is the effect of 'doxic expectations generated by a constructed family history' (ibid, 341). In this chapter, I adopt the view that family is a field that inculcates students' habitus after Bourdieu (1998); the asymmetry of power relations and distribution of capital in the family field enables parents to exert symbolic violence on their children. This argument adds to the current debate in the literature about 'familial habitus' (Reay 2010) and 'familial doxa' (Atkinson 2011) a new theoretical conceptualisation of parental influence as the exercise of 'symbolic violence' from parents on their children in the family field.

Reflection on the use of Bourdieu's theory in educational research

The aim of this chapter is to reflect on the use of Bourdieu's theoretical framework for understanding and theorising students' perceptions of parental influence on their educational choices for future studies in HE. It also questions whether Bourdieu's conceptual tool of capital is adequate as an analytic tool in educational research. This study highlighted how familial capital, in its different forms is used in various ways by middle class families to enhance their children's educational choices. A common pattern in the data was utilising the economic capital of the family for buying private tutorials, cultural goods and overseas studies. The enactment of social capital of the family was mediated by visits to the parents' workplace for seeking crucial information about future studies in HE. As far as parents' cultural capital is concerned, although most parents in the sample of this study had not studied at university themselves, they aspired for their children to study at university, thus their offspring's habitus was inculcated in the family field in a manner that predisposed students for studies in HE. However, is this an in-depth analysis and interpretation of the data or is capital just a descriptive tool? How can sociological knowledge get challenged and Bourdieu's framework be developed and extended, if capital is dominating in most educational research projects about parental influence?

I argue that symbolic violence as a theoretical tool can help educational researchers investigate power relations in the family field and in conjunction with familial capital can help us understand how parental influence operates in adolescence. Beyond exploring symbolic violence's analytic potential, this chapter attempts to problematise the use of 'familial habitus' (Reay 2010) and 'familial doxa' (Atkinson 2011) as theoretical tools, in order to provide new theorisations of parental influence. If we go back to the original writings of Bourdieu, and some of his classic books such as *The logic of practice* (Bourdieu 1980) and *Practical reason* (Bourdieu 1998), we can see that there is no reference to neither of these terms, which researchers working within a Bourdieusian framework have coined. Bourdieu has never used the term 'familial habitus' or 'familial doxa' in his writings; on the contrary, he has written about the family as a field (Bourdieu 1998) which inculcates students' habitus as part of the pedagogic work of the family (Bourdieu and Passeron 1990). This is not to say that we cannot extend Bourdieu's theoretical framework, but any new conceptual terms researchers coin should be consistent and coherent with

Bourdieu's theory. I argue that symbolic violence (Bourdieu 1980) can help educational researchers theorise how parents inculcate students' habitus in the family field, even when adolescent students misrecognise their parents' influence and 'deny' it in their interviews, because parental influence is largely unconscious and this is consistent with Bourdieu's view on the family (Bourdieu 1996).

The concept of symbolic violence comes with theoretical scepticism and methodological challenges. One major concern is how we can theorise unconscious phenomena and publish our findings without strong empirical data supporting our argument. The concept of symbolic violence provides a helpful lens through which educational researchers can view power relations in the family field and especially in adolescence, when students are in the threshold of adulthood and 'deny' their parents' influence to assert their autonomy and identity. I found that symbolic violence is extremely useful as a conceptual tool, as long as we ensure that our empirical data lead the analysis rather than imposing the conceptual framework on the empirical data. Undoubtedly, it is hard to theorise unconscious phenomena such as parental influence in adolescence, and it is even more difficult to convince the educational research community for the usefulness of this theorisation without strong empirical evidence.

Since symbolic violence cannot be directly observed in empirical research and has to be understood interpretively, much of this section is devoted to the resistance this idea received from reviewers. Although for the wider study (Kleanthous 2012) both quantitative and qualitative data were collected, in this chapter I presented only a glimpse of the qualitative data. For the quantitative aspect of the study, mathematical habitus (Zevenbergen 2005) was operationalised with some statements in a questionnaire measuring students' dispositions towards mathematics (i.e. 'I have a mathematical mind'). The analysis of the quantitative data of the study showed that parental influence was not statistically significant for predicting students' dispositions towards studying mathematically-demanding courses in HE. A paper that used symbolic violence to interpret the non-statistically significant effect of parental influence as 'misrecognition' received strong critique from reviewers before it got accepted for publication (Kleanthous and Williams 2013). Although the mathematics education research community has embraced Bourdieu's theoretical framework in recent years (e.g. Zevenbergen 2005; Williams 2012), it is still hard for this research community to accept theorisations of unconscious phenomena without strong statistical evidence.

In another paper comparing indigenous and immigrant students' perceptions of parental influence (Kleanthous 2014), I found that immigrant students were more conscious of parental influence compared to their indigenous middle-class counterparts. This phenomenon was interpreted drawing on Bourdieu's theoretical tool of the 'hysteresis effect' that arguably immigrant students and their parents experienced when moving to a new country. The dislocation of their habitus and their interaction with a new educational field in the country they migrated was theorised as a 'hysteresis effect' after Bourdieu (1977). As Bourdieu (ibid) puts it:

Thus, as a result of the hysteresis effect necessarily implied in the logic of the constitution of habitus, practices are always liable to incur negative sanctions when the environment with which they are actually confronted is *too distant from that which they are objectively fitted.*

(ibid, 78, my emphasis)

I argue that the 'hysteresis effect' might result from the misalignment of immigrant students' and parents' habitus with the new social context (field) and their effort to adjust to this new field (Kleanthous 2014). Bourdieu (2000) acknowledges that a form of reflection and reflexivity can result from moments of hysteresis. The reflexivity the hysteresis effect entails made immigrant students more conscious of parental influence in their interviews, in the sense that they acknowledged their parents' effort to provide for them and adjust in the new field. The reason I refer to this paper is to exemplify how the concept of 'symbolic violence' worked well for analysing the data from middle-class indigenous students and their parents, who were like 'fish in the water' (Bourdieu and Wacquant 1992), but I had to use another tool from Bourdieu's theoretical toolkit for theorising immigrant students' explicit articulation of parental influence in their interviews.

In *Distinction*, Bourdieu (1984, 101) maps out a formula of his theoretical framework (Habitus X Capital) + Field = Practice. With this algebraic representation of his theory, he highlights the importance of the interaction between these theoretical concepts. The habitus is structured by engagement in practice with the field, but at the same time, it is thereby structuring the field. Bourdieu and Wacquant (1992) claim that 'such notions as habitus, field, and capital can be defined, but only within the theoretical system they constitute, not in isolation' (ibid, 96). This formula is a way of reminding educational researchers of the interrelation between Bourdieu's theoretical tools and a call for using all of his tools when analysing the data of any research project. Although symbolic violence and the hysteresis effect do not appear in this equation they are very central to Bourdieu's theory, thus it is legitimate to use them to theorise parental influence, but only in relation to the rest of his theoretical toolkit. We need to put symbolic violence and the hysteresis effect next to habitus, practice and capital in relation to a field in order to understand their potentials as analytic tools.

Arguably, the concepts of 'symbolic violence' and 'misrecognition' are still received with scepticism from other researchers working within a Bourdieusian framework, but what I tried to demonstrate in this chapter is how crucial these theoretical tools are for understanding 'unspoken' parental influence and that they are consistent with Bourdieu's original writings. Nevertheless, they are some methodological challenges when a researcher is investigating unconscious phenomena through interviews. Perhaps it would have been useful to collect data through observations of familial practices, but this was not feasible for the purposes of this study. Interviews and responses to questionnaires are both self-reports, thus all findings rely on the participants' account, who might not be telling the whole story. On the contrary, observations of familial practice might be more informative, but undeniably, it is an intrusive research method to study parental influence and almost impossible to observe familial practices longitudinally.

Costa et al. (2019) point out that researchers often try to acquire a longitudinal understanding of social conditions through a latitudinal approach. Due to the difficulty in obtaining funding for such approaches, 'researchers are left to devise methodological tools that aim to collect and analyse periods of agents' experiences through latitudinal techniques and approaches' (ibid, 27). In their interviews, students and their parents mentioned incidents ranging from when students were very young until the point they were about to make their choices for studying at university. This biographical narrative that was described in their interviews (i.e. a parent buying archaeology books for his daughter when she was little), would have been difficult to capture through observations or any other ethnographic research method.

Concluding remarks

In our attempt as educational researchers to understand the social phenomena we are studying, we choose a theoretical framework to inform the design of our research methodology and instruments, but this does not imply that we need to restrict ourselves to a single theoretical framework, if it proves to be inadequate for analysing our data. Wenger-Trayner argues in favour of what he calls the 'plug-and-play of theories' and he suggests that his theoretical framework of communities of practice can be interweaved with other social theories (Farnsworth, Kleanthous and Wenger-Trayner 2016). He claims that:

> the implication for researchers is that they need to find the right theory or mix of theories to fit their specific purpose – to sharpen the questions they ask and the story they want to tell. This requires a deep understanding of what each theory is about.
>
> (ibid, 142)

In particular, Wenger-Trayner suggests that his theoretical framework is compatible with Bourdieu's theory because practice is at the heart of both theoretical frameworks. 'I would say that Bourdieu would be a good candidate for plug-and-play with my theory because they both end up seeing practice as the place where things happen' (ibid, 152). This suggestion for combining Bourdieu's theoretical framework with Wenger's (1998) theory of communities of practice in future research could be useful for exploring familial practices and parental influence on adolescent students. This of course, should be done with caution.

> You need to be rigorous in bringing theories together: compare their purposes, their stances and their technical terms and look for

complementarities and incompatibilities. [...] Only then can you start to combine two theories to support your analysis of a situation and tell a bigger story than either theory would afford.

(Farnsworth, Kleanthous and Wenger-Trayner 2016, 142)

Wenger's (1998) theory of communities of practice is a theory that could be interweaved with Bourdieu's theory, to see how the 'plug-and-play' of theories that Wenger-Trayner suggests works for analysing the data of a study. What is perhaps more interesting to see in future research is interweaving Bourdieu's theory with other theoretical frameworks to compare and contrast their key conceptual tools, such as habitus against identity. Wenger-Trayner claims that 'a good theory is not static but amenable to revision as new empirical data are introduced or alternative theoretical perspectives challenge previous conceptualisations' (Farnsworth, Kleanthous and Wenger-Trayner 2016, 157). In line with this, the use of some theoretical tools, which are not so commonly used in educational research, such as 'symbolic violence' and the 'hysteresis effect' indicate how rich Bourdieu's theory is and how it can be extended in order to theorise the social phenomena educational researchers seek to explore.

Notes

1 In order to measure the socio-economic status (SES) of the family for the quantitative aspect of this study, I used a scale of occupational status, which is the standardised scale used in Cyprus for measuring SES by the Government and the Pedagogical Institute (Ministry of Education). There is no equivalent allowance such as FSM (Free School Meal) or EMA (Educational Maintenance Allowance) in the Greek–Cypriot educational system as a proxy indicator of SES.
2 All names are pseudonyms.

References

Atkinson, W. 2011. From sociological fictions to social fictions: Some Bourdieusian reflections on the concepts of 'institutional habitus' and 'family habitus'. *British Journal of Sociology of Education* 32, 3: 331–347.

Bourdieu, P. 1973. Cultural reproduction and social reproduction. In *Knowledge, education and cultural change: Papers in the sociology of education*, ed. R. Brown, 257–271. London: Tavistock.

Bourdieu, P. 1977. *Outline of a theory of practice*. Cambridge: Cambridge University Press.

Bourdieu, P. 1980. *The logic of practice*. Stanford, CA: Stanford University Press.

Bourdieu, P. 1984. *Distinction: A social critique of the judgment of taste*. Cambridge, MA: Harvard University Press.

Bourdieu, P. 1986. The forms of capital. In *Handbook of theory and research for the sociology of education*, ed. J.C. Richardson, 241–258. New York, NY: Greenwood Press.

Bourdieu, P. 1996. On the family as a realised category. *Theory, Culture and Society* 13, 3: 19–26.

Bourdieu, P. 1998. *Practical reason: On the theory of action*. Cambridge: Polity Press.

Bourdieu, P. 2000. *Pascalian meditations*. Cambridge: Polity Press.

Bourdieu, P. and J.C. Passeron. 1990. *Reproduction in education, society and culture.* 2nd edn. London: Sage.

Bourdieu, P. and L. Wacquant. 1992. *An invitation to reflexive sociology.* Cambridge: Polity Press.

Brooks, R. 2003. Young people's higher education choices: The role of family and friends. *British Journal of Sociology of Education* 24, 3: 283–297.

Costa, C., C. Burke and M. Murphy. 2019. Capturing habitus: Theory, method and reflexivity. *International Journal of Research & Method in Education* 42, 1: 19–32.

Farnsworth, V., I. Kleanthous and E. Wenger-Trayner. 2016. Communities of practice as a social theory of learning: A conversation with Etienne Wenger. *British Journal of Educational Studies* 64, 2: 139–160.

Green, A. and M. Vryonides. 2005. Ideological tensions in the educational choice practices of modern Greek Cypriot parents: The role of social capital. *British Journal of Sociology of Education* 26, 6: 327–342.

Kleanthous, I. 2012. Perceived parental influence on adolescent students' mathematical dispositions: A Bourdieusian perspective. Unpublished PhD dissertation. University of Manchester.

Kleanthous, I. 2014. Indigenous and immigrant students in transition to higher education and perceptions of parental influence: A Bourdieusian perspective. *Policy Futures in Education* 12, 5: 670–680.

Kleanthous, I. and J.S. Williams. 2013. Perceived parental influence and students' dispositions to study mathematically-demanding courses in higher education. *Research in Mathematics Education* 15, 1: 50–69.

Lareau, A. and E.B. Weininger. 2004. Cultural capital in education research: A critical assessment. In *After Bourdieu*, eds. D.L. Swartz and V.L. Zolberg, 105–144. Dordrecht: Kluwer.

Levine-Rasky, C. 2009. Dynamics of parent involvement at a multicultural school. *British Journal of Sociology of Education* 30, 3: 331–344.

Reay, D. 1998a. Cultural reproduction: Mothers' involvement in their children's primary schooling. In *Bourdieu and education: Acts of practical theory*, eds. M. Grenfell and D. James, 55–71. London: Falmer Press.

Reay, D. 1998b. 'Always knowing' and 'never being sure': Familial and institutional habituses and higher education choice. *Journal of Education Policy* 13, 4: 519–529.

Reay, D. 2010. From the theory of practice to the practice of theory: Working with Bourdieu in research in higher education choice. In *Cultural analysis and Bourdieu's legacy: Settling accounts and developing alternatives*, eds. E. Silva and A. Warde, 75–86. London: Routledge.

Reay, D., J. Davies, M. David and S. Ball. 2001. Choices of degree or degrees of choice? Class, 'race' and the higher education choice process. *Sociology* 35, 4: 855–874.

Symeou, L. 2007. Cultural capital and family involvement in children's education: Tales from two primary schools in Cyprus. *British Journal of Sociology of Education* 28, 4: 473–487.

Wenger. E. 1998. *Communities of practice: Learning, meaning, and identity.* New York, NY: Cambridge University Press.

Williams, J.S. 2012. Use and exchange value in mathematics education: Contemporary CHAT meets Bourdieu's sociology. *Educational Studies in Mathematics* 80, 1: 57–72.

Zevenbergen, R. 2005. The construction of a mathematical habitus: Implications of ability grouping in the middle years. *Journal of Curriculum Studies* 37, 5: 607–619.

Part V
Derrida

12 Derrida and education research
An introduction

Jones Irwin

Introduction

The reception of Jacques Derrida's work (Irwin 2010a) in the discipline of the philosophy of education and, more generally, in the field of educational research has become increasingly positive in recent years. Theorists such as Michael Peters (2004b) and Peter Trifonas (2000) have argued persuasively and influentially that accusations of nihilism or textualism (Lather 2004) against deconstruction do not hold up and that his philosophical work has much to say concerning issues of 'power, violence and domination' (Lather 2004, 4), in a way not dissimilar to the work of critical theory. At the same time, the main representatives of the latter ideology in educational theory and research, the school of critical pedagogy, often express significant suspicion of the emancipatory potential of deconstruction and warn against its employment in educational theory and research (McLaren 1994; Giroux 2000).

In this chapter, I will explore the reasons for these tensions in the reading of the relationship between deconstruction and education. At the forefront of this analysis will be the question of the respective affinities and disaffinities between deconstruction and critical theory most especially, or what we might refer to more generally as the legacy of Marxist thinking in education (Balibar 2007). Mark Murphy and Cristina Costa (Murphy and Costa 2022), in their new essay for the second edition of this book, refer to the significance of such Leftist social theory for research in education while also noting how some of the significance of this legacy gets lost in translation. Thomas McCarthy, the seminal interpreter and translator of Habermas, has similarly argued that Derrida's critique of philosophy has a cogency that cannot be ignored by the Left. For McCarthy, Derrida's critique stems from a subversion of the attempt by philosophy to try to 'freeze the play of difference' (quoted in Peters and Marshall 1996: 164). For McCarthy, in agreement with Derrida here, 'such closure is impossible, philosophy cannot transcend its medium. The claim to have done so always relies on ignoring, excluding, marginalising or assimilating whatever escapes the grids of intelligibility it imposes on the movement of difference' (ibid, 164). Peters and Marshall (ibid) have also sought to draw out the affirmative potential in education which such a Derridean critique of reason can

DOI: 10.4324/9781003156550-17

have for 'the rise of new social movements' (ibid, 164). This connect to emergent social movements seems all the more important today in 2022, surrounded by climate and ethical–political global crises.

In exploring this affinity and disaffinity, I will delineate the relevance of Derrida and deconstruction for issues in educational research and especially for the current crises in the institution of the university per se (Irwin 2010b). The latter crisis in the university sector very clearly frames the issue of the future of educational research, both specifically in philosophy of education and more generally across educational studies. But we can also trace the influence of deconstruction on education across the full gamut of research areas, including programme evaluation (Stronach and MacLure 1997), emancipatory ethnographic research (Lather 2004), curricular reform (O'Cadiz et al. 1998) and practitioner-oriented research in early years and maths education (Brown and Jones 2001). Nonetheless, the primary influence of Derrida's work to date remains within the philosophy of education and related disciplines of education (Blake et al. 2003a; Pring 2004; Biesta 2013; 2020), in pedagogy (Trifonas 2000) and in specialised applications of the latter such as feminist poststructuralist educational interventions (St. Pierre and Pillow 2000; Lather 2004). My main focus in this chapter will thus be on the latter rather than the former, although I will seek to achieve a balance between these concerns.

The changing education context vis-à-vis Postmodernism

The relationship between later 20th-century French philosophical thinking and the ideology of Marxism has often been a fraught one. Slavoj Žižek (1994), for example, has recounted how, in former Yugoslavia, any attempt to explicate French thinking at an academic level had to justify the latter's relation to the orthodox state ideology of Marx.[1] We can trace a similar movement in the disciplines of education. While philosophy of education developed initially through an Anglo-American analytical lens, grounded in a rather strict conceptualism (Blake et al. 2003b), by the 1990s the discipline had broadened to accommodate the insights of critical theory and Marxism and a more sociopolitical interpretation of education (Blake and Masschelein 2003). A key figure here in the transition between a more analytical view of education and a more politicised conception was the Brazilian philosopher Paulo Freire (1996; Irwin 2012). Indeed, many of the theorists associated with the critical pedagogy movement take their cue from the work of Freire (Giroux 2000).

In this initial evolution of the discipline, philosophy of education demonstrated a clear suspicion of postmodernist thought (McLaren 1994) as, at least, apolitical and as, at worst, politically pernicious. However, there has been a gradual weakening of this antipostmodernist reading in pedagogy and, more and more, at least some aspects of postmodern thinking have become influential in both philosophy of education and in the wider realm of the discourse on educational research per se (Blake et al. 2003b; Peters and Wilson 2003). A key figure in the translation of Derrida and deconstruction into educational contexts, more recently, has been the Dutch pedagogue Gert Biesta (2013; 2017; 2020). Over more than a decade, Biesta's work has connected Derrida's vision to an intervention in educational discourses which can impact theory, practice and methodology. His earlier texts, such as *The beautiful risk of education* (Biesta 2013, 141ff.), develop McCarthy's aforementioned point that Derrida's critique of difference can lead to a renewed openness in educational thought and practice. Biesta links this to a renewed understanding of the relation between subjectivity and world, which occurs in Derrida's deconstructive thought. This also allows us to subvert the very heavy-handed culture of performativity and assessment which Biesta disparagingly refers to as the culture of 'learnification' (ibid, 141ff.). In two more recent texts, also influenced significantly by a Derridean philosophy, Biesta argues consequently for a renewal of our vision of 'teaching' (*The rediscovery of teaching* [Biesta 2017]) as well as an urgent need for a reconsideration of our approach to research methodology in education (*Educational research: An unorthodox introduction* [Biesta 2020]). This emergent understanding of the need to re-envision the relation between various kinds of social theory (here, deconstruction) and research methods is made powerfully by Murphy and Costa (2022) in this collection when they argue relatedly for the values of 'hybridity and critical reflexivity' in education.

Even in this renewed liberal context, however, it is perhaps Derrida's work which has been the most resisted within educational research and theory, whereas his contemporaries such as Lyotard, Deleuze and Badiou have become paradigm figures (Irwin 2010b). A powerful example of how postmodernist thinking has only been accepted on the terms of a more neo-Marxist approach to education is McLaren's distinction between what he terms 'resistance' and 'ludic' postmodernism (McLaren 1994). The first concept refers to a kind of postmodernist thinking, most especially for McLaren, identifiable with the work of Michel Foucault and postmodern feminism, which works to debunk hegemonic assumptions of the West. Thus, this approach to postmodern thinking is congruent with a more emancipatory approach to education. On the other hand, what McLaren terms a 'ludic' postmodernism is a more loose or 'nihilist' version of postmodernism which eschews the emancipatory potential of the former and which is thus unassimilable to any emancipatory pedagogy. Derrida's work is especially associated with this latter strain (ibid; Derrida 1977). Thus, while we might say that postmodernism has become increasingly influential in educational research (Peters and Wilson 2003), the relationship specifically between deconstruction and educational research remains complex and rather more fraught (Trifonas 2000; Lather 2004; Biesta 2020).

Alongside Biesta, the most notable examples of educational theorists working against this interpretation of Derrida are Michael Peters (Peters and Wilson 2003) and Peter Trifonas (2000). Both of these writers have been keen to point to the importance of Derrida's work for education, while not underplaying the tension which exists, for example, between deconstruction and more explicitly emancipatory projects such as critical pedagogy or neo-Marxism more generally (Giroux 2000). The significance of Derrida's work for education has also been enhanced by the publication in English in more recent years of several important collections of essays on education by Derrida. Many of these essays date from the early 1970s, showing the continuity of the educational problematic in Derrida's *oeuvre*, but the translation of these texts has brought this rather neglected aspect of his thinking to a much larger public (Derrida 2002). In so doing, it has given the lie to those who would see Derrida's work as simply anti-materialist (Lather 2004) and as being detached from political–educational or institutional questions. Derrida's early work with GREPH in France (focusing on the teaching of philosophy in French schools), for example, demonstrates his interest in, and commitment to, philosophy as a teaching discipline outside the university sector and with children (Derrida 2002). By the same token, his important and leading role in the development of the College of Philosophy in France in the 1980s (alongside Lyotard, amongst others) demonstrates his role in 'applying deconstruction' (Lather 2004) to educational and political contexts (Trifonas 2004b). We can also see in this a development of the '68 spirit, from the creation of the university at Vincennes onwards (a project which several key postmodernist thinkers were involved in, from Lyotard to Badiou) (Irwin 2010b).

Deconstruction and education

We can thus recognise the crucial importance of deconstruction as a philosophy for education and pedagogy, while also pointing to certain reservations which have been expressed in some quarters concerning its more radical implications (McLaren 1994; Giroux 2000). But, in clarifying this relevance, we are left with the more important question of the exact detail of this legacy. In what way can we understood the key implications of deconstruction for education research? One approach to this problematic is to argue that it is the very tensions which deconstruction generates in relation to education paradigms of research which constitute its strength as a relatively new perspective in this area. In the next sections, I will explore some of these relevant tensions. I will employ Peters and Trifonas' seminal reinterpretations of Derrida's work in dialogue with a significant essay by Patti Lather (2004), in one of the most important collections of essays on deconstruction and education (Peters and Trifonas 2004). We will explore these themes alongside a reading of some of Biesta's more recent employments of Derrida's concepts and methods (Biesta 2013; 2017; 2020). What makes Lather's essay so helpful, in this context, is that she precisely seeks to both do justice to the conceptual and theoretical innovations of Derrida's work while also developing the potential of the latter in the area of educational praxis and empirical research. Significantly, Lather's work develops out of an original Marxist context of ideology and she thus also thematises the complexity of the relationship between Derrida's philosophy and this latter tradition (Balibar 2007). Biesta's work also makes the application to research methodology overt, with his call for 'unorthodox methods' (Biesta 2020). Although congruent with critical theory, Biesta's interpretation of

Derrida's political vision tends more towards a social democratic vision, where ethics and politics are seen as constitutive of educational practice (Biesta 2013). Here, we can see related but distinct interpretations of Derrida's place within the tradition of social theory and its relation to education.

In their respective Introduction (Trifonas 2004a) and Preface (Peters 2004a) to their collection of essays (Peters and Trifonas 2004), Trifonas and Peters contextualise their renewed reading of Derrida's work and its acute relevance for current educational debates in theory and empirical research. The balanced emphasis on both the latter elements is significant in relation to what is often perceived as an overly-theoretical emphasis in Derrida's work. This tendency in education studies to be suspicious of certain theoretical emphases is the consequence of a move away from theory which, for example, Nigel Blake has examined in a British context of pedagogy (Blake et al. 2003b). For Blake, in the 1990s in education, the ideology of 'progressivism' (Darling and Nordenbo 2003) became a target for those wishing to indict the supposed decline of traditional educational standards, this targeting itself finding its original source in the Thatcherite ideology of the 1980s. The philosophy of education and its cognate disciplines came to be accused of an excessive liberalism and their theoretical aspects were regarded as a significant part of the problem, leading them to be viewed as out of touch with education and schooling on the ground. This obscurantist and confused set of ideas, essentially the basis of the New Right in political terms, ushered in a whole new culture of anti-theoreticism in education, culminating in the development of the contemporary culture of managerialism and performativity which became hegemonic in the late 1990s (Blake et al. 2003b). Paradoxically, however, as Blake is already elaborating in 2003, this repression of theory in education was to lead to a subsequent re-emergence of theory or what Blake calls a 'renewal of theory' by the early 21st century.[2] It is in the latter context that we can best understand the reinvocation of Derrida and deconstruction by Trifonas and Peters (Peters and Trifonas 2004).

As Trifonas elaborates in his Introduction to the volume of essays, 'the essays collected here take the premise that Derrida is indeed a most profound thinker of matters educational' (Trifonas 2004a, 1). Trifonas and Peters cite the opposition to deconstruction which comes not simply from within Marxist or analytical educational circles but from even within the postmodernist discourse itself. Here, they cite the vehement criticisms of Derrida by Foucault, who was in fact one of Derrida's original teachers of philosophy in Paris, at the École normale supérieure. 'Foucault suggested that deconstruction is nothing but the elaborate expression of a new didactic, a new pedagogy of the text' (ibid, 1). Against this view, they cite their own positive interpretation of the relevance of Derrida to pedagogy; 'Rather what deconstruction is seeking to do is to point to the undecidability [of the institution] at the expense of the metaphysical grounding of its architectonics' (ibid, 1). This concept of undecidability will become central to the analysis of the importance of deconstruction and Derrida, specifically for educational discourse. Unlike the clarity of the critical theory discourse of education which has been accused by some critics of a certain 'positivism' (Blake and Masschelein 2003), precisely because of its lack of undecidability (its excessive certainties), what is paradigmatic about deconstruction is the very instability of meaning it induces. Here, Trifonas and Peters invoke another central concept of Derrida's, that of 'aporia' or rather here, more specifically, they refer to the 'tensions of its aporias' (Trifonas 2004a, 1). In a similar vein, they also point to the need to eschew finalised solutions or completed understandings; 'and there is no need to enact the last word on this topic' (ibid, 1). In this context, Trifonas also refers significantly to both the 'ethics' and the 'politics' of deconstruction or the 'ethics of deconstruction' as it applies to what he terms the 'politics of education' (Trifonas 2004a). The latter problematic, in more recent times, connects directly to the issue of the status of the university, the politics of the university as it has come under siege from what has been referred to by some commentators as a new 'managerialism' in education (Blake et al. 2003b).

In some of his later essays, Derrida focuses more explicitly on ethical and political questions. Here two essays can be noted as significant, 'Cosmopolites de tous les pays, encore une effort!' (hereafter 'On cosmopolitanism'; Derrida 2001a) and 'On forgiveness' (Derrida 2001b). These essays foreground how deconstruction can inspire a more ethical-political vision of intercultural or 'cosmopolitan' education, as against more nationalist or anti-multicultural tendencies in our current predicament. The more recent emergence of Rightist ideology into mainstream politics is only the most obvious example of the latter. In his text 'On cosmopolitanism' (Derrida 2001a), Jacques Derrida attempts to delineate, in broad outline, the genealogy of the concept. What he locates in this tradition is an idea of cosmopolitanism which is focused on a notion of a 'city of refuge': 'We shall recognise in the Hebraic tradition, on the one hand, those cities which would welcome and protect those innocents who sought refuge from what the texts of that time call 'bloody vengeance' (ibid, 17).

For Derrida, this discourse on the city which provides protection to the most vulnerable outsiders first begins in the *Book of numbers*, and constitutes, in a rather retrospective Derridean language, an 'urban right to immunity and to hospitality' (Derrida 2001a, 17). It is also to be found, Derrida tells us, in *Joshua* where it is stated of the 'resident alien or temporary settler': 'if they admit him into the city, they will grant him a place where he may live as one of themselves' (Derrida 2001a, 17). What appears to be at issue here is not some deconstructive hermeneutics of the Biblical unsaid but rather the very literalism of Biblical command: God ordered Moses to institute six cities of refuge.

The development of this radical intercultural and cosmopolitan logic can be seen in Hellenistic philosophy, particularly in Cicero's Stoic philosophy. What is at issue here for Derrida is an 'ethics of hospitality', although this cannot be just one ethic amongst others. Rather, the ethics of hospitality, of welcoming and making an irreducible place for the other, constitutes for Derrida the very ethics or ethos of ethics itself: 'insofar as it has to do with the ethos, that is, the residence, one's home, the familiar place of dwelling, inasmuch as it is a manner of being there, the manner in which we relate to ourselves and to others, to others as our own or as foreigners, *ethics is hospitality*' (Derrida 2001a, 17).

Biesta in his Interview which concludes his text *The beautiful risk of education* (Biesta 2013), entitled 'Coming into the World, Uniqueness and the Beautiful Risk of Education' (ibid, 141ff.) takes up this Derridean challenge in the name of democracy and its intrinsic connection to education. As Biesta notes, very much in a Derridean ethos, 'I hope that it is clear that there is a strong democratic sentiment in the way in which I look at education … the democratic ethos and the educational ethos come together and perhaps even coincide. That is why, for me, the democratic is at the heart of the educational' (ibid, 148). In this context, we have a powerful testimony of how Derrida's concepts of renewed and radicalised ethics and politics, through cosmopolitanism and hospitality, might be translated into a contemporary democratic educational vision.

Applying Derrida to educational research

In her essay 'Applied Derrida: (Mis)Reading the work of mourning in educational research' (Lather 2004), Patti Lather seeks to provide a more specific focus to this analysis of deconstruction and its relation to education. Most significantly for our purposes, she is especially concerned with the issue of the relation between deconstruction and educational research. As Lather notes, '[my] primary interest is the uses of deconstruction in thinking about the improvement of educational policy and practice through research by way of a focus on reinscribing praxis under conditions of postmodernity' (ibid, 3). Clearly, for Lather, as for Trifonas, Peters and Biesta, deconstruction has something to say of worth not simply in an intra-philosophical sense or theoretically, but also to the context of educational research and policy. Here, Lather points to the possibility that taking on board the nuances and insights of Derrida might or should lead to an 'improvement' in this sector of analysis. She also invokes the Marxist term of *praxis*, the reciprocity of theory and practice, and her reading of this notion can be supplemented by the subtle reading of Marx, which Étienne Balibar gives in his *The philosophy of Marx* (Balibar 2007).

In thus invoking the relationship between deconstruction and Marxism, Lather is also aware, however, that not all Marxists or neo-Marxists see deconstruction in such positive terms. Citing the important example of Peter McLaren (1994), Lather points to his suspicions of Derrida's work which he interprets as being on the wrong side of his opposition between 'resistance postmodernism' and 'ludic postmodernism' (ibid). For McLaren, there is a real danger in employing deconstruction as a method in education, as the wrong kind of postmodernist turn, bringing about the 'decline of class politics and textualism' (Lather 2004, 4). Lather, herself coming from a neo-Marxist background, is not unaware of these criticisms of Derrida's work but, while acknowledging these dangers vis-à-vis the relation between Marxism and deconstruction, she points to a rather different approach as possible in this context. Unlike those theorists who read the implications of Derrida's work as diminishing political and ethical significance, Lather rather reads the situation in reverse. There are new 'relational structures' created by Derrida's work which point towards open ethical and political possibilities. This is due to what she terms the 'speculative force of Derrida's work': 'the speculative force of this excess works towards establishing new relational structures with a "greater emphasis on ethics and its relationship to the political"' (Spivak quoted in Lather 2004, 4). Here, in invoking Spivak's (1993) work, she also points to the impact that Derrida's work has had on a subversive political, and especially feminist, tradition of thinking. That notwithstanding the fact that Derrida has constantly warned against a simple emancipatory logic: 'one needs another language besides that of political liberation' (Derrida quoted in Kearney 1984, 122) As Lather observes, 'Derrida is clear that we "cannot not be" heirs of Marx's break with myth, religion and nationalism as ways to think the world and our place in it' (Lather 2004, 5). This she counts as Derrida's 'turn or return to Marx'. We can note here how this renewed political vision resonates with Biesta's reinterpretation of democracy and education cited above (Biesta 2013), itself connecting back to Derrida's renewed stress on an ethics of hospitality and cosmopolitanism (Derrida 2001a).

Specific implications of deconstruction for education research

In such a context, we can start to map what might be the specific implications of deconstruction for education research. Biesta and Lather both thematise the most significant implication of deconstruction for education research in terms of the need to overcome a certain scientism, which remains endemic in educational studies. 'It is tempting to revert to the quick and narrow scientism of the past. But the game has changed' (Lather 2004, 7). Biesta refers to the 'oppressive conditions' (Biesta 2013, 147) under which many educationalists (students and teachers alike) have to work. For both thinkers, the impact of Derrida's work on educational research should be seen as especially important in the current context. Whereas scientism opts for a narrow kind of calculability and reductionism, deconstruction allows the researcher in education to look at complexity and contingency, 'without predictability' (Lather 2004, 7). This is not anti-scientific; quite the contrary. It rather can be seen as enhancing our idea and practice of scientific understanding in educational research. 'Accounting for the complexity and contingency "without predictability" is what now shapes our conversations and expands our idea of science as cultural practice and practice of culture' (ibid, 7). Biesta notes why 'what works won't work' (Biesta 2013, 146) in that the application of the criterion of efficiency exclusively as the paradigm for successful education institutes a rather terrible kind of reductionism and flattening. 'The whole idea of evidence-based education is again based on the eradication of risk and a desire for total control over the education process' (ibid, 146). This is not a call for an eschewal of science but rather for a resituation of science and methodology in education.

We can thus hold onto a scientific model while avoiding scientism; this is very much in keeping with Derrida's claim that it is a complete misunderstanding to think of deconstruction as wholly capricious. Rather it invokes a deconstructive (scientific) rigor and logic, which is very strict in its own right.

How does this logic work? Lather's specific analysis is keen to explicate the key differences between this deconstructive approach and the critical theory approach which it is often confused with it. In the first case, Lather cites the key difference between a deconstructive and critical theory approach as one of a contrast between an emphasis on the principle of 'complicity' and the principle of 'unveiling' (the former associated with deconstruction, the latter with critical theory). 'Deconstruction; its interest is in complicit practices and excessive differences rather than unveiling structures and illuminating the forces and relations of production; deconstruction works against the critical righteousness of ideology critique' (Lather 2004, 6). This righteousness leads to a 'propaganda' which seeks to posit what is termed a 'correct consciousness' (ibid, 6). Again, what we have here encompassed is the whole complex history of the Marxist concept of ideology, as it relates to the notion of false consciousness and the related concept of the masses (Balibar 2007; Irwin 2012). It is clear that this rereading of ideology and false consciousness has significant implications for educational research, as it eschews any patronising reading of research subjects[3].

Crucially for educational research, there are also implications for the concept of subjectivity or the subject. Biesta takes up this theme persuasively when he argues that we cannot understand such subjectivity or 'uniqueness' as he refers to it as reducible to a measurable 'outcome'; 'Subjectivity is precisely not an outcome and even less a learning outcome; it is precisely not a thing that can be produced – which is why I like the idea of the event of subjectivity and of subjectivity-as-event so much' (Biesta 2013, 145). Lather puts this matter cogently concerning a deconstruction of the subject, perhaps Derrida's most significant contribution to this whole debate; 'in reading the subject, modes of investment are no longer based on traditional notions of categorical thinking such as false consciousness, on the one hand, or the more idealised model of intentional agency of reason or will' (Lather 2004: 7). The stable model of the individual or subject, so often the centre of educational research analysis, is thus undone by a fundamental instability: 'Indeterminacy and paradox become conditions of affirmative power by undoing finalities and mapping new possibilities of playing out relations between identity and difference, margins and centres' (ibid, 7).

What Biesta and Lather do here, with regard to subjectivity, is especially important for our purposes in the measure to which they eschew the tendency to keep the discussion at a purely intra-theoretical level. Rather they seek to 'apply deconstruction', as it were, to explore the very real possibilities for empirical research attendant on these new theoretical and philosophical innovations of Derrida's work. Lather's own work, in collaboration, has recently focused on stories of women living with HIV and she wants to exemplify the deconstructive method precisely in this context of empirical testimony: 'tell the stories of women living with HIV to ask hard questions about necessary com-plicities, inadequate categories dispersing rather than capturing meanings and producing bafflements rather than solutions' (Lather 2004, 7). This relates once again to Spivak's (1993) work, a key interlocutor in the debate concerning the status of the subaltern in education or politics. What this also debunks is the notion of some kind of self- sufficient or complete ontology, of, for example, the realist or Thomistic kind; as what Spivak calls a 'practical academic', I will draw on this work not so much to give flesh and blood to abstractions, as to evoke what Derrida terms a 'ghost effect' of spectral movement where ontol-ogy can only be a conjuration, a more demanding ontology of an other logic calling for other concepts' (Lather 2004, 7). Crucially, ontology is not dis-avowed here but rather resituated and reinscribed in a more complex and nuanced context.

The reading of Derrida here extends the Marxist paradigm in education and we can make reference, in this context, to Balibar's somewhat revisionistic account of Marxist thought (Balibar 2007). Employing Balibar's subtle reread-ing of Marx, we can argue that Marx's conception of *praxis* undoes the dualism between theory and practice. Instead, we get a loop effect or a proper dialec-tical relationship between theory and practice and theory must not be under-stood as contemplative in this regard. Theory rather is infused with a practical understanding. This also constitutes a significant redefinition of philosophy itself as a *praxis*; 'Marx put together a practice of material transformation that brought theory and practice together in a relationship of reciprocity, with a theorising quite other to contemplation, "proposing to philosophy that it view itself in the mirror of practice"' (ibid, 41). Philosophy must thus reinvent itself, and such a reinvention can generate a much more integrated relation between philosophy and educational practice. Overall in this book, which seeks a repositioning of social theory in relation to education and educational research, we can see how such a political understanding connects to what Murphy and Costa call for in a chapter in this collection; the need for a simultaneous *hybridity* and *critical reflexivity* (Murphy and Costa 2022).

The teaching of philosophy and the issue of the university

We can see the practical implications of this reinvention of philosophical endeavour after deconstruction, also in the pedagogical work of Egéa-Kuehne (2004), Trifonas (2004a; 2004b), Peters (2004a; 2004b) and Garrison (2004). In each case, these thinkers and educational practitioners apply Derrida's insights (like Biesta and Lather) to situations of educational complexity in the con-temporary era.

In her essay, 'The teaching of philosophy: Renewed rights and responsi-bilities', Denise Egéa-Kuehne (2004) begins by citing Derrida's renewed call with regard to the importance of philosophy in contemporary education and politics. This also relates to Derrida's later work, where there is a far more explicit engagement with the issue of pedagogy and education: 'never has philosophy appeared to me as vitally indispensable as today' (Derrida 2002). This is a debate which, in France, has raged throughout the 20th century in institutional philosophy and especially with regard to both the teaching of philosophy in schools and also the status of the university itself, especially with regard to the issue of the philosophical foundations of the university system and third-level education. As Egéa-Kuehne makes clear, there is a strong continuity in Derrida's work in education, as he has been arguing since the 1970s for the fore-grounding of philosophy in education: '[Derrida] agreed with Canguilhem's statement that "the defense of the teaching of philosophy would require a critical philosophy of teaching"' (Egéa-Kuehne 2004, 21). Thus, for Derrida, the link between pedagogy and philosophy is intrinsic rather than merely extrinsic. Derrida is also quoted reinforcing the centrality of this notion of education to his work, early to late: 'the question of teaching runs through all my work and all my poli-tico-institutional engagements whether they concern schools and the university or media' (quoted in ibid, 21). Egéa-Kuehne's essay draws on the renewed sig-nificance of this relation between education and institutional politics which, of course, has become even more acute in recent times, with mass student demon-strations in recent times, for example in the United Kingdom.

Trifonas develops this thematic in his own essay in the volume, entitled 'The ethics of science and/as research: Deconstruction and the orientations of a new academic responsibility' (Trifonas 2004b, 31). Here, Trifonas focuses on some Derridean texts with an explicitly pedagogical thematic (Derrida 2002). Derrida here elaborates the whole philosophy behind the College of Philosophy: '"the principle of reason" – 'I am defining the necessity for a new way of educating students that will prepare them to undertake new analyses in order to evaluate these ends and choose, when possible, among them all' (Derrida quoted in Trifonas 2004b, 35). As Trifonas makes clear, less than a year after the above comment, the Collège International de Philosophie would open its doors to students and scholars (during January 1984), providing perhaps a much antici-pated answer to the suggestion of a rethinking of the institution of 'higher' education. Derrida was to be its first acting director, followed by Jean Francois Lyotard and others, in a succession of one year appointments.

Thus, while Derrida's understanding of the university looks back to the original Kantian model, it also deconstructs that model relentlessly and critiques its limita-tions and restrictiveness. Thus, Trifonas links what he terms the 'meta-logic' of deconstruction (Trifonas 2004b, 39) with the *praxis* of a new understanding of institutional education. On Trifonas' terms, this can be described as follows:

> the meta-logic of deconstruction defines the site of the struggle for a new academic responsibility. To effectuate a change in the thinking of the being of the university and the academic responsibility of our roles in it as researchers and intellectuals; to avoid reproducing the classical architectonic of the Kantian institution (grounded in the principle of reason), thereby entrenching its effects still further.
>
> (ibid, 39)

Deconstruction and pedagogy

In his essay, 'Derrida, pedagogy and the calculation of the subject' (Peters 2004b), Michael Peters reinforces much of what we have seen Trifonas, Biesta and Lather argue for in terms of the importance of deconstruction for pedagogy and education. Peters make this point in a more general way but perhaps even more vehemently, against those accusations of textualism and nihilism we quoted earlier:

> The relation of both Derrida and deconstruction to pedagogy is as clear as it is fundamental; Derridean philosophy offers an active interpretation, resistance and reevaluation of humanist pedagogy, of forms of pedagogy based on the sovereign subject – which is to say, the predominant forms of pedagogy existing today that structure our pedagogical institutions, theories and practices.
>
> (ibid, 61)

The subtlety of the phrasing is crucial to see here; Derrida offers not a destruction of the subject but a *reevaluation*, perhaps we can say a reconstruction or certainly a 'resituation', as Derrida uses the term elsewhere.

In the final essay worthy of note in the volume, Jim Garrison takes up the fascinating problematic of the relation between deconstruction and pragmatism and most especially the relation which is complex between Derrida and the educational work of John Dewey (Garrison 2004). What is also at stake here is the aforementioned question of the status of progressivism as an educational ideology. As Garrison makes clear, Dewey's own philosophy itself is subject to the contingency which Derrida so well elaborates: 'Still every construction is contingent in a Darwinian universe; hence, every construction is subject to deconstruction and reconstruction' (ibid, 104). So, according to Garrison, Dewey's philosophy also contains a deconstructive component. From a pedagogical perspective, we might argue that this leaves the possibility of a greater rapprochement between progressivism, pragmatism and deconstruction in education. Often in educational research, these theoretical paradigms are seen as mutually exclusive and conflictual.

Some conclusions

In conclusion, we can say that there are certain key concepts in our analysis of deconstruction which provide a matrix for the analysis of deconstruction and education. Most notably, they are 'the subject' or subjectivity, reflection and the notion of *praxis* itself. Lather (2004) and Biesta (2013) refer to contemporary theory as post-enlightenment and there is a clear rereading of the notion of philosophy here, as we have noted especially in relation to Marx and specifically the interpretation by Balibar invoked (Balibar 2007). In this context, Lather sees herself as being faithful exactly to Derrida's own word, especially in his later work and revisions of the meta-level reading of deconstruction as a radicalisation of Marx: 'I have echoed Derrida's claim that deconstruction only ever made sense to him as a radicalisation of Marx' (Lather 2004, 13). At the beginning of the chapter, we mentioned the tensions which exist between the theories of deconstruction and critical theory in education. However, we have seen how Derrida's later work particularly holds out the potential for a rapprochement in this regard, with significant implications for educational research. By the same token, we can perhaps employ the suspicions of McLaren (1994), amongst others, in a constructive way to avoid a simple identification of these two philosophies which make such a significant contribution to contemporary educational research. We can avoid unnecessary conflict, while maintaining distinctiveness.

Notes

1 Žižek initially had his Master's thesis rejected in Slovenia until he added a chapter which argued for the affinities between French 'structuralism' (broadly understood) and Marx. On this point, see Žižek (1994).
2 What this analysis, alongside that of Lather's, also allows us to do is to unpack some of the misunderstandings which were attendant on the aforementioned critique of progressivist education in the 1980s and 1990s. The debate concerning the contested understanding of progressivism (Darling and Nordenbo 2003) is at the heart of the question of how we understand the educational enterprise itself as well as the vision we might have for educational research (Irwin 2012).
3 Certainly, not the least complicating factor in this regard is the fact that many neo-Marxists, from Gramsci (1988) onwards if not before, have complicated and rejected the false consciousness picture. Thus, the deconstructive version of ideology is not necessarily at odds with more refined conceptions of ideology in the Marxist tradition. Indeed, another more recent evolution of this debate concerns a more psychoanalytical or specifically Lacanian reading of ideology, whether through the work of Alain Badiou or Jacques Rancière or paradigmatically in Slavoj Žižek's seminal *The sublime object of ideology*, later developed in Žižek (1994).

References

Balibar, E. 2007. *The philosophy of Marx*. London: Verso.
Biesta, G. 2013. *The beautiful risk of education*. Abingdon: Routledge.
Biesta, G. 2017. *The rediscovery of teaching*. Abingdon: Routledge.
Biesta, G. 2020. *Educational research: An unorthodox introduction*. London: Bloomsbury.
Blake, N. and J. Masschelein. 2003. Critical theory and critical pedagogy. In *The Blackwell guide to the philosophy of education*. eds. N. Blake, P. Smeyers, R. Smith and P. Standish, 38–57. Oxford: Blackwell.
Blake, N., P. Smeyers, R. Smith and P. Standish. eds. 2003a. *The Blackwell guide to the philosophy of education*. Oxford: Blackwell.
Blake, N., P. Smeyers, R. Smith and P. Standish. eds. 2003b. Introduction. In *The Blackwell guide to the philosophy of education*. eds. N. Blake, P. Smeyers, R. Smith and P. Standish, 1–18. Oxford: Blackwell.
Brown, T. and L. Jones. 2001. *Action research and postmodernism: Congruence and critique*. Milton Keynes: Open University Press.

Darling, J. and S.E. Nordenbo. 2003. Progressivism. In *The Blackwell guide to the philosophy of education*. eds. N. Blake, P. Smeyers, R. Smith and P. Standish, 288–308. Oxford: Blackwell.

Derrida, J. 1974. *Of grammatology*. Trans. Gayatri Chakavorty Spivak. Baltimore, MD: John Hopkins University Press.

Derrida, J. 1977. *Margins of philosophy*. Trans. Alan Bass. Chicago, IL: Chicago University Press.

Derrida, J. 1981. *Dissemination*. Trans. with an introduction by Barbara Johnson. Chicago, IL: University of Chicago Press.

Derrida, J. 2001a. On cosmopolitanism. Trans. Mark Dooley. In J. Derrida. *Cosmopolitanism and forgiveness*. Abingdon: Routledge.

Derrida, J. 2001b. On forgiveness. Trans. Michael Hughes. In J. Derrida. *Cosmopolitanism and forgiveness*. Abingdon: Routledge.

Derrida, J. 2002. *Who's afraid of philosophy?: Right to philosophy* I. Stanford, CA: Stanford University Press.

Egéa-Kuehne, D. 2004. The teaching of philosophy: Renewed rights and responsibilities. In *Derrida, deconstruction and education: Ethics of pedagogy and research*. eds. M. Peters and P. Trifonas, 17–31. Oxford: Blackwell.

Freire, P. 1996. *Pedagogy of the oppressed*. London: Penguin.

Garrison, J. 2004. Dewey, Derrida and 'the double bind'. In *Derrida, deconstruction and education: Ethics of pedagogy and research*. eds. M. Peters and P. Trifonas, 95–108. Oxford: Blackwell.

Giroux, H. 2000. *Breaking in to the movies*. New York, NY: Routledge.

Gramsci, A. 1988. *The Antonio Gramsci reader: Selected writings 1916–1935*. ed. D. Forgacs. London: Lawrence and Wishart.

Irwin, J. 2010a. *Derrida and the writing of the body*. Aldershot: Ashgate.

Irwin, J. 2010b. Re-politicising education – Interpreting Jean-François Lyotard's May '68 texts and the postmodern condition in a contemporary educational context. In *Yearbook of the Irish Philosophical Society*. ed. C. McDonnell, 37–53. Maynooth: NUIM.

Irwin, J. 2012. *Paulo Freire's philosophy of education: Origins, development, impacts and legacies*. London: Continuum.

Kearney, R. 1984. *Dialogues with contemporary continental thinkers*. Manchester: Manchester University Press.

Lather, P. 2004. Applied Derrida: (Mis)Reading the work of mourning in educational research. In *Derrida, deconstruction and education: Ethics of pedagogy and research*. eds. M. Peters and P. Trifonas, 3–16. Oxford: Blackwell.

McLaren, P. 1994. Postmodernism and the death of politics: A Brazilian reprieve. In *Politics of liberation: Paths from Freire*. eds. P. McLaren and C. Lankshear, 93–215. Abingdon: Routledge.

Murphy, M. and C. Costa. 2022. Social theory and methodology in education research: From conceptualisation to operationalisation. In *Social theory and education research. Understanding Foucault, Habermas, Bourdieu and Derrida*. 2nd edn. ed. M. Murphy, 24–43. Abingdon: Routledge.

O'Cadiz, M., P. del Pilar, C.A. Torres and P. Lindquist. 1998. *Education and democracy: Paulo Freire, social movements and educational reform in Sao Paulo*. Oxford: Westview Press.

Peters, M. 2004a. Preface. In *Derrida, deconstruction and education: Ethics of pedagogy and research*. eds. M. Peters and P. Trifonas, viii–x. Oxford: Blackwell.

Peters, M. 2004b. Derrida, pedagogy and the calculation of the subject. In *Derrida, deconstruction and education: Ethics of pedagogy and research*. eds. M. Peters and P. Trifonas, 59–79. Oxford: Blackwell.

Peters, M. and J. Marshall. 1996. *Individualism and community: Education and social policy in the postmodern condition*. London: Falmer Press.

Peters, M. and Trifonas, P. 2004. *Derrida, deconstruction and education: Ethics of pedagogy and research*. Oxford: Blackwell.

Peters, M. and K. Wilson. 2003. Postmodernism/post-structuralism. In *The Blackwell guide to the philosophy of education*. eds. N. Blake et al., 57–72. Oxford: Blackwell.

Pring, R. 2004. *Philosophy of education: Aims, theory, common sense and research*. London: Continuum.

Spivak, G. 1993. *Outside in the teaching machine*. New York, NY: Routledge.

St. Pierre, B. and W. Pillow. eds. 2000. *Working the ruins: Feminist poststructural practice and theory in education*. New York, NY: Routledge.

Stronach, I. and M. MacLure. 1997. *Educational research undone: The postmodern embrace*. Milton Keynes: Open University Press.

Trifonas, P. 2000. *The ethics of writing: Derrida, deconstruction and pedagogy*. Oxford: Rowan and Littlefield.

Trifonas, P. 2004a. Introduction: Derrida and the philosophy of education. In*Derrida, deconstruction and education: Ethics of pedagogy and research*. eds. M. Peters and P. Trifonas, 1–3. Oxford: Blackwell.

Trifonas, P. 2004b. The ethics of science and/as research: Deconstruction and the orientations of a new academic responsibility. In *Derrida, deconstruction and education: Ethics of pedagogy and research*. eds. M. Peters and P. Trifonas, 31–43. Oxford: Blackwell.

Žižek, S. 1994. Introduction: The spectre of ideology. In *Mapping ideology*. ed. S. Žižek, i–xx. London: Verso.

13 'Derrida applied'

Derrida meets Dracula in the geography classroom

Christine Winter

Introduction

Derrida contends in his *Letter to a Japanese friend* that 'deconstruction is not a method' (Derrida 1988, 3). It is not a set of rules that can be instrumentally applied, neither is it an act or an operation. Instead, 'deconstruction takes place' (ibid, 4). In other words, things self-deconstruct or are opened up to deconstruction when they are read carefully. This contention presents an immediate challenge in the writing of this chapter when my designated purpose is to 'apply' theory in a research setting for an audience of educational researchers and advanced practitioners. Whilst expressing my apologies to Jacques Derrida and his followers as I write the chapter, at the same time, I note the need to interpret and engage with thinking about deconstruction in ways that allow for its dissemination, given the opportunities it accords for thinking differently about educational and curriculum matters. In order to pursue my purpose, I have divided the chapter into three sections. In the first section I provide my interpretation of deconstruction together with a brief account of the work of researchers who are concerned about 'applying' Derrida in education. As a link into the curriculum project itself, I explain the relevance of Derrida's ideas to the curriculum problem under study. The focus in section two is the school-based research project and how Derrida's ideas were engaged in the development, teaching and evaluation of a curriculum unit for a class of students aged 12–13 in a state comprehensive school in the north of England. The project was not without its challenges and high points and these are recounted in the third section of the chapter.

In this, the second edition of Mark Murphy's 2013 edited collection, I revisit the relationship between theory and method as presented in my original chapter for three reasons. The first is to provide a rationale for my decisions, the second to give a glimpse of the kinds of challenges researchers face in bridging the theory-method dyad, and the third to offer thoughts about future research. I achieve this by adding 'reflections' in italics to sections of the original text.

Deconstruction

Deconstruction involves the close reading of texts of any kind in such a way as to demonstrate the three tenets of Derrida's work: First, that meanings of words

DOI: 10.4324/9781003156550-18

are insecure and never fully under our control; second, that the metaphysics of presence implies the existence of an underpinning unity of knowledge that needs to be disrupted to expose its internal illogicalities as well as the source of its authorisation; and, third, that deconstruction opens up a space for justice – a space in which the other (something new, productive and unforeseeable) emerges. The first tenet (the insecurity of word meanings) rests on two ideas: *Différance* and deferral. Derrida argues against the proposal that the relationship between a word (sign or signifier) and its meaning (signified) is determined, concrete and stable. He proposes that an inscription or mark does not represent a thing or image, as if reflected in a mirror. Instead, the relationship between a word and its meaning is more diffuse and active, what he describes as 'the regulated play of differences' and 'the instituted trace' he calls *différance* (Derrida 1976, 62). The implication of this argument for the reading of texts suggests that word meanings escape accurate definition and conceptualisation because word meanings arise from differences to other words, allowing semantic slippage or deferral to occur, whereby meanings become parts of ever-emerging chains of signification:

> It is because of *différance* that the movement of signification is possible only if each so-called 'present' element, each element appearing on the scene of presence, is related to something other than itself, thereby keeping within itself the mark of the past element, and already letting itself be vitiated by the mark of its relation to the future element, this trace being related no less to what is called the future than to what is called the past, and constituting what is called the present by means of this very relation to what is not: what is absolutely what is not, not even if a past or a future as a modified present
>
> (Derrida 1972, 13)

Exceeding the metaphysics of presence, the second tenet in Derrida's way of thinking, suggests that the unity of knowledge which seemingly underpins arguments, concepts and frameworks of thinking, is an illusion and needs to be prodded and questioned to expose its cracks and crevices, to expose who authorised it and why. A deconstructive reading achieves this, first, by considering what the author intends or means to say and second, by considering what is going on in terms of language and meaning behind the author's back. The former requires the reader to engage in critical depth with the author's ideas, background, context, pre-suppositions and purpose. This first re-productive reading provides access to the author's intended meaning within which an initial interpretation can occur. But a second, productive, reading that exceeds the author's framework and parameters is required next:

> … The possibility must be kept alive of reading otherwise, which means passing through the classical discipline, and never having abandoned or jettisoned it, to explore what it omits, forget, excludes, expels,

marginalises, dismisses, ignores, scorns, slights, takes too lightly, waves off, is just not serious enough about!

(Caputo 1997, 79)

The latter approach opens onto a generative reading, a reading that transgresses the metaphysics of presence and looks through other frameworks, other parameters, other differential plays of the trace. Such a reading is described as providing exteriority because it goes beyond the assumed authority of the text and opens up the text to other ways of thinking that were not encountered during the first re-productive reading.

The third tenet, that 'deconstruction is justice' (Derrida 1992, 15) is problematical in the light of the denial of self-present meaning as argued above (ibid, 10). According to Derrida, justice here serves as an enframing concept, in need of deconstructive attention. Allowing justice to self-deconstruct will reveal it as beyond definition. Nevertheless, although justice remains 'an experience of the impossible' (ibid, 15) it should never be neglected. It is an unquestionable 'responsibility without limits' (ibid, 19) in the sense of opening up a space for a more just and democratic future than the experience of the present. The responsibility for justice rests on the act of bringing fresh eyes to a problem, on drawing on a unique and responsible interpretation of the problem in order to reinstitute and reinvent what was and what could be (*democratie à venir*). In the context of this study, the relation between justice and the curriculum is located in the questioning of the performative school culture and of traditional versions of curriculum knowledge about a place, leading to an openness towards other ways of knowing.

The aporia of 'Derrida applied'

I return briefly to the quandary expressed at the start of this chapter. If deconstruction is not a method or a tool that can be applied (Derrida 1997, 9; Brannington et al. 1996, xix), then, as educators we are faced with a dilemma when we wish to think about deconstruction in pursuit of ethical practice in the school classroom. We are confronted with an impossible situation, an aporia. The aporia, according to Derrida is 'the impossible or the impractical' (Derrida 1993, 13), 'the non-passage' (ibid, 12). When paralysed, immobilised by our confrontation with the aporia, we look around for another way, a space for the other, something Derrida describes as the *arrivant*. In other words, to recap: Deconstruction occurs whether we wish it to or not. It is automatic, non-applicable. It is not a programme that can be applied. Our role in education, is, then, to follow an-other way, in showing, disclosing, witnessing the event by revealing how the impossible is always and already the possible. Bennington describes our role as 'showing metaphysics in deconstruction' (Bennington 2000, 11) and in so doing, opening up a space for 'repeating metaphysics differently' (ibid). Our showing as teachers is an ethical experience because we are responsible for the future of the others in our care (Edgoose

2001, 131). It involves us in the disruption of the metaphysics of presence underpinning the knowledge and culture of our classroom practices that exclude the other (Biesta 2009a, 109; Blake et al. 1998, 38–39). It involves a responsibility for the engagement and engrossment of our students in their studies, a concern for and commitment to undecidability where fresh and free decisions can emerge and an openness to the arrival of the unforeseeable other, what Caputo describes as 'inventionalism' (Caputo 1997, 42; see also Biesta 2009b, 395). Egéa-Kuehne draws attention to the affirmation of otherness and alterity available when educators disrupt the safety and comfort of assumedly well-established, transparent, neutral knowledge and the illusion of cultural homogeneity by facilitating the bringing out for students that which is over-looked: controversy, multiple voices, risk-taking, difference and the unknown (Egéa-Kuehne 1996, 160; 2001, 203).

Addressing the first aporia encountered in the project and opening a space for 'repeating metaphysics differently' (Bennington 2000) requires some back-ground information. The school subject of geography for 11–14 year-olds (known as Key Stage 3 (KS3) in England) experienced a tough time during the first decade of the 21st century. The current Geography National Curriculum (GNC) bears a legacy from the first GNC of 1991, of out-dated subject knowledge (Rawling 2001). A steep decline in school-based curriculum development, a reliance on non-specialist teachers and on textbook teaching in some schools did not aid its recovery. In addition, the severing of links between university and school geography cut off access to the input of fresh and inno-vative thinking. Competition with other school subjects and the arrival of skills-based competency curricula in early 2000, in which humanities subjects such as geography, history and religious education were 'integrated', did little to enhance the status of the discrete subject. In 2005, Ofsted stated 'in many schools geography lacks rigour and fails to motivate young people' (Ofsted 2005, 8–9). In 2008, the same organisation reported school geography as '"boring" and lacking relevance'; 'heavy in content' and 'driven by textbooks' (Ofsted 2008, para 49, 23). Given this situation, any self-respecting geography educator who, believing that the word geo-graphy (meaning 'writing the earth'), carries responsibilities to investigate and improve the means available to students and teachers of writing/righting the earth, is motivated to act. I argued in 2009 (Winter 2009b), that the concepts underpinning the knowledge and language used in school geography curriculum policy traps meaning in certain ways that prevent other ways of knowing from emerging. Armchair theorising like this has its place, but some form of showing, disclosing, witnessing this argument inside the geography classroom was called for and took effect in the form of a commitment to attempt to revitalise school geographical knowledge through the development and teaching of a new KS3 curriculum unit for a class of youngsters.

Reflections: Here, I explain why I was attracted to Derrida's perspective in this pro-ject. My own study of the earth through the subject of geography in school and university contrasted sharply with my lived experience of it. For example, as a 17 year-old schoolgirl on an A-level fieldtrip to the Isle of Arran, I encountered my first U-shaped glaciated valley. I had drawn countless annotated diagrams of this geomorphological feature in lessons, for homework and examinations, but had never actually seen one until that day. I described this as an-'other way of knowing' the earth:

> *The valley was deeply sculptured, dark and chilling. The sight of this huge and magnificent place was breath-taking in its scale and awesomeness. I sensed I was knowing something exceptional, something unknowable, something that was quite different from my usual experience of knowing the landscape through my teacher's dictation and pages in books in the safety and comfort of my geography classroom. I was shocked, disturbed and disoriented by the emptiness and eeriness as I confronted this mysterious feature, which I had always felt I had under control – captured and neatly annotated using the correct technical terms in various exercise books – pyramidal peak, arêtes, hanging valleys, truncated spurs, corries, drumlins, scree slopes … during many hours of patient engagement as an obedient pupil in the geography classroom*

(Winter 2013, 281)

I was attracted to Derrida's ideas because they offered an opportunity to see and write the earth differently, by unshackling the earth from the constraints of totalising technical discourses of traditional academic geography, and regenerating it in more responsible and imaginative forms.

The school-based research project

The curriculum unit was developed and taught by two geography teachers (Sally and John) and myself between December 2008 and April 2009. The official policy context for the unit was the GNC (DCSF/QCA 2007, 100–109). The two teachers identified the need for a new unit focusing on the topic of coasts for Year 8 students, and we agreed that the overall scheme of work should be planned around an introduction to a stretch of coast in the United Kingdom; a study of the physical landscape of that coast and of a specific place located on the coast, followed by a fieldtrip. There is insufficient space here to report full details of discussions within the team about decisions made and actions taken, although these were all recorded, transcribed and analysed as part of the research project. For the same reason, I will be unable to recount the process and results of the entire curriculum project; instead, I will concentrate on the one section for which I took the main responsibility. Needless to say, a key and obvious dimension of this process of showing metaphysics in deconstruction in the classroom involved negotiation and compromise on the part of the team, for example, in complying with GNC requirements and school performativity pressures at the same time as reading these policy drivers differently, that is in accordance with the idea of *différance*. In respect to policy requirements, these comprised the following: An understanding of the physical and human characteristics of real places; developing 'geographical imaginations' of places; knowing where places are located; understanding the relationship between the physical and human worlds and developing cultural understanding and understanding of diversity. In respect to school performativity pressures, these will be discussed later. In respect to the third condition, of reading GNC requirements differently, the team sought to exceed the GNC requirements by bringing into being other knowledge about a place, not through the traditional conceptual gaze of the geographer, but through writing the earth differently (Winter 2009b, 64). The area chosen for study was that of the north-east coast of Yorkshire, England, between Whitby and Spurn Head because it is well-known to families of students attending the research school, being a traditional, popular and accessible holiday destination. Our task was to engage productively with knowledge about Whitby through disclosure of metaphysics in deconstruction: Disclosing an-other Whitby in a way that engaged our students by revealing something unexpected, inventive and unknown. The two teachers took the lead in developing a problem-solving activity about the problems of and solutions to coastal erosion in the southern part of the coast under study. I took the lead in a study of the coastal town of Whitby, which offers a multitude of opportunities for disrupting the metaphysics of presence assumed to reside within traditional conceptualisations of place study in the discipline of geography. In the descriptions of the student research enquiries to follow, the focus is on the planned lesson topics, activities and their rationales relating to the northern section of coast, specifically on the town of Whitby. This is followed by showing metaphysics in deconstruction with respect to data analysis, the performativity culture residing in the school and traditional conceptualisations of geographical knowledge held by the two project teachers. The chapter ends with an account of spaces for thinking otherwise created within the project and a reflection on the notion of 'Derrida applied'.

Reflections: Here, I make two reflections on theory. The first is that the two teachers with whom I worked kindly gave me time and space to develop the Whitby section of the project. Both were self-confessed 'physical' geographers, rather than 'human' or 'cultural' geographers who may have been attracted to a Derridean project. Both teachers felt more comfortable with coastal erosion than deconstruction. In this respect, I was not successful in disrupting the totalising divisions of geography as a school subject by the three of us working as a collaborative team across the whole curriculum unit. But, of course, the two teachers were accountable to the GNC, Ofsted and the future survival of their subject in the school. My second reflection relates to the dissonance between the Derridean approach I engaged for the knowledge content of the Whitby section and the technical methodological approach I engaged in the collection of data (I recorded and transcribed team planning meetings, student focus groups and teacher interviews; I observed lessons, analysed students' written work and kept a research diary). I suspect that, had I been supervising a student undertaking such a study, this would have formed a point of discussion at our first meeting! I admit that the rationale for my methodological approach was my familiarity with it, arising from previous experience together with an eye on the need for 'minimally-disruptive disruption' in the politically sensitive environment of a Geography Department under pressure. I discuss these methods, the school context and the challenges of data analysis later.

The curriculum unit: Introduction

After a lesson introducing the coastal area under study, students worked in groups to construct their own questionnaires to find out what their families, friends and neighbours thought about the area under study. The process involved a move away from a reliance on an authoritative textbook perspective of the place, en-framed through a traditional geographical lens to a more localised, multi-vocal and immediate view, from the perspectives of those who know the place well and have experienced it first-hand. We wanted students and those responding to the questionnaires to be aware of the range of different ways of understanding this place and to participate actively in contributing to those understandings. Students collected their data, analysed it and devised presentation methods to disseminate the findings to a wide audience, including their respondents. The section of the curriculum unit focusing on the harbour town of Whitby consisted of four research enquiries. Each group of Year 8 students conducted one enquiry.

The research enquiries

1 Whitby Abbey

An important attraction for tourists visiting Whitby is the Abbey ruins, owned and looked after by English Heritage. The Abbey is located on the site of an Anglo-Saxon Monastery dating from 657 AD. The famous 199 steps lead from the town to the site of the Abbey. The ruins of the Abbey are visible from miles around in the daytime because of its strategic position high up on a headland overlooking Whitby Harbour. At dawn and dusk, the ruins are sil-houetted against the sky, adding to the eerie atmosphere of the town. The Abbey is important because of its contribution to the town's history and pre-sent-day tourist economy. It is interesting to geographers and historians because of its strategic location on a promontory jutting out into the North Sea, high above the surrounding land and because of the significant role the monastery community played in the history of Christianity (Barnwell et al. 2003; Bede 731/1999, 731). The first curriculum activity used different sources (pictures in brochures, a painting by Turner and various kinds of maps) to encourage stu-dents to think about different ways to portray the location of Whitby Abbey. The second activity involved the analysis of a text about Whitby Abbey/ Monastery in which the language used plays on the idea of the 'head'. The third activity involved students searching websites to find images of Whitby Abbey showing the importance of its location high above the town. In the second activity, students explored how the text plays with the word 'head' in different ways. Students were asked to identify as many words as possible in the text which bore some connection to the word 'head' and to underline them before making a list of the words and explaining the connection of each to the word 'head'. This example was provided from the text below: 'High-up – the head is high-up at the top of the body'

A Monastery was founded in 657 AD on the Headland in Whitby. It is located high up on the cliff-top of the Headland, overlooking Whitby harbour. This is now the site of the ruins of Whitby Abbey.

In the seventh century Whitby Monastery was an important religious place, at the head of the Christian Church. It was at the top level of religious learning. It was the place where important religious people visited and were buried. It was also a place where people saw holy visions and experienced miracles.

The Monastery was situated on a high cliff overlooking the harbour where boats and ships of all kinds arrived and departed. Some of the ships carried new discoveries, inventions and ideas from the European continent into Britain. Whitby Monastery was an important nerve-centre of the region.

In 664 AD, the Monastery formed the focal point for an exciting event in the Christian Church called the Synod of Churches. This was where an argument was ended about two things:

1 the precise timing of Easter in the Christian calendar and
2 which hairstyle the monks should wear

2 The Whitby jet set

Anyone walking along Whitby's main Church Street cannot fail to notice the number of shops selling jewellery made from Whitby jet. Jet is one of the world's oldest gems, a black shiny material formed in the Jurassic period from decaying Araucaria araucana trees, more commonly known as monkey puzzle trees, and is called a 'mineraloid'. It was mined in the Whitby area in the past and pieces of jet eroded from the cliffs can still be found on Whitby beaches. Today the sale of jet in Whitby shops contributes to Whitby's economy and jet forms an important part of Whitby's cultural heritage and life. A traditional approach to studying Whitby in school geography would treat the geological formation of the gemstone as an aspect of the physical geography of the place and the production and sale of the stone as economic or human geography. In this study, the boundaries between physical and human geography are collapsed into a web-based enquiry into the place of a gemstone in a particular place. The activity involved using contemporary websites about Whitby jet to research its geological formation, history and politics. The final activity consisted of a close and critical analysis of three Whitby jet websites as cultural texts in order to understand how website designs, colours, language, styles of lettering, graphics and media are used in different ways to achieve different purposes.

3 The 'explorer' Captain James Cook

The explorer Captain James Cook served his apprenticeship as a trainee seafarer in Whitby from 1747 to 1756, working on the 'coal cats', small flat-bottomed ships carrying coal from the North-East of England to London. A skilled cartographer, Cook was employed by the British Admiralty to map the world on three successful 'voyages of discovery' in 1768 (on the *Endeavour* – to look for the 'Great Southern Continent' (GSC); 1772 (on the *Resolution* – again to look for the GSC) and 1776 (on the *Resolution* and the *Discovery* – to find out if a North-West Passage existed). All three ships were built in Whitby. Cook died on the shore in Kealakekua Bay, Hawaii in 1779. A range of explanations about his death exist, including the disappointment of locals when they discovered that the Captain and his crew were mere mortals and not the gods they had supposed them to be (Villiers 1967) and local resistance to the 'invaders' when Cook and his crew threatened to take a local leader as ransom for the theft of one of his cutters. Williams (2008) describes the rise in popular interest about 'How did Captain Cook meet his death?', with various interpretations by authors such as Dawes (1968), Beaglehole (1979), Sahlins (1985; 1995) and Dening (1996) There is a statue of Cook on the West Cliff in Whitby, overlooking the harbour.

Studying Cook's voyages raises interesting political questions for geographers which were covered in the curriculum unit. These included claims to British 'ownership' of coastal lands and their 're-naming' by Cook and his crew; the idea of 'discovery' of lands; the objectives of his voyages which were to secure trading destinations for British goods and manufactures; to acquire land and raw materials and to 'discover' and classify 'new' natural species, including 'new' human societies and intercultural issues focusing on power relations between indigenous people, Cook and his crews.

4 Dracula

Bram Stoker thought of the idea of a story about vampires when he was on holiday in Whitby in 1890 and published the novel *Dracula* in 1897 (Stoker 1897). The harbour port of Whitby figures strongly in several sections of the story – and two were selected for closer examination by the Year 8 students. The first extract is taken from the play *Dracula* adapted by David Calcutt (Stoker 1999, 40–41). It is the story of the arrival during a great storm of a Russian ship called the *Demeter*, into Whitby harbour. The ship carried Count Dracula from his home in Transylvania to England. Dracula's arrival in England was a little unusual and is portrayed vividly in the script. The second extract is taken from the original novel. It describes how one of the novel's characters, Lucy first met Count Dracula in St. Mary's churchyard on the East cliff overlooking the harbour. The students were asked to trace the route taken by Lucy as she sleep-walked from her lodgings on the West Cliff, to learn about the geography of the town using the novel, maps and photographs. The two extracts illustrate how the real place of Whitby can be thought about in a different way from the ways in which geographers usually think about real places, this time through fiction. Both extracts emphasise the mystery, suspense, thrill and chill that still remain around the harbour town. The Whitby tourist industry takes advantage of the Dracula connection in several ways: Shops selling Goth clothing and artefacts, a twice-yearly Goth weekend which attracts visitors from around the world, the 'Dracula Experience' and regular guided ghost walks around the town 'in search of Dracula'. A significant shift in tone and subject matter will be experienced by the reader in the next section, as I debate about the nature of data and its analysis in the context of this deconstructive study.

Challenges and high points

Showing the metaphysics of data analysis

The school-based project described above was, on the one hand, a curriculum development project and, at the same time, an educational research project. Design of the project occurred with an eye on the importance of 'dissemination', 'impact' and 'publication' of educational research findings as valued currency for transaction within the contemporary era of performativity in the educational research community. Adopting a traditional research approach, I conducted a logical sequence of research stages, moving from research questions to literature and theory to methodology, methods, analysis and presentation of findings. I organised comprehensive, rigorous and systematic data collection and analysis during the project's duration. I made audio recordings of all the planning meetings held with the two project teachers. I interviewed each project teacher individually on two separate occasions and conducted four student focus group interviews with students who had studied each of the topics described above. I collected samples of student work throughout the project as well as recording lesson observations and keeping a research diary. It was not until the point when I begin data coding, analysis and interpretation that I hit the second aporia of the project. It consisted of an obstacle to the showing of metaphysics in deconstruction with regard to the orthodoxy of analysis in educational research. I realised the danger that treating the 'data as given' reduces it to an inert raw material awaiting the application of procedure; that the tight framing of the project with certain instrumental goals and time frame in mind shapes the end result; that an assertive, logical analytical procedure applied to 'the data' serves as a one-way track to fast and efficient completion that can easily overlook the messiness and the ethical importance of the whole experience (Standish 2001, 498). Faced with the metaphysics of objectifying systematic analysis, the identification of recurring themes and anomalies and the measurement of their degree of correspondence with, or challenge to the findings of previous studies, I took a walk:

> When you go for a walk you must let your thoughts flutter randomly, letting them have a go now here, now there. That is how to arrange one's housekeeping. Themata are the accidents that the week should deliver to you in abundance. But the more you see to it that the dividends are

uncertain, the freer, better, richer they will become, and the more striking, surprising, penetrating.

(Kierkgaard 1996, 454, cited in Standish 2001, 504)

Deconstructive reading of the interview transcriptions showed the metaphysics of presence lurking beneath the language of educational, school and subject policy discourses engaged with by project teachers. I identified two dominant themata or totalising discourses embedded within the 'data'. These emerged as challenges during the project to impede the unrolling of a more dangerously inventive approach. One is the performativity-driven culture of the school and other is constraining versions of school geographical knowledge.

Reflections: The performative culture of the neoliberal education system was playing out for me as a researcher in higher education, through the importance of 'dissemination', 'impact' and 'publication' in the sense of my job security and career development through the project. This pressure of accountability and self-responsibilisation was felt also by the two project teachers in the context of the accountability culture of their school. The extent of the latter circumstance is discussed next.

Showing the metaphysics of performativity culture

Ball (2007) describes performativity as 'a culture and mode of regulation' which 'ties the effort of management to the information systems of the market and customer choice-making and/or to the target and benchmark requirements of the state' (ibid, 27). The curriculum project began several months after the school received an Ofsted report which was not as favourable as expected, and the agreement of the school to work with the project was linked to the Ofsted report in the sense that the project was 'steered' by the two teachers to comply with Ofsted requirements to some degree, thus limiting the project's aim of undermining dominant totalising discourses to make way for the Derridean incoming of the other. The thrust of the report focused on the need to raise standards of attainment in the school through, among other things, increased challenge in lessons, improvements in students' learning skills and curriculum development in line with students' needs. A clear directive was given to improve the school's management and leadership capacity in order to achieve these and other goals. At the start of the project, Sally reported the Head-teacher's reference to the school as 'coasting' in a meeting. This term refers to schools which are 'underperforming', 'drifting' and 'content to muddle along without trying hard to improve' (Number 10 2012). In the case of examination attainment in geography in this school at GCSE level 2007–09, results were consistently below the regional average for grades A*–A and grades A*–C.

Two further issues were evident as contributing to the school's willingness to participate in the project. The first was the decline, year-on-year in the numbers of students opting to study geography at Key Stage 4 (KS4, GCSE) and the second was the increasing pressure to move from a curriculum in which the subjects of geography, history and religious studies were taught discretely, to an integrated, competency-based humanities curriculum. This was a change John and Sally were determined to resist as they identified themselves as established subject specialists. Alongside the teachers' aims to improve the teaching of geography in the school in a general sense, the aims of the strategies introduced in response to the Ofsted report were two-fold: first to improve examination attainment at KS4 by appropriate development of the curriculum at KS3 and second, to increase the attractiveness of geography to KS3 students in order to improve recruitment to the KS4 course. The project contributed to the achievement of these aims by presenting opportunities for integrating into the KS3 programme of study knowledge and activities that would prepare students to achieve at higher levels at KS4 and the addition of a fieldtrip to the new KS3 curriculum unit would attract students to continue their study of the subject beyond KS3. The metaphysics of performativity demonstrates, by its instrumentalism and emphasis on outcomes of improved examination grades and increased subject recruitment, the kinds of constraints that limit the scope for in-ventionalism and the incoming of the other. Another metaphysics was at work in the project to influence its possibilities – that relating to totalising concepts underpinning subject knowledge and teacher identities.

Showing the metaphysics of school geography knowledge

The second obstacle to the incoming of the other through the curriculum project was the conceptualisations of knowledge operating between Sally and John with regard to the subject of geography. Both teachers had a strong commitment to 'physical' geography and understood the geographical world through long-established scientistic ideas. Scientism or quasi-science assumes the ascendance of scientific objectivity in the form of concepts, principles and procedures and applies them to matters that lie outside the realm of science. Examples include the domination of school geography by universalising dis-courses that attempt to impose 'true' order and control on the world through, for example, notions of physical and human geography as separate domains of knowledge; cause and effect and the existence of regular patterns and processes that exist 'out there' in the 'real world', awaiting identification, description and explanation as if they were objective truths (Cloke, Philo and Sadler 1991, 187). Examples in the project include references by teachers in the interviews and planning meetings to 'the interaction between people and the natural world', 'the way in which the physical features have, I suppose, led to eco-nomic activities' and '... an awful lot of the culture comes from the sea ... so the culture and the sort of economic activity are inextricably linked'.

In the division of labour within the project, I took the lead in planning the section which focused on the historical, literary and cultural geography of Whitby, the harbour town located in the north of the stretch of coast under study. Sally and John developed the unit sections focusing on the interaction between the physical and human environments in the southern coastal region, together with planning the fieldtrip. This allocation of tasks highlights our respective identities as 'human/cultural' and 'physical' geographers, keen to remain in the comfort zone of our knowledge, skills and experience within the subject domain. This idea of the teacher's subject identity and desire to remain in their comfort zone are illustrated through an example which arose during a planning meeting when we contemplated different activities associated with Whitby which might be developed. Two suggestions came up: Goths and whaling. John, whose undergraduate degree was in geology said:

> I like the idea of the whaling more than the Goths, because I think I'd feel a bit out of my depth with the Goth thing to be honest. I don't think I'd know enough, because they'd [students] know quite a bit as well. I think … you know when you can see how much you're going to have sit at home and go 'right … how am I going to plan this lesson?'

Opening a space …

A key limitation to collaborative curriculum development in the research school prior to the introduction of the project under examination here was the senior management responsibilities of geography teachers and the scattered location of their offices in the school building. The time demands of management and infrequency of serendipitous meetings in a common staff room reduced opportunities for discussion about the curriculum amongst geography teachers. Prior to the arrival of John, responsibility for developing the curriculum lay in the hands of Sally, as Head of Department. She worked alone and passed on new ideas to senior colleagues who made their own interpretations of these ideas and taught accordingly. This situation was exacerbated by the increasing use of ICT whereby each geography teacher developed and saved their own electronic resources, compared to the situation in more collaborative contexts where curriculum materials are held on and accessed via a shared drive.

The first space opened by the project was a space for collaboration. Its arrival was welcomed by John and Sally as an opportunity to participate in a different kind of curriculum planning based on co-operation and discussion. Sally described the project as 'extra work, but it's come from sort of discussion where we've talked about and been enthusiastic about a new direction we're going in. And I suppose the best measure of extra work is whether you look up and think 'oh crikey I didn't realise it was that time' (1 April 2009, 13).[1] She believed there was strength in three people working together because of the generation of ideas: 'we bounced a lot of ideas around to start with' (ibid, 14), continuing:

> when there's three of you, we looked at, talked about, rejected some things introduced things that anyone of us would never have come up with, that we did have lots of good discussions about loads and loads of interesting and different ways of doing things. I think it was a learning experience for us all.

(ibid, 14)

John concurred:

> Well, the good thing is the sort of fact that we actually sit down and have time to think about it which is huge … and it's more than one person. Because sometimes you sit by yourself and you go: 'I don't know …'
>
> (23 February 2009, 11)

The second space was one which was opened up for the students by the introduction of the study of places with which most were familiar in some ways, but not in those ways to which the project introduced them. Sally summed it up:

> we are taking kids where they know but are not familiar with and looking at something from a perspective that they normally wouldn't take. So they come away from it with a greater depth of knowledge and, hopefully enthusiasm, for something that is quite close to them but far away enough not to be too familiar
>
> (1 April 2009, 15)

Third, the teachers themselves felt that they participated in the opening of a space for new geographical knowledge and understanding entering the curriculum through their rejection of pre-made text-book based resources about case study places and their preference for their own ideas and materials:

> The fact that everything is fresh and new and developed really from the ground-up is good … it is that creativity thing, because we do know our kids and we know how well they'll respond. And I think what we've designed and what we've presented plays to their strengths as well
>
> (Sally, 1 April 2009, p.15)

This creativity was not without its risks, as all three of us engaged with the new knowledge and felt insecure about no longer relying on our well-established, well-practiced knowledge and skills in teaching the subject.

The questionnaire activity at the start of the project opened up a fourth space not only for the students' voices to be heard, but for those of their parents, families, neighbours and friends. As John said: 'we just wanted to get what they [students] already knew about it rather than teaching them' (06–04–09, 4). Several parents remarked positively and curiously about the project at the parents' evening which took place towards the end of the project. A fifth space for the emergence of a new kind of geography was created out of the breakdown of the binary of physical and human geography. John, the geologist said: 'it's kind of quite varied and I like the fact that there's no real "just physical" [geography] lessons, it's a sort of mix all the way through …' (23 April 2009, 12). An earlier point made by John a few days before is appropriate here: 'I think it's made us think a little bit more about doing cultural stuff, which we didn't really touch on before, maybe in discussion but not to the same extent' (6 April 2009, 3). The final space was space for the incoming of the unknown, something that is noticeable by its absence in conventional geography lessons. The idea of the unknown is not so much that students do not know something before a lesson and consider this as unknown, before learning it during the lesson and then knowing after the lesson. It is more that, through the study of Dracula and Captain Cook's death, students encountered, in the first example, the unknown beyond the human form and the feelings of mystery, thrill and chill previously unknown in the geography classroom. In the second example, the cause of Cook's death remains an anathema today, and yet, unsurprisingly is subject to a variety of perspectival explanations. Some mysteries are never solved.

Did the curriculum project open up a space for a more just and democratic future? In the first place, the project involved thinking other-wise about a place, in ways that were very different from those constrained by the protocols of conventional place studies in school geography. In bringing a fresh interpretation to place study, it opened spaces for knowing an-other side of Whitby, even opening up spaces for knowing the unknown associated with the town. This re-invented knowledge, knowledge of the other, transgressed place knowledge enframed within a disciplinary discourse to demonstrate a more just way of thinking. Second, elements of justice emerged through the research enquiries themselves, for example, through the study of the struggle for power between the Irish and the Roman churches that was resolved at the Synod at Whitby Monastery in 664 AD, the politics of jet jewellery making and its wearing, Cook's 'discovery' of foreign lands for British imperialist gain and views about the novel Dracula from a feminist stance. Justice came closer through the project in a third way, that is, through revealing the constraining influences of totalising discourses of performativity and of those enframing the subject. The former influenced the project, for example, in the school's initial agreement to participate and also in the selection of activities and resources. The latter influenced the project in terms of the division of labour within the project and the inability of cultural and physical geographers to work in a truly collaborative fashion within time constraints.

Reflections: I considered and responded to the question at the beginning of the previous paragraph post-hoc in 2012, after the project had ended. I am embarrassed to admit that I was so engrossed in the practicalities of the project and navigating my route through it that I lost sight of orienting the focus within the student enquiries explicitly towards justice. Needless to say, such a project was personally time-consuming and emotionally demanding, since it was conducted in a highly charged school environment with which I was unfamiliar. It also involved additional labour for the two project teachers, who I appreciated were already over-worked, so, being mindful of this, I consciously tried to minimise the pressure on them. This current discussion, then, is a reflection-on-reflection, and involves my reflection on a notion of justice that extends beyond totalising discourses of geographical knowledge and performativity described earlier, and beyond post-hoc reflections.

In studies I conducted subsequent to this one, and with the goal of opening up a space for justice, I turned to the work of Emmanuel Levinas (1996; 1998). I will explain why. Albeit with the help of the two geography teachers in this project, I had conceptualised, designed and resourced the student enquiries in the Whitby curriculum unit myself. This action I understand now, however, to have been hypocritical, given my regular critique of Government prescription and imposition of curriculum content on schools, and my ethical responsibility to the students whom I serve as educator. Levinas argues that justice can only be strived for by understanding and responding to our ethical responsibility to the other, which takes us beyond totalising discourses of subject knowledge, external instrumental interests and efficient 'delivery' (Winter 2014, 281–282). Our ethical response to the other is of the prime importance.

Curriculum knowledge forms the 'symbolic raw material' of education in the sense that students engage with, dis-engage from or re-imagine that knowledge in the context of their schooling (Todd 2001 , 446). Whatever the relationship between students and curriculum knowledge, it influences their subjectivity or who they are and who they will become, because they are changed by exposure to it. Curriculum knowledge has a language, an epistemology and an ontology. In the case of geography, these form the building blocks of the subject's enduring concepts, models, classifications and systems which prevail through the school curriculum. According to Chalier (1995), Levinas argues that the relationship to the other supersedes such manifestations of assumed 'truth'. Instead, chasing relationships back to a time before Western constructions of 'autonomy', 'rationality' and 'freedom' dominated our thinking, we can engage in relationships more basic, primordial and good, that is, our ethical responsibility to respond to the difference, suffering, vulnerability and oppression of the other. Breaking free of the constraints of technical rule-bound curriculum knowledge and political instrumentalism gives one freedom to engage, face to face, with the backgrounds, life experiences and cultural dispositions of the other (Levinas 1996) – whether these may be teachers or students.

But how can this ethical encounter be achieved in a school-based research project along the lines of the one described, but with attention to the ethical relation to the other? Three fundamental conditions seem to be necessary. The first is the need for the researcher to know the school context, the teachers and the students really well. Ethnographic methodology is a key solution, although constraints of time, resources and the self-protective shield schools erect to protect their reputations against critical comments in a high-stakes performative environment often preclude such approaches in current times. Ethnography enables the researcher to access the school culture first-hand and to understand the perspectives of teachers and students in the natural setting (Woods 1996, 2–3). It gives 'voice' to those who would not normally be heard because of their powerlessness (ibid, 3), provides insight into how students construct curriculum knowledge for themselves as they interact with the dominant curriculum knowledge system and opens a space for the incoming of the other. The ethnographer becomes integrated into the school system, 'reducing the resistance of the group members' and ethnography 'permits the investigator to experience and observe the group's norms, values, conflicts and pressures' (Hargreaves 1967, 193). Nevertheless, harking back to Stenhouse's 'teacher-as-researcher' and Action Research movements (Stenhouse 1975; see also Carr and Kemmis 1986), those best *placed to conduct ethnographies in classrooms are teachers themselves, when given appropriate professional and academic training and support.*

A second suggestion, which is not mutually exclusive of the first, is the co-production of the research project by students, working together with their teachers. The idea of students identifying a problem in their world and working together with their teachers to design an investigation of that problem avoids the imposition of an externally imposed study and research design that does not address the issues experienced and understood directly by the learners themselves. Liddiard et al. (2019) provide a clear and succinct review of the literature in this field. Such participatory methodologies require a third consideration – that of students and their teachers becoming critical researchers in order to develop and engage the skills of identifying educational problems, designing investigations, conducting studies and presenting findings in relation to their lived experiences, on their own terms, unshackled from the constraints of technical subject knowledge and traditional research methodologies. These inventive methodologies carry the potential to disrupt the illusion of cultural homogeneity by introducing unforeseen controversy, multiple perspectives, risk, imagination, difference and the unknown. Related to this discussion, and connected to my more recent work focusing on the Eurocentricity and whiteness of geography curriculum knowledge (Winter 2018), such methodologies open the ethical relation to the other as called for by Levinas.

'Deconstruction is not a method or some tool that you apply to something from the outside' (Derrida 1997, 9). Is Derrida's warrant for deconstruction a sufficient reason for *not* engaging his help in the process of classroom-based curriculum development? Perhaps it is a question of different kinds of texts. When showing the metaphysics in deconstruction in the classroom, the number, scale and complexity of things involved are far greater than when examining a single text. The politics and ethics of the educational system, of school culture, of school subject policy, of teacher professional identities, of relationships between the participants, between researcher and participants, their histories and the researcher's vested interests in the project are only a few examples of the multiple texts that make showing the metaphysics in deconstruction of curriculum policy and practice in – and through – practice a very different undertaking from deconstructive reading of an education policy or curriculum document.

Reflections: While deconstructing texts represents a first step in the quest for curriculum justice, reflections on the extension of this task into the enactment of curriculum in the classroom indicate a need for serious thinking about the relationship between theory and method in research.

I would like to thank Sally and John for their enthusiasm and commitment to the project, to thank their students and school geography. Both teachers approved the interpretation of events presented in this chapter. Thanks also to my colleague Jane Ferretti for her valuable comments on an earlier draft.

Note

1 Sources for these quotes are transcripts of interviews with the project teachers.

References

Ball, S.J. 2007. *Education plc: Understanding private sector participation in public sector education*. Oxford: Routledge.

Barnwell, P.S., L.A.S. Butler and C.J. Dunn. 2003. The confusion of conversion: Streanaeshalch, Strensall and Whitby and the Northumbrian Church. In *The cross goes north: Processes of conversion in Northern Europe AD 300–1300*. ed. M. Carver, 311-326. York: York Medieval Press.

Beaglehole, J.C. 1979. *The death of Captain Cook*. 2nd edn. Wellington, New Zealand: Alexander Turnbull Library.

Bede. 731/1999. *The ecclesiastical history of the English people*. Oxford: Oxford University Press.

Bennington, G. 2000. *Interrupting Derrida*. London: Routledge.

Biesta, J.J.G. 2009a. Education after deconstruction. In *Derrida, deconstruction and the politics of pedagogy*. eds. M.A. Peters and G. Biesta, 97–113. New York, NY: Peter Lang.

Biesta, J.J.G. 2009b. Witnessing deconstruction in education: Why quasi-transcendentalism matters. *Journal of Philosophy of Education* 43, 3: 391–404.

Blake, N., P. Smeyers, R. Smith and P. Standish. 1998. *Thinking again: Education after postmodernism*. London: Bergin and Garvey.

Brannington, J., R. Robbins and J. Wolfreys. eds. 1996. *Applying: To Derrida*. Houndmills: Macmillan Press.

Calcutt, D. ed. 1999. B. Stoker. *Dracula*. Oxford Playscripts. Oxford: Oxford University Press.

Caputo, J. 1997. ed. *Deconstruction in a nutshell*. New York, NY: Fordham University Press.

Carr, W. and S. Kemmis. 1986. *Becoming critical: Education, knowledge and action research*. Lewes: Falmer.

Chalier, C. 1995. The philosophy of Emmanuel Levinas and the Hebraic tradition. In *Ethics as first philosophy*. ed. A.T. Peperzak, 3–12. London: Routledge.

Cloke, P., C. Philo and D. Sadler. 1991. *Approaching human geography: An introduction to contemporary theoretical debates*. London: Arnold.

Dawes, G. 1968. Kealakekua Bay revisited: A note on the death of Captain Cook. *Journal of Pacific History* 3: 21–23.

DCSF/QCA. 2007. *The National Curriculum statutory requirements for key stages 3 and 4*. London: DCSF/QCA.

Dening, G. 1996. *Performances*. Chicago, IL: University of Chicago Press.

Derrida, J. 1972. Différance. In *Margins of philosophy*. Trans. A. Bass, 1–7. Chicago, UL: University of Chicago Press.

Derrida, J. 1976. *Of grammatology*. Trans. G.C. Spivak. Baltimore, MD: Johns Hopkins University.

Derrida, J. 1988. Letter to a Japanese friend. Trans. D. Wood and A. Benjamin. In *Derrida and Différance*. eds. D. Wood and R. Bernasconi, 1–5. Evanston, IL: Northwest University Press.

Derrida, J. 1992. Force of law: The 'mystical foundation of authority'. In *Deconstruction and the possibility of justice*. eds. D. Cornell, M. Rosenfeld and D.G. Carlson, 4–67. London: Routledge.

Derrida, J. 1993. Finis. In *Aporias*. Trans. T. Dutoit, 1–43. Stanford, CA: Stanford University Press.

Derrida, J. 1997. The Villanova roundtable: A conversation with Jacques Derrida. In *Deconstruction in a nutshell*. ed. J. Caputo, 3–28. New York, NY: Fordham University Press.

Edgoose, J. 2001. Just decide! Derrida and the ethical aporias of education. In *Derrida & Education*. eds. J.J.G. Biesta and D. Egéa-Kuehne, 119–133. Oxford: Routledge.

Egéa-Kuehne, D. 1996. Neutrality in education and Derrida's call for 'double duty'. In *Philosophy of Education 1966*. ed. F. Margonis, 154–163. Urbana, IL: Philosophy of Education Society.

Egéa-Kuehne, D. 2001. Derrida's ethics of affirmation: The challenge of educational rights and responsibility. In *Derrida & Education*. eds. J.J.G. Biesta and D. Egéa-Kuehne, 186–208. Oxford: Routledge.

Hargreaves, D. 1967. *Social relations in a secondary school*. London: Routledge and Kegan Paul.

Levinas, E. 1996. Meaning and sense. In *Emmanuel Levinas: Basic philosophical writings*. eds. A.T. Peperzak, S. Critchley and R. Bernasconi, 33–64. Bloomington, IN: Indiana University Press.

Levinas, E. 1998. Philosophy and the idea of infinity. In *Collected philosophical papers*. ed. A. Lingis, 47–59. Pittsburgh, PA: Duquesne University Press.

Liddiard, K., K. Runswick-Cole, D. Goodley, S. Whitney, E. Vogelmann and L.Watts, MBE. 2019. 'I was excited by the idea of a project that focuses on those unasked questions': Co-producing disability research with disabled young people. *Children and Society* 33, 2: 154–167.

Number 10. 2012. Transcript: PM speech at coasting schools meeting. Available at: www.number10.gov.uk/news/coasting-schools/ (accessed 20 June 2012).

Ofsted. 2005. 2004/5 Annual report on curriculum and assessment. Available at: www.geography.org.uk/download/GA_NKS3QCAreport.pdf (accessed 20 June 2012).

Ofsted. 2008. Geography in schools changing practice. Available at: https://webarchive.nationalarchives.gov.uk/ukgwa/20141107071800/http://www.ofsted.gov.uk/resources/geography-schools-changing-practice (accessed 20 June 2012).

Rawling, E.M. 2001. *Changing the subject: The impact of national curriculum policy on school geography 1980–2000*. Sheffield: The Geographical Association.

Sahlins, M. 1985. *Islands of history*. Chicago, IL: University of Chicago Press.

Sahlins, M. 1995. *How 'natives' think: about Captain Cook, for example*. Chicago, IL: University of Chicago Press.

Standish, P. 2001. Data return: The sense of the given in educational research. *Journal of Philosophy of Education* 35, 3: 497–518.

Stenhouse, L. 1975. *An introduction to curriculum research and development*. London: Heinemann.

Stoker, B. 1897. *Dracula*. Hertfordshire: Wordsworth Classics.

Stoker, B. 1999. *Dracula*. Adapted by D. Calcutt. Oxford: Oxford University Press.

Todd, S. 2001. 'Bringing more than I contain': Ethics, curriculum and the pedagogical demand for altered egos. *Journal of Curriculum Studies* 33, 4: 431–450.

Villiers, A. 1967. *Captain Cook: The seaman's seaman*. London: Penguin.

Williams, G. 2008. *The death of Captain Cook: A hero made and unmade*. London: Profile Books.

Winter, C. 2009a. Progress report. Geography and education I: The state of health of geography in schools. *Progress in Human Geography* 33, 5: 667–676.

Winter, C. 2009b. Places, spaces, holes for knowing and writing the earth: The geography curriculum and Derrida's Khora. *Ethics and Education* 4, 1: 57–68.

Winter, C. 2013. Enframing geography: Subject, curriculum, knowledge, responsibility. *Ethics and Education* 7, 3: 277–290.

Winter, C. 2014. Curriculum knowledge, justice, relations: The Schools' White Paper (2010) in England. *Journal of Philosophy of Education* 48, 2: 276–292.

Winter, C. 2018. Disrupting colonial discourses in the geography curriculum during the introduction of British values policy in schools. *Journal of Curriculum Studies* 50, 4: 456–475.

Woods, P. 1996. *Successful writing for qualitative researchers*. London: Routledge.

14 Engaging with student teachers on reflective writing

Reclaiming writing

Duncan P. Mercieca

Introduction

Reflective teaching and writing is now a fundamental aspect and practice of being a teacher. It is seen as 'an effective tool in democratizing teaching and learning processes' (Galea 2012, 245) that counter balances the 'positivistic technicist approach to teaching and learning that has overwhelmed the educational sector' (ibid). The move towards greater accountability has led to an emphasis on measurement, and this gives rise to a search for that which can be measured. 'The most insidious danger', as Jennings and Kennedy (1996) argue, 'is that only that which can be measured will be considered worthwhile, thereby leading to a revision to the worst excess of behaviourism and a blinked focus on behavioural objectives' (ibid, xi). Managerial discourses and market forces, particularly at a time of world financial crises, are more than ever pressing on educational aims. Political expediency has become the norm. In such circumstances, there is the need for teachers to stand back and reflect upon their professional lives and interactions with children and others. It is in this light that the majority of teacher training schools are putting a lot of effort into training, nurturing and guiding student teachers to become reflective practitioners. There seems to be a need for the 'search for meaning' at the heart of the process of becoming-teachers.

When I first wrote this chapter, I was working in Malta and I asked volunteer student teachers who had just finished their teacher training what they considered to be reflective writing. My desk was piled high with numerous files and bits of writings that the student teachers provided as reflective writings during the course of four years. I was amazed and flabbergasted at the volumes that each student teacher sent to my office: Parts of assignments and tasks assigned; activities aimed specifically at encouraging reflection; and, of course, all those activities that involved working directly with children and their parents, in schools and in carrying out lessons.

I gradually became more aware of the process of writing involved in reflective writings that the student teachers carry out in the course of their training. For, apart from 'reflective conversations' that occur at different moments in the training of teachers, most reflective processes involve the act of writing. Having

DOI: 10.4324/9781003156550-19

engaged with Derrida's ideas, I started to question the process of writing involved in reflective writing. Derrida's preoccupation with writing has been his lifetime concern, with his concepts on writing scattered throughout his work, while certain of his texts problematise the issue further.

Derrida cannot be reduced to a model of analysis often known as deconstruction. Jacques Derrida (1991) warns us that '[it] is not a method and cannot be transformed into one' (ibid, 273). Gert Biesta (2009) reminds us that 'we should not aim to deconstruct anything, but rather engage in witnessing the *event* of deconstruction' (emphasis in original, Biesta 2009, 400). We need to give witness to 'those moments where conditions of possibility and impossibility "cross" each other and in their crossing provide a deconstructive opening ... an entrance for the incoming of something new, something unforeseen' (ibid). We do not make deconstruction happen – deconstruction occurs whether we like it or not, but we can acknowledge it and give witness to it.

This has been my driving question in reading my students' writings: Do their writings allow for witnessing the event of deconstruction? Do their writings allow, give space or even create space for the impossible to cross the possible? What other models of writing could allow for more acknowledgment and witness of the possible and impossible crossing each other?

The difficulty and limitation with this chapter is that it is caught in its own economy of exchange (Derrida 1992; 1995; Standish 2001). The chapter questions the process of writing through writing itself. Therefore, in its own very nature there is a limitation to what can be questioned with regard to writing, yet it is this impossibility that the chapter tries to capture and acknowledge (Derrida 1993). This takes me to the heart of social science research where most of the research is written and the assumption made that it is read. The act of writing seems to constitute the foundations of research – writing is often assumed throughout the research process. Spoken words in interviews are transcribed into written words, as are also tones of voice, inflections and other non-verbal behaviours in an attempt to capture what would otherwise be lost. As a supervisor, I encourage my research students to start writing from early in their research process – in the belief that, eventually, writing will become easier.

This chapter is divided into four parts. Each part explores the process that I engaged in during my research. If I wanted to categorise this research project it would fall under the term 'action-research', which Carr and Kemmis (1986) 'regard [...] as a form of "self-reflective inquiry" by participants, undertaken in order to improve understanding of their practices in context with a view to maximizing social justice' (Cohen et al. 2000, 227).

In the next section I put forth some ideas from Derrida that have challenged my ideas on writing. I give an idea about how these Derridean concepts helped me to make strange the familiarity I am accustomed to in reading the student teachers' reflective writings. In the last section, I show how my reading of Derrida calls for a political action on my part, calling me to take up my responsibility – my ability to respond and act – by trying out a different model of writing with the student teachers.

Derrida on writing

Before engaging in some of the ideas developed in this chapter, it is important to remind ourselves that Derrida's writing style is itself his philosophy (see Rorty 1978). The way in which numerous Derridean texts are presented to us readers, texts which often are difficult to read and 'understand' within the Western philosophical tradition, are playing this double articulation between the text and the concepts. Texts and concepts are in infinite play with each other, both being inseparable and mutually contaminating for each other. Since my initial reading of Derrida's text, this has always fascinated me: How does writing create one's philosophy? And how does one's philosophy create one's writing?

In *Force and signification*, Derrida is engaging with French structuralism (Derrida 1978). In particular, he uses the text of Jean Rousset *Forme et signification* to create his argument (Rousset 1989). One can immediately see Derrida's play with the words *form* and *force*, where he is using the latter to correct Rousset's idea of form. Rousset developed geometrical schemas for studying literary texts and Derrida argues that this process is one of reductionism. This reductionism 'appears to give exhaustive descriptions of the "structures" or "formal constants" underlying the texts' (Johnson 1993, 13). Derrida argues that these structures become ends in themselves, and rather than the text being under study, the structure is. Also the structures from their nature are spatial entities and are applied to the text. As Christopher Johnson (1993) argues 'the nature of Rousset's method is indeed appropriately expressed in his choice of title, *Forme et signification*: his own forms (spatial, geometrical) are imposed upon different textual significations' (ibid, 13–14). Derrida furthers his analysis of Rousset and argues that his approach is 'performist', the idea that organisms develop from miniature complete versions of themselves. Each small part reflects and resumes the whole, and the temporal dimension is therefore always of the present. This implies 'the idea that the totality of the literary work is contained in germinal form at its beginning, the end of the work being implicit in its origin' (ibid, 15). These are Derrida's two main concerns: Structures and time, what Derrida calls the 'flatness' of structuralism (two-dimensions):

> the panoramagram, the very image of the structuralist instrument, was invented in 1824, as Littré states, in order to 'obtain immediately, on a flat surface, the development of depth vision of objects on the horizon'. Thanks to a more or less openly acknowledged schematization or spatialization, one can glance over the field divested of its force more freely or diagrammatically
>
> (Derrida 1978, 5)

It is this removing of, or hiding of, the 'force' in order for things to seem simpler, ordered, systematic and clean, that Derrida wants to recuperate in structuralism. Derrida does this by wanting to think in terms of three dimensions, rather than two. He wants duration (instead of the present time) and becoming (rather than geometrical structures) to play a part in flat structures, in order to give volume (i.e. the third dimension) to structures: 'in its demand for the flat and horizontal, what is intolerable for structuralism is indeed the richness implied by the volume, every element that cannot be spread into the simultaneity of a form' (Derrida 1978, 25).

The questions that follow from this are: How do we do this? How do we produce volume in flat structures? As often happens, we introduce opposites to help us to overcome the linearity of things, to find some sort of (Hegelian) synthesis between the opposites. Derrida will take a different stance to this – he will suggest 'that it is necessary to seek new concepts and new models, an economy escaping this system of metaphysical oppositions' (Derrida 1978, 19). This *economy* takes us to the heart of the Derridean project which is nutshelled in the term 'logocentrism'. This term is relevant to this chapter as in *Of grammatology*, Derrida examines the relationship between speech and writing (Derrida 1976). He argues that the latter is subordinate to the former: We think, speak and then maybe write what has been spoken. Logocentrism is the idea that the *logos* (speech) and not writing is central to language. The assumption is that speech is clear and transparent. We can understand the speaker and know what they are talking about – 'the subject is the "master" of language' (Usher and Edwards 1994, 121). But writing is seen as a suspect and untrustworthy because it can be interpreted in various ways and have different interpretations from what author meant and implied. However, writing for Derrida is able to escape the control of the speaker/writer/reader and we are in a position where language controls us.

This, obviously, 'plunges us into a realm of strangeness' (Usher and Edwards 1994, 121) as we have lost control of language. 'Grammatology', a term Derrida uses to refer to writing, can free our ideas of writing from being subordinated to our ideas of speech/writer/reader. In this way, the logos is a presence, what Derrida refers to as the 'metaphysics of presence' – a centre or original guarantee of all meaning, which for Derrida has characterised Western philosophy since Plato. The 'metaphysics of presence' is motivated by a desire for a 'transcendental signified', a signified that transcends all signifiers, as meaning that transcends all signs. What happens is that we measure everything in relation to the logocentric, so writing is measured in relation to speech, or to give another example, woman is measured in relation to man, and so on.

The 'economy' that Derrida writes about that escapes this system of metaphysical oppositions, i.e. the logocentrism,

> can be announced only through a certain organization, a certain strategic arrangement which, within the field of metaphysical opposition, uses the strength of the field to turn its own stratagems against it, producing a force of dislocation that spreads itself through the entire system, fissuring it in every direction and thoroughly delimiting it.
>
> (ibid)

In order to answer the questions posed above: How do we do this? How do we produce volume in flat structures? Derrida's answer in *Force and signification* is to bring form and force in an economy, allowing for fissures to appear when doing so (Derrida 1978). Although Derrida wants duration and becoming to give volume to flat structures, pure duration and pure becoming still need a 'certain organisation' – a form. Without a form these would never actualise. 'The point of articulation between force and form' (Johnson 1993, 23) is the 'inscription'.

Inscription is the line, the moment, between force and form. The 'scribble' (see Derrida 1979) that the writer engages in automatically brings death! It brings death because the moment I scribble something down, I have not opted for the other thousand possible words and ideas that potentially could have been scribbled down. I did not choose these other words and ideas. For Derrida (following Kierkegaard), this is a moment of madness – the aporia of infinite possible words has been summed in some scribbling. Scribbling is violent – it leaves a mark, a scratch. This is painful. Derrida uses the term 'anguish' (Derrida 1978, 9), which from its Latin roots means 'narrowness' and 'difficulty'. Derrida uses Artaud's 'description of the painful experience in writing' (ibid, 22). The following rather long quote aims to show the difficulties of writing and the painful experiences that Derrida himself experienced in writing:

> Each time I write something, and it feels like I am advancing into new territory, somewhere I haven't been before, and this type of advance often demands certain gestures that can be taken as aggressive with regard to other thinkers or colleagues… or even hurt others. So, every time I make this type of gesture, there are moments of fear. This doesn't happen at the moments when I'm writing. Actually, when I write there is a feeling of necessity, of something that is stronger than myself that demands that I must write as I write. I have never renounced anything I have written because I have been afraid of certain consequences. Nothing intimidates me when I write. I say what I think must be said. That is to say, when I don't write, there is a very strange moment when I go to sleep. At that moment when I am in a sort of half sleep, all of a sudden, I'm terrified by what I'm doing. And I tell myself 'You're crazy to write this!'… 'Stop everything! Take it back! Burn your papers! What you're doing is inadmissible!'.
>
> (Kirby and Ziering 2002)

Yet, Derrida argues that anguish is the condition from which all expression proceeds. It is as though infinite words and expressions are pressing on the writer – all wanting to be scribbled. It is in this light that Derrida (1978, 22) argues:

> To write is only to know that through writing, through the extremities of style, the best will not necessarily transpire … It is also to be incapable of

making meaning absolutely precede writing: it is thus to lower meaning while simultaneously elevating inscription

(ibid, 10)

Therefore, the inaugural moment[1] is writing and not speaking/thinking about something. It is writing, re-writing and re-re-writing that 'is, in a certain way, the condition of meaning and of the concept' (Johnson 1993, 28). The process of writing is that which constitutes the condition of sense, and not sense which is then written down.

As a final note on this section, I would like to emphasise the process of writing the above section. Authors such as Derrida are daunting, not only because ideas presented are complex and dense to access, but also because the volume of writing is just breath-taking. My experience of engaging with Derrida is that his texts require multiple readings. When at moments I feel that I think I am making sense of particular ideas, this feeling very quickly slips away and I am again lost in a reading that is breath-taking and painful. Even when I feel I am engaging with a concept, transforming it into a written text, despite pages of notes, is still daunting, and often the feeling of incompleteness haunts me, as is the case with this section. This begs the question, Why do I continue engaging in this process? The moment that my reading starts engaging with some of Derrida's ideas, the experience of that is unique – his ideas challenge me, question my very way of thinking about and being in research. The ideas challenge the social constructed world, particularly that focusing on education, which I live and inhabit. There has now developed a love–hate relationship, maybe in the way that Melanie Klein (1997) talks about the depressive position in her writing about splitting. I am often called by Derrida's text; there is a desire to be in the text, and I often return to his writings to re-read them, although I know that most ideas will escape me. Indeed, it is a very humbling position to be in. To those starting to engage with Derrida's work, my recommendation is be patient with themselves and let themselves 'be' with Derrida – slow reading, slow note-taking, slow writing, slow re-reading, slow re-note-taking, slow re-writing. There will be an 'aha' moment soon.

The research project

This chapter reflects on an action-research project that I engaged in a few years ago when I was working in a School of Education. I was engaged with supporting student teachers on their practice placement in Maltese primary schools. The aim of this research was not to capture a holistic picture of the teaching practice experience, but to focus on my reflections about my role in this process, and subsequently develop a module of reflective practices. In any professional course such as one focusing on training and forming teachers, the practical component is paramount. As will be discussed in the next section, the focus is not only on 'the doing' but also on reflecting on such a process. This action-research project focused on my reflections on student teachers' reflections on the processes of reflections. I felt challenged when reading the module description and assessment criteria of the teaching practice. In particular, I questioned the use and implication of the term 'reflective writing'. The issue was that the lived experience of being in a classroom and engaging with students was being transformed into a practice of writing that had to be 'reflective'.

As Bridget Somekh (2006) argues, the aim of doing an action-research project goes beyond describing and analysing, but to 'reconstruct and transform those practices' (ibid, 1). While aware of the need to bring about 'transformative practices', I wanted to resist performative transformations. The focus for me was not to find a better method of engaging in 'reflective writing' for student teachers, but to 'make-sense' of this process. The term 'making-sense' is influenced by the philosophy of Gilles Deleuze (1990), where he makes a distinction between understanding and making-sense. The former implies for him elements of certainty, while the latter focuses on the rhizomatic connections (multiple connections and each and every constantly changing connection) that are formed between ideas, people, spaces and time. Understanding is understood as 'sedentary', while making-sense is seen as flowing (see Wang 2015). This flow tends to resist 'shorthand' that often is part of the performative discourses that have embodied education. In the fast-paced society in which we live, we find ourselves using convenient 'shorthand' to help our work become conveniently more practical. We often resort to shorthand for the sake of efficiency, and sometimes in the belief that it makes us more professional. In so doing, we risk forgetting the contradictions in the language and practices that we use as these are suppressed in the shorthand (Mercieca and Mercieca 2012). The danger is of ironing out the complexity of the processes and, therefore, 'otherness' is left out. The risk (see Biesta 2013 on the use of the term 'risk') is that in using shorthand, we are in turn being produced by it. It is not only a tool, but it is also a way that constructs us, therefore becoming a methodology. John Law's (2004) writing on methodology can be applied in this context as he reminds us that the statements we use are not just 'about reality' but also produce the realities themselves.

> It is not just a philosophy of method, a methodology. It is not even simply about the kinds of realities that we want to recognise or the kinds of worlds we might hope to make. It is also, and most fundamentally about a way of being. It is about what kinds of social sciences we want to practice. And then, and as a part of this, it is about the kinds of people that we want to be, and about how we should live.
>
> (Addleson 1994, cited in Law 2004, 10)

This action-research project involved reading and engaging with the student teachers' reflective writings, reading on reflective writing and reading Derrida on the act of writing. The process ended with writing reflective comments to students on their reflective writing, and then writing the module specifications.

Derrida was important for me as his idea provided an 'in-between' that disrupted my urge for performativity, shorthand and clean method. Derrida's idea kept opening closures in the research. Derrida was not a method per se, but a force that did not allow method to calcify itself – there was a constant challenge that came from within as I had opted to include him in this research. Often, he provided me with an alternative language or, better still, to question the language that I assumed I knew already. Derrida for me was almost a natural choice. I was already acquainted with some of his ideas, and I was aware of the importance of the act of writing for Derrida, not only in questioning the act of writing (for example in relation to speech), but particularly in the way he wrote. It is a writing that tries to disrupt writing, as discussed in the previous section. The next two sections elaborate on this process, and in so doing I hope to show how Derrida's idea impacted on the methodology.

Routinised writing

> Such 'reflective writing' is a very effective and worthwhile exercise. There are many ways of doing this, but the most effective one is to find *your own* system of how to write about your feelings and thoughts regarding your own professional and personal development as teachers. In the portfolio you are being given several reflective tasks which will help you to focus your thoughts and ideas and reflectively question your choices and learning experiences
> (Professional Development Portfolio n.d., 7)

The Professional Development Portfolio starts off by stating that student teachers need to find their own voice in how to write about feelings and thoughts, regarding their professional and personal development as teachers. Yet, when one goes through the portfolio, one cannot not observe that it is made up of numerous tasks under various subheadings, which student teachers have to complete during their second academic year. Now (in 2017), the School of Education had shifted from hardcopies to online portfolios where student teachers are also given word limits for certain online tasks, and an automated system will not allow the student teachers to move forward if they have not inputted every part as expected.

The Professional Development Portfolio is just one example of the many reflective activities that student teachers are asked to do. Similarly, when on teaching practice[2] student teachers are asked to reflect on practice (see Schön 1983; 1987; 1991). Student teachers are given a *Reflective questions* booklet (Cardona 2005), which 'is designed to assist you with your reflections as you as you write up your weekly self-evaluations during Teaching-Practice' (ibid, 1). Even though it is specifically said in the introduction that the questions provided for each week should not be seen as a 'comprehension exercise' (ibid, 2), a closer look at the document suggests this is the case, as do the student teachers' answers. The following is an example of one of the questions suggested for the second week:

The effectiveness of any classroom management depends on a teacher's attitudes and practical intelligence. Reflect on these basic principles:

a   Have you established a friendly relationship with your students?
b   What did you establish the relationship on?
c   Do you consider yourself to have established a supportive and trusting relationship?
d   What is your regard towards disruptive students?
e   Can you honestly say that you have a positive regard towards disruptive students?
f   Do you consider your approach to be optimistic and no-nonsense approach?
g   If you do, how did you set about establishing it?

(Cardona 2005, 5)

From reading through the students' work, I found that when student teachers are not given models of reflective-practices, most of them still develop a very systematic approach to writing their reflections. The following excerpt is taken from a reflection diary that student teachers are asked to keep during their teaching practices.

How to improve:

1   I should repeat over and over again and remind students continuously about the present perfect, as it was difficult for the students to understand. The worksheet given for group work was not ideal one. I should have provided a worksheet with various examples where children would decide if the examples were simple past and present perfect. Another thing which I could do is to have an exercise with examples copied on their copybooks. The examples will then be worked out as a whole class to make sure that everyone is following and understanding.
2   The worksheet which I have given today for group work should have been given another time, when children would have understood the concept better.
3   I could have put the slideshow on the classroom computers and shown the PowerPoint presentation from there. In fact I gave every child a copy of the PowerPoint on the USBs, so that they could see it again at home.

(Student teacher, personal communication, June 2011)

This particular student teacher, when reflecting-on-practice about the lessons she delivers, divides her reflections into three sections: Things I did wrong; How to improve; and What went well. A number of bullet points are written under each section. Similarly, when she is writing about particular children, she has another list of subsections: 'General overview of the child'; 'The child's abilities'; 'Support areas needed to be addressed'; and 'How to intervene with child'. Every bit is compartmentalised, split into sections and seems to fit nicely into place within the larger picture. It is like when one finds a missing piece in a big jigsaw puzzle. The pieces fit nicely together. The moment one fills in a piece of writing it is as though a piece of the puzzle has been fitted into the larger picture. What also becomes evident in this example is how the present is made manifest to us. With the student teacher's writing we can come to know exactly how things are, what she did, what her intentions and actions are. We seem to be present during her lesson delivery. There is a clear end in the writing of the student teacher. Every point mirrors her whole lesson, thus allowing the totality of the lesson to be permanently present in any of one of the points written down. The beginning and end of the lesson can be seen through each point written down.

Structures, whether imposed by lecturers or by student teachers themselves on themselves, seem to have taken over most of reflective writing. And it is here that I question, in light of Derrida's arguments, whether structures of reflective writing have become ends in themselves, and whether these structures are just promoting the present. Content seems to take second place. Form has taken over the force or, to explain it in another way, force has been channelled into paragraphs, subtitles and bullet points that seem to dilute, stifle or even kill this force.

It is not only the reflective writing which seems to be too structured, but also the way we teach and theorise reflective practice. One of the texts used with our student teachers is that by Anthony Ghaye and Kay Ghaye (Ghaye and Ghaye 1998). In this text we are presented with a model of reflection which has four characteristics: 'it is cyclical, flexible, focused and holistic' (ibid, 6). Then we are presented with four foci which are in the heart of this model:

> Reflection on Values: self → others → action (which influences the self)
> Reflection on Practice: political → professional → personal (which influences the personal)
> Reflection on Improvement: construction → interpretation → validation (which influences the construction)
> Reflection on Context: Partnership→ culture → empowerment (which influences the partnership)
>
> (ibid, 8)

Not that there is anything wrong with such structures of how to think and engage in reflective practices, but the concern is that we tend to follow these structures to the letter. This could be seen as the flatness of structure, where a certain kind of geometry and a certain conception of time are at play. From the above, it was evident for me, viewing through a Derridean framework, that how we teach reflective-practice to student teachers and how they write their reflective practices may not be giving space for force and duration to manifest themselves. Rather, what this writing seems to be reinforcing is a logic of identity – through writing the student teacher can arrive at the origin of themselves and what it means to be a teacher. Writing is seen as that means through which we are able to master and control ourselves. What this writing leaves out or what it eliminates is the other of ourselves. We see ourselves as one having a particular identity which excludes alterity. 'The otherness which is excluded and suppressed in order to maintain the myth of a pure and uncontaminated original presence is actually constitutive of that which present itself as pure, self-sufficient, self-present, and therefore as totally different from this otherness' (Biesta 2001, 44).

In the next section I will 'reflect' about second phase of my research.

Student teachers writing the self

According to Richard Rorty (1978), 'for Derrida, writing always leads to more writing, and more, and still more' (ibid, 145). Probably this quote puts 'in a nutshell' (Caputo 1997) the ideas of this section. As part of my research, after I read extensively the reflective-writings written by my students, I wanted to take up Derrida's invitation of trying to come up with an economy that escapes closure as much as possible. As already pointed out, force still needs form. So I thought of shifting from reflective-writing to narrative writing. Beginning with this year, while student teachers were still engaged in reflective teaching and writing, I was able to create a study-unit for the student teachers with the title of this section. What this study-unit does is to give space for writing to take place, hoping that Rorty's suggestion holds true. No formula of how to write is presented and any kind of writing is accepted. I give a brief description of the study-unit to situate the reader of this chapter: The study-unit is carried out after the student teachers have a long period of being in schools, where they are mainly involved in teaching and working with students. During the course of the lectures they are presented with different policy documents, ideas from philosophers, pieces of poetry and novels (in particular Kafka and Woolf), photos of past and contemporary educational setting, they hear elderly people talking about their experience of schooling, read narratives written by teachers and watch movies of teachers. The student teachers are encouraged to write about their narratives of their just finished teaching experience in relation to these. The aim is to stimulate the student teachers to write about themselves, their ideas of teaching, about the process of working with children, their families and the experience of teaching classes. They are asked to write events that they experienced in the light of these stimulations.

The aim of these stimulations together with the experience of their just finished teaching-practice is to help escape the idea that the self is transparent and can be seen or spoken of through writing by the student teachers. Rather than seeing the self as transparent and clear which is accessible to oneself, the idea is to see the self as multi-layered and strange to oneself. The self is made up of various ideas and connections and the other of the self is given space to disrupt the identity that we built or assume that we have. Not only that, but this process questions the idea of 'the self' of the student teacher as something fixed which can be understood and known. This obviously questions the idea of agency that reflective-practice seems to be putting forth. The student teachers' experience and the stimulations give the possibility of the 'play of difference', which comes across through writing and re-writing. I am seeing this as a way how difference is not reduced to sameness. Here writing is not seen as a representation of a thought-out process by the student teacher, but rather the process of writing creates the student teacher and their 'sense' making of the teaching-experience. This would provide depth and volume to the flatness mentioned earlier.

In no way does this mean that this process has worked for all. Probably, the contrary. From reading the writings of the student teachers it is evident that some student teachers were struggling to engage in this experience of writing and re-writing. One student teacher emailed me to say that she was 'lost' as she did not know what she had to do. She wrote, 'I know that I have to write about my experience in relation to the various stimulations that we had, but HOW do I start writing … can you please consider giving us clear guidelines in how to do this writing' (personal communication – email by student, March 2011). The fear of getting 'lost' seems to be at the heart of what this student teacher is afraid to engage in, which is contradictory to the heart of the whole project, i.e. of getting lost. I do not offer structures to my student teachers, only exemplars (Woolf, Kafka, and many narratives of teachers) and a few suggestions. My first suggestion to the above student teacher was, 'start writing'; 'When you don't know what to write just start writing'; 'Start writing about your feeling of "getting lost" and see where that takes you'; 'Not all writing takes you somewhere – but you are on the road'; 'Writing is a painful process'. A student teacher reacted very vociferously to the latter phrase, saying to me 'why does writing need to be painful? The kind of writing that is being suggested opens up things that I don't want to deal with. It is not like the other reflective-practice writing – that closes up things'. This comment was very revealing to me. First, it is interesting that for her reflective-practice writing (as she called it) closed down her experience. Yet she did not want, or was finding it difficult, to engage into another writing that opened things up. This could have been painful for her. But, it seems that this pain or anguish, as Derrida (1978) refers to it, is a fundamental part of writing and re-writing.

Although at this stage of my research I also feel lost on how to present this to the student teacher, yet I feel that this 'feeling lost', 'strangeness', is a driving force. Derrida's idea of aporia – to be caught in moments of uncertainty, to have all possibilities available – is fundamental here. Daniela Mercieca (2009; 2011) draws upon Klein to explain how the psyche is engaged in a constant move towards integrity, that the discomfort experienced in the unknown is anxiety-provoking.

It is very difficult to produce an account which acknowledges contradictions, and describes the detail and diversity of events and analyses experience in terms which go beyond the unitary, rational subject. Defences are maintained to achieve integrity with an energy which is equivalent to the energy of the original repressed desire (Mercieca 2011, 30).

Mercieca quotes a number of papers written by professionals, whose aim is to explore ways of reducing the uncertainty using systematic procedures. However, she (Mercieca 2009; 2011) suggests to us to attempt to befriend the contradictory state of being and to view it as part and parcel of who we are.

> I maintain that it is incumbent upon us to make sure that they do have a place. It is only through maintaining a healthy level of doubt that the complexities and contingencies of the situations which children present us can be received and listened to. It is only by allowing ourselves to be uncertain that we are open to shock and surprise. It is through being more tolerant of the feelings that accompany not knowing, rather than resisting that which we do not expect, that we can be more open to children. And it is this that will enable our continuous development of professionalism, as opposed to a 'restriction of the role of the professional practitioner to that of the technical operative'
>
> (Nixon 2004, 33; Mercieca 2009, 178)

Bridging theory and method

In this research, reading with Derrida's texts and engaging with his ideas was woven throughout. Derrida's ideas, or his idea of deconstruction, are not a method, but act as a catalyst to challenge the research process. Law's powerful statement that method constructs 'the truth' (Law 2004) is helpful here to understand how theorists such as Derrida may support research in relation to constructing truth. As has been emphasised in this chapter, Derrida's work aims at opening up closed spaces and allows for alternative discourses to emerge. From my experience based on this research, and other research, my recommendation is that the work of Derrida needs to be situated at the beginning of the research process as well as throughout the process. Authors such as Derrida cannot be an appendix. They are so powerful that they need to be participant actors in the research process. Quoting the introductory line of a research project I developed, this is how I introduced the study:

> A number of characters are the main protagonists of this book: five students, three French philosophers and myself. All of these will be introduced shortly. Let me start by giving names to these characters: the students are Ruth, Nina, Charles, Luke and Matthew. The three philosophers are Jacques, Gilles and Félix (to keep it on a first name basis). I am the author of this book and the person who has conducted this particular research, and has brought the nine people together, forming 'folds of friendship' (Stivale, 2003). The nine people 'seize upon the extremely distant relationships to nourish their thought and thereby to maintain a vital, if dispersed, community of friends of thought' (Stivale, 2003, p. 25).
>
> (Mercieca 2013, 1)

The distant relationship that Stivale (2003) argues in the above quote seems apt here to understanding research as made up of friends that nourish each other. When I am intrigued by an educational concern or problem, and a tentative research question is forming, from its very early emerging stages I start reading and engaging with theory. I let theory challenge me, 'play' (Allan 2008) with my ideas and questions, thus influencing the construction of my research question. Similarly, I actively strive to create spaces for a conversation to occur between methodology and theory. My starting assumption is that theory challenges methodology, and methodology challenges theory. Research methodology is not neutral to theory. The process of analysing data is also very interesting. I often start looking at the data from particular theoretical ideas and concepts. The process of writing the research is also very interesting. How can one develop the idea of volume in one's writing, rather than let it present as a flat structure?

Conclusion

Teacher training puts reflective-practice at the core of the student teacher becoming, with particular focus given to written reflective-practice. Using a Derridean framework, my action-research process, of which I have given highlights above, helped me to question the taken for granted familiarity that I was engaging with when teaching reflected-practice and reading reflective-writings. Through reading Derrida and engaging with his various writing styles, I started to become more aware of the process of writing and its complexity. This helped me to think about the possibility of offering such ideas to my students and also to open myself to various writings which do not follow structures to the letter and allow for some force to be demonstrated through the writing.

During the course of this action-research I have been caught in moments of aporia and 'madness of deciding', particularly when I was trying out with student teachers the new study-unit that asks of them to write their narrative. My many moments of doubt, of not knowing exactly where I was going, of correcting myself as I developed this course were part of a very strange feeling of uncertainty. Considering that performativity is fast becoming a characteristic even within universities (see Nixon 2001a; 2001b; 2003; 2004), where assessment and measurement of each study-unit is now in place, to carry out a study-unit that is fluid can have consequences. Yet Derrida comes to me as a comfort and also as a provocation: A decision takes place only when one is caught in a moment of aporia. If one follows structures and procedures then there is no decision. What I and my student teachers were doing, as described in the fourth section of the chapter, was mostly on my part to create structures of reflective-practice and for the student teachers to follow. Now I try to provide spaces for student teachers to escape these formulated structures and allow their otherness to come across and disrupt the identity. This process has also disrupted my identity as a lecturer and researcher. Maybe the word 'disrupted' is not the best word to use here. Rather, this process gave me the opportunity to let the other (the impossible) be made possible in my identity as a lecturer – challenging (at times violently) who I am as a lecturer. Not that the impossible is actualised, but that which cannot be foreseen, is made present in what I do and influences my decisions. This openness to the other is a possible way forward that allows for the 'incalculable' for me and my students. This is nothing, if not justice for Derrida. Therefore, writing that is just!

Notes

1 Derrida always asks why there is something and not nothing.
2 In Malta, teaching practice for student teachers is a six-week teaching block.

References

Addleson, K. 1994. *Moral passages: Towards a collectivist moral theory*. London: Routledge.
Allan, J. 2008. *Rethinking inclusion: The philosophers of difference in practice*. Dordrecht: Springer.
Biesta, G.J.J. 2001. 'Preparing for the incalculable': Deconstruction, justice and the question of education. In *Derrida and Education*, eds. G.J.J. Biesta and D. Egéa-Kuehne, 32–54. London: Routledge.
Biesta, G.J.J. 2009. Witnessing deconstruction in education: Why quasi-transcendentalism matters. *Journal of Philosophy of Education* 43, 3: 391–404.
Biesta, G.J.J. 2013. *The beautiful risk of education*. London: Paradigm
Caputo, J.D. ed. 1997. *Deconstruction in a nutshell. A conversation with Jacques Derrida*. New York, NY: Fordham University Press.
Cardona, A. 2005. Reflective questions. Available at: www.um.edu.mt/educ/downloads (accessed 17 September 2019).
Carr, W. and Kemmis, S. 1986. *Becoming critical*. Lewes: Falmer.
Cohen, L., L. Manion and K. Morrison. 2000. *Research methods in education*. London: Routledge Falmer.
Deleuze, G. 1990. *The logic of sense*. New York, NY: Columbia University Press.
Derrida, J. 1976. *Of grammatology*. Baltimore. MD: Johns Hopkins University Press.
Derrida, J. 1978. Force and signification. In *Writing and difference*, 3–30. London: Routledge and Kegan Paul.
Derrida, J. 1979. Scribble (writing-power). *Yale French Studies* 58: 117–147.
Derrida, J. 1991. Letter to a Japanese Friend. In *Reading de Man Reading*, eds. W. Godzuch and L. Waters, 1–5. Minneapolis, MN: University of Minnesota Press.
Derrida, J. 1992. *Given time*. Chicago, IL: Chicago University Press.
Derrida, J. 1993. *Aporia*. Stanford, CA: Stanford University Press.
Derrida, J. 1995. *The gift of death*. Chicago, IL: Chicago University Press.
Galea, S. 2012. Reflecting reflective practice. *Educational Philosophy and Theory* 44, 3: 245–258.
Ghaye, A. and K. Ghaye. 1998. *Teaching and learning through critical reflective practice*. London: David Fulton Publishers.
Jennings, C. and E. Kennedy. eds. 1996. *The reflective professional in education: Psychological perspective on changing contexts*. London: Jessica Kingsley Publishers.

Johnson, C. 1993. *System and writing in the philosophy of Jacques Derrida*. Cambridge: Cambridge University Press.

Kirby, D. and A. Ziering. directors. 2002. *Derrida J*. Documentary [Motion picture]. New York, NY: Jane Doe Films.

Klein, M. 1997. *Envy and gratitude and other works 1946–1963*. London: Vintage.

Law, J. 2004. *After method – Mess in social science research*. London: Routledge.

Mercieca, D. 2009. Working with uncertainty: Reflections of an educational psychologist on working with children. *Ethics and Social Welfare* 3, 2: 170–180.

Mercieca, D. 2011. *Beyond conventional boundaries: Uncertainty in research and practice with children*. Rotterdam: Sense Publishers.

Mercieca, D.P. 2013. *Living otherwise: Students with profound and multiple learning disabilities as agents in educational contexts*. Rotterdam: Sense Publishers.

Mercieca, D.P. and D. Mercieca. 2012. How can the use of petit narratives create space and possibility when shorthand is used in educational psychology practice. *Educational and Child Psychology* 29, 2: 67–76.

Nixon, J. 2001a. 'Not without dust and heat': The moral bases of the 'new' academic professionalism. *British Journal of Educational Studies* 49, 2: 173–186.

Nixon, J. 2001b. Towards a new academic professionalism: A manifesto of hope. *British Journal of Sociology of Education* 22, 2: 227–244.

Nixon, J. 2003. Professional renewal as a condition of institutional change: Rethinking academic work. *International Studies in Sociology of Education* 13, 1: 3–15.

Nixon, J. 2004. What is theory? *Educar* 34: 27–37.

Professional Development Portfolio. n.d. Malta: University of Malta.

Rorty, R. 1978. Philosophy as a kind of writing: Essay on Derrida. *New Literary History* 10, 1: 141–160.

Rousset, J. 1989. *Forme et signification: Essais sur les structures littéraires de Corneille à Claudel*. Paris: J. Corti.

Schön, D.A. 1983. *The reflective practitioner: How professionals think in action*. New York, NY: Basic Books.

Schön, D.A. 1987. *Educating the reflective practitioner: Toward a new design for teaching and learning in the professions*. San Francisco, CA: Jossey-Bass.

Schön, D.A. 1991. *The reflective practitioner: How professionals think in action*. Aldershot: Ashgate Publishing Ltd.

Somekh, B. 2006. *Action research: A methodology for change and development*. Milton Keynes: Open University Press.

Standish, P. 2001. Data return: The sense of the given in educational research. *Journal of Philosophy of Education* 35, 3: 497–518. doi:10.1111/1467-9752.00240.

Stivale, C. 2003. Deleuze/Parnet in dialogues: The fold of post-identity. *The Journal of Midwest Modern Language Association* 36, 1: 25–37.

Usher, R. and R. Edwards. 1994. *Postmodernism and education*. London: Routledge.

Wang, C.L. 2015. Mapping or tracing? Rethinking curriculum mapping in higher education. *Studies in Higher Education* 40, 9: 1550–1559.

Index

Made in the USA
Middletown, DE
27 June 2022

67877831R00161